Office 2013
All-In-One

ABSOLUTE
BEGINNER'S
GUIDE

Patrice-Anne Rutledge, et al.

800 East 96th Street
Indianapolis, Indiana 46240

Office 2013 All-In-One Absolute Beginner's Guide

ISBN-13: 978-0-7897-5101-0
ISBN-10: 0-7897-5101-1

Library of Congress Control Number: 2013943455

Printed in the United States of America

First Printing: August 2013

Trademarks

Warning and Disclaimer

Bulk Sales

Que Publishing offers excellent discounts on this book when ordered in quantity for bulk purchases or special sales. For more information, please contact

U.S. Corporate and Government Sales
1-800-382-3419
corpsales@pearsontechgroup.com

For sales outside of the U.S., please contact

International Sales
international@pearsoned.com

Editor-in-Chief
Greg Wiegand

Acquisitions Editor
Michelle Newcomb

Development Editor
Charlotte Kughen

Managing Editor
Sandra Schroeder

Project Editor
Mandie Frank

Indexer
Brad Herriman

Proofreader
Anne Goebel

Technical Editor
Vince Averello

Editorial Assistant
Cindy Teeters

Cover Designer
Matt Coleman

Compositor
Mary Sudul

Contributors
Sherry Kinkoph-Gunter
Diane Poremsky
Tracy Syrstad

Contents at a Glance

Table of Contents

About the Author

Patrice-Anne Rutledge is a business technology author and consultant who specializes in teaching others to maximize the power of new technologies. Patrice has used—and has trained others to use—Microsoft Office for many years. She is the author of numerous books about Office for Pearson Education, including *Easy Office 2013* and *PowerPoint 2013 Absolute Beginner's Guide*. She can be reached through her website at www.patricerutledge.com.

Dedication

To my family, with thanks for their ongoing support and encouragement.

Acknowledgments

Special thanks to Michelle Newcomb, Charlotte Kughen, Todd Brakke, Vince Averello, Mandie Frank, Sherry Kinkoph Gunter, Tracy Syrstad, and Diane Poremsky for their many contributions to this book.

We Want to Hear from You!

As the reader of this book, *you* are our most important critic and commentator. We value your opinion and want to know what we're doing right, what we could do better, what areas you'd like to see us publish in, and any other words of wisdom you're willing to pass our way.

We welcome your comments. You can email or write to let us know what you did or didn't like about this book—as well as what we can do to make our books better.

Please note that we cannot help you with technical problems related to the topic of this book.

When you write, please be sure to include this book's title and author as well as your name and email address. We will carefully review your comments and share them with the author and editors who worked on the book.

Email: feedback@quepublishing.com

Mail: Que Publishing
ATTN: Reader Feedback
800 East 96th Street
Indianapolis, IN 46240 USA

Reader Services

Visit our website and register this book at quepublishing.com/register for convenient access to any updates, downloads, or errata that might be available for this book.

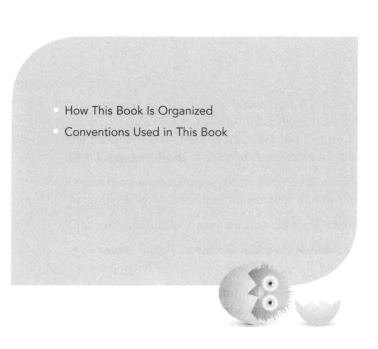

INTRODUCTION

Microsoft Office 2013 is the latest version of Microsoft's popular suite of business software applications. Using Office, you can quickly create documents such as letters, reports, and resumes; calculate and analyze data in spreadsheets; design and deliver presentations; send and receive email; and store data in digital notebooks.

The world is becoming increasingly mobile, and so is Office 2013. This new version is integrated with SkyDrive, Microsoft's online storage solution. In addition to web-based file-sharing, SkyDrive also gives you access to the Microsoft Web Apps for Word, Excel, PowerPoint, and OneNote. Office 2013 makes it easy to access, edit, and create Office files on the go using a mobile device such as a tablet or smartphone.

Office 2013 All-In-One Absolute Beginner's Guide is designed to get you up and running on Office as quickly as possible. This book covers five of the most popular Office applications— Word, Excel, PowerPoint, Outlook, and OneNote—and provides step-by-step instructions that help you master tasks with little effort. For now, turn to Chapter 1, "Getting Started with Microsoft Office 2013," to begin exploring this powerful application suite.

How This Book Is Organized

Office 2013 All-In-One Absolute Beginner's Guide is divided into six parts.

Part I, "Introducing Microsoft Office 2013," presents Office fundamentals, such as navigating applications, using the Ribbon and Backstage view, getting help, and saving and opening files.

In Part II, "Microsoft Word 2013," you continue on to one of the most popular Office applications: Microsoft Word. In this section, you learn how to create and format documents, modify page layout, and perform a collaborative review of your documents before you print, publish, or send.

Next, you explore Excel, Office's spreadsheet application. Part III, "Microsoft Excel 2013," shows you how to create and format Excel worksheets and master cell formulas and functions. Finally, you can analyze your worksheet data using visual tools such as charts, PivotTables, and sparklines (mini charts).

Part IV, "Microsoft PowerPoint 2013," shows you how to create eye-catching presentations using PowerPoint's powerful collection of ready-made tools. You also learn how to edit and format presentations; incorporate audio, video, and animation; and prepare for delivery, either in person or on the Web.

Part V, "Microsoft Outlook 2013," helps you get up and running quickly with Office's email, calendaring, and scheduling tools.

And finally, you explore OneNote, Office's digital notebook application that helps you organize data. Part VI, "Microsoft OneNote 2013," introduces you to OneNote basics, including creating notebooks; inserting text, images, and external content; and using tools such as Linked Note Taking and Send to OneNote.

Conventions Used in This Book

Office 2013 All-In-One Absolute Beginner's Guide uses a number of conventions to provide you with special information. These include the following elements:

 TIP Tips offer suggestions for making things easier or provide alternative ways to perform a particular task.

 NOTE Notes provide additional, more detailed information about a specific Office feature.

 CAUTION Cautions warn you about potential problems that might occur and offer advice on how to avoid these problems.

IN THIS CHAPTER

- Exploring the Start Screen
- Setting Up Your Office Account
- Using the Ribbon Tabs
- Using Backstage View
- Using Toolbars
- Using Task Panes
- Getting Help

1

GETTING STARTED WITH MICROSOFT OFFICE 2013

Although Microsoft Office 2013 is intuitive and easy to use, it's worth spending several minutes exploring its interface and navigation tools. The most common of these include the Ribbon, Backstage view, the Quick Access Toolbar, the mini toolbar, contextual tabs, and task panes.

If you're upgrading from Office 2007 or 2010, the basic Office interface should be reasonably familiar. There are enhancements to the Ribbon and Backstage view, but these key features still work in much the same way. If you're upgrading from a previous Office version, however, take your time exploring the new ways to use and navigate Office.

The first thing to notice when you start most Office 2013 applications is the new start screen that welcomes you. This screen is color-coded: blue for Word, green for Excel, and red for PowerPoint. Outlook and OneNote, however, open directly to the Home tab, bypassing the start screen.

For now, start with a quick tour of Microsoft Office 2013.

 NOTE   Be aware that although common functions and features are similar throughout Microsoft Office, there are slight variations in each individual application.

Exploring the Start Screen

When you first open an Office application, the new start screen greets you (see Figure 1.1 for an example of the Word start screen).

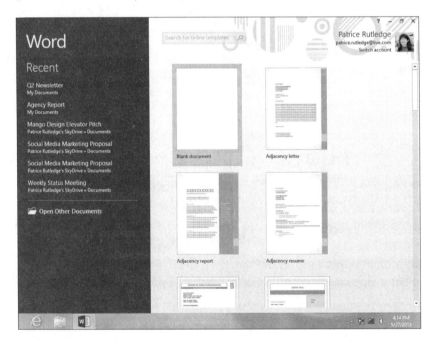

FIGURE 1.1

Getting started with Office applications is easy.

From here, you can perform any of the following tasks:

- Open a recent file.
- Open other files (the Open window displays).
- Create a new file, either a blank file or one based on the available themes or templates. (These vary based on the application.)
- Search online for themes and templates.
- Switch to another account.

NOTE If this is your first time using Office 2013, no recent files display.

Setting Up Your Office Account

The *Account window* is where you set up your Microsoft account and connected services, which are both important for taking full advantage of Office 2013. When you first open this new version of Office, be sure to take a few minutes to handle this important task.

To open the Account window, click the File tab and select Account (see Figure 1.2 for an example of the Account window in PowerPoint). Alternatively, select Account from the start screen.

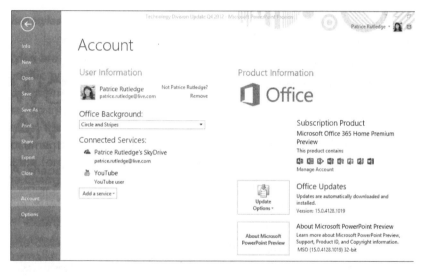

FIGURE 1.2

Set up your Microsoft account and connected services in the Account window.

Here's what you can do in this window:

- **Specify the Microsoft account to use with Office**. Office 2013 connects you to the Web with your Microsoft account—an email and password you use to access all Microsoft services such as SkyDrive, Messenger, Hotmail, and Outlook.com. Formerly, this was called a Windows Live ID.

     TIP If you don't have a Microsoft account, you can sign up for one at https://signup.live.com.

- **Select the Office background you prefer**. The default background is Circle and Stripes, but you can also select from a variety of other options, including Clouds, Straws, or no background.

- **Specify the services you want to connect with**. The Account window displays the services you've already connected with. (Office finds some services automatically based on your Microsoft account email address.) Click the Add a Service button to add more services, including Flickr, YouTube, Office 365 SharePoint, SkyDrive, Facebook, LinkedIn, and Twitter.

- **Manage your Office account**. Click the Manage Account link to sign in to your Microsoft account.

- **Specify how you want to update Office**. By default, Office updates happen automatically, but you can disable this if you prefer.

Using the Ribbon Tabs

Although the Ribbon isn't a new Office feature (it was introduced in Office 2007), it does represent a new experience for anyone upgrading from version 2003 or earlier.

The *Ribbon*, which replaces the menu structure found in previous versions of Office, provides an easy way to access common commands and buttons using the least amount of space possible. The Ribbon is divided into tabs, which vary by application. For example, in Word the available tabs include File, Home, Insert, Design, Page Layout, References, Mailings, Review, and View. Each Ribbon tab includes groups and buttons of related features.

Figure 1.3 shows the Home tab in PowerPoint.

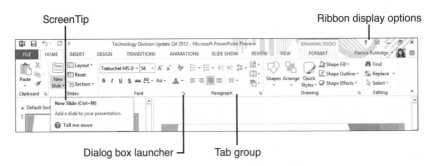

FIGURE 1.3

Ribbon tabs are where you find all your Office commands.

TIP By default, Office displays both the Ribbon tab and its related commands and buttons. If you want to save screen space, you can choose to show tabs only or hide the Ribbon entirely. If you show tabs only, you can click a tab to display its commands temporarily. To customize what displays, click the Ribbon Display Options button in the upper-right corner of the screen and make your selection from the menu.

To quickly determine the function of tab buttons and commands, pause your mouse over each option to display a basic description in a ScreenTip. If a hotkey is available (such as pressing Ctrl+C for Copy), it also displays in the ScreenTip.

Common Ribbon features include the following:

- **Galleries**—Galleries offer a menu of visual choices that pertain to a selected button or command. For example, when you click the down arrow next to the Themes group on the Design tab, a visual gallery of theme images displays (see Figure 1.4).

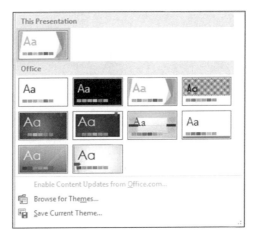

FIGURE 1.4

Galleries offer a quick overview of potential visual effects.

- **Live Preview**—Most, but not all, galleries provide a live preview of each option before you actually apply it. As an example, the Themes gallery enables you to see how each theme appears on your document when you pause your mouse over it. That way, you can quickly try out several options before making any actual changes.

- **Dialog box launcher**—Clicking one of these small diagonal arrows in the lower-right corner of a group opens a dialog box of related options. For example, in Figure 1.3, you can see dialog box launchers in the Clipboard, Font, Paragraph, and Styles groups. The Clipboard dialog box launcher, interestingly enough, doesn't launch a dialog box, but rather a task pane. All the other launchers launch a traditional dialog box. See "Using Task Panes," later in this chapter, for more information about task panes.

- **Contextual tabs**—Although the main tabs always display on the Ribbon, Office also includes several contextual Ribbon tabs that appear only when you're performing specific tasks. For example, when you select a chart, the Chart Tools tab displays, which includes two contextual tabs: Design and Format (see Figure 1.5). They remain as long as you work on your chart. When you click elsewhere, they disappear.

Chart Tools–Design tab ⌐   ⌐ Chart Tools–Format tab

FIGURE 1.5

Office opens additional contextual tabs depending on the task you perform.

See Chapter 2, "Working with Office Applications," for more information about customizing the Ribbon tabs.

 NOTE   A few buttons include two sections: The upper portion performs a default action, and the lower portion (with a down arrow) opens a drop-down menu or gallery of options. For example, clicking the upper portion of the New Slide button on the Home tab of PowerPoint automatically inserts a new slide using the default Title Slide layout. Clicking the lower portion opens a gallery of options.

Using Backstage View

Backstage view enables you to perform the most common file-related tasks in one place. For example, Backstage view is the place where you create, open, save, share, and print Office documents.

To access Backstage view, click the File tab. Figure 1.6 shows Backstage view in Excel.

FIGURE 1.6

Perform all your file-related tasks in one place: Backstage view.

On the left side of the screen, you see a list of buttons and tabs. Clicking one of the tabs (Info, New, Open, Save, Save As, Print, Share, Export, Close, Account, and Options) displays related content on the right side of the screen. See Chapter 2 for more information about the features available in Backstage view.

Using Toolbars

Although Office 2013 uses far fewer toolbars than earlier versions of Office, you need to know about two types of toolbars: the Quick Access Toolbar and mini toolbar.

Using the Quick Access Toolbar

The *Quick Access Toolbar* is a small toolbar that displays in the upper-left corner of your screen (see Figure 1.7) and is available no matter which Ribbon tab you select.

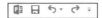

FIGURE 1.7

Common commands are at your fingertips no matter what you're doing.

By default, this toolbar contains three buttons: Save, Undo, and Repeat, but you can customize it to include almost any command. See Chapter 2 for more information about customizing the buttons on this toolbar and moving it to another location.

Using the Mini Toolbar

The *mini toolbar* is a small contextual toolbar that appears when you perform specific tasks. For example, when you select text, a mini toolbar appears with options related to text formatting (see Figure 1.8).

FIGURE 1.8

When you edit text, the mini toolbar appears with common text-editing commands.

Although you can perform the same tasks using the commands on the main Ribbon tab, using the mini toolbar makes these commands available in a more convenient location.

Using Task Panes

A *task pane* is a window inside an Office application that enables you to perform common tasks without covering your main work area, such as a document, presentation, or spreadsheet window. You can keep more than one pane open at a time, but keep in mind that too many open task panes can clutter your screen. Many dialog boxes are now panes in Office 2013. Some common Office task panes include Format Shape (see Figure 1.9), Format Picture, Revisions, and Clipboard.

FIGURE 1.9

The Format Shape pane is one of many time-saving panes in Office.

You can make the task pane wider or narrower if you prefer by pausing the mouse pointer over the left edge of the pane until the pointer becomes a two-headed arrow. Click the mouse and drag the left edge to either the left or right until the task pane is the width you want.

To close a task pane, click the Close (x) button in the upper-right corner.

Getting Help

Although Office is an intuitive program, there are times when you might need additional help in completing an in-progress task or figuring out how to do something. Fortunately, help is just a click away. Microsoft continuously updates its help system, so if you're connected to the Web while you search for help, you always get the latest help content.

To search for help on a specific topic, follow these steps:

1. Click the Help button in the upper-right corner of the screen (a small question mark) or in the upper-right corner of a dialog box to open the Help window. Pressing F1 is another way to access help.

2. To search for help on a specific topic, enter keywords in the text box. For example, if you want to search for help on creating sections, you could enter sections.

3. Click the Search button to initiate the search. The Help window displays a list of search result articles.

4. Click the article title that best matches your search to view the help content.

The top of the Help window includes the following navigation buttons: Back, Forward, Home, Print, and Use Large Text.

Office.com (http://office.microsoft.com) also offers searchable help, tutorials, and downloads.

THE ABSOLUTE MINIMUM

Here are the key points to remember from this chapter:

- When you start Word, Excel, and PowerPoint, the new start screen welcomes you. Outlook and OneNote, however, open directly to the Home tab.

- The Account window is where you set up your Microsoft account and connected services, such as Facebook, LinkedIn, Twitter, and YouTube.

- The Ribbon offers easy access to common commands and buttons using the least amount of space possible. The Ribbon is divided into tabs, which vary by application.

- Backstage view enables you to perform the most common file-related tasks in one place. For example, Backstage view is where you create, open, save, share, and print Office documents.

- Office 2013 offers two important toolbars: the Quick Access Toolbar that displays in the upper-left corner of your screen and the contextual mini toolbar that appears when you perform specific tasks, such as formatting text.

- A task pane is a window inside an Office application that enables you to perform common tasks without covering your main work area. Common task panes include the Format Shape, Format Picture, and Clipboard panes.

- Although Office is an intuitive program, you can access updated online help with the click of a button.

2

WORKING WITH OFFICE APPLICATIONS

Spending some time mastering the basics of Microsoft Office pays off in the long run, particularly if you're new to Office or could use a refresher.

First, explore how to perform Office's most common tasks: opening, saving, renaming, closing, deleting, and printing files. Next, explore the Backstage view options for sharing and exporting files. Finally, spend a few minutes customizing Office defaults to suit your own work style and preferences.

Although these tools and options should be familiar if you're upgrading, Office 2013 does include some changes and new features.

Working with Files

This section applies primarily to Word, Excel, and PowerPoint. Working with files is similar in OneNote, but it doesn't include the Start screen options. Because the goal of Outlook isn't to create a file, many of these options don't apply.

Creating a New File

To create a new file, click the File tab and select New. In the New window, you can create a blank file, select a template, or search online for a template. The exact content of this window varies by application. For example, the New window in Word offers the option to create a blank document or select from one of many templates (see Figure 2.1).

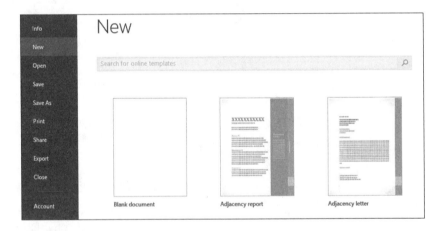

FIGURE 2.1

Use the New window to get started on a new document.

 NOTE   The Start screen also enables you to create a blank document or choose from a template.

Opening a File

Office offers a variety of ways to open a file, including the following:

- On the Start screen, select one of the files in the Recent list or click the Open Other [*file type*] link to open the Open dialog box (see Figure 2.2). The exact wording of the Open Other link varies by application, such as Open Other Documents, Open Other Workbooks, or Open Other Presentations. This option isn't available for OneNote or Outlook.

- Press Ctrl+O to open the Open dialog box.

- Click the File tab and select Open to display the Open window where you can open recent files or open files stored on SkyDrive or your computer.

- Double-click the name of an Office file in Windows Explorer.

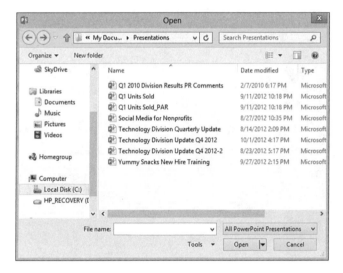

FIGURE 2.2

The Open dialog box includes many additional features, including file management and search capabilities.

If you choose a method that displays the Open dialog box, select the file you want and then click the Open button.

Renaming a File

To rename a file, select it in the Open dialog box and perform one of the following actions:

- Press F2.

- Right-click and select Rename from the shortcut menu.

- Click the Organize button and select Rename from the shortcut menu.

- Click the filename, wait a second, and then click it again.

Office converts the filename to an edit box in which you can overwrite the existing name.

Saving a File

To save an open file, follow these steps:

1. On the Quick Access Toolbar, click the Save button. Alternatively, press Ctrl+S. If this is the first time you've saved the file, the Save As window opens, as shown in Figure 2.3.

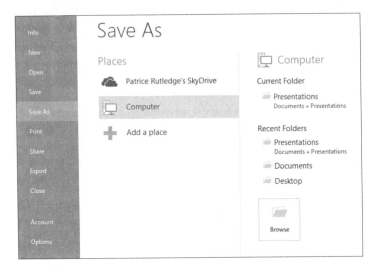

FIGURE 2.3

Choose between several save options in the Save As window.

2. On the left side of the window, specify where you want to save your file, such as on your computer or on SkyDrive.

3. Click the Browse button to open the Save As dialog box (see Figure 2.4).

 TIP Optionally, you can save time by selecting one of the options in the Recent Folders list. If you often save your files to the same folder, pause your mouse over that folder name and click the Pin This Item to the List icon to ensure that this folder is always at the top of the list for easy convenience.

4. Select the folder in which to save your file. Office automatically selects your default folder, but you can change this if you want. You can customize the default folder on the Save tab in the Options dialog box. (Choose Tools, Save Options from the Save As dialog box.)

5. In the File Name field, type a name.

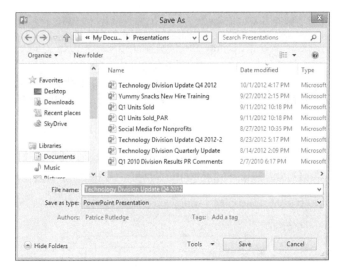

FIGURE 2.4
Specify save parameters in this dialog box.

6. Choose the file format from the Save as Type drop-down list. If you want to save as a PDF or XPS document, see "Saving as a PDF or XPS Document," later in this chapter.

7. Click the Save button to save the file.

 TIP After you save a file for the first time, press Ctrl+S or click the Save button to save new changes without opening the Save As dialog box. If you want to save an existing file to a new location or change its name, click the File tab and select Save As.

Closing a File

At times, you might want to close a file without exiting the application itself. This is particularly useful if you have many files open and want to save memory.

To close an open file, you can do one of the following:

• Click the File tab and select Close. If you haven't saved your file, Office prompts you to do so. If your file has been saved, Office closes it immediately.

• Click the Close (x) button in the upper-right corner of the screen to close an open file. Note, however, that if this is the only file you have open, this action also closes the application itself.

• Use the shortcut key Ctrl+W.

Deleting a File

If you no longer need an Office file, you can delete it. To delete a file you no longer want, select it in the Open dialog box and press the Delete key on your keyboard. A warning dialog box appears, verifying that you want to delete the file and send it to the Recycle Bin. Click Yes to confirm the deletion.

Printing a File

The Print window in Backstage view enables you to specify print settings as well as preview and print your documents. Click the File tab and select Print, as shown in Figure 2.5.

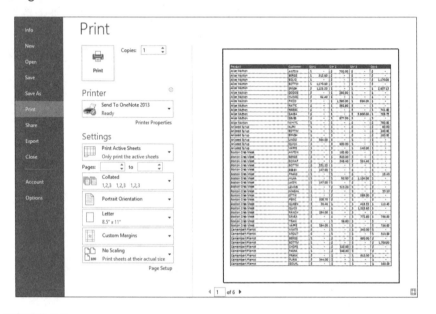

FIGURE 2.5

Prepare, preview, and print from the Print window in Backstage view.

Before you print, apply any special print settings. The Settings section includes several boxes with drop-down lists where you can specify these options. The text that displays in each box varies depending on the last selection you made.

Select your printer (if it doesn't display in the Printer section by default), specify the number of copies, and click the Print button.

 NOTE See Chapter 12, "Printing Documents," Chapter 22, "Preparing Workbooks for Distribution and Printing," and Chapter 36, "Creating and Printing Presentation Materials" for more information about application-specific print options in Word, Excel, and PowerPoint.

Sharing Files

Office offers numerous ways to share your documents with others, including several that are new to Office 2013. You find a variety of sharing options in the Share window in Backstage view.

Preparing to Share Files

Before you share an Office file with others or post it online, you should consider doing several things: protect it, inspect it for confidential information, validate its accessibility, and check for compatibility with previous versions.

The Info window in Backstage view enables you to accomplish all these tasks in one place. To open the Info window, click the File tab.

On this window, you can do the following:

- **Protect files**—Click the Protect button to open a menu of options, shown in Figure 2.6, for protecting a file. For example, you can apply a password, make it read-only, or apply a digital signature to control access. Whether you choose to protect your Office files depends on the group of people you work with, your need for security, and your audience. Obviously, if you post a document in a public location directed at a wide audience of viewers, you wouldn't want to protect with a password or otherwise limit access.

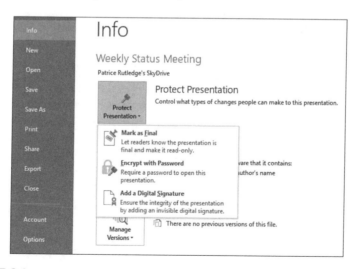

FIGURE 2.6

Prepare to share files using tools in the Info window.

- **Check your file for issues**—Click the Check for Issues button to open a menu of options that enables you to inspect files, check file accessibility, and check file compatibility. For example, you can:

  - Inspect a file for hidden data and personal information such as comments, notes, author name, or document properties (see Figure 2.7).

FIGURE 2.7

Use the Document Inspector to find and remove hidden and personal information before sharing.

 CAUTION Because you might not be able to undo changes the Document Inspector makes, it's a good idea to run the Inspector on a copy of your original.

- Review and fix potential accessibility issues based on the comments in the Accessibility Checker pane. For example, the Checker might identify missing alt text or find issues with the reading order of your content, problems that would cause difficulty for someone with a visual impairment who uses a screen reader.

- Check for compatibility issues if you want others to be able to open your files in a previous version of Office. You could lose features that weren't yet available in that version.

Sharing Files with Others

You can save your Office files to SkyDrive and then invite other people to view, edit, or collaborate on them.

 TIP See Chapter 6, "Using Microsoft Office on the Web and Mobile Devices," for more information about SkyDrive, Microsoft's online storage and collaboration solution.

To share a file with others, follow these steps:

1. Click the File tab and select Share.

2. In the Share window, select Invite People to display the Invite People section on the right side of the window (see Figure 2.8).

FIGURE 2.8

Sharing files with others is easy in Office 2013.

 NOTE If you haven't saved your file to SkyDrive yet, Office prompts you to click the Save to Cloud button to do so.

3. Enter the names or email addresses of the people you want to share with.

4. By default, Office enables the people you share with to edit your files. Select Can View from the drop-down list if you want to restrict this to viewing only.

5. Optionally, select the Require User to Sign In Before Accessing Document if you want to require a sign-in.

6. Click the Share button.

7. Click the Proceed button in the warning dialog box to confirm that you want to share. Office notifies the people about the file you want to share with them.

 NOTE *Co-authoring* is an Office feature that enables you to work on the same document simultaneously with other colleagues no matter where they're located. Co-authoring requires either a SkyDrive account or Microsoft SharePoint. To activate this feature, more than one person needs to open the same file in either SkyDrive or SharePoint.

Sharing via a Link

If you've saved your file, you can share it with a link. To create a link, follow these steps:

1. Click the File tab and select Share.

2. In the Share window, select Get a Sharing Link to display the Get a Sharing Link section on the right side of the window (see Figure 2.9).

 CAUTION The Get a Sharing Link option doesn't display if you saved your file only to your computer.

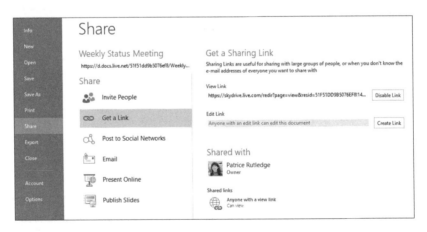

FIGURE 2.9

Share links to files stored online.

3. Click the Create Link button next to either View Link or Edit Link, depending on the rights you want to provide.

4. Copy the link provided and share with the appropriate people.

To disable a link, click the Disable Link button next to the link you no longer want.

Sharing on Social Networks

You can share your online Office documents on social networks such as Facebook, Twitter, and LinkedIn. To share a file on a social network, follow these steps:

1. Click the File tab and select Share.

2. In the Share window, select Post to Social Networks to display the Post to Social Networks section on the right side of the window (see Figure 2.10).

FIGURE 2.10

Get social by sharing files on your favorite sites.

 CAUTION   The Post to Social Networks option doesn't display if you haven't saved your file online.

 NOTE   If you haven't connected with any social networks yet, click the Click Here to Connect to Social Networks link to do so. You're prompted to log into your Microsoft account and connect with your preferred social sites.

3. Select the check box next to each social site on which you want to share.

4. By default, Office enables the people you share with to view your file, but you can choose Can Edit from the drop-down list if you want to provide editing functionality.

5. Optionally, add a personal message about the file you're sharing.

6. Click the Post button to post on your selected social sites.

Sharing via Email

Office provides numerous options for sharing your files with others via email. To do so, follow these steps:

1. Click the File tab and select Share.

2. In the Share window, select Email to display the Email section on the right side of the window (see Figure 2.11).

FIGURE 2.11

Choose one of several email-sharing options.

3. Choose from one of the following options: Send as Attachment, Send a Link, Send as PDF, Send as XPS, or Send as Internet Fax. See "Saving as a PDF or XPS Document" later in this chapter for more information about saving in PDF or XPS format.

Exporting Files

In the Export window in Backstage view, you can save a file as a PDF or XPS document as well as change its file type.

 NOTE   The Export window in PowerPoint also includes options to create a video, package your presentation for a CD, or create handouts, all covered in the PowerPoint section of this book. The Export window in OneNote enables you to export pages and sections as well as entire notebooks.

Saving as a PDF or XPS Document

Office enables you to save directly as a PDF or XPS document without requiring an add-in.

 TIP   Be sure to save your file before you save as a PDF or XPS documents.

To save as a PDF or XPS, follow these steps:

1. Click the File tab and then click Export to open the Export window (see Figure 2.12).

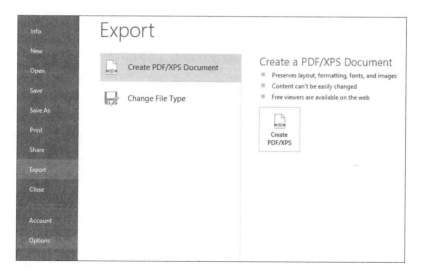

FIGURE 2.12

The Export window enables you to export your file to different formats.

2. On the left side of the window, select Create PDF/XPS Document.

3. Click the Create PDF/XPS button to open the Publish as PDF or XPS dialog box (see Figure 2.13).

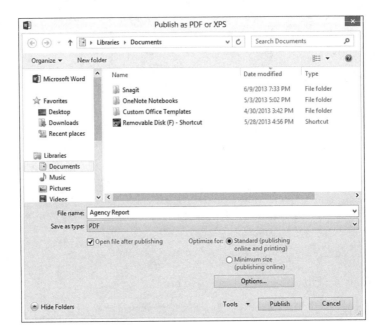

FIGURE 2.13

Save your file as a PDF or XPS document in this dialog box.

4. Select the folder in which to save your document.

5. In the File Name field, type a name.

6. In the Save as Type drop-down list, select either PDF or XPS Document.

7. Select the Open File After Publishing check box if you want to open your PDF or XPS document after saving.

8. If you want to create a document that's suitable for both online viewing and printing, select the Standard option button. If you just want people to view it online, select the Minimum Size option button.

9. Optionally, click the Options button if you want to customize your document, such as specifying a specific page range.

10. Click the OK button to return to the Save As dialog box.

11. Click the Publish button to publish your document based on your specifications.

Changing to Another File Type

If you save your file in one format and want to convert it to another, you can easily do so. For example, you could convert a PowerPoint slide to an image, a Word document to a text file, or a file to a previous version of Office.

To change file type, follow these steps:

1. Click the File tab and select Export to open the Export window (refer to Figure 2.12).

2. On the left side of the window, select Change File Type.

3. On the right side of the window, select one of the available file types, which vary by application (see Figure 2.14).

FIGURE 2.14

Quickly change a file type.

4. Scroll down to the bottom of the list and click the Save As button to open the Save As dialog box (refer to Figure 2.4).

5. Enter a new filename, if desired.

6. Click the Save button. Office saves your file in the format you specified.

Customizing Office

Although you can use Office as is without any customization, it's worthwhile to review Office's customization options at least once to verify the default settings suit your needs. In this section, you find out how to customize Office, including the Quick Access Toolbar and Ribbon tabs.

Customizing the Quick Access Toolbar

The Quick Access Toolbar is a customizable toolbar that contains popular commands you might use regardless of which tab currently displays. By default, the Save, Undo, and Repeat buttons are available from the Quick Access Toolbar, shown in Figure 2.15.

FIGURE 2.15

The Quick Access Toolbar gives you ready access to popular Office commands.

Moving the Quick Access Toolbar

The toolbar's default location is in the upper-left corner of the screen. If you prefer, you can move the toolbar to just below the Ribbon. To move the toolbar, click the down arrow to its right, next to the Repeat button, and select Show Below the Ribbon from the menu that displays.

 NOTE There are only two options for placing the Quick Access Toolbar. You can't move it to any other location on your screen.

Adding and Removing Quick Access Toolbar Commands

To quickly add the most popular commands to the toolbar, click the down arrow to its right and choose from the available options, including New, Open, Quick Print, and more.

A check mark is placed before each active command on the toolbar, such as the default commands Save, Undo, and Repeat. To add another command from this menu to the toolbar, click it. To remove one of these commands from the toolbar, click it again and the check mark disappears.

To add a command button from another tab to the toolbar, right-click it on the Ribbon tab and select Add to Quick Access Toolbar from the menu that displays. For example, let's say you want to add the New Slide button to the Quick Access Toolbar. To do so, go to the Home tab, right-click the New Slide button, and select Add to Quick Access Toolbar. The New Slide button is placed on the Quick Access Toolbar to the right of the Repeat button.

To remove a button, right-click it on the toolbar and choose Remove from Quick Access Toolbar from the menu that displays.

 TIP You can perform advanced customizations to the Quick Access Toolbar in the Options dialog box, described in the next section of this chapter.

Customizing Office Options

Office offers numerous customization options in the Options dialog box. The name of this dialog box varies by application, such as the Word Options dialog box, Excel Options dialog box, and so forth. Although many of the customization options are similar, others are specific to a particular application. Changes you make in the Options dialog box become your new default settings until you change them again.

To access the Options dialog box, click the File tab and choose Options. Figure 2.16 shows the Word Options dialog box.

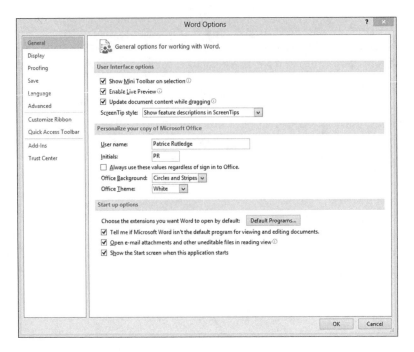

FIGURE 2.16

Use the Word Options dialog box to change many of Word's default settings.

The Options dialog box includes seveal tabs. The tabs cmmon to all Office applications are:

- **General**—Customize the most popular Office options, including the mini toolbar, Live Preview, ScreenTip styles, the default Ofice background and theme, startup options, and your user name.

- **Proofing**—Specify AutoCorrect and spelling options. AutoCorrect is a useful feature that can help save time and automatically correct mistakes you frequently make. By default, Office includes AutoCorrect substitutions for common misspellings, such as correcting "teh to "the," but you can also add your own.

- **Save**—Specify save options including automatic saves and backups, default file format, default local file location, and more. This tab is called Save & Backup in OneNote.

- **Language**—Select languages for editing, display, help, and ScreenTips. These options are most useful if you plan to create documents in a language other than English or want to enable a different version of English, such as English for the UK or Canada if your default is the United States.

- **Advanced**—Specify advanced options for editing, printing, and formatting.

- **Customize Ribbon**—Customize the Ribbon by adding and removing tab commands. Figure 2.17 shows the Customize Ribbon tab.

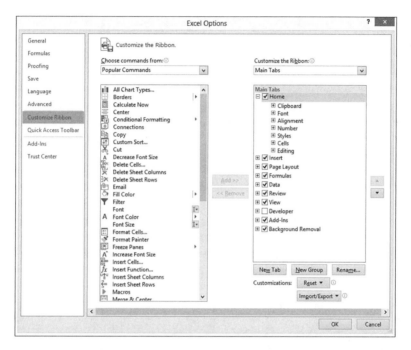

FIGURE 2.17

Customize the Ribbon or even hide it from view.

- **Quick Access Toolbar**—Perform advanced customizations to the Quick Access Toolbar, such as adding commands not accessible from the toolbar and rearranging the order of toolbar buttons.

- **Add-Ins**—View and manage Office add-ins, which offer supplemental features that enhance your Office experience. You can also download add-ins from the Microsoft Download Center (www.microsoft.com/downloads). Go to the Add-Ins tab on the Ribbon to access the features of the add-ins you've activated.

- **Trust Center**—Specify security and privacy settings.

NOTE Depending on the application you're using, the Options dialog box might include other tabs. For example, Word and OneNote include a Display tab for display options. Excel offers the Formulas tab where you can customize how Excel handles formulas. Outlook offers several additional tabs for customizing its specific features: Mail, Calendar, People, Tasks, and Search.

Setting File Properties

As you create and modify your files, you automatically change many of their properties. To view and modify properties, click the File tab to open Backstage view. On the right side of the Info window, you can view basic details about your file properties. To view more information or edit properties, click the Properties button (it's just below the thumbnail image) and select Show Document Panel from the menu. Office opens the Document Properties dialog box.

In this dialog box, the name of the file author displays by default. (Change this by clicking the File tab, selecting Options, and entering a new user name.) You can also optionally enter a title, subject, keywords, category, status, and comments.

TIP To remove this data from a file before sharing, use the Document Inspector (File tab, Info, Check for Issues).

For more options, click the down arrow to the right of Properties and choose Advanced Properties from the menu. A dialog box with the name of your file appears. This dialog box enables you to specify file details, enter a custom summary, display detailed statistics, and create custom properties.

THE ABSOLUTE MINIMUM

Here are the key points to remember from this chapter:

- Office offers numerous—and easy—options for handling common tasks such as saving, opening, renaming, closing, deleting, and printing files.

- The Share window provides several ways to share your documents with others, including sharing on SkyDrive, via a link, on social networks, or via email.

- The Export window enables you to save a file as a PDF or XPS document as well as change its file type.

- Customization options are numerous in Office. You can customize the Quick Access Toolbar and the Ribbon, as well as display, proofing, save, and other settings.

3

WORKING WITH TEXT

Adding and formatting text is a straightforward process in Microsoft Office. The Home tab in Word, Excel, OneNote, and PowerPoint (and the Message tab in Outlook) are "home" to a solid collection of text-formatting tools, giving you the option to select a font style and size, change text color, or apply bold, italic, and underlining to your text.

If the standard formatting isn't enough, however, Office also offers sophisticated text formatting and customization. In addition, it automates many formatting tasks if you're in a hurry or have limited design skills. In this chapter, you find out how to add and format text, text boxes, bullets, numbered lists, WordArt, symbols, and equations. You also discover how to spell check the text in your documents.

CAUTION Be aware that although working with text is similar throughout Microsoft Office, there are variations between applications. This chapter identifies the most common differences, but you might find other small inconsistencies. If you can't find a specific feature or button, it could have a different name or location on the Ribbon.

Formatting Text

Office themes include colors, fonts, and other design elements designed to work well and look good together. In this way, Office frees you to focus on your content. For maximum flexibility, however, Office offers numerous options for text formatting and customization.

You can format text in several ways:

- Use the options available on the Home tab. (These are on the Message tab in Outlook.)
- Use the Font and Paragraph dialog boxes to make a number of changes in one place and to set defaults. Open these dialog boxes by clicking the dialog box launcher (down arrow) in the lower-right corner of the Font and Paragraph groups.
- Apply text formatting individually by right-clicking the target text and using options on the mini toolbar.
- Use the text formatting options on the Format Shape pane. (Right-click text and select Format Shape from the menu.) See Chapter 5, "Working with Shapes and SmartArt," for more information about this pane.

Enhancing Text

The following are some changes you might consider to enhance your documents:

- **Enlarge or reduce font size**—Before changing font size, be sure that the size is still appropriate for the document. Verify that all text is still readable and appropriate for the type of document.
- **Replace one font with another**—You might have a particular font you prefer to use in documents. Be careful, however, not to be too creative with unusual fonts. You want to be sure that everyone can read your document clearly.
- **Add boldface, italic, or color**—Use these to emphasize a point with a certain word or words.
- **Add text effects**—Apply text effects such as shadow, reflection, glow, bevel, and 3-D rotation.

Using the Formatting Tools on the Home Tab

The Home tab includes an extensive collection of text formatting tools. (You find these on the Message tab in Outlook.) Figure 3.1 shows the Home tab in Microsoft Word.

FIGURE 3.1

The Home tab includes buttons for commonly used text effects.

Table 3.1 lists the formatting options in the Font group on the Home tab in Word. These options are similar in other Office applications.

TABLE 3.1   Font Group Buttons

Name	Description
Font	Apply a font to the selected text.
Font Size	Set the selected text's size. Choose any common size from 8 to 96 points, or type any size in the edit box.
Increase Font Size	Increase the selected text's size by a few points.
Decrease Font Size	Decrease the selected text's size by a few points.
Change Case	Change the case of the selected text. Options include Sentence case, lowercase, UPPERCASE, Capitalize Each Word, and tOGGLE cASE.
Clear All Formatting	Clear all formatting from selected text.
Bold	Bold the selected text.
Italic	Italicize the selected text.
Underline	Underline the selected text.
Strikethrough	Draw a line through selected text.
Subscript	Type small letters below the text line.
Superscript	Type small letters above the text line.
Text Effects and Typography	Apply special effects—such as a shadow, glow, reflection, or outline—to the selected text.
Text Highlight Color	Highlight selected text in a bright color.
Font Color	Apply the color you choose from the drop-down list to the selected text.

To apply one of these formatting elements, select the text you want to format and click the appropriate button. Clicking the Bold, Italic, Underline, or Strikethrough button a second time acts as a toggle and removes the formatting.

With the Font drop-down list, you can preview what each font actually looks like.

 CAUTION Remember that an unusual use of case might be difficult to read, particularly uppercase and toggle case. With text, go for readability and clarity.

Table 3.2 lists the formatting options in the Paragraph group on the Home tab in Word. These options are similar in other Office applications.

TABLE 3.2 Paragraph Group Buttons

Name	Description
Bullets	Apply or remove bullets to the selected text.
Numbering	Apply or remove automatic numbering to the selected text.
Multilevel List	Organize text with a list of one or more levels.
Decrease Indent	Decrease the indent level of the selected text.
Increase Indent	Increase the indent level of the selected text.
Sort	Sort selected text in alphabetical or numerical order.
Show/Hide	Show or hide formatting codes.
Align Left	Align text to the object's left margin.
Center	Center text within the object.
Align Right	Align text to the object's right margin.
Justify	Space words and letters within words so that the text touches both margins in the object.
Line and Paragraph Spacing	Determine the number of spaces between lines, such as single or double spacing.
Shading	Change the color behind the selected text.
Borders	Apply a border to all or part of selected text.

Formatting Text with Options in the Font Dialog Box

The Font dialog box offers some advanced formatting options not available on the Home tab. This feature is available in Word, Excel, and PowerPoint.

To format selected text with the options in the Font dialog box, follow these steps:

1. On the Home tab, click the dialog box launcher (down arrow) in the lower-right corner of the Font group. The Font dialog box displays, as shown in Figure 3.2.

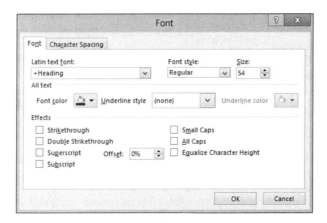

FIGURE 3.2

Make font changes quickly with the Font dialog box.

2. In the Font list, select the font you want to use. Scroll down the list to see the available fonts.

3. In the Font Style list, choose whether the font should be regular (neither bold nor italic), bold, italic, or bold and italic.

4. In the Size field, enter a specific font point size in the box or scroll through the available options.

5. Choose a font color from the palette that displays when you click the button next to the Font Color field. For additional color choices, click More Colors from the palette to open the Colors dialog box. See Chapter 4, "Working with Pictures," for more information about the Colors dialog box.

6. If you want to underline text, select an Underline Style and Underline Color from the drop-down lists.

7. Apply other effects by selecting the check box next to any of the following:

   - **Strikethrough**—Places a horizontal line through the selected text.

   - **Double Strikethrough**—Places two horizontal lines through the selected text.

   - **Superscript**—Raises the text above the baseline and reduces the font size. Sets the Offset to 30%, which you can adjust.

   - **Subscript**—Lowers the text below the baseline and reduces the font size. Sets the Offset to –25%, which you can adjust.

NOTE *Offset* refers to the percentage the text displays above or below the baseline, which is the invisible line on which the characters sit. For example, because subscript text is below the baseline, its offset is a negative number.

- **Small Caps**—Formats the text in small caps.

- **All Caps**—Capitalizes the selected text.

8. Click the OK button to close the dialog box and apply the font formatting.

Formatting Text with Options in the Paragraph Dialog Box

The Paragraph dialog box offers some advanced formatting options not available directly on the Home tab. To open this dialog box, select the text you want to format and click the down arrow in the lower-right corner of the Paragraph group on the Home tab. The Paragraph dialog box appears, as shown in Figure 3.3.

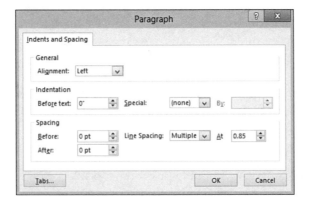

FIGURE 3.3

Set alignment, indentation, and spacing in the Paragraph dialog box.

In this dialog box, you can do the following:

- Set alignment, including right-aligned, left-aligned, centered, justified, and distributed text.

- Specify indentation requirements such as hanging and first-line indentation.

- Set line spacing. When a document looks crowded or too sparse, the *line spacing*, or the amount of space between lines of text, might be at fault. Adjust line spacing until the text looks right.

- Establish tab stop parameters by clicking the Tabs button and setting the tab stop position.

Formatting Text with the Mini Toolbar

To access the mini toolbar, right-click the text you want to format. The mini toolbar appears (see Figure 3.4) either above or below a menu that includes options for Font, Paragraph, Bullets, and Numbering.

FIGURE 3.4

The mini toolbar enables you to quickly access common text formatting options.

The mini toolbar contains selected text formatting buttons, most of which you should be familiar with from the Font and Paragraph groups on the Home tab. These include the following:

- Font
- Font Size
- Increase Font Size
- Decrease Font Size
- Format Painter
- Styles
- Bold
- Italic
- Underline
- Text Highlight Color
- Font Color
- Bullets
- Numbering

Using Bullets

To format text as a bulleted list, select the text and click the Bullets button on the Home tab. (In Outlook, this is on the Message tab.) Office uses the theme's default bullet style, but you can change to another bullet style if you want.

 TIP Consider using a list-style SmartArt graphic instead of a bullet list for greater visual impact. See Chapter 5 for more information about SmartArt options.

For more bullet options, click the down arrow to the right of the Bullets button.

In Word and Outlook, the Bullet Library opens and displays popular bullet options. Click the Define New Bullet link to open the Define New Bullet dialog box, where you can insert a symbol or picture as a bullet.

In PowerPoint, a list of bullet options displays. Click the Bullets and Numbering link to open the Bullets and Numbering dialog box where you can select from other bullet types or insert a picture or symbol as a bullet. (Click the Customize button to do the latter.) Figure 3.5 shows the Bullets and Numbering dialog box.

In OneNote, the Bullet Library displays. There are no additional options in OneNote.

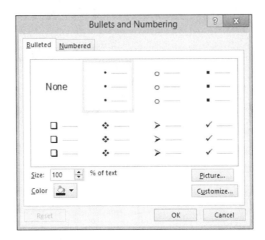

FIGURE 3.5

You can choose from many different bullet types.

 NOTE   Excel doesn't offer the Bullets button.

Using Numbered Lists

For a sequence of items, creating a numbered list is a good alternative to a bulleted list. For example, a series of procedural steps works well in a numbered list. You can create numbered lists with actual numbers, Roman numerals, or letters of the alphabet.

To format text as a numbered list, select the text and click the Numbering button on the Home tab. Office applies the default numbering to your text.

If the default numbered list formatting doesn't suit your needs, click the down arrow to the right of the Numbering button.

In Word and Outlook, the Numbering Library opens to display popular numbering options, including alphabetical lists. Click the Define New Number

Format link to open the Define New Number Format dialog box (see Figure 3.6) with even more choices.

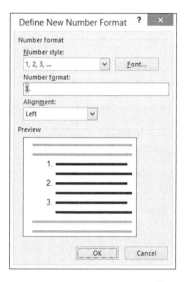

FIGURE 3.6

Create a numbered list in Office.

In PowerPoint, a list of numbering options displays. Click the Bullets and Numbering link to open the Bullets and Numbering dialog box to the Numbered tab where you customize your numbered list even further.

In OneNote, the Numbering Library displays. Click the Customize Numbers link to open the Customize Numbering pane where you can specify your exact sequence and format.

 NOTE Excel doesn't offer the Numbering button.

Using WordArt

WordArt enables you to create special text effects such as shadowed, rotated, stretched, and multicolored text in Word, Excel, and PowerPoint. Office treats WordArt as both an object and text, so you can apply object formatting such as fills and 3-D as well as apply text formatting. You can also check the spelling in your WordArt text.

CAUTION Be careful not to overuse WordArt in your document, or it can become cluttered and confusing. Use WordArt only for emphasis.

Inserting WordArt

Inserting WordArt is a simple, three-step process:

1. On the Insert tab, click the WordArt button. The WordArt gallery displays, as shown in Figure 3.7.

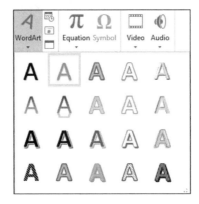

FIGURE 3.7

Preview WordArt styles before you choose one.

2. Click the WordArt style you prefer. A text box displays.

3. Replace the placeholder text with text you want to format using WordArt.

 TIP In Excel, click the Text button on the Insert tab and select WordArt to access this feature.

 TIP To move or resize a WordArt object, see "Moving and Resizing a Text Box" later in this chapter.

Formatting WordArt

If you want to change your initial WordArt selection, you can select a different style or customize it. Many WordArt formatting options are similar to those for shapes. See Chapter 5 for more information about these options.

To format WordArt, select a WordArt object and click the Drawing Tools – Format tab. Figure 3.8 shows the WordArt Styles group, where you can do the following:

- Click the down arrow to the right of the Text Fill button to choose another theme color, remove the fill color, or apply gradients and textures.

- Click the down arrow to the right of the Text Outline button to choose an outline color, remove the outline, or specify a weight or dash type.

- Click the down arrow to the right of the Text Effects button to apply special effects such as shadows, reflections, glows, bevels, 3-D rotation, and transforms (unusual text formations).

- Click the dialog box launcher (down arrow) in the lower-right corner of the WordArt Styles group to open the Format Shape pane. See Chapter 5 for more information about the text formatting options available on this pane.

FIGURE 3.8

Format your WordArt for additional emphasis.

- In Excel and PowerPoint, click the down arrow to the right of the sample styles that display in the WordArt Styles group. The WordArt gallery opens, where you can apply a new WordArt style to selected text or all text in the shape. You can also click the Clear WordArt option to remove WordArt formatting.

- In Word and Outlook, click the Quick Styles button to apply a new style to your WordArt.

If you click the Text Fill, Text Outline, or Text Effects button directly, you apply the default formatting. You must select the down arrow to the right of these buttons to view all available options.

 TIP You can also apply the formatting options in the WordArt Styles group to other text, not just WordArt.

Using Text Boxes

Use a text box when you need to add text in a special location in Word, Excel, or PowerPoint. Text boxes are also useful for wrapping text around an object.

Inserting a Text Box

To insert a text box, you can do the following:

- In Word and Outlook, click the Text Box button on the Insert tab and select Draw Text box from the menu.
- In Excel, click the Text button on the Insert tab and select Text Box.
- In PowerPoint, click the Text Box button on the Insert tab.

From here, click where you want to place the text box and enter your text. Figure 3.9 shows a text box.

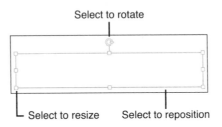

Select to rotate

Select to resize   Select to reposition

FIGURE 3.9

A text box calls attention to something you want to say and enables you to place the text exactly where you want it.

Moving and Resizing a Text Box

If your text box isn't exactly right when you first create it, you can take the following actions:

- Position the mouse over one of the text box handles to resize it. The mouse pointer displays as an arrow when you resize.
- Position the mouse over the text box outline and drag it to a new location. The mouse pointer displays as a crosshair when you reposition.
- Position the mouse over the rotation handle (the small circle at the top of the text box) to rotate the box. The mouse pointer displays as an open circle when you rotate.

 TIP   You can also move and resize placeholders, shapes, and WordArt objects using these techniques.

Formatting a Text Box

You can format text in a text box as you would any other text, including formatting the font, size, color, and style. See "Formatting Text" earlier in this chapter.

You can also format a text box using the Format Shape pane. To view the options available in this pane, follow these steps:

1. Right-click the text box you want to format.

2. Select Format Shape from the menu that displays to open the Format Shape pane.

3. In the Format Shape pane, click the Text Options link and then the Textbox button.

4. Modify your text box using the options available on the pane (see Figure 3.10). For example, you can specify alignment, text direction, margins, and more. For more information about these options, see "Using the Format Shape Pane" in Chapter 5.

FIGURE 3.10

The Format Shape pane offers a variety of text box formatting options.

5. When you're finished, click the Close (x) button in the upper-right corner of the pane to close it.

Inserting Symbols and Equations

Although the typical computer keyboard is jam-packed with plenty of characters, numbers, and symbols, there are some special symbols you can't find on a keyboard. These include symbols such as a copyright or registered trademark. You can use Office's Symbol dialog box to find special characters and other symbols to insert into your documents, including mathematical symbols, special quote marks, and wingdings (tiny graphics). In addition, you can use Office's equation functionality to enter complex equations in your documents.

To insert a symbol, click the Symbol button on the Insert tab. Word and OneNote display a list of common symbols; click the More Symbols link to open the Symbol dialog box (see Figure 3.11). Excel and PowerPoint open the Symbol dialog box directly. From here, you can select from a large collection of symbols and special characters.

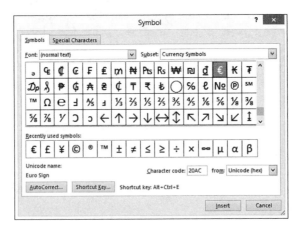

FIGURE 3.11

Select from a large collection of symbols.

To insert an equation, click the Equation button on the Insert tab. In Word and Excel, the Equation Tools – Design tab opens (see Figure 3.12), which enables you to create any equation you want to add to your document. To insert a ready-made equation—such as the Binomial theorem or the Pythagorean theorem—click the Equation button on the Equation Tools – Design tab and select an equation from the menu that displays.

FIGURE 3.12

Office makes it easy to enter complex equations.

In PowerPoint and One Note, a list of common equations displays initially. To view the Equation Tools – Design tab, select Insert New Equation from the bottom of the list.

Proofing Your Text

Creating a quality, error-free, and easy-to-read document is a natural objective. Fortunately, Office offers a spelling checker and a built-in thesaurus for finding just the right word. Keep in mind that, although an automated tool can help you catch errors, it isn't foolproof and doesn't take the place of thorough proofreading by a real person.

Setting Spelling Check Options

To set options for spelling, click the File tab, select Options, and go to the Proofing tab on the Options dialog box, as shown in Figure 3.13.

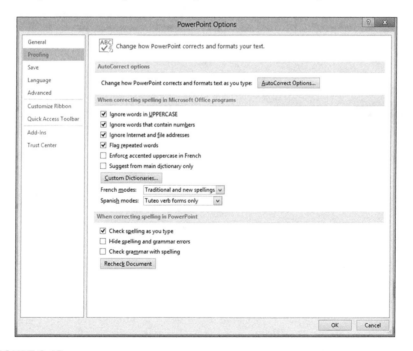

FIGURE 3.13

You can set several spell-checking options.

The options on the Proofing tab enable you to specify your preferences when you run the spelling checker, such as ignoring words in uppercase and that contain numbers, ignoring Internet and file addresses, flagging repeated words, checking spelling as you type, checking grammar, and more.

Checking Your Spelling

After you set the spelling options you want, you can spell check your document.

If you set the option to have Office check spelling as you type, you know immediately when you've possibly misspelled a word. Office places a red squiggly line under all suspected misspellings, as Figure 3.14 shows. You can either fix the error yourself or right-click to see some suggested alternatives from which to choose.

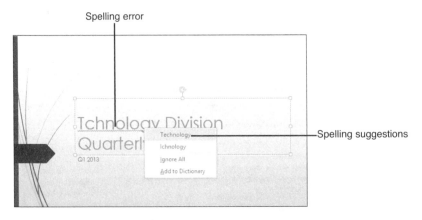

FIGURE 3.14

When you right-click a spelling error, Office suggests some possible alternative spellings.

You can also spell check your entire document at once. To check the spelling in your document, follow these steps:

1. On the Review tab, click the Spelling button. (This is called the Spelling & Grammar button in Word and Outlook.) Alternatively, press F7. When Office encounters an error, it displays the Spelling pane, shown in Figure 3.15.

    NOTE In Excel and Outlook, the Spelling dialog box opens rather than the Spelling pane.

2. Review the word that the spelling checker suspects is misspelled.

FIGURE 3.15

The Spelling pane offers several options for handling potential misspellings.

3. If the word is correct, click the Ignore button (to ignore this instance of the word) or the Ignore All button (to ignore all instances of the word).

4. If the word is misspelled and the highlighted suggestion is correct, click the Change button (to change the individual misspelled word) or the Change All button (to change all instances of this misspelled word).

5. If you want to add the suspect word to the custom dictionary as a correctly spelled word, click the Add button.

6. If the word is misspelled and none of the suggestions is correct, enter the correct spelling and click the Resume button.

7. Continue steps 2 through 6 until you finish checking your document's spelling. Office displays a dialog box that informs you the process is complete and closes the Spelling pane.

Looking Up a Synonym in the Thesaurus

If you ever have trouble coming up with just the right word, Office can help you with its thesaurus.

To find a synonym in the thesaurus, follow these steps:

1. Select the word you want to look up. If you can't think of the exact word, type a word that's close to it.

2. On the Review tab, click the Thesaurus button (or press Shift+F7). The Thesaurus pane opens.

3. Pause the mouse over the word you want to use. A down arrow displays to the right of this word.

4. Click the down arrow and select Insert from the shortcut menu that displays. Office places the new word in your document.

TIP   A quick way to find a synonym is to right-click the word in question and choose Synonyms from the menu. A list of possible synonyms displays.

NOTE   The Research pane also offers access to a thesaurus as well as a dictionary, translation tools, and several other research sources. Click the Research button on the Review tab to access this pane.

THE ABSOLUTE MINIMUM

Here are the key points to remember from this chapter:

- Office offers numerous ways to format text: the formatting tools on the Home tab, the mini toolbar, and the Format Shape pane.

- Creating a bulleted list is a common way to format text in Office, but be sure to consider other—often more effective—ways to communicate your message.

- For a sequence of items, creating a numbered list is an alternative to a bulleted list.

- WordArt lets you create special text effects such as shadowed, rotated, stretched, and multicolored text.

- Use a text box when you need to add text outside its original placeholders or when you need to frame special text.

- Office offers a vast collection of symbols and equations you can add to your documents.

- Create an error-free document with Office's proofing tools such as the spelling checker.

- If you have trouble coming up with just the right word, Office's built-in thesaurus can help.

WORKING WITH PICTURES

Office offers several ways to enliven your documents with pictures, including inserting pictures from your computer or the Web, inserting screenshots, and creating photo albums.

After you add pictures to your documents, Office provides a variety of customization and formatting options, including color correction, artistic effects, picture styles, borders, custom layouts, and much more.

Using Pictures in Office

You can insert a variety of pictures into your Office documents, including both illustrations and photographs. You do this by inserting a picture from your own computer or network or by inserting online pictures from the Office.com clip art collection, your SkyDrive account, or an external site such as Flickr.

Office works with two basic types of pictures. *Bitmap* pictures are composed of pixels: tiny dots of color. A single picture might contain hundreds of thousands of pixels. Bitmap pictures are the most common type of pictures on the Web. Photos from digital cameras are also bitmaps. Common bitmap file formats include .bmp, .gif, .jpg, .png, and .tif.

Vector pictures, on the other hand, are composed of points, lines, and curves. Because you can easily resize and change the color of vector pictures, they are popular for producing logos and other pictures that need to be repurposed. Common vector file formats include .eps and .wmf.

Table 4.1 lists the most common picture formats you can use in Office.

TABLE 4.1 Picture Formats

File Extension	Format
.emf	Windows Enhanced Metafile
.wmf	Windows Metafile
.jpg, .jpeg, .jfif, .jpe	JPEG File Interchange Format
.png	Portable Network Graphics
.bmp, .dib, .rle, .bmz	Windows Bitmap
.gif, .gfa	Graphics Interchange Format
.emz	Compressed Windows Enhanced Metafile
.wmz	Compressed Windows Metafile
.pcz	Compressed Macintosh PICT
.tif, .tiff	Tag Image File Format
.eps	Encapsulated PostScript
.pct, .pict	Macintosh PICT
.wpg	WordPerfect Graphics

Inserting Pictures

Office makes it easy to insert a picture from your computer or a network location. To do so, follow these steps:

1. On the Insert tab, click the Pictures button. The Insert Picture dialog box opens (see Figure 4.1), which is similar to the Open dialog box.

FIGURE 4.1

Find and insert a picture from the Insert Picture dialog box.

 NOTE See Chapter 2, "Working with Office Applications," for more information about the advanced features of the Open dialog box that are shared with the Insert Picture dialog box.

2. Select the picture you want to insert.

 TIP To select multiple pictures, hold down the Shift key as you select. If the pictures aren't contiguous, hold down the Ctrl key.

3. Click the Insert button to insert the selected picture. If you plan to make updates to this picture and would rather link to it instead, click the down arrow to the right of the Insert button and choose to link directly to the file. Alternatively, you can insert it and then link to it.

You can resize and reposition your picture and modify it in other ways. See "Modifying Pictures," later in this chapter, for more information.

Inserting Online Pictures

Office offers several options for inserting online pictures, including pictures from the Office.com clip art collection, your SkyDrive account, and other locations on the Web such as Bing Image Search and Flickr. After you insert an online picture, you can reformat, recolor, and redesign it to suit your needs.

Inserting Pictures from the Office.com Clip Art Collection

To insert a royalty-free photo or illustration from the Office.com clip art collection, follow these steps:

1. On the Insert tab, click the Online Pictures button. The Insert Pictures dialog box opens, as shown in Figure 4.2.

FIGURE 4.2

Insert pictures from Office.com.

2. Enter a keyword or keywords in the Search Office.com field and then click the Search button (the small magnifying glass to the right of the field). For example, you can search for pictures with computers, people, and so forth.

3. Scroll down the right side of the dialog box to view all results that match your keywords (see Figure 4.3).

Return to initial
dialog box.   Revise keywords.

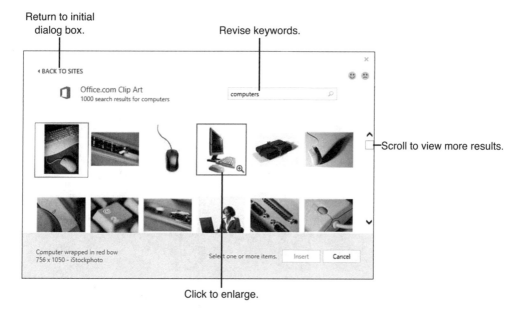

Scroll to view more results.

Click to enlarge.

FIGURE 4.3

Viewing matching results.

4. Pause your mouse over a picture to display a description.

5. Click the View Larger button in the lower-right corner of a picture to enlarge it.

6. Select one or more pictures from the matching results. To select multiple pictures, hold down the Shift key as you select.

7. Click the Insert button to insert the picture.

 TIP If your initial search doesn't yield the desired results, enter new keywords to search again.

Inserting Pictures from the Bing Image Search

To search Microsoft's search engine Bing for pictures licensed under Creative Commons, follow these steps:

 NOTE Creative Commons (creativecommons.org) enables content creators such as artists and photographers to let the public use their content under conditions they specify.

1. On the Insert tab, click the Online Pictures button to open the Insert Pictures dialog box (refer to Figure 4.2).

2. Enter a keyword or keywords in the Search Bing field and click the Search button (the small magnifying glass to the right of the field).

3. Scroll down the right side of the dialog box to view all results that match your keywords (see Figure 4.4).

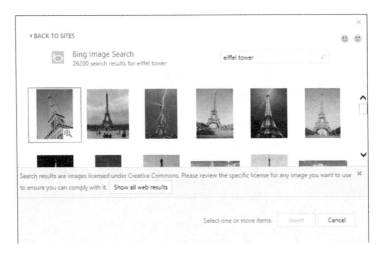

FIGURE 4.4

Bing displays matching pictures that are licensed under Creative Commons.

 CAUTION You can click the Show All Web Results button to view more options, but be aware that this could display pictures protected by copyright.

4. Pause your mouse over a picture to display a description.

5. Click the View Larger button in the lower-right corner of a picture to enlarge it.

6. Select one or more pictures from the matching results. To select multiple pictures, hold down the Shift key as you select.

7. Click the Insert button to insert the picture.

Inserting Pictures from Your SkyDrive Account

To insert pictures stored on your SkyDrive account, follow these steps:

1. On the Insert tab, click the Online Pictures button to open the Insert Pictures dialog box (refer to Figure 4.2).

2. Click the Browse button.

3. Navigate to the folder that contains the picture you want to insert (see Figure 4.5).

FIGURE 4.5

Insert pictures stored on SkyDrive.

4. Select one or more pictures from the matching results.

5. Click the Insert button to insert the picture.

 TIP You can also insert pictures from your Flickr account. Click the Flickr button in the lower-left corner of the Insert Pictures dialog box to connect your Flickr account to your Microsoft account, enabling you to view your Flickr photos and videos in Office.

 TIP If you use PowerPoint, another interesting way to use pictures is to create a photo album, a presentation composed of a series of pictures. For example, you could create a travel presentation consisting of a series of photos taken on a trip. To create a presentation based on a photo album, click the Photo Album button on the Insert tab.

Inserting Screenshots

Rather than using an external application to take screenshots, Office offers its own screen capture tool.

To take a screenshot and insert it into your document, follow these steps:

1. Open the application from which you want to take a screenshot. For example, you might want to capture something from another Office application or from an external website.

2. Return to your Office document.

3. On the Insert tab, click the Screenshot button (Screen Clipping in OneNote). A list of available windows appears, as shown in Figure 4.6.

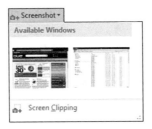

FIGURE 4.6

Insert a screenshot of an open window or clip a section of a screen.

4. If you want to take a screenshot of the entire window and insert it into your Office document, select that window from the list.

5. If you want to select a specific area for your screenshot, select the Screen Clipping option on the menu. This minimizes Office and displays open applications and the desktop with a white semi-transparent layer.

6. If you're taking a clip of a screenshot, select the area you want to include using your mouse pointer (which now appears as a crosshair).

Release the mouse and Office inserts the screenshot.

Modifying Pictures

After you insert a picture, you can modify it to suit your needs. Office includes many image-editing features that can eliminate the need to edit your pictures in an external application.

The Picture Tools – Format tab, shown in Figure 4.7, appears whenever you select a picture or when you select a shape that has a picture fill. Using this contextual tab, you can make both minor and major adjustments to a picture, such as changing its color or adjusting its contrast. Although the buttons on this tab use the term *Picture*, these features also apply to photos and screenshots.

FIGURE 4.7

The Picture Tools – Format tab offers a multitude of formatting options.

 CAUTION   OneNote doesn't offer the Picture Tools – Format tab and provides limited picture-formatting options.

 NOTE   Many of the options on the Picture Tools – Format tab include a link to the Format Picture pane, where you can customize a picture even further. You can also access this pane by right-clicking a picture and selecting Format Picture from the menu that appears. See the "Using the Format Picture Pane" section, later in this chapter, for more information.

Adjusting Pictures

The Adjust group on the Picture Tools – Format tab enables you to remove background areas from pictures, correct pictures, adjust color settings, and apply artistic effects. Be aware that not all these options are available, depending on the format of the picture you want to modify.

Removing a Picture Background

To remove the background of a selected picture, click the Remove Background button on the Picture Tools – Format tab. The Background Removal tab appears, as shown in Figure 4.8.

FIGURE 4.8

The Background Removal tab enables you to specify how and what to remove.

This tab offers the following options:

- **Mark Areas to Keep**—Designate the areas to keep with a Pencil tool.

- **Mark Areas to Remove**—Designate the areas to remove with a Pencil tool.

- **Delete Mark**—Remove the background areas you marked to remove.

- **Discard All Changes**—Restore the picture to its original state.

- **Keep Changes**—Save changes and close the Background Removal tab.

 CAUTION It takes some time to learn to use this powerful tool effectively. If you don't like the end result, click the Undo button in the upper-left corner of the screen to restore your picture's background.

Applying Picture Corrections

To brighten and sharpen a selected picture, follow these steps:

1. On the Picture Tools – Format tab, click the Corrections button.

2. From the gallery that appears, select an option in either the Sharpen/Soften section or the Brightness/Contrast section.

3. Pause your mouse over each style to preview what it looks like when applied to your picture.

4. When you find a style you like, click the style to apply it.

For additional picture correction options, click the Picture Corrections Options link at the bottom of the gallery to open the Format Picture pane.

Adjusting Picture Colors

To change or adjust a selected picture's colors, click the Color button on the Picture Tools – Format tab. In the gallery that appears, as shown in Figure 4.9, you can perform the following tasks:

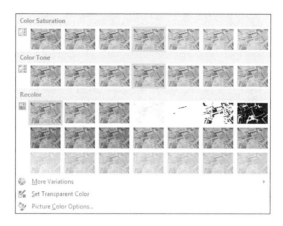

FIGURE 4.9

Specify exact colors for your picture.

- Modify your picture's color by specifying its purity based on a percentage (Color Saturation), specifying how light or dark the color is (Color Tone), or changing to a new color (Recolor).

- Click the More Variations link to open the Colors palette. You can choose a color from the palette or click the More Colors link to open the Colors dialog box. See Chapter 5, "Working with Shapes and SmartArt," for more information about this palette.

- Click the Set Transparent Color link to click a pixel in the selected picture, thereby making all pixels of the same color transparent.

- Click the Picture Color Options link to open the Format Picture pane.

Applying Artistic Effects

To apply artistic effects to a selected picture, such as a paintbrush effect or a pencil sketch effect, click the Artistic Effects button on the Picture Tools – Format tab. In the gallery that appears, select your desired effect. To apply additional effects in the Format Picture pane, click the Artistic Effects Options link.

Compressing Pictures

Compressing pictures enables you to reduce the file size of your document.

To compress a selected picture, follow these steps:

1. Click the Compress Pictures button on the Picture Tools – Format tab (a small button in the Adjust group). The Compress Pictures dialog box opens, as shown in Figure 4.10.

FIGURE 4.10

Specify compression options and select your target output.

2. The Apply Only to This Picture check box is selected by default. If you want to compress all the pictures, remove this check mark.

3. The Delete Cropped Areas of Pictures check box is selected by default, which permanently removes any areas you cropped and reduces file size. If you don't want to do this, remove this check mark.

4. By default, the Use Document Resolution option button is selected as your target output. Optionally, you can switch to a resolution suited to print, screen, or email. Depending on your picture format, all these options might not be available.

5. Click the OK button to compress your picture.

 NOTE If you remove the check mark next to the Apply Only to This Picture, Office compresses all pictures. This process could take a while, especially if you are working on a large document with many pictures.

Changing to a Different Picture

If you decide to insert a different picture, but want to retain all the formatting you've applied to an existing picture, on the Picture Tools – Format tab, click the Change Picture button.

The Insert Pictures dialog box opens, where you can select a new picture from your computer or the Web. Office inserts the new picture and keeps all existing formatting.

Resetting a Picture

If you've made a lot of changes to a picture and then decide you want to go back to the original, on the Picture Tools – Format tab, click the Reset Picture button.

Office restores your picture to its original appearance. If you want to reset picture formatting *and* size (from compression, for example), click the down arrow to the right of the Reset Picture button and select Reset Picture & Size from the menu.

 NOTE   If you compress a picture and select the Delete Cropped Areas of Pictures check box, you can't reset your picture.

Working with Picture Styles

The Picture Styles group on the Picture Tools – Format tab enables you to apply one of many preselected styles to your pictures. You can also add a border, apply special effects, and modify your layout.

Applying a Picture Style

To apply a picture style, select one of the styles in the Picture Styles group, or click the down arrow to the right of the group to open a gallery of additional options, as shown in Figure 4.11.

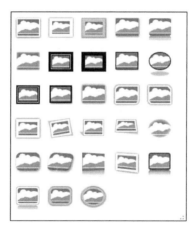

FIGURE 4.11

Choose to apply a picture style, such as a rotated white border or a soft-edge oval shape, to your picture.

This gallery displays additional picture styles such as Reflected Bevel Black, Rotated White, and Soft Edge Oval. Pause your mouse over each style to preview what it looks like when applied to your picture. When you find a style you like, click it to apply.

TIP You can also apply a picture style by right-clicking a picture and then selecting the Style button that displays either above or below the shortcut menu depending on where you right-click the picture.

Applying Picture Borders

To add a border to a selected picture, on the Picture Tools – Format tab, click the Picture Border button. The Picture Border palette appears, as shown in Figure 4.12.

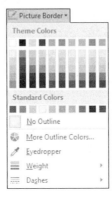

FIGURE 4.12

Specify the type of picture border to apply.

Choose from the following options:

- Apply one of the theme or standard colors. The theme colors are compatible with your color scheme.

- Select No Outline to hide the existing border.

- Select More Outline Colors to open the Colors dialog box, in which you can select from many other colors or create a custom color. See Chapter 5 for more information about this dialog box.

- Select Eyedropper to select a fill color by clicking an existing color on the screen.

- Select Weight to specify the border weight—from 1/4 point to 6 points.

- Select Dashes to specify a dash style, such as square dot, dash dot, or long dash. Unless you create a thick outline, dashes probably won't be visible.

Applying Picture Effects

You can add shadow, glow, bevel, and 3-D effects to pictures by using the tools on the Picture Effects palette. To apply picture effects to a selected picture, on the Picture Tools – Format tab, click the Picture Effects button. The Picture Effects menu appears. Each menu choice leads to a gallery of additional options.

Depending on the shape you select, not all options are available. To preview a potential effect, pause the mouse over it in the gallery.

Choose from the following options on the Picture Effects menu:

- **Preset**—Apply one of 12 ready-made effects designed to work well with your picture.

- **Shadow**—Apply an outer, inner, or perspective shadow to the shape. Select No Shadow to remove the shadow.

- **Reflection**—Apply one of several reflection variations, such as a half or full reflection. Selecting No Reflection removes the shape effect.

- **Glow**—Apply one of several glow variations in different colors and sizes. Select No Glow to remove the glow effect. Select More Glow Colors to open the Colors palette, where you can select another color.

- **Soft Edges**—Apply a soft edge, ranging in width from 1 to 50 points. Select No Soft Edges to remove the effect.

- **Bevel**—Apply one of several bevel options, such as a circle or divot. Select No Bevel to remove the effect.

- **3-D Rotation**—Apply a parallel, perspective, or oblique rotation to the selected shape. Remove the effect by selecting No Rotation.

 TIP For more options, select the Options link at the bottom of each gallery to open the Format Picture pane. The exact wording of the Options link varies based on the name of the gallery, such as Shadow Options or 3-D Rotation Options.

Converting Pictures to SmartArt Graphics

If you want to convert a picture, or a series of pictures, to a SmartArt graphic, select the pictures and then on the Picture Tools – Format tab, click the Picture Layout button. From the gallery that appears, select the SmartArt style you want to apply to your pictures.

See Chapter 5 for more information about SmartArt graphics in Office.

Arranging Pictures

Like with other objects, you can arrange the pictures you insert into your document. The Arrange group on the Picture Tools – Format tab offers numerous options for arranging pictures. For example, you can align, group, and rotate pictures and send overlapping pictures backward or forward to achieve a desired effect.

Cropping Pictures

If you don't want to include an entire picture in your document, you can crop it to your exact specifications. For example, you might want to zero in on an object in the center of a picture, or remove extra content at the top of a picture.

To crop a selected picture, on the Picture Tools – Format tab, click the Crop button.

 TIP You can also crop a picture by right-clicking it and then selecting the Crop button that displays either above or below the shortcut menu depending on where you right-click the picture.

From the menu that appears, select one of the following options:

- **Crop**—Drag the mouse to determine your cropping area. Handles surround the picture, enabling you to specify the exact content you want to retain.

- **Crop to Shape**—Select a shape from the gallery that appears. Office modifies the picture to fit the selected shape.

- **Aspect Ratio**—Crop to a specific aspect ratio, such as a 1:1 square, 2:3 portrait, or 3:2 landscape.

- **Fill**—Resize the picture to fill the entire picture area, maintaining the original aspect ratio.

- **Fit**—Resize the picture to fit the specified picture area, maintaining the original aspect ratio.

Modifying a Picture's Height and Width

To modify a selected picture's height or width, on the Picture Tools – Format tab, enter a new measurement in the Shape Height and Shape Width boxes, located in the Size group. Alternatively, use the scrolling arrows to make incremental adjustments either smaller or larger.

For more picture-sizing options, click the arrow in the lower-right corner of the Size group to open the Format Picture pane, where you can specify size, rotation, scale, and more.

Using the Format Picture Pane

You can use the Format Picture pane to apply numerous formatting changes all in one place. This pane duplicates many of the functions available on the Picture Tools – Format tab, but also has some special features of its own.

To open the Format Picture pane, shown in Figure 4.13, right-click a picture and choose Format Picture from the menu that displays.

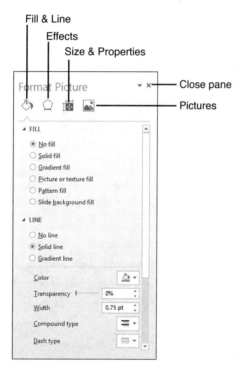

FIGURE 4.13

The Format Picture pane enables you to make many changes in one place.

 TIP You can also access this pane from the Options menu in many of the palettes and galleries on the Picture Tools – Format tab. For example, click the Artistic Effects button and select Artistic Effects Options from the gallery to open the Artistic Effects section on the Format Picture pane.

Click one of the following buttons to display related content on the pane:

- **Fill & Line**—Format fills and lines.

- **Effects**—Apply shadows, reflections, glows, soft edges, 3-D formats, 3-D rotations, and artistic effects.

- **Size & Properties**—Format size, position, text boxes, and alt text. In Word and Outlook, this is called Layout & Properties.
- **Pictures**—Apply picture corrections, color, and cropping.

The tools available on the Format Picture pane are nearly identical to those found on the Format Shape pane. See Chapter 5 for more information about this pane.

THE ABSOLUTE MINIMUM

Here are the key points to remember from this chapter:

- You can insert a variety of pictures, photos, and illustrations into your Office document, including both bitmap and vector images.

- Inserting a picture from your computer or a network location is one of the most common ways to add pictures to a document.

- Office offers several options for inserting online pictures, including pictures from the Office.com clip art collection, your SkyDrive account, and other locations on the Web such as Bing and Flickr.

- You don't need to use an external application to take screenshots. Office provides its own screen capture tool that lets you insert full or cropped screenshots.

- You can use the Picture Tools – Format tab or the Format Picture pane to modify a picture's color, appearance, or size as well as apply artistic effects, styles, borders, and layouts.

WORKING WITH SHAPES AND SMARTART

A *shape* is an object such as a line, arrow, rectangle, circle, square, or callout. You can quickly insert basic shapes in your documents, but after you use Office for a little while, you'll probably want to modify the default shape formats. Fortunately, Office offers a variety of shape-formatting options that enable you to quickly customize a shape to meet your exact needs.

If you want something a bit more sophisticated than a simple shape, consider SmartArt. SmartArt offers ready-made, color-coordinated designs that display lists, processes, organization charts, matrices, and more—in a way that makes the most of Office's many design features.

Inserting Shapes

Office offers dozens of ready-made shapes that you can add to your documents.

 NOTE In OneNote, you insert shapes on the Draw tab. See Chapter 54, "Inserting Notebook Content," to learn more about the Draw tab and adding shapes in OneNote.

To insert a shape, follow these steps:

1. On the Insert tab, click the Shapes button. The Shapes gallery opens, as shown in Figure 5.1.

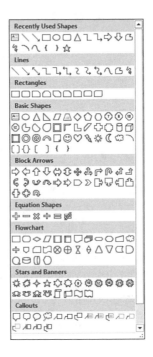

FIGURE 5.1

The Shapes gallery offers a variety of options.

 TIP If you've already inserted another shape and the Drawing Tools – Format tab appears, you can access the Shapes gallery from this tab as well.

2. From the gallery, select the shape you want to insert. Gallery options include lines, rectangles, arrows, callouts, circles, and more.

3. In your document, click where you want the shape to appear and then drag until the shape is the size you want. You can then format the shape as you would any other object.

 TIP   Keep in mind that although shapes make it easy to create an attractive image, they aren't designed for complex graphic needs. If you need something more detailed, consider using SmartArt, covered later in this chapter.

Inserting Lines and Arrows

You can add lines and arrows to draw attention to something, show how things are connected, or show how one thing leads to another. For example, you might want to add a line to connect two shapes. Or you might use an arrow to point to text or an object of special importance. You can also create simple images with the line, rectangle, and oval shapes.

To draw a line or arrow, follow these steps:

1. On the Insert tab, click the Shapes button to open the Shapes gallery (refer to Figure 5.1).

2. Click one of the buttons in the Lines section of the Shapes gallery. The mouse pointer becomes a plus sign.

3. Click and hold down where you want the line to begin and then drag to where you want the line to end.

If the line looks crooked or is the wrong length, you can adjust it. First, select the line. Then pause your mouse over one of the handles that appear at the ends of the line. The mouse pointer becomes a line with an arrowhead at both ends. Click and drag the circle to lengthen the line or adjust its angle.

If the line isn't in the right place, you can move it. First, select the line. Then pause your mouse over the line. The mouse pointer becomes a cross with arrowheads at all four ends. Click and drag the line to move it.

 TIP   Press the Shift key as you drag the mouse to create straight horizontal or vertical lines. This enables you to draw lines at angles evenly divisible by 15 (0, 15, 30, 45, and so forth), which makes it much easier to create a straight line. Press the Ctrl key as you drag the mouse to draw a line from a center point, lengthening the line in both directions as you drag.

NOTE By using the options in the Shape Outline palette, you can easily change the appearance of a line or arrow by adjusting its width or converting it to a dashed line. See "Specifying Shape Outlines," later in this chapter, for more information.

Inserting Rectangles and Ovals

You can also draw rectangular and oval shapes. Using rectangular shapes enables you to emphasize important information, group information, or illustrate other ideas or concepts.

To draw a rectangle, click one of the buttons in the Rectangles section of the Shapes gallery. The mouse pointer becomes a plus sign. Click where you want the rectangle to appear and then drag to draw the rectangle.

 TIP To draw a square, press the Shift key while you draw the shape.

To draw an oval, click the Oval button in the Basic Shapes section of the Shapes gallery. The mouse pointer becomes a plus sign. Click where you want the oval to appear and then drag to draw the oval.

 TIP To draw a perfect circle, press the Shift key while you draw the shape.

You can then reshape and resize these images or apply other formatting to them.

Another option is to add text to a rectangular or oval shape. If you want to add only a word or two, select the shape and type the text you want to enter. Alternatively, click the Text Box button on either the Insert tab or the Drawing Tools – Format tab and create a text box inside the original object. Be sure, however, that the text box fits into the object without overlapping its borders.

Formatting Shapes Using the Drawing Tools – Format Tab

When you create or select a shape, the contextual Drawing Tools – Format tab appears, shown in Figure 5.2.

FIGURE 5.2

The Drawing Tools – Format tab offers numerous options for shape creation and formatting.

The Insert Shapes and Shape Styles groups on the Drawing Tools – Format tab are the centerpieces of Office's suite of shape-creation and shape-formatting tools. They offer a multitude of options for modifying and enhancing shapes, such as specifying a shape's fill, outline, and effects. The rest of this section focuses on the many shape-formatting options available on this tab.

Working with Shape Quick Styles

One way to format a shape quickly is to apply a Quick Style. Quick Styles offer numerous fill, shading, and border options in colors that coordinate with your chosen theme.

To apply a Quick Style to a shape, follow these steps:

1. Select the shape to which you want to apply the style.

2. On the Drawing Tools – Format tab, click the down arrow to the right of the Shape Styles box to open the Shape Styles gallery, as shown in Figure 5.3.

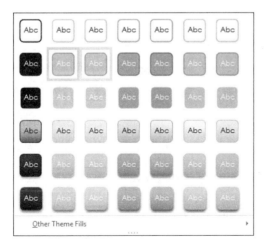

FIGURE 5.3

Choose a shape style that coordinates with your document theme.

3. Pause your mouse over an available style to preview the style's effect on your shape.

 TIP You can also open the Shape Styles gallery by right-clicking a shape and clicking the Style button that displays either below or above the contextual menu.

4. Optionally, click Other Theme Fills at the bottom of the gallery to open a palette of additional options, including several grayscale options.

 TIP As a shortcut, you can click one of the styles that display in the Shape Styles box on the tab itself without opening the gallery. The default view shows several possible styles.

5. Click a style to apply it to the selected shape.

Specifying Shape Fill Color

To set a shape's fill color, select it, and on the Drawing Tools – Format tab, click the Shape Fill button. A palette displays, as shown in Figure 5.4.

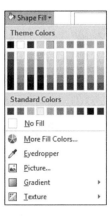

FIGURE 5.4

Add colors or patterns to fill an object.

You can do any of the following in this palette:

- Apply one of the theme, recent, or standard colors. The theme colors are compatible with your chosen color scheme.

- Select No Fill to make the object transparent. You see the document background through the object.

- Select More Fill Colors to open the Colors dialog box, where you can choose from many other colors or create a custom color.

- Select Eyedropper to choose a fill color by clicking an existing color on the screen. (This option is available only in PowerPoint.)

- Select Picture to fill your shape with a picture you select.

- Select Gradient to apply a light or dark gradient pattern.

- Select Texture to fill the shape with one of the available texture patterns in the gallery that appears.

 TIP You can also access fill options by right-clicking a shape and clicking the Fill button that displays below the contextual menu.

Using the Colors Dialog Box

Select More Fill Colors in the Shape Fill palette to open the Colors dialog box, as illustrated in Figure 5.5.

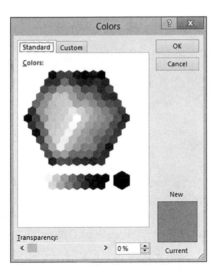

FIGURE 5.5

Choose from many common colors in the Colors dialog box.

To choose a new color, select it in the palette on the Standard tab. The color appears in the New section of the preview box to contrast with the Current color.

Click OK to keep the color or click Cancel to return to the original color.

TIP You can set transparency (making the color appear transparent) by dragging the Transparency scrollbar or by entering a specific transparency percentage. The higher the percentage, the more transparent the color, which enables things behind the object to show through.

Using a Custom Color

To add a custom color, click the Custom tab on the Colors dialog box, as shown in Figure 5.6.

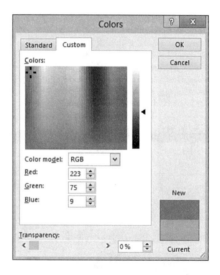

FIGURE 5.6

Create a custom color to suit your exact needs.

You can create a custom color in two ways. One way is to click and drag the crosshair in the Colors area until you find the color you want. The other way is to choose either RGB or HSL in the Color Model drop-down field and then adjust the color's level of red, green, and blue (for RGB) or hue, saturation, and luminance (for HSL). Click OK to keep the color or click Cancel to discard it.

NOTE *Red, green,* and *blue* represent the amount of each of these primary colors in the color you create. The RGB color wheel is based on projected light—the kind you see with computer screen projection.

Hue represents the actual color, *saturation* represents the color's intensity, and *luminance* represents the color's brightness. In general, the lower the number, the lighter or less intense the color is.

Applying a Picture Fill

You can even fill an object with a picture. For example, you could create a shape such as a circle and fill it with a logo, product image, or photo.

To apply a picture fill, follow these steps:

1. Select the shape to which you want to apply the picture fill.

2. On the Drawing Tools – Format tab, click the Shape Fill button and then choose Picture from the menu.

3. In the Insert Pictures dialog box, do one of the following:

    *   Click the Browse button next to the From a File field to open the Insert Picture dialog box, where you can select a picture on your computer to insert.

    *   Enter keywords in the Search Office.com field and press the Enter key to search the Office.com online clip art collection.

    *   Enter keywords in the Search Bing field to search Bing for relevant pictures.

    *   Click the Browse button next to the SkyDrive field to insert a picture you stored on your SkyDrive account.

    *   Click the Flickr button to insert a picture from your Flickr account.

See Chapter 4, "Working with Pictures," to learn more about the Insert Pictures dialog box.

CAUTION   Some pictures just don't work well as fills. Look at yours carefully. If it doesn't look good, press Ctrl+Z to undo it and then apply another fill.

Applying a Gradient Fill

A gradient creates a smooth transition from one color to another, using gentle blending. To apply a gradient to a selected shape, on the Drawing Tools – Format tab, click the Shape Fill button and select Gradient from the menu. From the gallery that appears, you can apply a light or dark gradient. Pause your mouse over each available gradient to preview its effect. Click the gradient to apply to your document. To remove a gradient, select No Gradient in the gallery.

TIP   For more gradient options, click More Gradients in the gallery to open the Format Shape pane. See "Using the Format Shape Pane," later in this chapter, for more information.

Applying a Textured Fill

To apply a texture to a selected shape, on the Drawing Tools – Format tab, click the Shape Fill button and then choose Texture from the menu. Select your preferred texture from the gallery, pausing your mouse over each option to preview it.

 TIP For more options, click More Textures in the gallery to open the Format Shape pane, described in the "Using the Format Shape Pane" section later in this chapter.

Specifying Shape Outlines

To specify the outline of a shape—either a line or any other shape such as a circle or rectangle—select the shape and click the Shape Outline button on the Drawing Tools – Format tab. The Shape Outline palette appears, as shown in Figure 5.7.

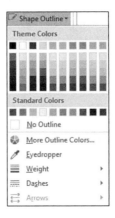

FIGURE 5.7

Specify the format of a shape's outline in the Shape Outline palette.

 TIP You can also access outline options by right-clicking a shape and clicking the Outline button that displays below the contextual menu.

Choose from the following options:

- Apply one of the theme or standard colors. The theme colors are compatible with your color scheme.

- Select No Outline to hide the existing line.

- Select More Outline Colors to open the Colors dialog box, where you can select from many other colors or create a custom color.

- Select Eyedropper to choose an outline color by clicking an existing color on the screen. (This option is available only in PowerPoint.)

- Select Weight to specify the outline weight—from ¾ point to 6 points.

- Select Dashes to specify a dash style, such as square dot, dash dot, or long dash. Unless you create a thick outline, dashes probably won't be visible.

- Select Arrows to specify an arrow style. Note that this option is available only for open shapes with a distinct beginning and end such as lines, arrows, curves, freeforms, and scribbles.

 TIP   For more options, select More Lines or More Arrows from the Weight, Dashes, or Arrows menus to open the Format Shape pane, described in the "Using the Format Shape Pane" section later in this chapter.

Applying Shape Effects

You can add shadow, glow, bevel, and 3-D effects to shapes by clicking the Shape Effects button on the Drawing Tools – Format tab. The Shape Effects menu offers numerous effect choices, each leading to a gallery of additional options.

Depending on the shape you select, not all options are available. To preview a potential shape effect, pause the mouse over it in the gallery.

Choose from the following shape effects:

- **Preset**—Apply one of 12 ready-made effects designed to work well with your shape.

- **Shadow**—Apply an outer, inner, or perspective shadow to the shape. Select No Shadow to remove the shadow.

- **Reflection**—Apply one of several reflection variations, such as half or full reflection. Selecting No Reflection removes the shape effect.

- **Glow**—Apply one of several glow variations in different colors and sizes. Select No Glow to remove the glow effect. Select More Glow Colors to open the Colors palette, where you can select another color. See "Using the Colors Dialog Box," earlier in this chapter, for more information about colors.

- **Soft Edges**—Apply a soft edge, ranging in width from 1 to 50 points. Select No Soft Edges to remove the effect.

- **Bevel**—Apply one of several bevel options, such as a circle or divot. Select No Bevel to remove the effect.

- **3-D Rotation**—Apply a parallel, perspective, or oblique rotation to the selected shape. Remove the effect by selecting No Rotation.

Editing Shapes

On the Drawing Tools – Format tab, click the Edit Shape button in the Insert Shapes group to open a submenu with the following choices:

- **Change Shape**—Change the applied shape to another shape available in the Shapes gallery.
- **Edit Points**—Edit the points of selected shapes. This enables you to select and drag a shape's existing points to create a new shape design.
- **Reroute Connectors**—Force a connector (line connecting two shapes) to be the shortest distance. Be aware that although doing this creates a more direct connection, the connector might overlap other shapes or text.

 CAUTION Be aware that depending on the type of shape you select, not all editing options are available.

Merging Shapes

Office 2013 introduces the capability to merge shapes. This feature is available only in PowerPoint.

To merge two or more selected shapes, follow these steps:

1. Select the shapes you want to merge.
2. On the Drawing Tools – Format tab, click the Merge Shapes button. (It's a small button in the Insert Shapes group.)
3. From the menu that displays, specify the merge option you want to apply: Union, Combine, Fragment, Intersect, or Subtract. Figure 5.8 shows several examples of these merge options.

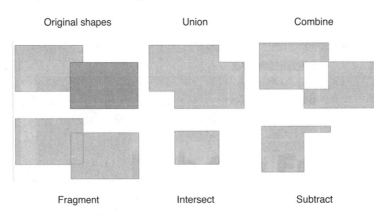

FIGURE 5.8

Try out some creative shape merge options.

Using the Format Shape Pane

You can use the Format Shape pane to apply numerous formatting changes all in one place. The Format Shape pane duplicates some of the functions available on the Drawing Tools – Format tab, but also has some special features of its own.

 NOTE If you select a picture to format, the name of the pane is Format Picture, but contains many of the same features as the Format Shape pane.

To open the Format Shape pane, right-click a shape and choose Format Shape from the menu that displays. Figure 5.9 shows the Format Shape pane.

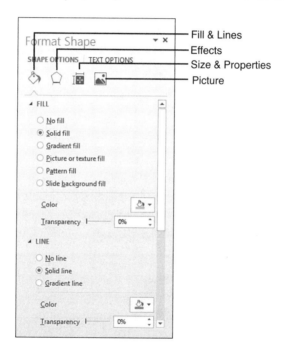

FIGURE 5.9

The Format Shape pane enables you to make many changes in one place.

The specific buttons and fields available on the Format Shape pane vary by application, but in general you can apply

- A variety of fill and line options. You can also modify transparency, customize gradient presets, and change the scale and alignment of picture and texture fills.

- Special effects, including shadow, reflection, glow, soft edge, and 3-D effects.

- Text and picture effects (available only for shapes with picture or texture fills), including text box formatting and picture color correction and cropping.

Working with SmartArt Graphics

SmartArt takes the power and flexibility of shapes one step further. SmartArt enables you to combine shapes and text to create informative lists, matrices, pyramids, and more. Then, using Office's shape and text formatting options, you can create a custom graphic that both conveys your message and gives your document an extra polish.

 NOTE SmartArt isn't available in OneNote.

For example, you can create a detailed organization chart with SmartArt (see Figure 5.10). Or you can create a graphic that explains a step-by-step process (see Figure 5.11).

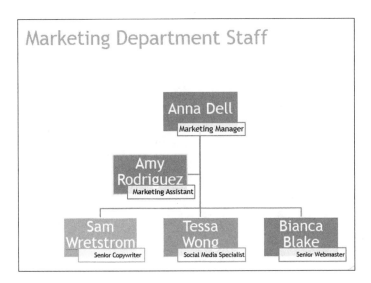

FIGURE 5.10

Use one of SmartArt's many organization chart layouts.

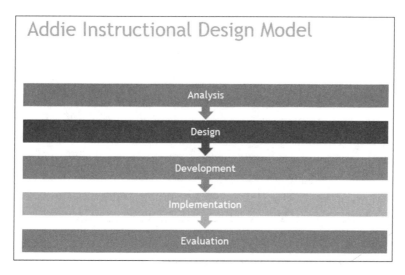

FIGURE 5.11

Highlight a process.

Table 5.1 lists SmartArt types, each offering a variety of layouts to choose from.

TABLE 5.1 SmartArt Types

Choose This SmartArt Type	To Display
List	Nonsequential data
Process	Steps in a process or a sequential timeline
Cycle	An ongoing process
Hierarchy	Hierarchical data such as an organizational chart
Relationship	Connected data
Matrix	Parts in relation to a whole
Pyramid	Proportions from small to large
Picture	A graphical representation of data

Inserting a SmartArt Graphic

To insert a SmartArt graphic, follow these steps:

1. On the Insert tab, click the SmartArt button. The Choose a SmartArt Graphic dialog box opens (see Figure 5.12).

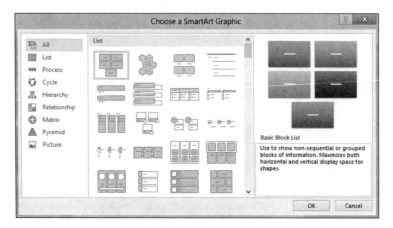

FIGURE 5.12

Choose from a variety of SmartArt graphic layouts.

2. Select the button for the SmartArt layout types you want to view. Alternatively, select the All button to scroll through a list of all options. Refer to Table 5.1 for an explanation of each SmartArt type.

 NOTE If you're new to SmartArt, it's often difficult to determine which graphic best suits your needs. When you click each graphic icon in the Choose a SmartArt Graphic dialog box, the right side of the screen displays a detailed example of the selected SmartArt graphic and describes its use in the box below. Reviewing all your options at least once gives you a clearer idea of what's available and can provide some inspiration as well.

3. Select the icon for the graphic type you want to insert and click the OK button. The graphic displays in your document (see Figure 5.13).

Enter text in the placeholder

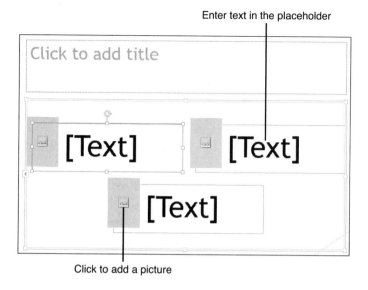

Click to add a picture

FIGURE 5.13

Your initial SmartArt graphic is blank, awaiting your content.

Each SmartArt graphic includes text placeholders where you can enter the appropriate text. To enter text, click the [Text] placeholder and start typing. If you enter more text than the shape can hold, Office resizes the text. You can also enter text in the Text pane, described in the "Using the Text Pane" section, later in this chapter. If you choose a graphic that includes pictures, click the picture placeholder to open the Insert Pictures dialog box.

Office offers two contextual tabs that enable you to modify the design and format of your SmartArt graphics: the SmartArt Tools – Design tab and the SmartArt Tools – Format tab.

Note that these contextual tabs display only when you have selected a graphic. If they disappear, select your graphic again to view them. Also, be aware that depending on your choice of SmartArt graphic, not all options are available on the SmartArt Tools tabs.

Using SmartArt Design Tools

The SmartArt Tools – Design tab, shown in Figure 5.14, enables you to create additional graphic objects, specify layout and style options, and convert your SmartArt graphic to other formats.

FIGURE 5.14

The SmartArt Tools – Design tab is one of two SmartArt Tools contextual tabs.

Adding a Shape to a SmartArt Graphic

Although SmartArt graphics already contain shapes by default, you can add more shapes if you need. For example, you could create a basic cycle graphic, which comes with five shapes, and then decide you need to add a sixth.

To add a shape to a SmartArt graphic, follow these steps:

1. Select the SmartArt graphic to which you want to add a shape.

2. On the SmartArt Tools – Design tab, click the down arrow to the right of the Add Shape button to display a menu of options.

3. Select from the following menu choices:

    *   **Add Shape After**—Add an identical shape after a selected shape.

    *   **Add Shape Before**—Add an identical shape before a selected shape.

    *   **Add Shape Above**—Add an identical shape above a selected shape.

    *   **Add Shape Below**—Add an identical shape below a selected shape.

    *   **Add Assistant**—Add an assistant shape to an organization chart.

 NOTE The options available are based on your choice of SmartArt. For example, the Add Assistant menu option is available only if your graphic is an organization chart.

If you want to place an additional shape in the default location for your graphic type (such as at the end of a list), you can click the Add Shape button directly, without viewing the menu options.

Adding Bullets

If your SmartArt graphic supports bulleted lists, you can add a text bullet by clicking the Add Bullet button on the SmartArt Tools – Design tab. You must select a specific graphic object for this button to become active.

Using the Text Pane

Although you can enter text directly on your SmartArt graphic, using the Text pane is a good idea if you have a lot of text or your graphic is more complex.

To open the Text pane, click the Text Pane button on the SmartArt Tools – Design tab.

In this pane, you can enter and revise text, use the buttons in the Create Graphic group to promote or demote objects, and edit any pictures if you selected a graphic type that includes pictures.

To close the Text pane, click the Close button (x) in the upper-right corner or click the Text Pane button on the SmartArt Tools – Design tab again, which acts as a toggle.

Organizing SmartArt Content

The Create Graphic group on the SmartArt Tools – Design tab (refer to Figure 5.14) also includes several buttons that help you organize the content in your graphic. For example, you can promote, demote, or reorder objects to customize your graphic exactly the way you want. Be aware that like other options on the SmartArt Tools – Design tab, the availability of these buttons depends on your graphic type and what object is selected.

The buttons include the following:

- **Promote**—Move selected object up a level. You can also use this with the Text pane.

- **Demote**—Move selected object down a level. You can also use this with the Text pane.

- **Right to Left**—Change layout from the right to the left.

- **Move Up**—Move selected object up in a sequence.

- **Move Down**—Move selected object down in a sequence.

- **Layout**—Modify the layout of an organization chart, such as displaying subordinates to the left or to the right.

Modifying Your SmartArt Layout

The Layouts group on the SmartArt Tools – Design tab offers several layout options that you can apply to your SmartArt graphic. Three options appear on the tab itself, but you can click the down arrow to the right of the group to open a gallery of additional options. Pause the mouse over each option to preview it.

These layouts correspond to the layouts that appear on the Choose a SmartArt Graphic dialog box.

Changing SmartArt Colors

If you don't like your graphic's default color scheme, you can quickly change it by clicking the Change Colors button on the SmartArt Tools – Design tab.

You can choose a primary theme color, select something more colorful, or opt for one of your theme's accent colors.

Applying a SmartArt Style

If you want to quickly dress up your SmartArt graphic, apply one of the many ready-made styles designed to complement your chosen theme. To do so, select a style in the SmartArt Styles group on the SmartArt Tools – Design tab. For more options, click the down arrow to display a gallery where you can chose a style that's a good match for your document, or try out a 3-D style.

Resetting a SmartArt Graphic

If you've made a lot of changes to your SmartArt graphic and decide you don't like what you've done, click the Reset Graphic button on the SmartArt Tools – Design tab. Office deletes all the formatting changes you've made to your graphic and restores its original format. It doesn't delete any text you've added, however.

Converting a SmartArt Graphic

If you decide that you don't want to use a SmartArt graphic you created but would like to retain your text as a bulleted list, click the Convert button on the SmartArt Tools – Design tab and then select Convert to Text from the menu.

Another option is to convert your SmartArt graphic to a shape so that you can take advantage of shape-formatting options. To do this, click the Convert button and then select Convert to Shapes from the menu.

Formatting SmartArt Graphics

The SmartArt Tools – Format tab, as shown in Figure 5.15, offers numerous SmartArt formatting options, many of which are shared with other objects.

FIGURE 5.15

Create a custom look with the options on the SmartArt Tools – Format tab.

On this tab, you can perform the following tasks:

- Edit a 3-D graphic in 2-D.

- Format and change individual SmartArt shapes.

- Apply shape style, fills, outlines, and effects.

- Apply WordArt styles, fills, outlines, and effects to SmartArt text. Learn more in Chapter 3, "Working with Text."

- Arrange SmartArt objects, such as moving objects forward and backward and aligning, grouping, and rotating objects.

- Change the height and width of your SmartArt graphic by clicking the Size button.

Editing in 2-D

If you applied a 3-D style to your SmartArt graphic, you can temporarily return to 2-D to edit it by clicking the Edit in 2-D button on the SmartArt Tools – Format tab. When you finish editing, click this button again to return to your 3-D style.

Changing the Appearance of SmartArt Shapes

Although SmartArt graphics include default shapes, you might prefer a different shape. For example, if you select a Basic Block List, your graphic includes several basic rectangles. Your preference, however, might be rounded rectangles.

To change the appearance of the shapes in your SmartArt graphic, follow these steps:

1. Select the shape or shapes you want to change. To select multiple shapes, press the Ctrl key while clicking the shapes you want to change.

2. On the SmartArt Tools – Format tab, click the Change Shape button. A gallery of shape options appears (refer to Figure 5.1).

3. Select the shape option you prefer to change your selected shapes.

Resizing Shapes

If you want to resize selected shapes on your graphic, click either the Larger or Smaller button on the SmartArt Tools – Format tab. You can continue clicking these buttons until you reach your desired size.

THE ABSOLUTE MINIMUM

Here are the key points to remember from this chapter:

- Office enables you to insert a variety of shapes, including lines, arrows, rectangles, circles, squares, callouts, and more.

- The Drawing Tools – Format tab provides an extensive array of shape-formatting tools.

- Using the Format Shape pane is another option for modifying and customizing shapes.

- SmartArt graphics combine shapes and text to create informative, eye-catching content.

USING MICROSOFT OFFICE ON THE WEB AND MOBILE DEVICES

Even if you're away from the computer where you installed Office 2013—or away from any computer, for that matter—you can access your Office documents. In this chapter, you find out how to access Office on the Web and from mobile devices. You also discover how to make the most of Office's integration with SkyDrive and Office Web Apps.

Using SkyDrive

By default, you can store and share your Office files on SkyDrive, Microsoft's online storage solution. SkyDrive offers several gigabytes of free online storage that you can use to collaborate with colleagues anywhere in the world using a PC, Mac, or mobile device (such as a smartphone, iPad, or other tablet). SkyDrive requires a free Microsoft account to access. If you have an existing account with another Microsoft application such as Hotmail or Messenger, you already have an account. If you don't, you can sign up for a free account when you access SkyDrive.

 CAUTION Because SkyDrive is a web-based application, be aware that it could change or include new features in the future.

 NOTE You can also share Office files on SharePoint. Because installing and deploying SharePoint is normally the domain of a corporate information technology (IT) department, it's beyond the scope of this book. To learn more about SharePoint, go to http://sharepoint.microsoft.com.

Getting Started with SkyDrive

To log in to SkyDrive, go to http://skydrive.com (see Figure 6.1) and enter the username and password for your Microsoft account. If you don't have a Microsoft account, sign up for a free account by clicking the Sign Up Now link.

FIGURE 6.1

Getting started with SkyDrive takes only a few minutes.

On SkyDrive, shown in Figure 6.2, you can perform the following tasks:

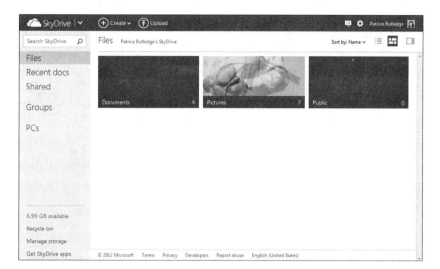

FIGURE 6.2

Store, share, and collaborate on SkyDrive.

- Create new folders by clicking the Create button and selecting Folder from the menu. You can share folders with everyone (a public folder), only people in your network, or select people you have provided access to. Alternatively, you can make your folder private so that only you can access it.

- Add files to your folders by clicking the Upload button. From here, you can browse your computer and select the files you want to upload. You can upload files up to 300MB on SkyDrive.com or up to 2GB from the SkyDrive app that you install on your computer. See "Uploading Files to SkyDrive," later in this chapter, for more information.

- Open individual files by clicking a folder icon and then clicking the file's icon.

- Manage an individual file by right-clicking it and selecting a menu option, such as Sharing, Embed, Rename, Delete, Move To, and so forth.

- Create a new file by clicking the Create button and selecting the type of file you want to create. See "Creating a New File Using Office Web Apps" later in this chapter.

- Share folders and files by right-clicking them and selecting Sharing from the menu. From here, you can send a link by email, share on social sites such as Facebook and Twitter, and share a link that enables others to view or edit your content.

- Create groups of people to share and collaborate with by clicking the Groups link.

- Increase your storage capacity by clicking the Manage Storage link in the lower-left corner and choosing a paid storage plan.

- Get free SkyDrive apps by clicking the Get SkyDrive Apps link in the lower-left corner. Options include a Windows desktop app as well as apps for the Windows phone, iPhone, iPad, or an Android device. See "Using SkyDrive Mobile Apps" later in this chapter for more information.

TIP This chapter covers just a subset of what you can do on SkyDrive. For more details, go to http://windows.microsoft.com/en-US/skydrive/help-center.

Uploading Files to SkyDrive

Although you can save your Office files to SkyDrive by default or in the Save As window (refer to Chapter 2, "Working with Office Applications," for a reminder on how to do this), you can also upload them manually.

TIP Adding files to SkyDrive isn't limited to those you create in Office. You can also store any other files on SkyDrive, such as photos, PDFs, and so forth.

To upload an existing file to SkyDrive, follow these steps:

1. In the SkyDrive main window (refer to Figure 6.2), select the folder where you want to store your file.

2. Click the Upload button.

3. Navigate to the file you want to upload and then click the Open button. SkyDrive uploads the file to the selected folder.

Using SkyDrive Mobile Apps

If you want to access SkyDrive from your mobile device, Microsoft offers three mobile apps that enable you to view, share, and upload files on the go. These include

- SkyDrive for Windows Phone (http://bit.ly/WindowsPhoneSkyDrive)

- SkyDrive for iPhone, iPod touch, and iPad (http://bit.ly/iPhoneSkyDrive)

- SkyDrive for Android (http://bit.ly/AndroidSkyDrive)

NOTE Because the URLs to these SkyDrive apps are lengthy, this section offers shortened Bit.ly links for your convenience.

Using Office Web Apps

Microsoft Office offers web-based versions of its most popular applications, including PowerPoint, Word, Excel, and OneNote. To use Office Web Apps, you need either Microsoft SharePoint (primarily for use in large organizations) or a SkyDrive account (for use by anyone with web access).

With Office Web Apps, you can view and edit Office documents from any computer or mobile device. It's important to note, however, that the app's editing features comprise a subset of the features available in the desktop version of Office. You should plan to perform only basic edits in the Office Web Apps.

NOTE This section focuses on accessing Office Web Apps on SkyDrive. Installing and deploying SharePoint is normally the domain of a corporate IT department, and someone from that department would set up your access rights via SharePoint.

Creating a New File Using Office Web Apps

You can create Microsoft Office files directly in Office Web Apps, including the following: Word documents, Excel workbooks, PowerPoint presentations, OneNote notebooks, and Excel surveys. You can edit these files in the app or download them later for use in the desktop version of Office.

To create a new file, follow these steps:

1. In the SkyDrive main window (refer to Figure 6.2), select the folder where you want to store the file you create.

2. Click the Create button and select the type of file you want to create, as shown in Figure 6.3.

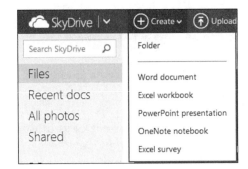

FIGURE 6.3

Create an Office file directly on SkyDrive using Office Web Apps.

3. Enter a filename and then click the Create button, as shown in Figure 6.4.

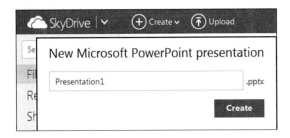

FIGURE 6.4

Enter a name for your new file.

The relevant Web App opens in edit mode, where you can add, edit, and format content. See "Editing Files in Office Web Apps," later in this chapter, for more information.

Exploring Office Web Apps

The menu options available in each Web App vary. These include:

- **Excel Web App**—File, Home, Insert, View, Open in Excel
- **OneNote Web App**—File, Home, Insert, View, Open in OneNote.
- **PowerPoint Web App**—File, Home, Insert, Design, Animations, Transitions, View, Open in PowerPoint
- **Word Web App**—File, Edit Document, Share, Find, Comments

Figure 6.5 displays a sample Web App, the Excel Web App.

FIGURE 6.5

Access Excel on the Web with the Excel Web App.

 TIP Clicking the File tab opens Backstage view.

 NOTE Word is the only Web App that doesn't have an option to return to the desktop version on the main menu. To do so, select Edit in Word from the Edit Document menu. To edit in the Web App, select Edit in Word Web App from the Edit Document menu. The Web App opens with new menu options: File, Home, Insert, Page Layout, View, and Open in Word.

To return to SkyDrive, click the SkyDrive link in the upper-left corner of the screen.

Editing Files in Office Web Apps

You can edit any Office file that you create or store in SkyDrive. To edit a file, click it. The selected file opens in its associated Web App. Figure 6.6 provides an example of editing a Word document in the Word Web App.

FIGURE 6.6

Edit Word documents on the go in the Word Web App.

NOTE Office Web Apps don't have a Save button because they save your changes automatically.

THE ABSOLUTE MINIMUM

Here are the key points to remember from this chapter:

- Microsoft Office works directly with SkyDrive, Microsoft's online storage and collaboration solution.

- SkyDrive mobile apps are available for Windows Phone; the iPhone, iPod touch, and iPad; and Android devices.

- Office Web Apps enable you to view, edit, and collaborate on Excel, OneNote, PowerPoint, and Word files on the Web and mobile devices.

7

WORD 2013 BASICS

Microsoft Word is the powerhouse of the Microsoft Office suite of applications, enabling you to present yourself or your business through polished, professional-looking documents. In this chapter, you discover the variety of document types you can create, explore new Word 2013 features, and learn how to start a new document and view your Word documents.

Exploring Word

If you have never worked with Microsoft Word before, you are in for a treat; and if you have worked with the application before, you'll be happy to know that this new version is better than ever. Microsoft Word is an amazingly powerful application and there's seemingly no end to the types of documents you can create with it. Yes, it's easy to write a simple letter in Word, but you can also use this powerful application to create:

- All kinds of reports, from year-end budget reports to company prospects and beyond
- Research papers, term papers, essays, and the like
- Résumés, business cards, and all manner of promotional materials
- Brochures, flyers, and newsletters
- Organized lists, menus, to-do sheets, and so on
- Personalized calendars for home, office, and school
- Greeting cards, postcards, and notecards
- Photo albums for every occasion
- Faxes, labels, and coordinated mailing materials
- Web pages—yes, even web pages!

You can see from this small list of typical projects, you can use Word to create a variety of documents for a multitude of purposes, even those that rely more on visuals than on text.

Exploring Word 2013 New Features

Microsoft has made quite a few improvements to Word since its last rendition. For starters, it is retooled a bit to work with the new Windows 8 operating system. If your computer is one of the newer touchscreen models, you can utilize touchscreen techniques to interact with the application, such as selecting text using your finger to drag across the screen or tapping the screen to activate a command. If your computer doesn't utilize touchscreen technologies, don't worry about it; you can use the traditional mouse, keyboard, or mousepad (on a laptop) methods to work in Word.

Here's a rundown of what else you can expect in the new Word 2013:

- A new, modern interface with a customizable watermark design in the upper-right corner.

- A new Start screen, also called a landing page, with quick access to recently used files, templates, and stored content.

- More templates than Word has ever had before. You can search for templates for every kind of document imaginable.

- New cloud connectivity—with an online connection and a Microsoft account, you can store documents online and access them from anywhere or any computer. Cloud connectivity includes Office 365 (a subscription-based software service) and SkyDrive (online file-hosting service).

- An improved Ribbon at the top of the window that organizes commands.

- Compatibility with apps for Word and other Microsoft Office applications, such as dictionaries.

- The new Reading mode, which works great on a tablet, lets you browse a document like you're reading a book.

- Bookmarks that let you pick up reading right where you left off in a document.

- Capability to open PDF file formats and edit their content just like any other Word document.

- Improved markup tracking to help multiple users keep track of changes in a shared document.

- Improved graphics features to help you work with artwork and pictures you add to a document, including alignment guides to help you position graphics with your text.

- Capability to insert online videos into your documents, such as content from YouTube.

Exploring Word File Types

Before getting started with Word, it's important to understand Word file types, also called file formats. By default, the files you create in Word are saved in Word's "document" file type, which means the filenames end with a .docx file extension. If you save a file and name it Bob, its actual full name is Bob.docx with the file extension. Most of the time you don't see file extensions in Windows unless you want to, but they determine what sort of application can read the file. Different applications read and create different file types. For example, you normally won't create Word document files in an illustration application, and you can't turn a Word document file into a graphic file—software applications are designed to make certain types of files, hence the distinguishing file extensions.

However, many apps can read and work with a wider variety of file types than just the ones they are designed to create. Microsoft Word enables you to open other text files, web pages, XML documents, OpenDocument files, PDF files, XPS files, and files created in older versions of Word. You can also save your documents as these other file types.

The default Word document type is mostly backward compatible, which means you can open your Word 2013 files in older versions of Word. The more you work with various types of files on your computer, the easier you can distinguish their types and which applications you can use to view the files.

 NOTE Ordinarily, you don't see file extensions unless you choose to display them. If you want to see them in Windows Explorer or File Explorer (depending on your version of Windows), open the Explorer window (click the Explorer icon in the Windows desktop taskbar), click the Tools menu, and click Folder Options. In the Folder Options dialog box, click the View tab and deselect the Hide Extensions for Known File Types check box. Click OK and you can now view file extensions, even in Word's Save As and Open dialog boxes.

Starting a New Document

Every time you open Word, you are presented with the option of starting a new document, opening a recent document, or opening another document stored on your computer, SkyDrive, or other location. The Word Start screen, as it is called, is a launching pad for deciding what you want to do in Word. To open a blank document, choose the Blank document option from among the list of templates, as shown in Figure 7.1. Yes, strangely enough, even a blank document is built on a template. You can learn more about using templates in Chapter 9, "Using Templates."

 NOTE The term *document* in the non-digital world generally refers to a written or printed paper bearing original, official, or legal information. In the realm of computers, the term *document* refers to a file. Typically, computer documents contain text, but not always. Documents can also include files generated by desktop publishing applications, web pages, and more. Just for the record, the files you create in Word are officially called *documents*.

Click here to start a new document.

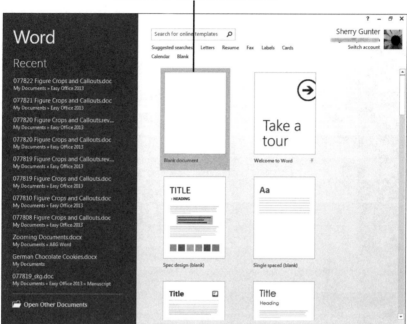

FIGURE 7.1

You can start a new document when you launch Word.

If you're already using Word and want to create a new document, follow these steps:

1. Click the File tab on the Ribbon.

2. Click New.

3. Click Blank document, shown in Figure 7.2, or any other template you want to use to start a new file.

Word opens a new, blank document onscreen and you're ready to go.

Click here to start a new document.

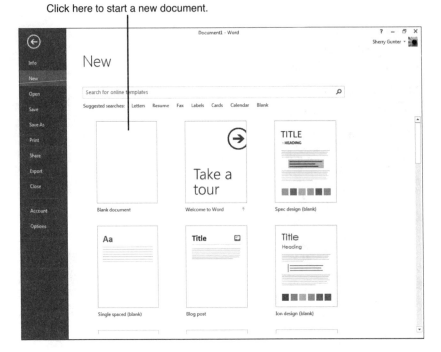

FIGURE 7.2

Use the New command to start a new document in Word.

 NOTE To learn more about other basic Word operations—such as saving, opening, and closing documents—see Chapter 2, "Working with Office Applications," which covers features common to multiple Office apps.

Viewing Multiple Documents

You can open more than one document at a time and switch between them as you work. This is particularly useful when you want to move text from one to the other. You can use the Windows taskbar to swap between open documents. Just move the mouse pointer to the taskbar and hover over the Word icon, as shown in Figure 7.3. A list of the open files appears and you can click the one you want to view.

FIGURE 7.3

Use the Windows taskbar to quickly switch between open Word documents.

You can also use Word's View tab to switch between document windows, as well as control the display of two or more windows onscreen at the same time. Click the View tab, shown in Figure 7.4, to find all the viewing options.

Use this option to arrange more than one document onscreen at a time.

Click here to switch between open documents.

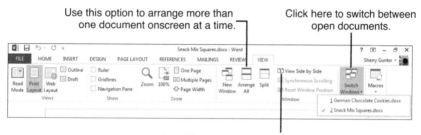

Use this option to view two documents side by side.

FIGURE 7.4

Find all kinds of viewing options on the View tab.

Here are a few ways to view multiple documents:

- To switch document windows, click the Switch Windows button and click the document you want to view.

- To view all open documents onscreen at once, click the Arrange All tool (see Figure 7.5).

CAUTION If you have multiple open documents, viewing all of them onscreen can make your screen pretty crowded. This option works best with only a few open documents.

- To view two documents side by side, click the View Side by Side tool. Click it again to return to one full document window.

FIGURE 7.5

Use the Arrange All option to view two or more documents onscreen.

Don't forget—you can use the Minimize, Restore, and Maximize tools in the upper-right corner of the document window to control individual windows. See Chapter 1, "Getting Started with Microsoft Office 2013," to learn more.

THE ABSOLUTE MINIMUM

Here are the key points to remember from this chapter:

- Before starting your first Word document, familiarize yourself with Word basics and explore the new features of Word 2013.

- You can start a new document through the File tab or you can add the New button to the Quick Access toolbar for easy access.

- Switch between open documents using the Windows taskbar, or the options found on Word's View tab.

IN THIS CHAPTER

- Setting Margins
- Creating Columns
- Changing Vertical Alignment
- Adding Headers and Footers to a Document
- Inserting Pages, Breaks, and Sections

8

FORMATTING PAGES

This chapter concentrates on formatting you can apply to entire pages to make them look polished and easy on the eyes. Page formatting includes features such as setting page margins, turning text into columns, adding headers and footers, and controlling vertical alignment. Whereas text formatting and paragraph formatting makes your document's content look good, page formatting is all about making your pages look good—and when your documents look good, you look good.

Setting Margins

Margins are the area between the content of your document and the actual edges of the printed or visual page. You can adjust the margins in Word to suit your needs. For example, if you plan on binding your printed pages in some sort of book or binder format, leaving ample right margins is key to making sure users can see everything when turning pages. If you are creating a single-page flyer, you might not want much space in terms of margins around the printed page. In some cases, making slight adjustments to the document's margins can help you cram everything onto one page.

Page margins are also where some special page elements hang out, such as page numbers, headers, and footers. (You learn more about these features later in this chapter.) By default, every blank document in Word starts with 1" margins on all four sides. This default margin scheme is known as the Normal margin setting. You can make adjustments to your margins using the Margins tool on the Page Layout tab, as shown in Figure 8.1. When you click the Margins button you can choose from several preset margins or you can create your own custom margin(s).

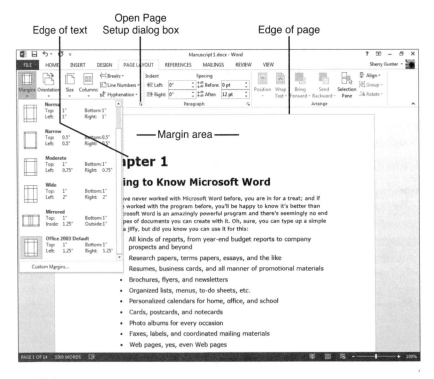

FIGURE 8.1

Find Word's margin controls on the Page Layout tab.

To set your own margins, click the Custom Margins option at the bottom of the Margins menu. This opens the Page Layout dialog box to the Margins tab, as shown in Figure 8.2. You can also access this same dialog box by clicking the dialog box launcher—the tiny icon with an arrow on it located in the bottom-right corner of the Page Setup group of tools on the Page Layout tab.

In the Page Setup dialog box, you can specify a value—measured in inches—for the top and bottom of the page, and the left and right sides. You can change just one margin, or as many as you want. Click the spinner arrows to adjust the value or type directly into the box you want to change. The Preview area at the bottom of the dialog box gives you a thumbnail preview of what the new margin(s) will look like. Click OK to exit the dialog and apply the changes.

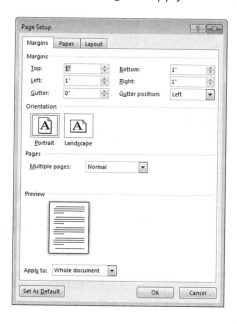

FIGURE 8.2

You can also open the Page Setup dialog box to set your own margins.

 TIP   When you create a two-page spread, the margins for the adjacent pages are called the *gutter*. You can control the amount of gutter space using the Page Setup dialog box.

 NOTE   Margins aren't the only setting you can adjust in the Page Setup dialog box. You can also use the settings within to change the page orientation (direction) for printing, choose a paper size for your printer, and control how page elements such as headers, footers, and vertical alignment affect the document.

You can also use a ruler to set margins. On the View tab, click the Ruler check box to display the horizontal and vertical rulers. The margin area is marked in a darker shade on the ends of the rulers. Move the mouse pointer over the edge of the margin shading and then click and drag the border to adjust the margin, as shown in Figure 8.3. As you drag the margin, a temporary line appears across the page, helping you to see where the new location for the margin will be when you release the mouse button.

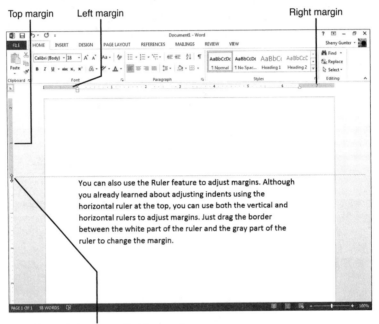

Drag the margin border to adjust the margin

FIGURE 8.3

You can use the rulers to set margins.

If you want to return to the default margins, display the Margins drop-down menu and choose Normal.

Creating Columns

You can turn your text into columns that run up and down the page, just like columns you find in a magazine or newspaper. The column format is perfect for newsletters, brochures, and other printed publications. You can choose between several preset column formats, including two specialized formats that create a narrower right or left column (appropriately called Left and Right)—in other words, the columns differ in width size. You can also create your own custom columns. Figure 8.4 shows an example of columns at work in a document.

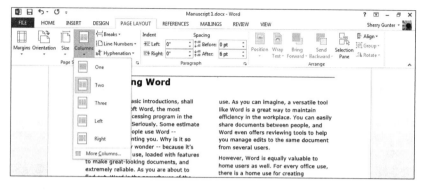

FIGURE 8.4

Use the Columns button to assign column formatting.

To create columns, follow these steps:

1. Select the text you want to turn into columns.

2. On the Page Layout tab, click the Columns button (refer to Figure 8.4).

3. Click the number of columns you want to create and Word immediately applies the column formatting to the selected text.

If you need to create custom columns, you can open the Columns dialog box, as shown in Figure 8.5. You can use the dialog box to specify the number of columns, their width and spacing, and even include vertical lines to separate the columns. To display the dialog box, click the More Columns command at the bottom of the Columns menu (shown in Figure 8.4).

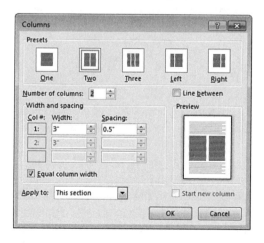

FIGURE 8.5

You can create custom columns using the Columns dialog box.

If you type new text at the bottom of the last column, Word assumes you want to keep using the column formatting. If you do, but need to insert a break of some kind, you can insert a column break. This breaks the column and starts a new column. To do this, on the Page Layout tab, click the Breaks button, and choose Column.

 TIP If you ever need to revert to a no-column format in your document, select the column text or just click anywhere in the column and use the Columns drop-down menu to choose One. This returns everything to the default page width for the text. You can also do this to turn off the columns and start a regular page again.

Changing Vertical Alignment

In Chapter 3, "Working with Text," you learn how to control all kinds of horizontal alignment on a page, including aligning text to a margin and setting indents, controlling spacing between lines of text, and using tabs. Did you know you can also control vertical alignment in your document? Word's vertical alignment controls mirror the horizontal ones, which means you can align text to the top, center, and bottom of the page, as well as justify it between the top and bottom margins. By default, the vertical alignment is set to Top. This means everything you type in starts out at the top of the page. You can use the other alignments to shift text to align at the center or bottom of the page.

Vertical alignment isn't quite as obvious as horizontal alignment, unless you only have a few lines of text or paragraphs on a page. However, you might find vertical alignment useful when creating title pages or other types of pages where vertical text is important.

 TIP The best way to see vertical alignment happen onscreen is to adjust the zoom setting to see the entire page. Use the Zoom slider (in the bottom-right corner of the program window) to zoom out and view more of your document page.

You can find Word's vertical alignment controls in the Page Setup dialog box, as shown in Figure 8.6. To display the dialog box, click the dialog box launcher (the tiny square with an arrow) in the lower-right corner of the Page Setup group on the Page Layout tab. After the dialog box is open, select the Layout tab and select another alignment from the Vertical Alignment drop-down list. Click OK to exit the dialog box and apply the new setting.

FIGURE 8.6

Control vertical alignment through the Page Setup dialog box.

 TIP You can choose to apply the vertical alignment setting to the current page rather than the whole document. You might do this for a title page, for example. To do so, select an option from the Apply To drop-down list at the bottom of the Page Setup dialog box. On the next document page, you can reopen the dialog box and choose another alignment to apply for that page onward.

Take a look at Figure 8.7 to see how vertical alignment affects a title page. In this example, the Bottom alignment is assigned and all the lines of text stack up against the bottom margin.

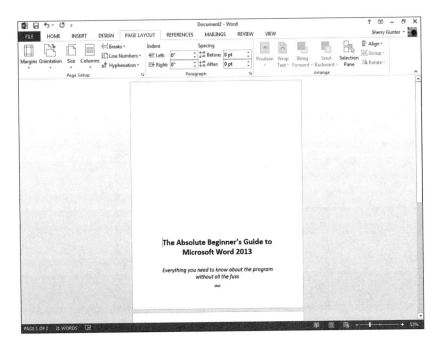

FIGURE 8.7

In this example, vertical alignment is set to Bottom.

Adding Headers and Footers to a Document

There's an invisible area that exists between the top and bottom margins and the actual edge of the page—this area is called the *header area* at the top of the page and the *footer area* at the bottom of the page (see Figure 8.8). You can use the header and footer areas to add extra elements to your documents such as page numbers, author name, dates, and other pertinent information about the document.

The great thing about this special area is that the information you place here prints on every page, which is quite helpful when organizing your documents. Longer documents can really benefit from page numbers, and in a busy workplace environment, including the author information, document title, or dates at the top of every page can help other users know where the document came from or when it was created.

Header

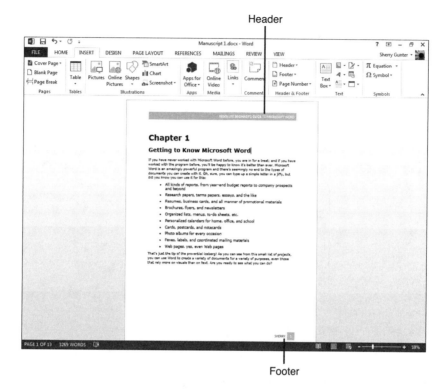

Footer

FIGURE 8.8

Headers and footers appear between the page margins and the actual edge of the page.

Adding Headers and Footers

The Ribbon's Insert tab offers access to headers and footers. As with a lot of things in Word, you can choose to create your own header and footer elements, or you can utilize one of the preset designs available. The presets are part of Word's built-in elements, *Quick Parts*, which are preformatted elements sporting a variety of designs and styles. Most of the preset headers and footers feature placeholder fields—spots you can fill in with your own text. If you see a "Type Here" spot, that's where you add your own stuff. Take a look at the drop-down menu for Header shown in Figure 8.9. You can scroll through the library of built-in headers to find something to suit your document.

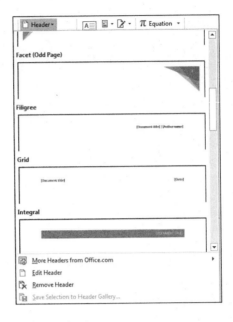

FIGURE 8.9

You can choose from a variety of preset headers.

If you don't see anything you like from the preset elements, you can look for more headers on the Microsoft Office website. You can also choose a header and edit to suit your own needs and then save it to the Header Gallery as a template piece to reuse again.

The Footer menu, shown in Figure 8.10, shows a similar setup but with some presets designed for the bottom of pages.

To actually assign a header or footer, choose it from the appropriate menu. After doing so, you can replace any placeholder text with your own, as shown in Figure 8.11. When you insert a header or footer, Word instantly puts the cursor in the header or footer area and one or more special tabs appear on the Ribbon. You can use the Header & Footer Tools – Design tab to add more preset fields (such as a date and time or filename) and customize your header or footer text, as well as assign any special options or positioning controls. You can also use the Design tab to navigate between the two areas of the page, if your document uses both header and footer information.

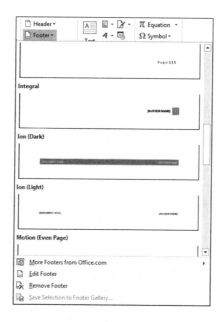

FIGURE 8.10

The Footer menu also has preset options.

Click here to close the editing mode

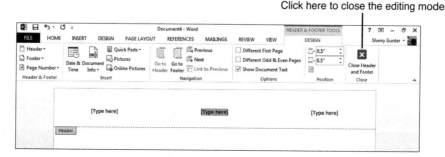

FIGURE 8.11

Word switches to a special editing mode to work on headers and footers, and displays special tabs of tools to help you with the task.

If the header or footer you choose utilizes a special design element, the Table Tools or Drawing Tools tabs might appear offering access to more tools for customizing header or footer appearance.

To start filling in header or footer information, click the placeholder text and type in your own. When you finish creating your header or footer, you can click the Close Header and Footer button on the Header & Footer's Design tab, or you can double-click anywhere else on the document page.

To return to the header or footer area and make changes, double-click in the header or footer area. To remove a header or footer, on the Insert tab, click the Header button or Footer button and choose Remove Header or Remove Footer.

TIP Headers and footers print on every page, unless you specify otherwise. To control printing, open the Page Setup dialog box to the Layout tab where you'll find options for placing different odd and even or first page headers and footers. Refer to Figure 8.6 to see the location of these controls.

Adding Page Numbers

You can insert simple page number headers or footers using the Page Number button on the Insert tab. You can choose from a library of preset designs for various locations on the page. You can also format the numbers the way you want.

To assign page numbers, on the Insert tab, click the Page Number button. Next, choose a position for the numbers and choose a design from the library. Word immediately applies the page numbers to your document (see Figure 8.12).

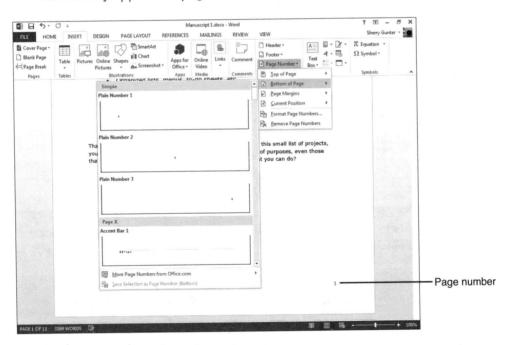

Page number

FIGURE 8.12

Use the Page Numbers feature to insert page numbers as headers or footers on your document pages.

Like regular headers or footers, when you insert page numbers, Word opens the special editing mode for working with header and footer text, depending on where you chose to insert the page numbers. You can double-click anywhere else in the document to exit the special editing mode. To return to the header or footer area and make changes to the numbers or formats, double-click in the header or footer area. To remove the page numbers entirely, on the Insert tab, click the Page Numbers button, and choose Remove Page Numbers.

 TIP Word keeps a running tally of pages and words down on the status bar.

 TIP When you need to navigate to a specific page in your document, on the Home tab click the Find button and then click Go To (or press Ctrl+G). Type in the page number and press Enter.

Inserting Pages, Breaks, and Sections

When working with documents longer than a single page, Microsoft Word automatically inserts page breaks for you as you type. However, sometimes you need to insert your own new pages or breaks, or divide the document into sections. Not that this comes to a surprise to you by now, but Word has tools for doing all of this. For example, maybe you suddenly need a new page in the middle of your report to add some more information or a graph. You can easily add new pages where you need them. Or maybe you decide to insert a page break and start the next chapter on a new page. You can control page insertions using the Insert tab on the Ribbon.

 TIP Word can also tally section numbers on the status bar. To turn on section number display, right-click the status bar and choose Section.

 TIP To navigate to a specific section in your document, press Ctrl+G to open the Find and Replace dialog box, which displays the Go To tab. Specify sections in the list box and then type in the section number and press Enter.

Inserting Pages

Ready for a blank page? Start by clicking in the page you want to appear after the newly inserted page. After you've done this, on the Insert tab, click the Blank Page button. Word inserts a new, empty page for you.

You can also insert instant cover pages for your documents. A cover page typically includes some sort of document title, and information about the author, company, or creation date. You can choose from a variety of cover page *built-ins*—preset designs in which you add your own original content. On the Insert tab, click the Cover Page button to display a drop-down menu of choices. Scroll through and click the one you want, and then replace any placeholder text with your own information.

Inserting Breaks

You can also control where a page breaks using Word's Page Break command. When you insert a page break, you're splitting an existing page into two pages. This is handy when you want to turn a paragraph into the start of a new page, or end one chapter and start another. Click where you want to insert a break and click the Page Break button on the Insert tab.

As you're typing, you can also use a keyboard shortcut to insert a page break: Press Ctrl+Enter.

On the Page Layout tab, as shown in Figure 8.13, clicking the Breaks button lists other page and section breaks you can add. You can use this menu to insert page breaks, column breaks, and several types of section breaks. Figure 8.14 shows an example of a page break.

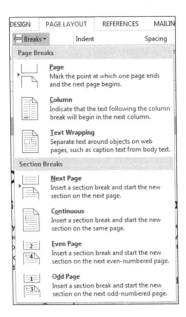

FIGURE 8.13

You can use the Breaks menu to insert page and section breaks.

Page break

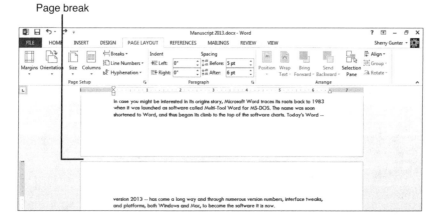

FIGURE 8.14

Here's what a page break looks like in Print Layout view mode.

Section breaks work a bit differently than forcing a new page. You can divide a page into sections and utilize section headers and footers for each section. Section breaks are typically used when you want to start a new area with new formatting. For example, maybe you're creating a report that utilizes regular portrait-oriented pages (the page is taller than it is wide), but you need to add a graph that fits on a landscape-oriented page (the page is wider than it is tall). You can do this with a section break. Or maybe your research paper uses regular numbered lists in one part, but Roman numerals in another—a section break can help you format both separately.

With page breaks, the new page retains the same formatting as the previous page, but with section breaks, you can use completely different page formatting, including different margins, columns, or page orientation. You can choose from four different types of section breaks:

- **Next Page**—Inserts a new page or continues text on the next consecutive page.

- **Continuous**—Starts a new section without adding a page (common for columns).

- **Even Page**—Inserts a new even-numbered page, or continues text on the next even-numbered page.

- **Odd Page**—Inserts a new odd-numbered page, or continues text on the next odd-numbered page.

TIP To remove a break, turn on the display of paragraph marks. (On the Home tab, click the Show/Hide button in the Paragraph group—this feature toggles on or off.) Now navigate to the page break in the file, select it, and press the Delete key to remove it.

THE ABSOLUTE MINIMUM

Here are the key points to remember from this chapter:

- To control page margins, display the Page Layout tab and click the Margins button.

- You can make your text flow nicely on a page using columns and the Columns drop-down menu on the Page Layout tab.

- You can position text vertically up and down a page using the Page Layout options found in the Page Setup dialog box.

- Headers appear at the top of pages between the margin and the actual edge of the page. Footers appear at the bottom of document pages.

- You can insert or remove new pages, page breaks, and section breaks wherever you want in your document.

USING TEMPLATES

You might not realize this, but as soon as you opened Word and started typing text you began working with templates. Every document in Word, including blank ones, are built with templates. If you've never worked directly with templates before, this chapter is just for you. Not only does this chapter define templates and introduce you to all the choices available in Word, but it also shows you how to create your own. Templates might sound a little intimidating at first, but after you know how they work and what to do with them, you'll soon be using them like a pro.

Understanding Templates

A *template* is a pattern or boilerplate document that gives you a starting point for building documents. Most templates offer preset formatting and placeholder text that you can replace with your own text. The placeholder text is there to give you an idea of the type of text you can use in the document, as well as an idea of what the preassigned formatting looks like.

So what's the difference between a template and a regular document, you might ask? Template files utilize a special file format and extension. If you turn on the file extension display in Windows Explorer, you can see Word template files listed with the .dotx, .dotm, or .dot extensions. (See Chapter 7, "Word 2013 Basics," to learn more about file types.) Don't let the special file format confuse you, however. When you assign a template, you're just placing a style overlay onto a regular Word document file, so the document remains a regular .doc file type. It doesn't suddenly become a template itself. It merely utilizes the design guide.

Applying a Template

You can apply a template to an existing document, or you can start a new document based on a template of your choice. To start a new document based on a template, click the Ribbon's File tab and click New. This displays a screen similar to Figure 9.1 listing templates you can peruse.

The blank document, even though it's blank, is still a template.

Use the search box to look for more templates online.

Use the scroll bar to peruse the full selection of suggested templates.

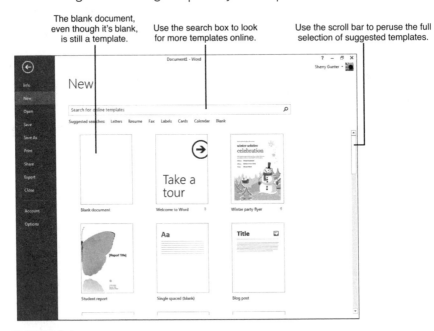

FIGURE 9.1

You can find templates listed on the New screen.

The top of the screen offers a search box you can use to look for a particular kind of template and lists some search categories you can inspect with a simple click. Or you can use the scroll bar to scroll along and view various templates displayed in the window. When you find something you actually want to use, click it to select it. A smaller screen pops up, similar to Figure 9.2, with details about the template, its popularity rating, and a button you can click to download and apply the template. If the template suits you, click the Create button. If not, click the Close button (X) or use the navigation arrows to view more template descriptions.

Click here to close without adding the template

Use the arrow buttons to look through more template descriptions and ratings.

Click here to download and apply the template

FIGURE 9.2

Read more about the template and decide whether you want to download and apply it.

 TIP If you find yourself using the same template over and over again, you can pin it so it's always on the top of the list of templates on the New screen. To do so, move the mouse over the template you want to pin and click the pushpin icon in the bottom-right corner of the highlighted template. The pushpin icon toggles on and off; a vertical pushpin indicates the template is pinned, a horizontal pushpin means the template is not pinned.

As soon as you download a template, Word applies it to a new document. You need to save the file when you finish adding your own text and fixing it the way you want. (See Chapter 2, "Working with Office Applications," to learn more about saving files.) The template you downloaded is automatically added to your template library. Word creates a new document file and applies the template. The file is not saved yet, so it still displays the Document2 filename at the top.

To start filling in a template, click the placeholder box and type away. Any placeholder text is replaced with the new text you add. You can easily move around and format text blocks. As soon as you click a box, it's selected and surrounded by *selection handles*, which you can drag to resize the box.

 NOTE You can apply templates from older versions of Word, or templates you have created and stored elsewhere. Click the Ribbon's File tab and then click Options in the left pane. This opens the Word Options dialog box. Click Add-Ins. From the Manage drop-down list at the bottom of the dialog box, select Templates and then click the Go button. This opens the Templates and Add-ins dialog box. You can click the Attach button to navigate to the folder or drive where your template file is stored and then open the template and attach it to your document.

Finding More Templates

You can use the search box on the New screen to look for more templates online (refer to Figure 9.1). Tapping into the vast resources of the Microsoft Office website, you can look for specific types of templates based on the keyword(s) you enter. With the New screen displayed (click the Ribbon's File tab and click New to display it), click in the search box and type in your search word. Press Enter or click the Search button and a page opens displaying any matching results. Naturally you need an online connection to utilize this feature.

Click the Home button to return to the main New screen. Also on the New screen, just below the search box, is a list of suggested search categories. You can click a category to view a list of corresponding templates.

 NOTE By default, Word 2013 saves templates in the following folder path: %appdata%\Microsoft\Templates\. If you type this path into the Explorer window's Address bar, you can view all the template files stored within the default folder.

You can also use your web browser to check the Office website for more templates. Browse to office.microsoft.com, click the Templates link, and then click the link for Word. The web page displays all kinds of templates, categories, and links. When you find a template you want, click the Download button. You're prompted to save the file to a folder you designate, or you can choose the default Templates folder as its home.

> **TIP** Finding downloaded templates can sometimes be a bit frustrating, especially if you don't remember to specify a folder. You can use Explorer to search for templates (.dotx file extensions). In the Explorer search box, type *.dot or *.dotx to search for all templates, or if you know the exact name, you can type it instead.

Saving Templates

You can turn any document into a template file to reuse, or, after customizing a template, you can turn it into a new template to apply again and again. When you have finished making the document look just the way you want and are ready to save it as a template file, follow these steps:

1. Click File.

2. Click Save As.

3. On the Save As screen, specify where you want to save your template and click the Browse button.

4. Navigate to the folder or drive where you want to store the file; for best results, save your templates in the Custom Office Templates folder in the Documents library.

5. From the Save As Type drop-down list (see Figure 9.3), select Word Template (*.dotx).

6. Type a name for the template.

7. Click Save.

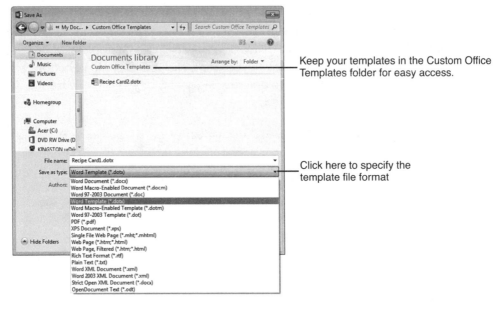

Keep your templates in the Custom Office Templates folder for easy access.

Click here to specify the template file format

FIGURE 9.3

You can save any file as a template using the Save As Type drop-down list.

You can click the Personal category on the New screen to view the templates stored in your Custom Office Templates folder.

THE ABSOLUTE MINIMUM

Here are the key points to remember from this chapter:

- Templates can help you whip up great-looking documents in a jiffy.

- With an online connection, you can peruse a vast library of Word templates from the Office website.

- You can customize any template to suit your own needs, or you can turn a document into a template to use again and again.

- To make things easy, store your templates in the Custom Office Templates folder in the Documents library.

10

APPLYING ADVANCED FORMATTING

Just when you thought you had learned all there is to make your Word documents look their best, there are a couple more tools and features to consider. This chapter covers the finishing touches you can apply to your documents to make them look extra special and attractive. Some of these extra features can be, quite simply, timesavers and/or lifesavers. If you're looking for quick polish for a document, then look no further than Word's special text effects. They can add instant pizzazz to a document. If uniformity is more your goal, then themes and styles can help you keep your document's major plot points looking groomed. When it's overall background elements you need, borders and shading can help you out, as well as applying a subtle, yet serious, watermark. This chapter shows you how to make a real show of your text.

Applying a Theme

One of the best ways you can apply an overall consistent look and feel to a document is to utilize one of Word's many themes. A *theme* includes a coordinating set of colors, fonts, and text effects you can apply to make sure your documents share a harmonious appearance. Themes control the primary design aspects of your document, such as colors, fonts, styling of charts and tables, and shapes and diagrams. You can choose from a variety of preset themes, or browse for more themes online. Figure 10.1 shows a document before a theme is applied, and Figure 10.2 shows a document after a theme is applied. It's like a makeover for your file!

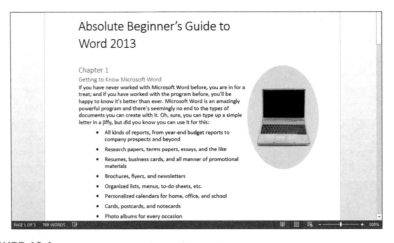

FIGURE 10.1

Before a theme is applied.

FIGURE 10.2

After applying a theme.

Themes work best with *styles* you apply in a document, which are covered in the next section. Themes and styles work hand-in-hand to help ensure design efficiency in your documents. Although at first glance, themes and styles seem a lot alike in Word, they're actually different in their focus. A *theme* defines the overall appearance of your document, whereas *styles* help you control various design options within the document. When you assign a theme, a set of styles is included with the design. Naturally, you can make changes to the various parts of a theme or a style to your liking.

To apply a theme, click the Themes button on the Design tab and select a theme from the gallery (see Figure 10.3) to immediately apply it.

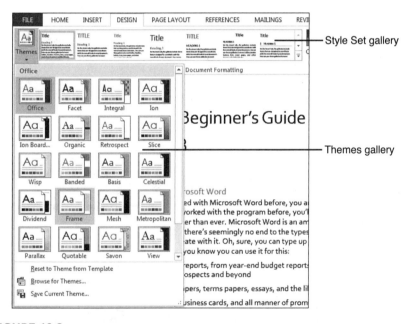

FIGURE 10.3

The Themes gallery lists preset themes you can apply.

You can preview each theme by hovering the mouse pointer over the theme in the gallery menu. Word's Live Preview feature previews the theme on the document page, just to show you what things will look like if you decide to use that particular theme.

CAUTION   Just a warning: Unless your document already has some styles applied, you might not see many theme elements reflected with Live Preview.

As you can see in the Themes gallery, each theme has a color strip of coordinating colors. When you activate a theme, the Style Set gallery (see Figure 10.3) displays coordinating styles designed for that particular theme.

 TIP If you find yourself using themes for every document you create, add the Themes gallery to Word's Quick Access toolbar—that toolbar in the upper-left corner of the program window where the Save and Undo buttons sit, ready for action. To add the gallery, right-click over any theme name in the Themes drop-down menu and then click Add Gallery to Quick Access Toolbar. This immediately puts a button on the toolbar; click the button to view the gallery of themes.

To turn off a theme and return to the default Office theme, click the Themes button on the Design tab and choose the Office theme from the gallery.

Themes aren't terribly useful until you start assigning styles, so let's proceed with the rest of the story—learning all about styles.

Applying Styles

Styles are sets of formatting you can apply to create a uniform look throughout your document. Figure 10.4 shows an example of text without styles, whereas Figure 10.5 shows the same document with styles applied. Notice the change in formatting and text color.

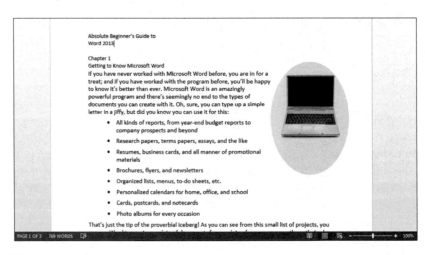

FIGURE 10.4

Before styles.

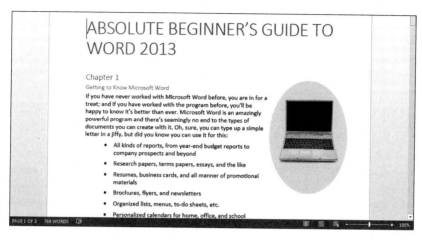

FIGURE 10.5

After styles.

Styles are particularly useful when you need to apply the same formatting to specific types of text in a document, such as headings and subheadings, pull quotes and book titles, references, captions, and all the various parts and pieces that go into building longer documents that require a great deal of consistency. Rather than tediously assigning the same formatting manually for each spot in the document where it's needed, you can assign the formatting to a style and apply all the formatting at one time. If you update a style in one spot in the document, the changes are made to all the other text sporting the same assigned style throughout the document—automatically.

For example, say your corporate report uses headings throughout the document with the formatting set to Times New Roman font, 16-point size, and bold. Normally, you would have to use three steps to assign the different formatting settings to the selected line of text. With a style, you just perform one step to assign all three formatting commands at once.

Styles can consist of the typical text formatting you might think of—such as fonts, sizes, bold or italic—or paragraph formatting, such as indents and spacing. Just about any formatting you can think of as it applies to your document text can be used with styles. Styles can also include colors, borders and shading, text effects, and anything else you need to apply to create a uniform appearance throughout your document. As you can imagine, styles really come in handy for multilevel, complex documents.

NOTE There are technically two types of styles: paragraph and character styles. Paragraph styles contain both text formatting and paragraph formatting, whereas character styles work for single words and characters—that is, text.

As mentioned in the previous section, style sets are part of themes you can apply to a document. Each theme offers different *style sets*—a collection of styles that coordinate nicely with the chosen theme. Style sets hang out over in the Style Sets gallery on the Design tab, as shown in Figure 10.6. But individual styles are listed in the Styles gallery on the Home tab. A little confusing, isn't it? Most people who worked with previous versions of Word are used to the styles appearing with the rest of the text-building tools, which are located on the Home tab, but the document formatting tools are on the Design tab, hence the placement of themes and style sets.

Are you ready to view some style sets? Glance through the Style Sets gallery and see what you like. You can click the More button in the Style Sets gallery to view all the associated sets, as shown in Figure 10.7.

Choose a style set here.

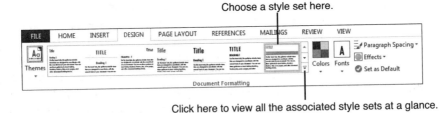

Click here to view all the associated style sets at a glance.

FIGURE 10.6

Use the Design tab's Style Sets gallery to choose a style set.

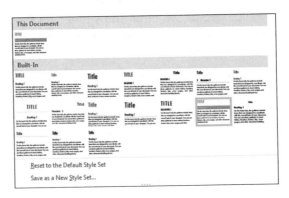

FIGURE 10.7

You might want to expand the gallery to see everything at a glance.

After you designate a style set from the gallery, you can apply individual styles from that set using the Styles gallery on the Home tab, as shown in Figure 10.8. You can also create your own styles and add them to the style set.

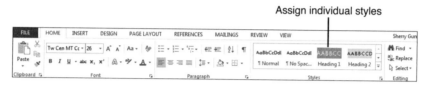

FIGURE 10.8

Use the Home tab's Styles gallery to assign individual styles to document text.

Choosing Style Sets

By default, Word starts you out with the Office theme and a default Office style set. It includes some basic styles for heading levels, titles, and a few other items. For example, it assigns the Normal Quick Style to the body text of your documents, unless you change it.

To choose a style set, select one of the options in the Document Formatting group on the Design tab (refer to Figure 10.6).

You can use the tools located to the right of the style sets to tweak the overall design, such as changing the color scheme, font, or spacing.

Assigning Styles

You can apply a style to specific text by selecting it first, or you can apply a style to an entire paragraph just by clicking anywhere in the paragraph.

To assign a style to selected text, select a style in the Styles group on the Home tab (refer to Figure 10.8).

The Styles gallery on the Home tab is a bit limiting in what styles appear (unless the one you want is always shown first). To see more, click the dialog box launcher—the tiny icon with an arrow in it displayed in the lower-right corner of the Styles group (refer to Figure 10.8). After you click the launcher, the Styles pane opens as shown in Figure 10.9. This pane lists all the styles for the style set currently applied to the document. You can choose a style from the list to apply it to text in your document. You can keep the pane open to assign more styles throughout your document.

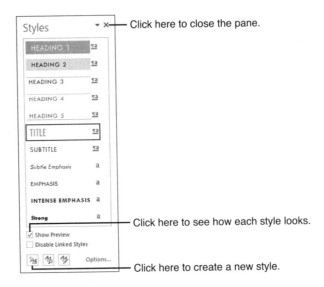

Click here to close the pane.

Click here to see how each style looks.

Click here to create a new style.

FIGURE 10.9

The Styles pane.

TIP If you don't see all your styles listed, then click the Options link at the bottom of the Styles pane and select All Styles from the Select Styles to Show drop-down list.

Creating New Styles

You can modify an existing style and save it as a new style in the list. You can also create a new style from scratch. Start by applying all the necessary formatting and then click the New Style button at the bottom of the Style pane (refer to Figure 10.9). This opens the Create New Style from Formatting dialog box, as shown in Figure 10.10. You can type in a name for the style, and change any other settings as needed. Click OK when you finish and Word adds the style to the Styles gallery. Now it's ready to go the next time you need it.

If you want the new style available in other documents as well as the current one, you need to select the New Documents Based on This Template option in the dialog box.

If you want to update all the uses of the new style throughout the document (in case you tweak the formatting or something), select the Automatically Update check box.

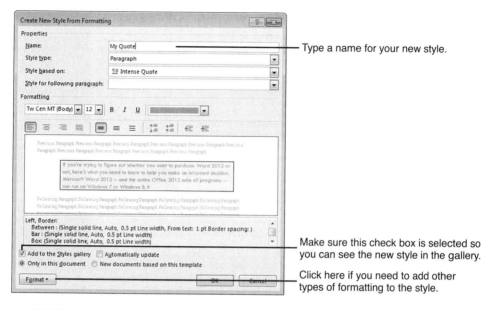

Type a name for your new style.

Make sure this check box is selected so you can see the new style in the gallery.

Click here if you need to add other types of formatting to the style.

FIGURE 10.10

Use this dialog box to create a new style.

TIP If you notice that unexpected formatting changes keep happening to your paragraphs, you probably have the Automatically Update option on and need to change the setting. To turn this off, right-click the style name in the Styles pane and choose Modify. This opens the Modify Style dialog box. Uncheck the Automatically Update check box to turn the feature off.

Adding Special Effects

In this section, you find out how to apply the classic drop caps technique, give your formatting some pizzazz with text effects, and insert a subtle behind-the-scenes watermark.

Inserting Drop Caps

Drop caps have long been a part of the publishing industry, commonly used in books to present the first character of the chapter in a prominent fashion. Typically, a drop cap is an enlarged first letter of the first word of the first paragraph, an initial—check out Figure 10.11 to see what a drop cap looks like.

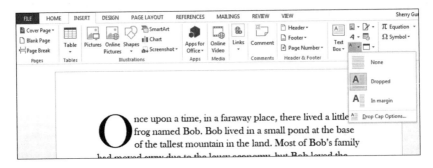

FIGURE 10.11

Here's an example of a drop cap, plus a peek at the Drop Cap menu.

Drop caps can appear below or above the text baseline (the invisible horizontal line that characters sit on). They work best with a longer paragraph that has more than three lines of text.

To create your own drop cap, follow these steps:

1. Select the text character you want to turn into a drop cap.

2. On the Insert tab, click the Drop Cap button to display the menu shown in Figure 10.11.

3. Select Dropped, and Word turns the character into a drop cap.

You can edit a drop cap using the Drop Cap dialog box, shown in Figure 10.12. To open this box, either click the Drop Cap button and choose Drop Cap Options, or right-click over a selected drop cap's border and choose Drop Cap. You can use the tools in the dialog box to adjust the font style, how many lines to drop, and the distance from the rest of the text. If you decide you need to remove the drop cap, select it and activate the None command.

FIGURE 10.12

The Drop Cap dialog box.

Applying Text Effects

Word's text effect tools can add some serious flair and style to your text. Utilizing such techniques as outlining, shadows, glow, and reflection, you can create a variety of artsy looks. To use the feature, click the Text Effects and Typography button on the Home tab. (It's on the second row of the Font group.) A menu of effects categories appears, and each one offers a submenu of choices presented in a gallery. Figure 10.13 shows the Glow gallery and the text displays a preview of the highlighted effect. To assign an effect, just click it.

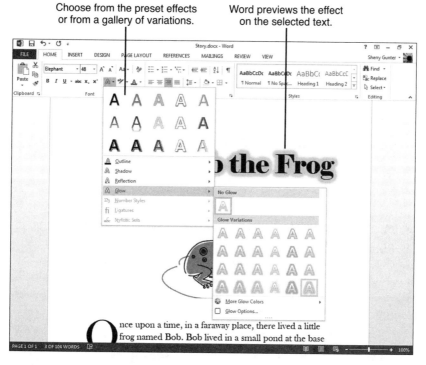

FIGURE 10.13

You can add text effects to turn text into fancy-looking typography.

To turn off an effect, select the text, reopen the gallery, and choose the No command offered, such as No Glow.

Adding a Watermark

It sounds like a fancy term for something involving liquid, which is never a good idea near a computer, but a *watermark* is actually text or an image that appears faded in the background of a page. Take a look at Figure 10.14. Can you make out the DRAFT watermark, printed on an angle?

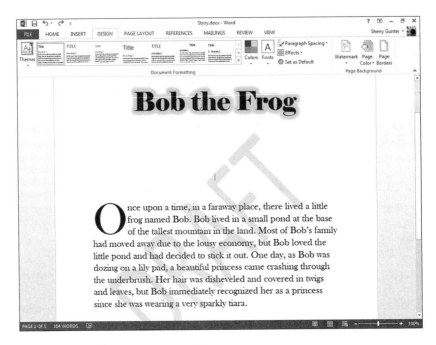

FIGURE 10.14

Watermarks appear behind text on a page.

Watermarks are commonly used in corporate and industrial settings; for example, to identify documents as confidential or drafts, or in the case of government agencies, top secret. Watermarks appear behind the document text as a background element. You can use text or pictures as watermarks, including photos. Word's Watermark tool includes several default choices presented in the Watermark gallery (see Figure 10.15).

To insert a simple watermark, click the Watermark button on the Design tab and select a watermark design from the gallery (see Figure 10.15).

To create a custom design, you can open the Printed Watermark dialog box. Click the Custom Watermark command at the bottom of the Watermark menu. This opens the Printed Watermark dialog box, as shown in Figure 10.16. To use a picture as a watermark, click the Picture Watermark option and navigate to the file. To use a different word or phrase than the gallery offers, click the Text drop-down menu and make a selection. You can also use the settings to control the font, size, color, and layout of the watermark.

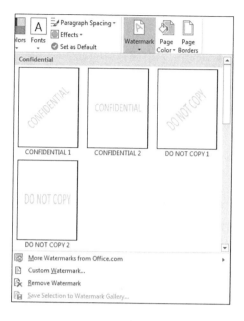

FIGURE 10.15

You can use the Watermark tool to add a watermark from the scrollable gallery.

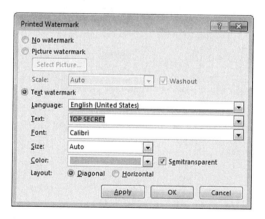

FIGURE 10.16

Use this dialog box to add a picture as a watermark or create custom text.

To remove a watermark, click the Watermark button and choose Remove Watermark.

Adding Borders and Shading

You can add borders and background shading to text, paragraphs, or entire pages. Borders are a great way to section off parts of your document or draw attention to special areas. The use of color as a background can do the same. This section shows you how to utilize the borders and shading tools, and the skills you learn here can help you as you continue to work with other document elements you add, such as tables and clip art.

 TIP Colors, borders, and all manner of formatting are great, but always keep legibility in mind. If any of the extra formatting makes reading your text too difficult, then you've defeated the purpose.

Adding Text Borders

You can create custom borders in Word and control the color and thickness of the lines. You can also customize the line style and even choose which sides you want bordered. Options, options, options—so many options!

To add a border around text, whether it's a single word or paragraph, follow these steps:

1. Select the text you want to add a border to.

2. On the Home tab, click the Borders drop-down arrow (see Figure 10.17).

3. Choose a border option.

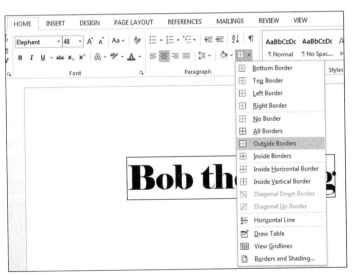

FIGURE 10.17

Use the Borders tool to add borders to your text.

You can customize a border using the Borders and Shading dialog box, shown in Figure 10.18. To find your way to this feature, click the Borders and Shading command at the bottom of the Borders drop-down menu. With the Borders tab displayed, you can choose a border setting, line style, color, and line width. When you've set all the options you want, click OK to apply them to the selected text.

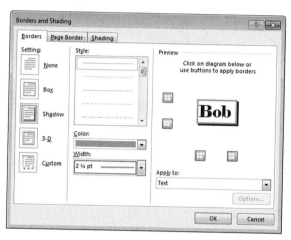

FIGURE 10.18

The Borders and Shading dialog box.

Adding Page Borders

You can add a border to the entire page using Word's Page Borders tool, which is on the Design tab. Click the Page Borders button to open the Borders and Shading dialog box to the Page Border tab, as shown in Figure 10.19. This tab shows the exact same tools as the Borders tab shown in Figure 10.18, but anything you set here applies to the page instead of selected text. You can set a custom border and specify sides, or choose from a regular box, shadow, or 3-D border. You can also control the line style, line width, and color.

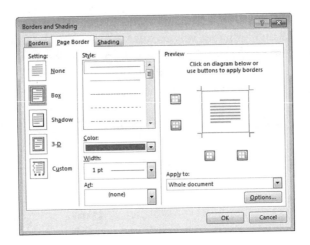

FIGURE 10.19

The Borders and Shading dialog box, again.

Adding Shading

Word's Shading tool adds a background color behind the selected text or the entire page:

1. Select the text you want to be shaded.

2. On the Home tab, click the Shading drop-down arrow (see Figure 10.20).

3. Choose a color option. You can choose from the palette of standard colors or theme colors.

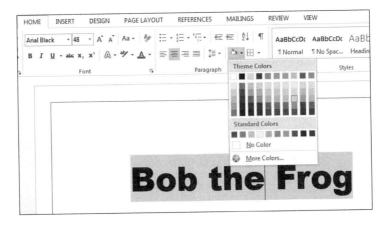

FIGURE 10.20

Use the Shading tool to add background color to your text.

You can use the same technique to add shading to the entire page, but the command for shading the whole page is on the Design tab. Click the Page Color button to display the exact same drop-down palette of colors.

 TIP You can open the Colors dialog box to find more customized colors than what the color palette presents. Click the More Colors command below the color palette to open the dialog box and explore more choices.

Adding Text with Quick Parts

To help you build better documents faster, Microsoft Word offers a library of premade content you can insert, called *Quick Parts* or building blocks (because you can use them to build onto your document). These building blocks include all kinds of elements, such as headers and footers for the tops and bottoms of your pages, salutations for letters, page numbers, special formatting for quote inserts, tables, cover pages, and more. In fact, you can turn any piece of text you use over and over again into a building block and keep it in the Quick Part library ready to use at a moment's notice.

Acting just like parts of a template, Quick Parts offer preformatted text and designs, which often include more than placeholder text. You can customize the placeholder text with your own text. For example, a quote box (shown in Figure 10.21) includes placeholder text for a quote. Just type in your own quote text and it's good to go.

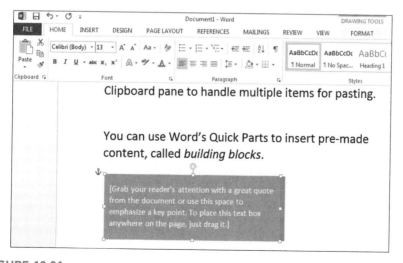

FIGURE 10.21

Here's an example of a quote box, a premade building block you can insert and use by substituting your own text in place of the placeholder text.

TIP Quick Parts are perfect for smaller bits of preformatted text elements, but if you're looking to create a whole document, then templates are the thing to use. See Chapter 9, "Using Templates," to learn more about using Word's versatile templates—premade documents.

Inserting a Quick Part

To use any of Word's premade building blocks, follow these steps:

1. On the Insert tab, click the Quick Parts button (see Figure 10.22).

A gallery of your own Quick Parts appears in the drop-down menu.

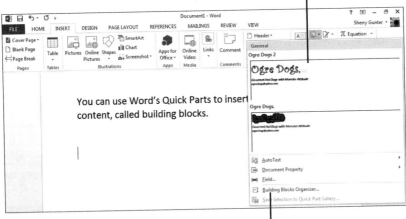

You can use Word's Quick Parts to insert content, called building blocks.

Click here to open the Building Blocks library.

FIGURE 10.22

Use the Quick Parts drop-down menu to access your own Quick Parts as well as the Building Blocks library.

2. Select Building Blocks Organizer to open the Building Blocks Organizer dialog box (see Figure 10.23).

3. Select the building block you want to preview.

4. When you find one you want to use, click the Insert button and Word adds it to the document.

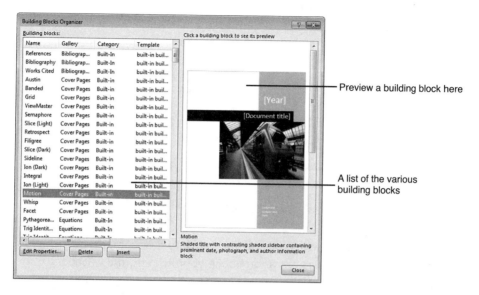

Preview a building block here

A list of the various building blocks

FIGURE 10.23

The Building Blocks Organizer.

Creating Your Own Quick Parts

As you might already suspect, creating building blocks for text elements you use a lot in your documents can be a real timesaver. For example, if you use a company logo, motto, and contact information at the bottom of every letter document you create in Word, you can turn the information into a building block and reuse it again and again. Saving an item as a building block automatically adds it to the Quick Part Gallery for easy access.

To turn text into a building block, follow these steps:

1. Select the text you want to turn into a Quick Part.

2. On the Insert tab, click the Quick Parts button.

3. Select Save Selection to Quick Part Gallery. This opens the Create New Building Block dialog box, as shown in Figure 10.24.

4. Type a name for your building block.

5. Fill out any additional details you want to save along with the text element.

6. Click OK to save the building block.

Create New Building Block		
Name:	Salutation	
Gallery:	Quick Parts	▾
Category:	General	▾
Description:		
Save in:	Building Blocks.dotx	▾
Options:	Insert content only	▾
	OK	Cancel

— Name your building block

— Enter any other details

FIGURE 10.24

Create your own Quick Parts using this dialog box.

Any time you want to add your building block to a document, click the Quick Parts button on the Insert tab and choose your item from the Gallery.

THE ABSOLUTE MINIMUM

Here are the key points to remember from this chapter:

- Themes control the primary design aspects of your document, such as colors, fonts, styling of charts and tables, and shapes and diagrams, and you can change themes using the Themes button on the Design tab.

- Styles help you control various design options within the document. Every theme includes a set of styles, also found on the Design tab listed in the Style Set gallery.

- Text effects add artsy typography techniques to your text, such as glows and shadows; click the Text Effects button on the Home tab to assign them.

- You can use Word's borders and shading tools to add borders and shading to text or entire pages.

- You can use Quick Parts to insert premade content, such as quotes, corporate salutations, page numbers, and other repetitive text.

ADDING TABLES AND CHARTS

Tables in their simplest form are a grid of interconnecting rows and columns. The areas made by this interconnectivity are called *cells*. You can fill cells with text, numbers, artwork and pictures, or even with other tables. You can choose to create tables with or without borders, or add borders around certain cells, add background shading, and numerous other options.

Tables present data in an easy-to-read fashion. For example, you might need to present side-by-side lists in a document, or type up a household budget, create a form, or even design a web page. Because a table's columns and rows are so easy to resize the way you want, there's no limit to the things you can do with tables. Tables are ideal for making invoices, catalogs, newsletters, or any kind of situation in which text requires defined structure.

In addition, Word provides numerous options for modifying and styling tables and their data. Sometimes you might need to nudge a row or column size to add a little space around the cell contents, or add and subtract cells, columns, and rows. Other times, your table might require a complete makeover with new fonts and styles.

Charts offer another way to present related data, but with less detail and more visual impact than tables. Word includes 10 different chart categories—each with a unique purpose—such as column, line, pie, bar, or area charts. Like tables, you can edit, modify, and format charts to suit your exact needs.

Inserting Tables

Word offers several ways to create a table, from simple to sophisticated. You can

- Insert a basic table from a grid
- Insert a table using the Insert Table dialog box
- Create a Quick Table
- Draw a custom table
- Insert an Excel spreadsheet as a table

Inserting a Basic Table

The easiest way to create a table is to click the Table button on the Insert tab and specify how many columns and rows you want simply by dragging the mouse across the grid, as shown in Figure 11.1. As soon as you release the mouse button, your new table instantly appears in the document at the current cursor location, as shown in Figure 11.2.

Any time you add a table or click anywhere in one, the Ribbon immediately displays the Table Tools tabs, which include the Design tab, which is filled with various table style options and design features, and the Layout tab, which includes tools for changing the table's columns, rows, cell size, alignment, and so on.

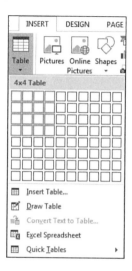

FIGURE 11.1

For an instant table, look for the Table tool on the Insert tab.

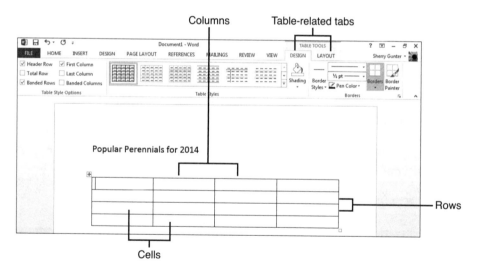

FIGURE 11.2

A newly inserted Word table, measuring 4 × 4 (rows and columns).

Word assumes you want to begin filling your table starting with the first cell, so the cursor sits in the first table cell ready for you to type in text. At this point, you might be wondering how to navigate your tables. Here are a few methods to help you move around in them:

- Press the Tab key on your keyboard to navigate from cell to cell.

- Press Shift+Tab to move back to the previous cell.
- Use the arrow buttons on your keyboard to navigate up and down, right and left in a table. Each click of the button moves the cursor to the next cell.
- Press Ctrl+Home to move to the first cell in the table.
- Press Alt+Page Up to move to the top cell in the current column.
- Press Alt+Page Down to move to the last cell in the current column.

Of course, you can always use the mouse to navigate between cells, clicking which cell you want to work in.

Inserting a Table Using the Insert Table Dialog Box

If you want to control not only columns and rows, but also how text behaves within the table cells, you can create a table using the Insert Table dialog box, shown in Figure 11.4, and choose from the AutoFit options available. To do so, follow these steps:

1. On the Insert tab, click the Table button.

2. Click Insert Table.

3. Specify the number of columns and rows (see Figure 11.3); click the spinner arrows or just type in a value in the appropriate box.

4. Select an AutoFit behavior; you can choose a particular column width, fit the contents to the table (which means the columns expand to fit whatever you type), or fit the table to the window (which means the table fits the size of your document).

5. Click OK. Word creates your table.

FIGURE 11.3

You can also use the Insert Table dialog box to insert tables.

TIP You can convert existing text into a table using Word's Convert Text to Table command. First select the text you want to turn into a table, click the Table button, and then choose Convert Text to Table from the menu. You can then specify the number of columns you want or let Word determine the quantity for you, and instruct Word how you want the text separated (such as paragraphs or commas). Click OK, and Word carries out your instructions.

Inserting and Creating a Quick Table

Although design-it-yourself tables are fun, you might prefer to speed up your table creation using one of Word's built-in Quick Tables, which are part of Word's library collection of Quick Parts and built-in *building blocks*. You can use the Quick Tables gallery to insert calendars, tabular lists, and preformatted tables with preset subheadings. Basically, building blocks are tiny templates you can reuse for formatting new content. To access the gallery, click the Table button on the Insert tab and click the Quick Tables command to view the gallery, shown in Figure 11.4.

FIGURE 11.4

You can choose from several preset tables to insert into your document.

When you see a Quick Table you like, click it in the gallery to insert it into your document and add your own text to personalize the table. All the built-in tables include placeholder text for things such as column headings or calendar months. Figure 11.5 shows an example of a Quick Table with subheadings.

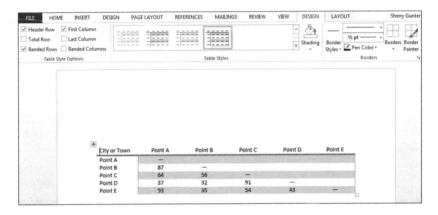

FIGURE 11.5

Here's one of Word's Quick Tables.

TIP To learn more about using building blocks or Quick Parts, see Chapter 10, "Applying Advanced Formatting."

When you customize a Quick Table, or any table for that matter, you can turn it into a Quick Part and use it again. Click the finished table's upper-left corner icon to select the table, click the Table button and choose the Quick Tables command, and then click Save Selection to Quick Tables Gallery. This opens the Create New Building Block dialog box where you can name the table and add a description. By default, the table you save becomes part of the building blocks library and appears in the Quick Tables gallery along with the other table templates.

Drawing a Custom Table

Another way to insert a table into your document is to draw it yourself. For example, you might have a plan for a particular layout for your table that includes one really wide column and several smaller ones, or perhaps your content needs both small and large cells in the same table. With Word's Draw Table feature, you can control how big the table is, how many columns and rows it contains, and the size and spacing of those columns and rows.

To draw a table, follow these steps:

1. On the Insert tab, click the Table button.

2. Select Draw Table. The mouse pointer turns into a pencil icon.

3. Click and drag the size of the table you want to create.

4. Click and drag each row and column you want to appear inside the table, as shown in Figure 11.6.

5. When the table is finished, click the Draw Table button on the Table Tools – Layout tab to turn off drawing mode.

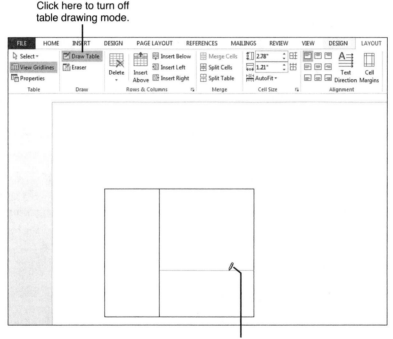

FIGURE 11.6

Customize the table by drawing in the columns and rows.

You can edit your table by drawing new lines, erasing existing lines, or dragging lines to resize cell borders. Try some of these techniques to fine-tune your newly drawn table:

• To erase a line, click the Eraser tool on the Table Tools – Layout tab and drag across the line you want to erase.

- To add a new line to create a new column or row, click the Draw Table button on the Table Tools – Layout tab and draw the line. The button toggles the drawing mode on or off.
- To reposition a row or column border, drag the border line.

Inserting an Excel Spreadsheet as a Table

What if you need a table that acts more like a spreadsheet than like Word content? Word has a tool for that—the Excel Spreadsheet command inserts a spreadsheet right into your document. Best of all, when you activate this feature, you can tap into tools for adding formulas and functions, sorting and filtering, and more, thus putting powerful spreadsheet features at your fingertips.

When you insert a spreadsheet, you might suddenly think you've opened the Excel program window. As you can see in Figure 11.10, Word's Ribbon immediately switches to reveal Excel tabs and tools. Don't worry; as soon as you click outside the Excel spreadsheet table, you're back in the familiar Word environment again.

To insert an Excel spreadsheet as a table, click the Table button on the Insert tab and select Excel Spreadsheet.

Word opens a blank spreadsheet for you, as shown in Figure 11.7. Excel spreadsheets act a lot like a regular Word table; you can enter text or numbers, resize columns and rows, add pictures, and so on. The row and column labels (numbers for rows and letters for columns) don't print with your table; rather, they are used with formulas and functions you might add to the table. The table gridlines appear in printouts, but you can format them to your liking.

 TIP   You can also use the universal Copy and Paste commands to copy Excel data into Word. See Chapter 2, "Working with Office Applications," to learn more.

Excel tabs filled with tools for spreadsheet tasks.

You're still in Word, as shown in the title bar.   Use the Formula Bar to build mathematical equations.

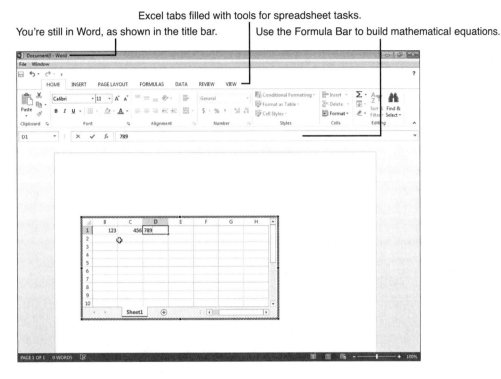

FIGURE 11.7

You can insert an Excel-style table into Word and use Excel tools to populate the table.

Selecting Table Parts

Before you can apply formatting or other changes to your table data, you need to learn how to select the various parts of your table. Selecting table parts is similar to selecting regular document text. Figure 11.8 shows an example of a selected row; notice all the row cells are highlighted in gray to signify that they're selected.

Use the Select menu to select
individual parts of the table.

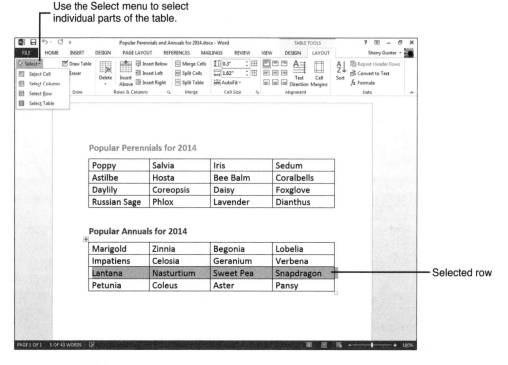

FIGURE 11.8

You can easily select parts of the table in order to apply formatting or make other modifications.

Use these selection techniques to select parts of the table:

- Select a single word or number by double-clicking it.

- Select a cell by moving the mouse pointer to the left border of the cell until the pointer looks like a thick arrow icon and then click.

- Select a cell by triple-clicking it.

- Select multiple cells by dragging across them.

- Select an entire row by moving the mouse pointer to the left border of the row until it takes the shape of a thick arrow pointer and then double-click.

- Select an entire column by clicking the top border of the column. (The mouse pointer turns into a thick downward-pointing icon when you're hovering over the column border.)

- Select the whole table by clicking the tiny square in the upper-left corner of the table.

- Select parts of your table by clicking the Select button on the Table Tools – Layout tab and choosing an option from the menu.

To deselect any selected area or item in a table, just click anywhere outside the selected element.

Modifying Tables

Word tables are extremely flexible. You can modify columns and rows, add and delete cell content, merge and split cells, modify alignment, reposition and resize tables, and enhance tables with styles and borders.

Changing Column Widths and Row Heights

Every column and row in a table is resizable. You can expand and contract columns and rows to modify the appearance of your table. For example, if the cell contents look too tight, adjust the column width, or if you need to insert more lines of text in a cell, you can adjust the row height to fit more text.

Resizing by Dragging

One of the most direct ways to change the column width or row height is to move the border yourself. You can do this by dragging the row or column border. Move your mouse pointer over the border you want to adjust until the icon changes to a double-sided arrow pointer, as shown in Figure 11.9. Next, click and drag the line to the size you need. When you drag a row or column border, it affects the entire row or column. Depending on what line you're dragging and which direction you're dragging it, the column width grows or shrinks, or the row height gets taller or smaller.

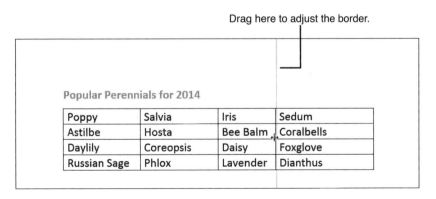

FIGURE 11.9

Manually dragging a column or row border is an easy way to adjust your table.

Using the Tab Tools

You can also adjust the cell size using the controls found on the Table Tools – Layout tab, one of the two Table Tools tabs displayed whenever you work with a table. In the Cell Size group, shown in Figure 11.10, you can see and set measurements for columns and rows. The first measurement (Table Row Height) shows row height, and you can adjust it using the spinner arrows or you can type in a precise measurement (based on inches). The second measurement (Table Column Width) shows column width, and again, you can click the spinner arrows or type in a value to change the setting. Simply click in a cell in the row or column you want to change and then specify another value on the Table Tools – Layout tab.

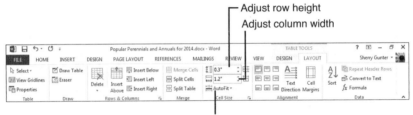

Adjust row height
Adjust column width

Specify an AutoFit option.

FIGURE 11.10

You can use the tools on the Table Tools – Layout tab to adjust your table.

Under the Table Row Height and Table Column Width controls on the Table Tools – Layout tab sits the AutoFit command. AutoFit does exactly as its name suggests—it automatically adjusts the row or column to fit the content, resizes to fit the page, or enables you to set a fixed width. Click the AutoFit button and make your selection. AutoFit Contents is the default setting unless you specify something else.

Using the Table Properties Dialog Box

Yet another way to set column width and row height is through the Table Properties dialog box, shown in Figure 11.11. You might use this route if you want to set a few additional options along with resizing your columns and rows, such as controlling how a row or column breaks across pages; specifying a minimum width or height; or changing the measurement from inches to percentage.

Use one of the following options to open the dialog box:

- Click the dialog box launcher in the lower-right corner of the Cell Size group on the Table Tools – Layout tab.

- Right-click the table and choose Table Properties from the pop-up menu.

- Click the Properties button on the Table Tools – Layout tab.

Next, click either the Row tab or the Column tab within the dialog box to view the associated settings.

FIGURE 11.11

You can also use the Table Properties dialog box to adjust rows and columns.

Here's something interesting about the Table Properties dialog box: The Row and Column tabs both offer two buttons labeled Previous and Next that you can use to set different row height or column width values for each row or column in your table. Set a value for the current row or column, click the Previous or Next button (depending on which direction in the table you're going), and set another value for the next row or column.

Adding and Deleting Columns and Rows

An essential part of working with tables is the ability to add and subtract columns and rows. For example, you might need to add some columns to include more data in a table, or you might want to remove rows you no longer need.

One technique that's quick and easy is to just move your mouse pointer over to the left of a row line, as shown in Figure 11.12, and click. Word inserts a new row immediately. If it's a new column you want, move the mouse pointer over the top of a column border line, as shown in Figure 11.13, until it becomes a plus icon, and then click to instantly insert a column.

Popular Annuals for 2014

Marigold	Zinnia	Begonia	Lobelia
Impatiens	Celosia	Geranium	Verbena
Lantana	Nasturtium	Sweet Pea	Snapdragon
Petunia	Coleus	Aster	Pansy

└ To add a row, click when you see this symbol.

FIGURE 11.12

You can instantly insert a row by hovering to the left of the row border.

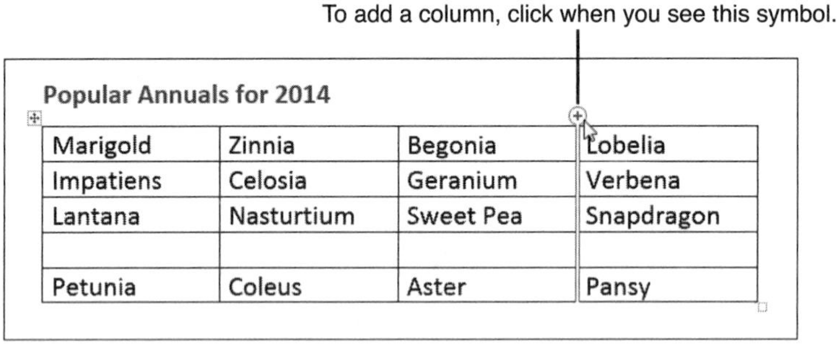

To add a column, click when you see this symbol.

Popular Annuals for 2014

Marigold	Zinnia	Begonia	Lobelia
Impatiens	Celosia	Geranium	Verbena
Lantana	Nasturtium	Sweet Pea	Snapdragon
Petunia	Coleus	Aster	Pansy

FIGURE 11.13

You can instantly insert a column just by hovering over the column border.

Another option is to right-click a cell in the column or row to display the pop-up shortcut menu, click the Insert command, and then click an Insert option. You can insert a column to the left or right of the current location in the table, or insert a row above or below the current location.

Just as easy as the right-click method is to use the tools on the Table Tools – Layout tab (refer to Figure 11.10). The Rows and Columns group offers four buttons for managing your layouts: Insert Above, Insert Below, Insert Left, and Insert Right. For example, clicking Insert Above adds a new row directly above the current row, clicking Insert Left adds a new column directly to the left of the current column, and so forth.

If it's removal you want, you can click the Delete button on the Table Tools – Layout tab (refer to Figure 11.10), and remove columns and rows using the Delete Columns or Delete Rows commands. To remove multiple columns or rows, first select them, and then activate the appropriate command.

Do you want to add multiple rows and columns? That's easy—first select the number of columns or rows adjacent to the spot where new columns and rows are to be inserted. Now when you activate the Insert command, Word inserts the same number of new rows and columns. (Repeat, if necessary; for example, if you want to insert four columns but can't select that many because you have only three columns, select two of the columns and then choose Insert twice.)

You can also remove multiple rows or columns by selecting them before applying a deletion technique.

TIP Did you make a mistake and delete the wrong column or row? No problem; just click the Undo button on the Quick Access toolbar (upper-left corner of the program window, above the Ribbon's tabs).

Adding and Deleting Cells

Adding and removing columns and rows might seem like a no-brainer, but adding and removing individual cells might require a little more thinking. When you insert a new row, you're inserting new cells spanning the entire table. However, some table structures you work with might only require an additional cell, not a bunch of cells. You can choose to add and delete individual cells in a table.

The Delete Cells dialog box, which you were introduced to in the previous section, enables you to remove a cell and specify how you want the other cells to adjust. For example, if you remove a cell in a column, you might want the cells below the deleted cell to shift up, filling the hole created by the removal process.

To access the Delete Cells dialog box, right-click over the cell you want to remove and choose Delete Cells. You can also click the Delete button on the Table Tools – Layout tab and choose Delete Cells. Click either Shift Cells Left or Shift Cells Up, and then click OK to apply the changes to your table.

The Insert Cells dialog box works in a similar fashion, except your table cells are making room for the new cell you add. Start by clicking where you want to insert a new cell; then right-click and choose Insert, Insert Cells. Next, click either Shift Cells Right or Shift Cells Down; click OK to apply the changes.

NOTE Naturally, you might assume the Delete key on your keyboard deletes table elements, such as cells, but that's not the case. Pressing Delete only deletes the cell contents. Pressing Insert also doesn't insert table elements.

TIP Do you need to delete the whole table? On the Table Tools – Layout tab, click the Delete button and then select Delete Table.

Merging and Splitting Table Cells

You can use the Merge Cells command to turn two or more separate table cells into one big cell (see Figure 11.14). For example, you might combine two side-by-side cells to create a large cell for a title across the top of your table, or combine two cells vertically to insert a large logo or picture.

Popular Annuals for 2014			
Marigold	Zinnia	Begonia	Lobelia
Impatiens	Celosia	Geranium	Verbena
Lantana	Nasturtium	Sweet Pea	Snapdragon
Petunia	Coleus	Aster	Pansy

FIGURE 11.14

Three cells merged into one.

To merge selected cells, click the Merge Cells button on the Table Tools – Layout tab. Word immediately merges the cells, including any content each might have held.

Splitting cells is the reverse of merging them. When you split a cell, you are creating two new separate cells out of one cell (see Figure 11.15).

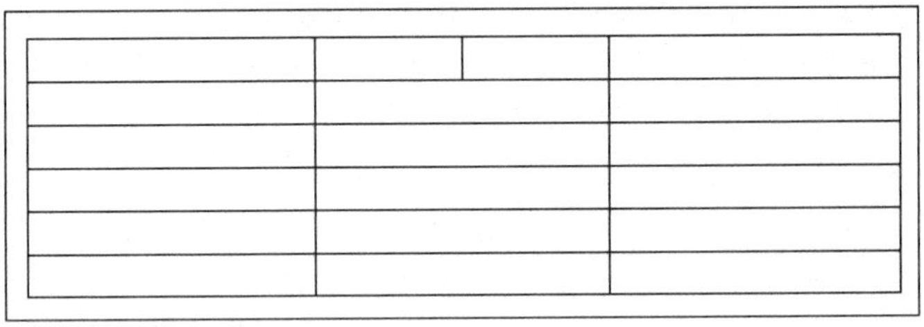

FIGURE 11.15

The top center cell is now two cells.

To split cells, follow these steps:

1. Select the cells you want to split.

2. On the Table Tools – Layout tab, click the Split Cells button. The Split Cells dialog box opens, as shown in Figure 11.16.

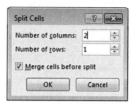

FIGURE 11.16

Specify how you want to split a cell using the Split Cells dialog box.

3. Specify the number of columns or rows you want to create; type in a number or click the spinner arrows to set a number.

4. Click OK.

 TIP   You can also split a table into two separate tables using the Split Table button on the Table Tools – Layout tab.

Changing Cell Alignment and Margins

Don't forget you can use any of Word's formatting tools to enhance the appearance of your table, such as changing the font, size, color, and so forth. You can also change table alignment—the way in which text is positioned within a cell. The Table Tools – Layout tab offers all the alignment options as buttons listed in the Alignment group (refer to Figure 11.10). Not only do these commands pertain to horizontal positioning of text (left, center, right), but also the vertical positioning (top, center, bottom). To assign an alignment to a cell, click in the cell or select the group of cells and activate an alignment setting.

 TIP   Pause your mouse over each button in the Alignment group to view a description of what it aligns.

Word automatically assigns some default margins to your table cells, giving them a little bit of breathing space between the text and the sides of the cell. You can make adjustments to these inner margins using the Table Options dialog box, shown in Figure 11.17. Click the Cell Margins tool on the Table Tools – Layout tab to open the dialog box.

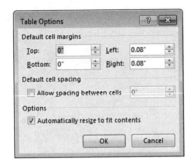

FIGURE 11.17

You can control cell margins using the Table Options dialog box.

You can change the margin settings by clicking the spinner arrows or by typing a value (measured in inches). Click OK to exit the dialog box and apply the changes to the current cell. Be sure to select the entire table if you want to apply the margins to all the cells.

NOTE You can use the Text Direction button on the Table Tools – Layout tab to change the direction of text in a cell, thus creating text that reads vertically in the cell. Each click of the button rotates the cell's text.

Repositioning and Resizing Tables

When you insert a table into your document, default settings determine its positioning on the page. Mainly, the table is automatically left-aligned on the page itself, and no text wrapping is applied. *Text wrapping* refers to how text flows around an object you add to a page, such as a picture, logo, drawn shape, or, in this case, a table.

To find positioning controls for the entire table, click the Properties button on the Table Tools – Layout tab. This opens the Table Properties dialog box to its Table tab, shown in Figure 11.18. You can use the options on this tab to set a different alignment and turn on text wrapping, which is helpful for a smaller table that you want paragraphs to flow around. You can even use the Table Properties dialog box to indent the table's position from the left margin or set a preferred width for the table.

FIGURE 11.18

The Table Properties dialog box offers positioning settings for the table.

If the Table tab is not displayed, click it to view its contents. After you make changes to the settings, click OK to exit the dialog box and apply them to the current table.

You can move a table and drop it anywhere you want it to appear in your document. When you click inside a table, the table icon appears in the upper-left corner of the table, as shown in Figure 11.19. You can click and drag the icon to move the table.

Drag this handle to move the table.

Popular Annuals for 2014			
Marigold	Zinnia	Begonia	Lobelia
Impatiens	Celosia	Geranium	Verbena
Lantana	Nasturtium	Sweet Pea	Snapdragon
Petunia	Coleus	Aster	Pansy

FIGURE 11.19

Use the table's selection handle to drag the table to a new location.

You can also resize a table by dragging the bottom-right corner of the table. Resizing a table automatically resizes all the rows and columns in the table to fit.

Enhancing a Table with Table Styles and Borders

If you need to speed up your table design work without all the effort of applying various formatting, consider assigning a style instead. Table styles let you enhance a table using one of Word's built-in table designs that include colors, borders, background cell shading, fonts, and more. You can find the Table Styles gallery on the Table Tools – Design tab, shown in Figure 11.20.

Marigold	Zinnia	Begonia	Lobelia
Impatiens	Celosia	Geranium	Verbena
Lantana	Nasturtium	Sweet Pea	Snapdragon
Petunia	Coleus	Aster	Pansy

Drag this handle to resize the table.

FIGURE 11.20

The Table Styles gallery offers a variety of preset table formatting.

A style gives your table an instant makeover. For example, Figure 11.21 shows a simple table, and Figure 11.22 shows the same table with a style applied. As you can see, a style adds immediate impact and gives the table visual depth and emphasis in the document. Styles are a great way to make your table stand out, plus you can tweak the style after you assign it to make the table look the way you want. As part of Word's Quick Parts, templates, and built-ins, table styles are easily modified.

2014

Quarterly Sales

	Quarter 1	Quarter 2	Quarter 3	Quarter 4
Ralph	8,905	9,975	10,425	8,700
Lulu	7,800	10,680	12,250	10,200
Eddie	9,100	9,900	10,700	9,300
Bob	5,750	8,890	11,050	11,500

FIGURE 11.21

Before a table style.

2014

Quarterly Sales

	Quarter 1	Quarter 2	Quarter 3	Quarter 4
Ralph	8,905	9,975	10,425	8,700
Lulu	7,800	10,680	12,250	10,200
Eddie	9,100	9,900	10,700	9,300
Bob	5,750	8,890	11,050	11,500

FIGURE 11.22

After a table style.

To assign a preset style to selected table content, choose a style in the Table Styles group on the Table Tools – Design tab (see Figure 11.23). Word immediately applies the chosen style. You can preview all the styles from the Table Styles gallery simply by moving your mouse pointer over each style. Word previews the effect on the current table.

Use the Table Style options to customize your table style.

Table Styles gallery   Click the More button to open the full gallery.

FIGURE 11.23

Use the Table Tools – Design tab to make changes to your table's design and style.

 NOTE You can modify an existing table style and save it as a new style in the gallery. Start by applying all the necessary formatting to the table and then click the New Table Style button at the bottom of the full Table Styles gallery. This opens the Create New Style from Formatting dialog box where you can type a name for the style and change any other settings as needed. Click OK when you finish, and Word adds the style to the gallery. Now it's ready to go the next time you need it.

To the left of the Table Styles gallery sit the Table Style Options. You can turn these on or off to customize your table style. For example, if you choose a style with banded rows, you can turn off the shading for the bands to change the appearance of the style. You can experiment with the options to see what looks best on your particular table.

To the right of the Table Styles gallery is a Shading drop-down menu, shown in Figure 11.24. Click the button to display a palette of background shading you can add to your table cells. You can apply shading to a selected cell or the entire table.

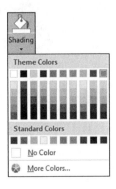

FIGURE 11.24

Add background shading to your table with the Shading drop-down palette.

The far-right side of the Table Tools – Design tab offers a variety of tools to create borders in your tables. You can change the border style, line thickness, and color, and create custom borders for certain sides of a cell. For example, to change the border style, click the Border Styles drop-down arrow and choose from the Theme Borders gallery. You can experiment with the various formatting features here to create just the right framework for your table or table cells.

Inserting Charts

Microsoft Word's charting feature taps into the power of spreadsheets and helps you create visuals to illustrate quantitative and qualitative data, such as a graph showing sales figures for last month or a pie chart of total expenses. You can access charting tools directly in Word without ever having to open Excel or another spreadsheet program. Figure 11.25 shows an example of a pie chart.

If you're new to creating charts, review what chart types are available and familiarize yourself with chart terminology. Then, you can start inserting charts and learning how to tweak them with a little formatting.

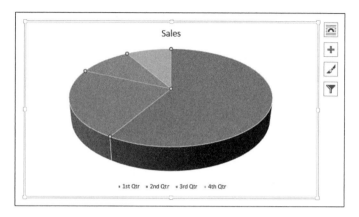

FIGURE 11.25

Pie charts show how individual values are proportional to the sum of the whole.

Understanding the Chart Types

First, determine what sort of chart you want to create. You can choose from 10 different chart categories, and each one has a specific purpose. Word enables you to create the following chart types: column, line, pie, bar, area, X Y (scatter), stock, surface, radar, and combo. Within each category, you can find a variety of styles to depict the data. For example, if you go with a bar chart, the bars measure something of quantity, such as dollar amounts, and you can choose stacked or clustered bars, or bars rendered in 3-D style. Before thinking about styles, decide on a chart type. To help you out, take a look at this list describing the categories:

- **Column**—Shows changes in data over a period of time or compares data.

- **Line**—Shows trends in intervals, such as time.

- **Pie**—Shows how individual values are proportional to the sum of the whole.

- **Bar**—Compares data using rectangular horizontal bars.

- **Area**—Shows trends or amounts of change over time or across categories.

- **X Y (Scatter)**—Illustrates relationships between numerical values or trends across uneven time periods.

- **Stock**—Illustrates fluctuating stock prices.

- **Surface**—Looks like a topographical map; illustrates combinations between data values.

- **Radar**—Shows changes in values relative to a center point. This chart type looks like a spider web.
- **Combo**—Uses a combination of chart types to illustrate up to three data series.

 NOTE Two more categories are listed in the Insert Chart dialog box: Recent and Templates. The Recent category keeps track of recently used charts so you can quickly insert them again without wading through the chart types. The Templates category lists any charts you've saved as templates to reuse in more chart creation.

Understanding Chart Parts

Not all charts look the same, but the general elements are fairly common. Charts are typically composed of several key parts, and naturally those parts have distinct names:

- **Data points**—The individual values you plot in a chart. For example, if you're creating a chart that tracks monthly sales, the total for each salesperson is a *data point* on the chart.

- **Data series**—A group of related values in a chart. Back to the monthly sales total example used previously, if you're charting three months' worth of sales for each salesperson, you're using a *data series*—three totals for the same person makes it a series, you see.

- **Data categories**—When you organize data for a chart, such as the three months you're tracking for sales, the name of each month becomes a *data category* in your chart.

- **Axes**—The display of horizontal and vertical scale upon which the data is plotted. The X axis, also called the *category axis*, is the horizontal scale, and the Y axis, also called the *value axis*, is the vertical scale. In the monthly sales example, the X axis lists the individual salespeople by name and the Y axis lists the monetary values by which you are measuring their success, such as increments of $1,000 or $10,000.

- **Axis labels**—Text that identifies what data is being plotted on the chart, such as time intervals, categories, or monetary scale.

- **Plot area**—Shows the measurement for the given values in the chart, such as how much money each salesperson generated displayed in bars or lines, and so on.

- **Legend**—A summary or key indicating what the chart is mapping. Depending on the type of chart, the legend identifies the data series or differentiates between the series.

- **Chart area**—Refers to the entire chart and all its parts, including any borders you assign.

- **Gridlines**—Also called *tick marks*, these are the lines that appear in the plot area to help you read your chart and line up the chart data with the scale it's illustrating.

- **Data table**—The chunk of worksheet cells you use to enter the chart data. You can include the cells in the final chart, if you want, if you need to show how you built the chart.

- **Chart text**—You can add chart titles, subtitles, and other information text to a chart. You can also format the text to correspond with the rest of the document.

Figure 11.26 shows some of these chart terms pointed out on an actual chart.

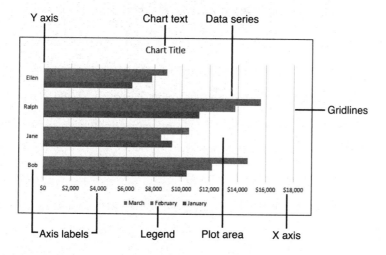

FIGURE 11.26

The parts of a chart.

Inserting a Chart

Decide where you want your chart to appear with a click on the page and then follow these steps:

1. On the Insert tab, click the Chart button to open the Insert Chart dialog box (see Figure 11.27).

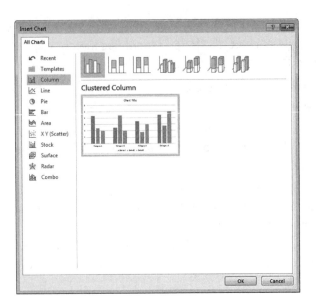

FIGURE 11.27

The Insert Chart dialog box lists the various chart types you can apply.

2. Select a chart type.

3. Select the chart you want to create.

4. Click OK. Word creates the chart, similar to Figure 11.28.

The Word program window displays a worksheet grid, a large chart area filled with placeholder chart elements. In addition, two new tabs appear on the Ribbon: Chart Tools – Design and Chart Tools – Format.

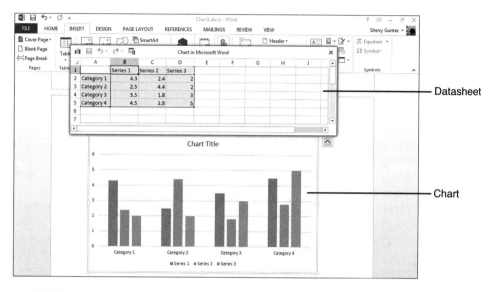

FIGURE 11.28

When you first create a chart, it's empty.

Entering Chart Data

Now it's time to start entering chart data. On a chart, the grid of columns and rows is the datasheet, the spot where you record all the data you want to turn into a chart. The datasheet window even presents some helpful placeholder data to help you get started, and names it appropriately to give you a clue as to what might go where.

To begin, click in a cell and type your data. As soon as you type something, Word updates the chart with the new data. Let's reuse that monthly sales totals example we've been talking about so far. For this example, use a Column chart. To display three salespeople's totals across three months, you can type the month names as your column headings, as shown in Figure 11.29.

Type sales months starting here.

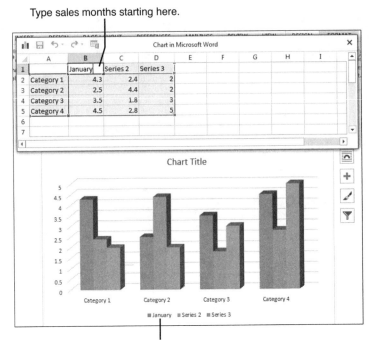

The chart immediately reflects edits.

FIGURE 11.29

This example shows months as column headings.

Next, add the individual names of your sales force in the row headings, shown in Figure 11.30.

Type salespeople's names in these rows.

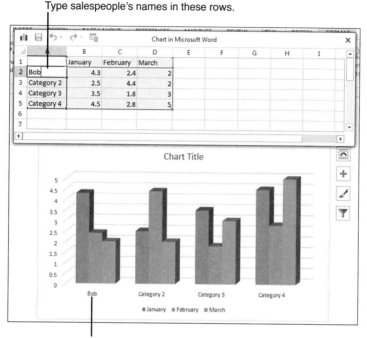

The chart immediately reflects edits.

FIGURE 11.30

Type in each salesperson's name in the row headings.

The intersecting cells hold all the sales figures for each person, as shown in Figure 11.31. Type in the sales amounts for each person in their corresponding columns and rows.

Type sales figures in the cells.

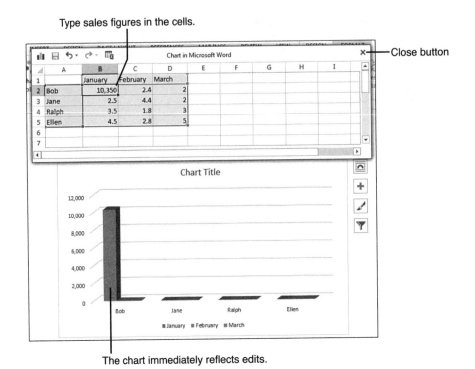

Close button

The chart immediately reflects edits.

FIGURE 11.31

Type in all the sales figures.

When you finish typing in all the chart data, you can close the datasheet by clicking the little window's Close button. You can also drag it by its title bar to move it out of the way, or minimize it. If you do close it and want to open it again, right-click the chart and click Edit Data or click the Edit Data button on the Chart Tools – Design tab.

Editing Charts

As soon as you click anywhere on a chart, the Chart Tools – Design and Chart Tools – Format tabs appear. The Chart Tools – Design tab offers tools for fiddling with the design elements of the chart, and the Chart Tools – Format tab has tools for changing the appearance of chart shapes, text, and arrangement.

To add items to your chart, go to the Chart Tools – Design tab, shown in Figure 11.32. If you click the first button on the tab, the Add Chart Elements button, a drop-down menu appears listing various elements you can add. Click a category to open a submenu and then click the item you want to insert. For example, if you want to include a legend—a key to what all the colors or data series stand for—click the Legend category and click a location for the item. You can easily experiment with each of the items listed to see what they look like in your chart. As you move the mouse pointer over each, the chart reflects the addition.

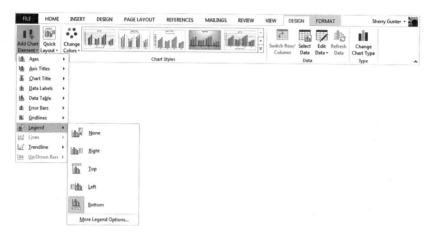

FIGURE 11.32

You can add elements to enhance your chart using the Add Chart Elements menu.

The Chart Tools – Design tab offers other chart-changing tools you can apply:

- Don't like your original layout? Click the Quick Layout button to select another. (These are the same layouts you viewed in the Insert Chart dialog box.)

- Don't like the chart color scheme? Click the Change Colors button and choose another color set to apply.

- Don't like the chart's overall style? Swap it out with something different from the available styles listed in the Chart Styles gallery. Chart styles include colors, fonts, and backgrounds.

- Don't like your chart type? Click the Change Chart Type button to open the Change Chart Type dialog box and select another chart type.

If you need to edit your chart's data, you can click the Edit Data button and select Edit Data from the drop-down menu. This opens the datasheet window you used to enter all the chart data. If you would rather do your editing in Excel instead, click the Edit Data in Excel 2013 option.

The Chart Tools – Format tab, shown in Figure 11.33, displays tools for changing the formatting attributes of your chart parts and controlling the position of the chart. Most of the tools are the same tools used to format SmartArt, shapes, and pictures, so this section doesn't discuss them, except to talk about a few unique to charts.

FIGURE 11.33

Use the tools on the Chart Tools – Format tab to change the appearance of various chart elements.

On the left side of the tab is a group of tools labeled Current Selection. You can use these tools to format a particular selection in your chart, such as the legend or data series. When you click the Format Selection button, a pane opens with additional options you can apply to format the selection, as shown in Figure 11.34. The pane changes based on what item you're formatting and you can click the tools within the pane to make different types of changes, such as changing a fill color or plotting the series on another axis. Many of the tools duplicate what's already offered on the Chart Tools – Format tab, such as the Shape Fill or Shape Effects tools. But the pane handily groups tools related to the task at hand in one spot so you can easily change the settings for the selected item all at once. When you finish using the pane, click its Close button.

Format Selection button

Click an arrow to expand or collapse a group of tools.

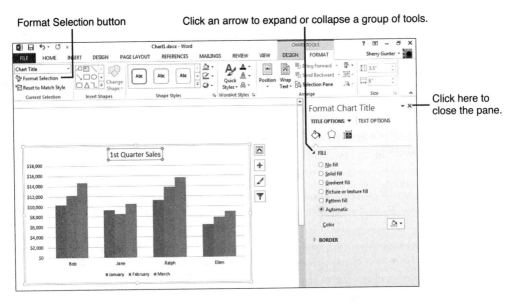

Click here to close the pane.

FIGURE 11.34

Formatting panes help you quickly assign attributes to a selected chart element.

TIP You can also double-click a chart to open the pane of formatting tools.

In addition to Ribbon tabs, you can also jump right to task-related chart-editing features using some special shortcuts, shown in Figure 11.35. When you work with a chart, four icons appear to the right of the chart:

- **Layout Options**—Displays text wrapping settings to control how the chart interacts with the rest of the document page.

- **Chart Elements**—Add or subtract chart elements using this pop-up list.

- **Chart Styles**—Gives you quick access to the Chart Styles gallery to change the chart appearance.

- **Chart Filters**—Edit data points and names on the chart using this pop-up list.

Click an icon to view its related information.

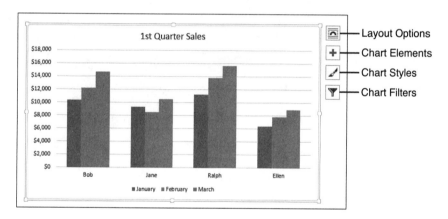

FIGURE 11.35

Use the task-related editing features as shortcuts to chart commands and tools.

TIP You can right-click on a chart to view a shortcut menu of commands to help you edit and format chart elements.

THE ABSOLUTE MINIMUM

Here are the key points to remember from this chapter:

- Word offers several ways to create a table. You can insert a basic table from a grid, insert a table using the Insert Table dialog box, create a Quick Table, draw a custom table, or insert an Excel spreadsheet as a table.

- To edit and format parts of the table, you need to learn a few selection techniques.

- Word offers a multitude of table modification, editing, and formatting options. You can modify columns and rows, add and delete cell content, merge and split cells, modify alignment, reposition and resize tables, and enhance tables with styles and borders. You find these tools on the Table Tools – Layout tab and on the Table Tools – Design tab.

- If you need to display numerical data, use Word's charting features to create your own chart. Click the Chart button on the Insert tab to get started. Word offers 10 different chart categories you can choose from, and each type includes a variety of layouts.

12

PRINTING DOCUMENTS

After you create, format, and perfect your Word documents, it's time to print them. In this chapter, you find out how to preview documents before printing, adjust printer settings, and print accompanying envelopes and labels. In addition, you explore the secrets to performing a simple and painless mail merge, enabling you to quickly create a mass mailing rather than prepare documents one at a time.

Previewing and Printing a Document

You can preview and print from the same place in Microsoft Word: the Print window. To open this window, click the File tab on the Ribbon, and then click Print. Shown in Figure 12.1, the Print window features printer controls and options on the left and a preview area on the right. You can control how many copies you print, which printer you use (if you have more than one), and which pages print out, plus a whole lot more.

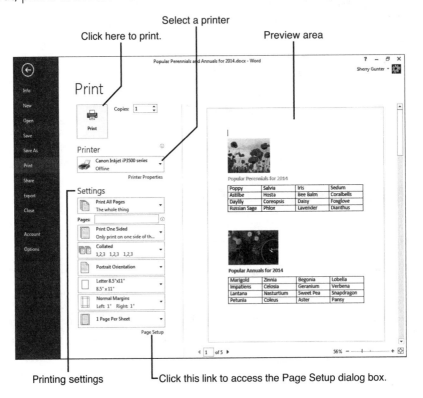

FIGURE 12.1

You can preview and print from the same window in Microsoft Word 2013.

 NOTE You can add shortcut buttons for both printing and opening the Print window to your Quick Access toolbar—the toolbar that sits in the upper-left corner of the program window above the Ribbon. Click the Customize Quick Access Toolbar button (the arrow button at the right end of the toolbar). From the drop-down menu, click Print Preview and Print if you want to add a shortcut to the Print screen (refer to Figure 12.1). You can bypass the whole Print screen and go directly to printing if you add the Quick Print command to the toolbar.

Previewing Pages

The preview area is scrollable, as you can tell from the scrollbar that appears on the far right side of the window. You can use the navigation arrows at the bottom of the preview area to display different pages. Click a navigation arrow button to move forward and backward among the document pages. To view a specific page, type its number in the box and press Enter.

Another nice control is the ability to zoom in and out to view a page. Drag the Zoom slider left to zoom out or drag it right to zoom in, as indicated in Figure 12.2. You can also click either end of the Zoom bar to quickly zoom your view. If you zoom in, the horizontal scrollbar appears so you can move around to view different parts of the page. To return to full page view again, click the Zoom to Page button.

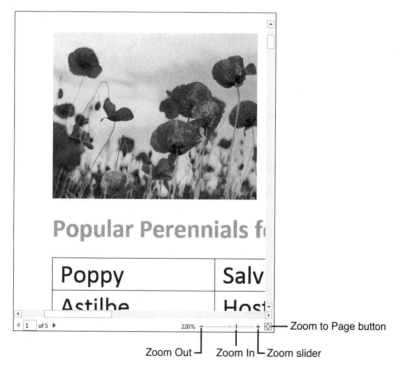

FIGURE 12.2

The preview area offers several controls you can use to check out your pages.

Managing Print Settings

If you're ready to print and you're confident all the settings are accurate as they are, you can simply click the Print button (refer to Figure 12.1) to print your document. However, if you need to adjust a few things first, such as specifying how many copies to make, then you should explore the settings available in the Print window.

 TIP Before you get ready to click the Print button, you first need to make sure your printer is connected, turned on, and ready to go. If you have more than one hooked up, you have an opportunity to choose which printer you want to use. If you run into any kind of printing problems, most of the time it's a hardware problem, like running out of ink or paper. A printer precheck can sometimes eliminate problems before they arise.

Next to the Print button, you can use the spinner arrows or type in a number for the number of copies you want to print. One copy is the default setting, so if you need two or more, you need to change the value.

To change the printer used for the job (if you happen to have more than one connected), click the Printer drop-down arrow and choose one from the list. The list also reveals options for faxing, sending the file to Microsoft's OneNote program, and so forth. At the bottom of the menu is a command for adding a printer, in case you just hooked up a new one that you want Word to recognize.

To view settings pertaining to your particular brand of printer, click the Printer Properties link located just below the Printer drop-down menu.

You can control what prints using the first option listed under Settings. By default, Word assumes you want to print all the pages in your document and sets the option to Print All Pages. But if you click the drop-down arrow, you can choose to print just the current page, particular pages (which you then have to specify), or just the selected text (which you select in the document before flipping over to the Print window for printing). The menu also lets you choose to print extra document info, such as a list of styles used or file properties. The bottom of the menu enables you to control odd and even page printing and whether any markup edit marks print.

 NOTE See Chapter 14, "Collaborating, Reviewing, and Sharing Documents," for more information on Word's document markup capabilities.

If you need to print on both sides of the paper, click the next setting and select your printing preferences. Some printers can print both sides without any intervention, but others require some manual help to do this (such as home printers). You can choose the manual option and Word prompts you when to switch the paper load for the second side's printing. The default setting, Print One Sided, does exactly as its name implies—just prints one side of the paper.

If you need to collate the pages for stapling together or binding, click the Collated drop-down arrow and choose whether to collate or not. If you're making two copies of a 10-page document, for example, you can choose to print each set of 10-pages in order, which is the Collated option. If you want to print out two or more copies of each page at a time, such as two copies of page one followed by two copies of page two, then choose Uncollated.

To change the page orientation, click the next setting and specify whether the page is taller than it is wide (portrait) or wider than it is tall (landscape).

If you need to specify a paper size, such as legal size, click the Size drop-down arrow and choose your paper size. The menu list includes label sizes, business card sizes, envelope sizes, and more. Plus, you can click the More Paper Size command at the bottom of the menu and open the Page Setup dialog box to more paper size settings. Letter size (8.5" × 11") is the default setting.

 TIP Have you ever wondered why some drop-down menus drop up instead of down? It's because of how much display space is available onscreen. If there's not enough room to display the menu in a downward direction, Word displays it upward instead.

To adjust your margins before printing, click the Margins drop-down arrow and make a selection. You can learn more about setting margins in Chapter 8, "Formatting Pages." Be careful, though; adjusting margins might create some issues for your pages, changing the layout and flow of text. Thankfully, you can preview everything you do in the preview area before committing the changes to a printout.

Lastly, you can adjust how many pages appear on a single printed page with the Page per Sheet drop-down menu. In general, you only want to print one page on one piece of paper, but occasions might arise when you want to print 2, 4, 6, 8, or 16 pages on a single piece of paper.

Any changes you make to the printer settings remain in effect for any additional printing for the document, unless you change them again.

Controlling Page Setup

You can find plenty of tools for setting printing options before you actually get to the Print window. The Page Layout tab, for instance, lets you set margins, page orientation, and paper size with a click of a button. As shown in Figure 12.3, you can click the Page Layout tab to view the settings, all of which are grouped under the heading Page Setup. You can set these options before you even begin building a new document, or you can assign them at any point of the document creation process. Just click the tab and then click a drop-down arrow to display a menu of choices.

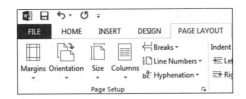

FIGURE 12.3

You can find page layout controls on the Page Layout tab for setting margins, page orientation, and paper size.

The following Page Setup group commands can help you control aspects of your pages before printing:

- **Margins**—View a menu of margin settings you can apply.

- **Orientation**—Switch between portrait and landscape page orientation.

- **Size**—Specify a paper size, such as letter or legal, using this drop-down menu.

You can also adjust page settings through the Page Setup dialog box. Click the dialog box launcher (located in the lower-right corner of the Page Setup group) to open the dialog box, shown in Figure 12.4. The dialog box has three tabs: Margins, Paper, and Layout. On the Paper tab, you can choose a paper size and source for your printer. Simply make your changes and click OK to apply them to the document.

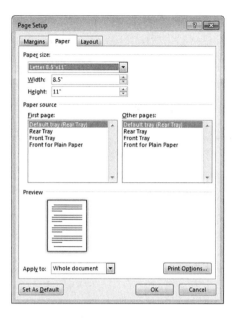

FIGURE 12.4

The Page Setup dialog box.

 TIP You can learn more about setting margins in Chapter 8, as well as how to use the Page Setup dialog box to add headers and footers, and set vertical alignment options.

Printing Envelopes and Labels

Printing document pages is fairly straightforward; simply click the Print button to print your documents. But did you know you can also print envelopes and labels with ease using special Word tools?

Printing Envelopes

You can grab the address information off any letter you create in Word and turn it into a printed envelope. Using Word's Envelopes command, you can quickly print an envelope containing both the sender and delivery addresses, and control how the envelope prints out of your printer. Plus, you can change the font, envelope size, and position of the addresses on the envelope, such as moving an address to make room for a preprinted logo on the envelope.

By default, Word is set up to process a standard size 10 envelope, which measures 4⅛" by 9½". If you need another size, you can specify one before printing. Also by default, Word assigns 12-point type for the envelope text, but you can change the font and size if you prefer something else.

To print an envelope, follow these steps:

1. Open the letter document containing the address information you want to turn into an envelope, similar to what's shown in Figure 12.5.

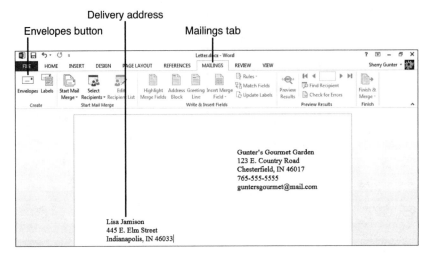

FIGURE 12.5

To print envelopes in Word, click the Envelopes button on the Mailings tab.

2. On the Mailings tab, click the Envelopes button.

3. Word opens the Envelopes and Labels dialog box shown in Figure 12.6 to the Envelopes tab. (If the Envelopes tab is not already selected, click it.) Based on the letter document, Word guesses which lines of text comprise the recipient's address. To type another one instead, click in the Delivery address box and type another.

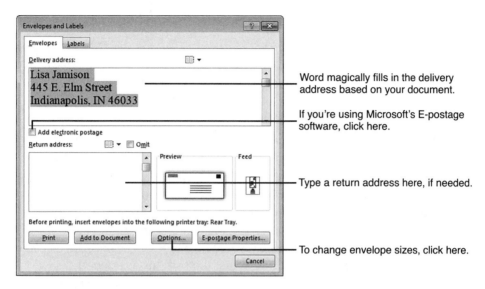

Word magically fills in the delivery address based on your document.

If you're using Microsoft's E-postage software, click here.

Type a return address here, if needed.

To change envelope sizes, click here.

FIGURE 12.6

The Envelopes and Labels dialog box.

4. Click the Return address box and type in a return address, if needed.

5. Click the Options button to open the Envelope Options dialog box, shown in Figure 12.7.

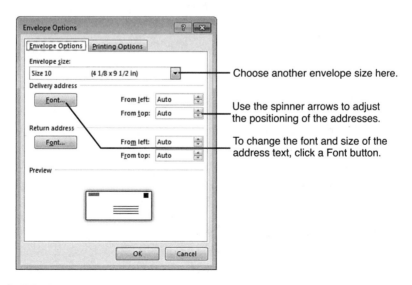

Choose another envelope size here.

Use the spinner arrows to adjust the positioning of the addresses.

To change the font and size of the address text, click a Font button.

FIGURE 12.7

Use the Envelope Options dialog box to change the envelope size or reposition the addresses.

6. From the Envelope Options tab, click the Envelope size drop-down arrow and select a size.

7. If you need to control any positioning settings for either the delivery address or the return address, make your adjustments using the spinner arrows.

8. Click OK.

9. Click Print and feed your envelope through the printer per your printer's configuration.

If you use electronic postage, you can print it out on the envelope as well, but only if you install the electronic postage software from the Microsoft Office website. Click the Add Electronic Postage check box (refer to Figure 12.15) and Word displays a prompt box with some instructions for visiting the website to download the software. If you already have the software installed, you can click the E-postage Properties button to adjust the settings as needed.

If you need to tweak how an envelope is processed through your printer, such as changing the feed method or which printer tray to use, click the Printing Options tab in the Envelope Options dialog box and make your changes.

 TIP Tired of typing in your return address for envelopes and labels? Why not add it to Word's customizing info so it's automatically added each time? Start by clicking the File tab and clicking Options to open the Word Options dialog box. Next, click the Advanced tab and then scroll down the page to find the General options. In the big Mailing Address text box, type in your return address and click OK to exit the dialog box. Next time you use the Envelopes and Labels dialog box, the address is already there.

Printing Labels

Word also has tools to help you print labels for addresses. You can print a single label or a sheet of labels. If you use label paper from a particular manufacturer, you can feed them into the printer, choose that manufacturer and label size, and print them from Word, too. When you create labels in Word, they're turned into a table with cell size matching that of the designated label vendor size you select. Most label paper is self-adhesive, and the entire sheet of labels is constructed of individual labels spaced out across the page. Your Word-based labels need to match the layout of your label paper, so you need to know the manufacturer and product number. There are lots of label vendors, including Microsoft, 3M, and Avery, so chances of finding a match among the labels listed in Word are pretty good. Even if you don't find a match, you can designate your own new label size and layout.

You have the choice of printing a single label from your label sheet, which is handy so you don't waste label paper, or printing a full sheet of the same label. You can also print a sheet of different addresses. To do a full sheet of the same or different addresses, you instruct Word to create a new document. When you do, the addresses are all positioned across the page according to the label type you specify. To create a sheet of differing addresses, you can use this new document to type them. You can save the document to use over and over again.

To create and print a full sheet of labels, follow these steps:

1. On the Mailings tab, click the Labels button (see Figure 12.8).

FIGURE 12.8

Use the Labels button to get started with printing labels in Word.

2. Word opens the Envelopes and Labels dialog box to the Labels tab, shown in Figure 12.9. (If the Labels tab is not already selected, click it.) If you're creating a sheet of the same address, click in the Address box and type the text you want on the label.

Select this option to print a full sheet of labels.

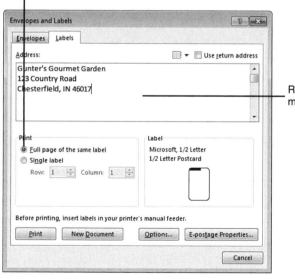

Right-click here to display the shortcut menu for formatting the font.

FIGURE 12.9

The Envelopes and Labels dialog box with the Labels options displayed.

3. If you need to apply any special formatting to the text, right-click in the Address box and choose Font or Paragraph to open the corresponding dialog box and make your changes.

4. To print all the same label, click the Full Page of the Same Label option.

5. Click the Label section to open the Label Options dialog box shown in Figure 12.10 (or click the Options button to do the same thing).

Choose your product number from the list box.

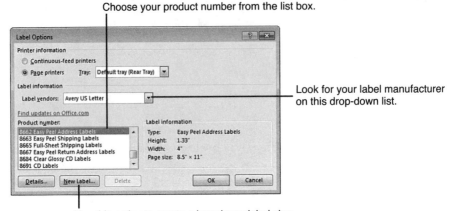

Look for your label manufacturer on this drop-down list.

Use this option to create a brand new label size.

FIGURE 12.10

Use the Label Options dialog box to choose your label vendor and product number or style.

6. Select the type of label you're going to print on; if you can't find a match, choose New Label and enter the correct dimensions for your labels.

7. Click OK to return to the Envelopes and Labels dialog box.

8. Click New Document.

9. Word opens a new document with the label table in place (similar to what you see in Figure 12.11). If you're printing different addresses, this is the place to type them all up. Click in a table cell and start typing them in.

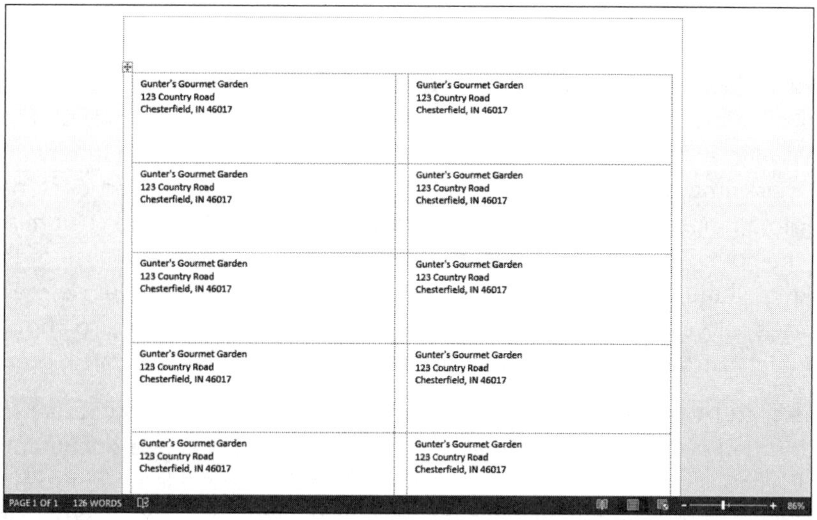

[A new document showing a label table with multiple cells each reading:]

Gunter's Gourmet Garden
123 Country Road
Chesterfield, IN 46017

PAGE 1 OF 1   126 WORDS   86%

FIGURE 12.11

A new document filled with a label table to match your label manufacturer's label page layout.

 TIP Saving the page is a good idea if you want to reuse the labels again. Click the Save button on the Quick Access toolbar or press Ctrl+S to save the file.

10. When you're ready to print the sheet, press Ctrl+P and feed your labels through the printer per your printer's configuration.

 TIP To avoid wasting your expensive labels, print a test set first. In step 10, use a blank sheet of printer paper rather than a sheet of labels. Place the newly printed page in front of a page of blank labels and hold the two sheets up to a light. If the printed text appears to be positioned correctly over the individual labels, you're ready to print on the labels. If not, adjust your settings and repeat the test until the printed sample and the labels are perfectly matched.

If you want just a single label, you can type it in the Address box and click the Single label option, and then specify which label on the sheet to put it in before printing.

 NOTE You can grab mailing addresses from your contacts database, such as Microsoft Outlook. Click the Address Book icon in the Envelopes and Labels dialog box to start the process of using a contacts profile.

Using Word's Mail Merge Tool

Word's Mail Merge tool has been available for several editions of Word, but it's still a pretty nifty feature even if it hasn't changed much through the years. Basically, you can use it to create mass mailings, such as form letters, invitations, or mass emails. You create a form letter in which you can insert personalized information, such as names and addresses, and end up with a customized letter to mail out. The Mail Merge Wizard walks you through each phase of the process, taking all the guesswork out of it. You can type up a form letter before you get started, or you can stop and do so when prompted. You can also choose to insert contacts and addresses from an existing table (database) or start a brand-new list.

The secret to personalized mail merge documents is designating merge fields. A *merge field* is preset information for automating parts of a document. Merge fields act as placeholders for information that is inserted later. For example, if your letter starts with a contact's address, you can insert an Address Block field. If your form letter uses an opening salutation, you can insert a Greeting Line field that uses the contact's first name and a salutation. When you merge the form letter document with your list of contacts, Word grabs the data from the designated fields (such as a contact's address or first name) and inserts it into the document where you told it to.

To show you how this procedure works, begin with an existing form letter. On the Mailings tab, click the Start Mail Merge button, as shown in Figure 12.12. You're going to use the wizard for this procedure, which is simply a step-by-step walkthrough using a pane, so click the Step-by-Step Mail Merge Wizard option to open the Mail Merge pane, shown in Figure 12.13.

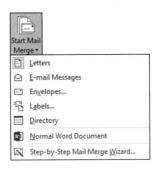

FIGURE 12.12

Start a mail merge using the Mailings tab.

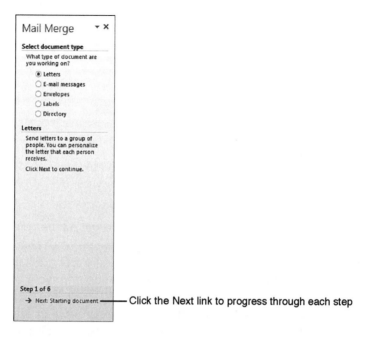

Click the Next link to progress through each step

FIGURE 12.13

The Mail Merge pane walks you through each step.

Step 1, shown in Figure 12.13, is to select the type of document for the mass mailing. For this example, choose Letters (but you can choose something else, if needed). After you make your selection, click the Next link at the bottom of the pane. You can click the Next link every time you finish a step to progress to the next step.

Step 2, shown in Figure 12.14, asks you to specify a starting document. Unless you want to use another file as the form letter, leave the Use the Current Document radio button selected. You can also use a template or another document. Click the Next link at the bottom of the pane to continue.

FIGURE 12.14

Specify a document for the form letter.

Step 3, shown in Figure 12.15, is where it starts to get a little complicated. You need to choose your source for names and addresses—your contacts list. You can go several different directions here. You can use an existing database of contacts from a file or database, you can grab the information from your contacts list in Microsoft Outlook (if you happen to use Outlook), or you can type a brand-new list of contacts. Just in case you don't use Outlook or have an existing list, build a new one now. This route is going to take a little longer, but it's good practice and you just might need a separate list file for other activities on your computer. Click the Type a New List option and then click the Create button to open a window to start typing names and addresses, as shown in Figure 12.16. Of course, if you use an existing list or Outlook contacts, you're prompted to specify those files before continuing to step 4.

FIGURE 12.15

Choose the source of your contact data.

A blank record awaits you

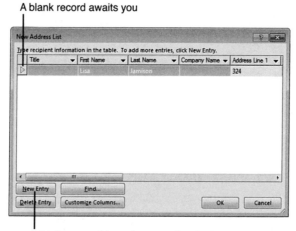

Click here to add another record to the list.

FIGURE 12.16

Use the New Address List window to build a brand-new database of contact information.

Meanwhile, back at the build-your-own list task, start typing the first *record* (that's what they call a contact's information, in this case, a row of entries). Click the Tab key to move from one column to the next. The default list format is pretty basic; each column represents a portion of the contact information, starting with title, first name, last name, address, city, state, and ZIP code. After you finish entering all the data you want for the first contact, click the New Entry button and type another. Keep repeating this procedure until you've completed your contacts list. When you're done, click OK (see Figure 12.17). Word prompts you to save and name the new list you just made, as shown in Figure 12.18. Word saves this data as a database file format (.mdb file extension), which can be opened in a database program, such as Microsoft Access.

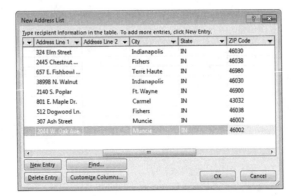

FIGURE 12.17

Click the OK button when you're done creating your list.

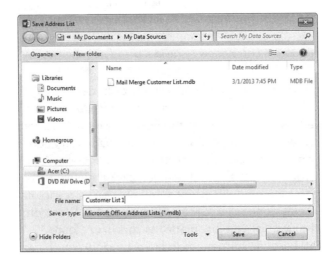

FIGURE 12.18

Word prompts you to save your list file.

 TIP You don't have to use the default fields offered in the New Address List box. You can customize the bits of data you want to use for each record. To do so, click the Customize Columns button and start tailoring the record fields.

The Mail Merge Recipients box appears next, shown in Figure 12.19, listing everything again. Names in the list with a check mark next to them are going to be included in the mail merge. You can take this opportunity to uncheck anyone you don't want included. Click OK to exit the dialog box. The newly created list name now appears in the Mail Merge pane as your list source. Click Next to continue.

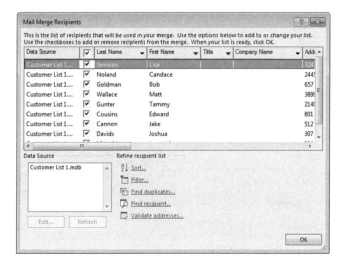

FIGURE 12.19

Now you have a source for the contact information needed for your mail merge.

Step 4 involves adding the special merge fields needed to grab contact information. Using the current letter, click where you want to insert the address and click the Address Block link in the Mail Merge pane, shown in Figure 12.20. Word opens the Insert Address Block dialog box (see Figure 12.21), previewing a contact from your designated list. Check to make sure the information is what you want. (In this example, look for the standard address info: three lines that include the person's name, street address, city, state, and ZIP code.) You can turn check boxes on or off for other options regarding the address information. Click OK when everything is to your liking.

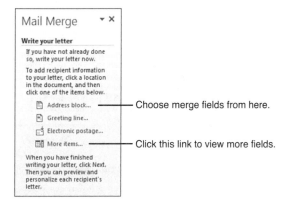

FIGURE 12.20

Step 4 involves inserting merge fields into your form letter.

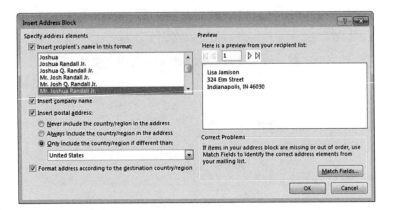

FIGURE 12.21

The Insert Address Block dialog box.

Word inserts the field, as shown in Figure 12.22. You can continue adding more fields to your form letter in places where you want to customize it, such as a greeting. Figure 12.23 shows the Insert Greeting Line dialog box where you can choose an opening salutation and control how you want the greeting to appear in the letter. A similar type of dialog box appears for each field you add to your letter. After you've placed all your merge fields, click Next in the Mail Merge pane to keep going.

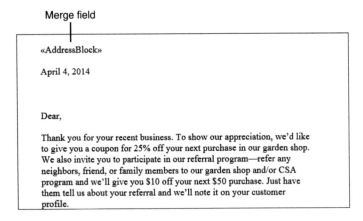

FIGURE 12.22

Merge fields appear with special markings in your document.

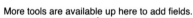

FIGURE 12.23

The Insert Greeting Line dialog box.

In Step 5, you preview what your merged letter looks like with an actual merging of contact info into the letter, as demonstrated in Figure 12.24. You can use the navigation arrows in the pane to view different contacts' data in the letter. You can also use this preview time to make adjustments to your letter or merge fields. Notice the Mailings tab has a group of tools under the heading Write & Insert Fields. You can use the tools to add more fields, highlight them in the letter so you can see where they are, and more.

More tools are available up here to add fields.

Use the navigation arrows to view different contact info in the form.

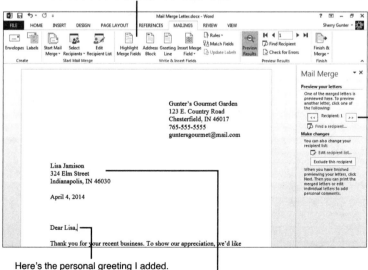

Here's the personal greeting I added.

The Address Block merge field is the actual address.

FIGURE 12.24

Step 5 lets you preview your form letter with actual contact information inserted into it.

If everything looks good and you're ready to merge, click the Next link at the bottom of the Mail Merge pane. Step 6, shown in Figure 12.25, instructs you on how to complete the merge. You can choose to print the letters directly, or open them in a new document file. Make your selection and away it goes. If you choose Edit Individual Letters, Word opens a new document with letters for each contact. If you go this route, a Merge to New Document dialog box opens and you can specify whether you want to merge all the records or only certain ones. If you merge them all, you might end up with a very long document depending on how many contacts you're mailing.

The mail merge process might seem a bit complicated, but it's much easier than typing individual letters. It's especially speedy if you already have a contacts list available and don't have to build a new one.

FIGURE 12.25

Step 6 is the last phase of the process: choose whether you want to start printing letters right away or view them all in another Word document file.

Done

THE ABSOLUTE MINIMUM

Here are the key points to remember from this chapter:

- The Print window offers a multitude of printing options.
- You can use the Print window to preview how your document is going to look when printed on paper.
- Printing envelopes is easy with a little help from the Envelopes and Labels dialog box. You can find a huge list of label vendors and label sizes to match your printer product; but if you can't, you can create a new label size to suit your situation.
- A mail merge takes a generic form letter and customizes it with information from a contacts list, such as names and addresses.

IN THIS CHAPTER

- Structuring Documents with Outline View
- Inserting Footnotes and Endnotes
- Adding Captions
- Inserting Cross-References
- Creating an Index
- Creating a Table of Contents
- Inserting Bookmarks
- Navigating Long Documents with the Navigation Pane

WORKING WITH LONGER DOCUMENTS

Word's versatility kicks into high gear when you create long documents. Unless you're a professional blurb writer and your documents are destined to always be one-page in length or less then you might be interested to know about all the features Word offers for longer types of documents. If you use Microsoft Word to write research papers, term papers, legal contracts, manuscripts, and other lengthy tomes, you can take advantage of a variety of tools for outlining, inserting footnotes, endnotes, captions, indexes, cross-references, and so on. The References tab is the place to look for most of these features, and this chapter shows you how to put several of these tools to work.

Structuring Documents with Outline View

Often an overlooked feature in Word, Outline view can help you construct documents based on a hierarchy of headings, subheadings, and body content. Use Outline view when you want to focus on the document's structure rather than its formatting. When you're crafting any type of document that requires you to group ideas or arrange thoughts in a hierarchical fashion (which means top to bottom with levels of importance), switch to Outline view and get busy organizing your thoughts. You can assign and change heading levels (such as Heading 1, Heading 2, and so on) as needed as your document develops. This hierarchical framework is incredibly practical for planning elements that go into your document, whether you're formulating a letter or list or plotting a full-blown script for the next big television series.

Let's say you're working on a particularly lengthy document, like a thesis, report, or dissertation. Chances are you're going to use headings and subheadings throughout to plan and develop your topic and coverage. You might start with a rough outline of all the main points you want to make, so your outline might look like Figure 13.1. Then within each of those main points you add subtopics, much like you see in Figure 13.2. Within each of the subheadings, you start adding content. You can do all of this in Word using Outline view.

⊕ Raising Your Own Flock of Chickens
    ⊖ Pros and Cons of Raising Chickens
    ⊖ Determining a Breed
    ⊕ Raising Chicks
    ⊕ Housing Your Chickens
    ⊕ Caring for Your Chickens
    ⊖ Chicken Eggs

FIGURE 13.1

An outline in Outline view showing the headings for a report.

⊕ Raising Your Own Flock of Chickens
      ⊖ Pros and Cons of Raising Chickens
      ⊖ Determining a Breed
      ⊕ Raising Chicks
          ⊖ Hatching Chicks
          ⊖ Caring for Chicks
          ⊖ Feeding Chicks
      ⊕ Housing Your Chickens
          ⊖ Building a Coop
          ⊖ Roosting Ideas
      ⊕ Caring for Your Chickens
      ⊖ Chicken Eggs
—

FIGURE 13.2

Here's the same outline, but with subheadings developing under each main topic point.

At first glance you might think "Hey, I can do that in Word without using a special view," in which case you would be right. But you're overlooking something. When you use Outline view, you're tapping into some powerful tools to help you work with your outline—namely the Outlining tab, shown in Figure 13.3. This tab offers tools to help you promote and demote items in the hierarchy with a click; you can also expand and collapse groups so you can focus on important points. It also offers a menu of heading levels you can select from as you build the document.

FIGURE 13.3

The Outlining tab offers a variety of tools to help you build and work with your outline.

To turn on the Outline view, click the Outline button on the View tab. Word displays the Outlining tab, and the text you type into the document is organized into levels, starting with a default level until you specify another. Notice in Figure 13.3 that the headings and subheadings have icons in front of the text. A plus sign indicates that subheadings exist within that heading level, and a minus sign indicates no subheadings.

You can click in the document and start typing; press the Enter key to start a new topic. You can use the following tools to make changes to the outline:

- To assign a heading level, click the line of text, click the Outline Level drop-down menu, shown in Figure 13.4, and choose a level.

- To promote text one level, click the Promote button.

- To promote text to heading 1, click the Promote to Heading 1 button.

- To demote text one level, click the Demote button.

- To demote text to body text, click the Demote to Body Text button.

- To move a topic up in the hierarchy, click the Move Up button (see Figure 13.5).

- To move a topic down in the hierarchy, click the Move Down button.

- To expand a group to view all the subpoints and body content, click the Expand button.

- To collapse a group and just view its main heading level, click the Collapse button.

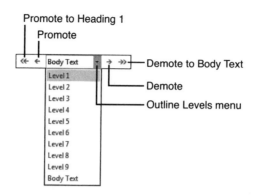

FIGURE 13.4

Assign levels with the Outline Levels menu.

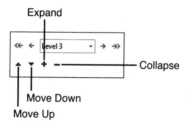

FIGURE 13.5

Use the Outlining tools to move your document points around.

 TIP Many people are confused by Word's heading styles and the idea of promoting/demoting levels, but it's a simple system: The lower the heading *number*, the higher the *ranking* of that heading. So Heading 1 style is applied to the most important topics you address in your document. (Think of them as "number one points to get across to my audience.") Apply Heading 2 styles to subtopics within your Heading 1 topics, Heading 3 styles to issues that are subordinate to your Heading 2 topics, and so on. Word has nine heading levels you can apply to the various topics and sections in your document to organize its structure.

You can drag and drop lines of text in your document to change their positioning in the hierarchy. You can also choose to view only certain levels in your document, which simplifies reviewing the overall structure and organizing the outline. For example, maybe you need to print out a copy of the main points of your report without all the subheadings and body content. You can use the Show Levels drop-down menu, shown in Figure 13.6, to choose to view all the Level 2 text, for example.

FIGURE 13.6

Control what levels appear in the document view using this menu.

You can use the Show Text Formatting check box to show or hide formatting. Click the Show First Line Only check box to reveal only the first line of body text and not the whole paragraph of body text. This might come in handy when reviewing a longer outline.

After you've finalized your document's structure in Outline view, you can switch over to Print Layout view and make it look nice with formatting attributes. To close Outline view, click the Close Outline View button. This returns you to Word and the outline appears as normal text—with all the proper headings and levels assigned, of course.

Inserting Footnotes and Endnotes

If you're working with the type of document that requires resource notations—extra explanations or comments in addition to the text, or other references—you can insert footnotes and endnotes. A *footnote* is an explanatory flagged note inserted at the bottom of a page to cite a source. *Endnotes* appear at the end of a section or at the end of a document rather than at the bottom of a page. You can find buttons for adding footnotes, endnotes, and other reference features on the References tab, shown in Figure 13.7.

To insert a footnote or endnote, use these steps:

1. Click where you want to add the numeral or symbol indicating a footnote or endnote.

2. On the References tab, click the Insert Footnote button or the Insert Endnote button.

3. Word inserts a superscripted reference mark to flag the note.

4. Type your footnote or endnote text at the bottom of the page or section.

Insert Endnote button

Insert Footnote button | Footnote & Endnote icon

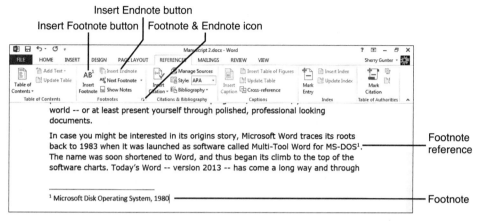

world -- or at least present yourself through polished, professional looking documents.

In case you might be interested in its origins story, Microsoft Word traces its roots back to 1983 when it was launched as software called Multi-Tool Word for MS-DOS[1]. The name was soon shortened to Word, and thus began its climb to the top of the software charts. Today's Word -- version 2013 -- has come a long way and through ——— Footnote reference

[1] Microsoft Disk Operating System, 1980| ——— Footnote

FIGURE 13.7

Find footnote and endnote tools on the References tab.

NOTE As you keep adding footnotes or endnotes throughout your document, Word keeps track of the sequencing and continues the numbering automatically. To customize how the footnotes and endnotes appear, including what type of numbering format is used (such as Arabic numbers or Roman numerals), open the Footnote and Endnote dialog box shown in Figure 13.8. To display the dialog box, click the dialog box launcher in the lower-right corner of the Footnotes group on the References tab. You can also right-click a footnote or endnote and choose Note Options to open the dialog box.

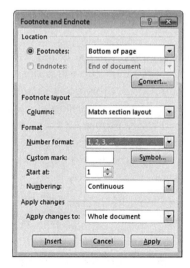

FIGURE 13.8

The Footnote and Endnote dialog box has customizing options you can apply.

The dialog box offers several ways to customize your notes. For example, to control where on the page the footnote or endnote should appear, click the corresponding location drop-down arrow and choose a placement. To change the number format, choose the format you want from the Number Format drop-down list. To control the sequence of numbering, such as continuing the sequence throughout the whole document or just within a particular section, choose an option from the Numbering drop-down list. You can also insert a custom mark or symbol to use in place of a superscripted number. After you make your changes to the customizing options, click Apply.

 TIP The cool thing about using Word's automatic footnote/ endnote numbering is that if you move the text containing the note, Word automatically fixes the numbering for you.

To work with footnotes or endnotes, you can use these options:

- You can move your mouse pointer over a note's superscripted character to view a ScreenTip with the footnote or endnote text.
- To edit a footnote or endnote, click in the footnote or endnote text and make your changes.
- To move between footnotes, click the Next Footnote drop-down arrow on the References tab and choose which direction to move in the document.
- To remove a footnote or endnote, select the superscripted numeral or symbol that flags the note and then press the Delete key.

Adding Captions

You can add captions to pictures, charts, tables, text boxes, and other graphic objects you place in a document. A caption is basically a numbered label. In fact, you can see them throughout this book to alert you to screen captures that go along with whatever topic you're learning about. Every time you see a figure reference—where the text reads Figure 13.1 or 13.2, and so forth—those numbers refer to caption numbers assigned to each figure in the book. (In this example, you're reading Chapter 13 and the figure numbers start at 1, so 13.1 is the first figure reference in the sequence.)

Word's captioning feature includes preset labels to use: Figures, Equation, or Table. If those preset labels don't work for you, you can create your own custom label.

Word also handles the caption numbering for you, such as Figure 1, Figure 2, and so forth. As with footnote/endnote numbering, Word keeps your captions in order even if you move everything around in the document. Another cool thing about captioning using the official caption styles is you can use the captions in cross-references. (See the next section to learn more about this concept.)

To add a caption, use these steps:

1. Select the object to which you want to add a caption.

2. On the References tab, click the Insert Caption button.

3. The Caption dialog box opens, as shown in Figure 13.9. Choose your label type from the Label drop-down list.

FIGURE 13.9

The Caption dialog box.

4. You can position the caption above or below the object; below is the default setting. Click the Position drop-down list to change the position.

5. Click OK.

6. Word inserts the caption, similar to Figure 13.10. Type in any additional text you want the caption to include.

You can apply formatting to your captions to make them look good. Look for text formatting tools on the Home tab.

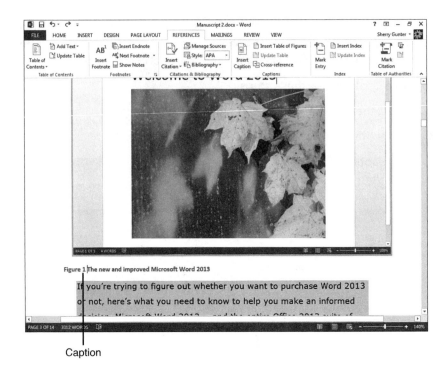

Caption

FIGURE 13.10

Captions can appear above or below the figure, table, or equation.

Inserting Cross-References

You can use cross-references in your documents to refer readers to another section of the document or to additional information. You can insert cross-references to refer readers to existing text that is styled as a heading, to footnotes or endnotes, to captions and bookmarks, figures, and even to numbered paragraphs. The key to make them work properly is to make sure your document has that reference type somewhere within the document. For example, if you want to refer the reader to another section, make sure you assign the section title a heading level using Word's styles (see Chapter 10, "Applying Advanced Formatting," to learn more about styles), or if you want to refer the reader to a figure located elsewhere, make sure the document has captioned figures to refer to. So before you attempt to insert a cross-reference, first make sure you include the reference types in the document. After you have the reference types in place, follow these steps to insert a cross-reference:

1. Click in the document where you want to insert a cross-reference.

2. On the References tab, click the Cross-Reference button.

3. The Cross-Reference dialog box opens, as shown in Figure 13.11. Click the Reference type drop-down arrow and choose the type of document element to which the cross-reference refers.

FIGURE 13.11

The Cross-Reference dialog box.

4. From the Insert Reference to drop-down list, select the type of information to include in the cross-reference.

5. Select the specific item to which the cross-reference should refer.

6. Leave the Insert as Hyperlink check box selected if you want readers to be able to navigate directly to the cross-reference item.

7. Click Insert and Word inserts the cross-reference, as shown in Figure 13.12.

8. Click Close.

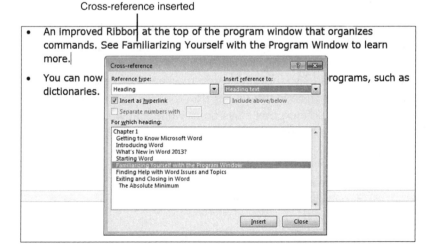

FIGURE 13.12

You can pick which reference to insert from the list of choices.

After you insert a cross-reference, you can tweak it with additional text and punctuation as needed. To remove a cross-reference you no longer want, select it and press the Delete key.

Creating an Index

Would your lengthy document benefit from an index? An *index* is a list of important terms that appear in the document along with the page numbers on which they appear. Indexes help readers look up content and topics, and typically appear at the end of a document. You've probably encountered plenty of indexes in various types of books, such as reference books or even how-to manuals. It turns out that adding an index in Word is fairly easy, as long as you're not frightened by paragraph marks and indexing fields. Don't worry, there's nothing scary about either of these.

To start the process, you have to mark your index words using a special field. After you've marked all the important words you want to include in the index, you can turn them into a tabbed columnar list that Word automatically updates for you. Word's indexing feature enables you to customize your index to include leader characters and preset index designs.

To start building an index, begin marking words you want to designate as index terms. Select the word or phrase in the document and click the Mark Entry button on the References tab. Word opens the Mark Index Entry dialog box, shown in Figure 13.13. Click the Mark button to create an entry for the word or phrase on this page only, or click Mark All to create entries for all occurrences in the document.

When you mark the entry, Word adds a special XE indexing field to your document and turns on paragraph marks, as shown in Figure 13.14. The indexing field is enclosed in braces ({}) and marked with an XE tag (for "index entry"). You can continue adding more indexing markers; just keep selecting words and clicking the Mark button in the dialog box to mark them as you read through the document. The dialog box stays open while you work. When you finish, click Cancel to close the dialog box.

 TIP You don't have to mark all of your document's index entries in a single session. You might prefer to mark entries in multiple sessions, refreshing the index as you go along.

Select the word or phrase to index   Mark Entry button

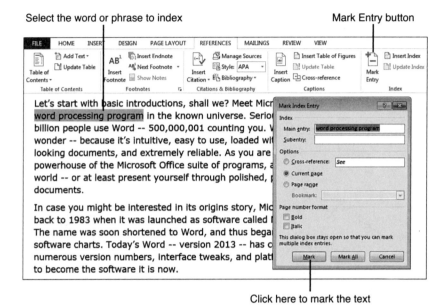

Click here to mark the text

FIGURE 13.13

You can use the Mark Index Entry dialog box to mark words and phrases for indexing.

XE indexing field

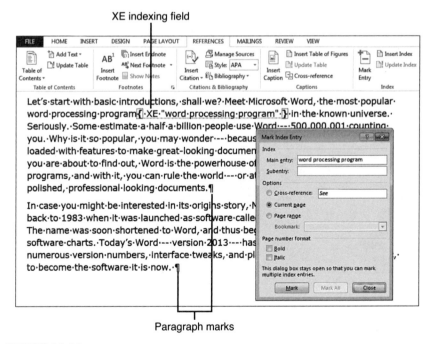

Paragraph marks

FIGURE 13.14

Word turns on the display of paragraph marks and adds an indexing field to the document.

TIP You can drag the dialog box around the screen to move it out of the way while you mark words and phrases. Drag it by its title bar and drop it somewhere out of the way.

The next part of making an index is clicking at the end of the document, or wherever you want the index to appear. On the References tab, click the Insert Index button. This opens the Index dialog box, shown in Figure 13.15.

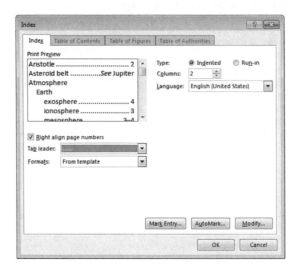

FIGURE 13.15

The Index dialog box.

Click the Right Align Page Numbers check box and choose a design from the Tab Leader drop-down list. Click OK and Word inserts an alphabetical index, similar to Figure 13.16.

Section Break (Continuous)

Bookmarks	4¶	Ribbon	3¶
Cloud	2¶	**Scroll·bar**	9¶
Desktop	5¶	SkyDrive	3¶
Internet·Explorer	12¶	Start·screen	6¶
Maximize	8¶	**Status·bar**	9¶
Microsoft·Office·suite	1¶	**Title·bar**	8¶
Minimize	8¶	Windows·Explorer	4¶
Program·Window·Controls	9¶	word·processing·program	1¶
Quick·Access·Toolbar	8¶		
¶

FIGURE 13.16

Here's an example of an index.

TIP   You can turn off paragraph marks by clicking the Show/Hide ¶ button on the Home tab. Look for it in the upper-right corner of the Paragraph group.

To remove an XE field, select the entire field and press the Delete key, and then update the index. On the References tab, click the Update Index button.

NOTE   Fields are special containers you add into your Word documents to hold data that often requires updating, such as dates or page numbers. Word updates fields automatically when the reference changes. However, sometimes you need to update a field manually. To quickly update a single field, click it and press F9.

Creating a Table of Contents

The front end of your long document might benefit from a *table of contents*—a quick reference of where to find what content within your document. You can instruct Word to generate a table of contents, or TOC for short, based on the predefined heading styles you assigned throughout the document. Of course, first assigning the headings is up to you. (You can find headings listed in the Styles gallery on the Home tab.) After your headings are ready to go, you can create a table of contents using these steps:

1. Click where you want to place your table of contents. For best results, place your TOC on a blank page at the front of the document.

2. On the References tab, click the Table of Contents button.

3. Click a TOC style from the menu, as shown in Figure 13.17, and Word immediately inserts it, similar to Figure 13.18.

Here's what you can do with your table of contents:

*   When you click inside the TOC, two special tool buttons appear at the top. These duplicate the TOC tools found on the References tab. You can use either the shortcut buttons or the Ribbon buttons to edit your TOC, your choice.

*   You can edit your TOC by changing which level headings are listed. Click the Add Text button and choose a heading to add.

*   To switch to another TOC style, click the Table of Contents button again and choose another style.

*   If you make changes to your document headings and content, click the Update Table button to make your TOC current.

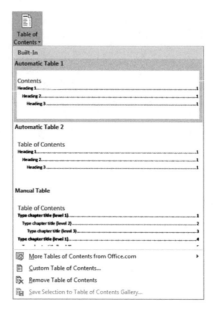

FIGURE 13.17

Use the Table of Contents drop-down menu to choose a TOC style.

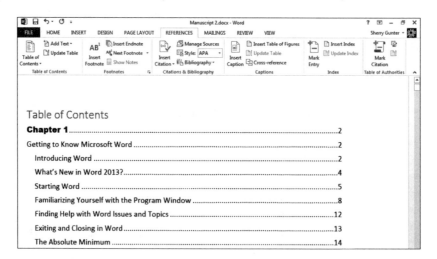

FIGURE 13.18

Word creates a TOC based on the headings assigned in your document.

Inserting Bookmarks

You can add *bookmarks* to help you navigate longer documents. Digital bookmarks act a lot like actual bookmarks, enabling you to mark a location in the document for easy access later. For example, you might use a bookmark to quickly navigate to a key word or phrase, or bookmark text you want to revisit after you've researched a few things. You might also use a bookmark to help you quickly jump to another spot in your document, such as a table of contents.

In order for Word to keep track of all the bookmarks in a document, you have to give the bookmarks individual names. When naming your bookmark, you must follow very strict naming rules. Bookmark names must begin with a letter, and names can include numbers along with letter characters. However, no spaces are allowed in the bookmark name. Instead of a space, use an underscore character, such as in Chapter_3.

Use these steps to add a bookmark:

1. Select the text you want to turn into a bookmark.

2. On the Insert tab, click the Links button.

3. Select Bookmark from the menu, as shown in Figure 13.19.

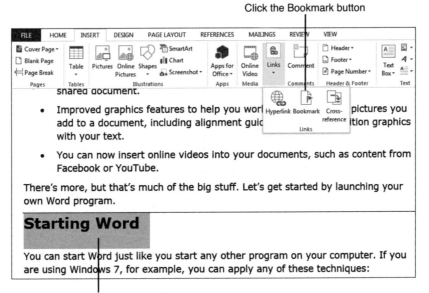

FIGURE 13.19

Find the Bookmark tool on the Insert tab.

4. The Bookmark dialog box opens. Type a name for the bookmark.

5. Click Add.

To use the bookmark later, on the Home tab, click the Find drop-down arrow, and choose Go To. This opens the Find and Replace dialog box (you can learn more about the Find and Replace tools in Chapter 3, "Working with Text") to the Go To tab, as shown in Figure 13.20. Click the Bookmark element, choose the particular bookmark you want to jump to, and then click the Go To button to transport yourself to the location in the document. To exit the dialog box when you're finished jumping around the document, click the Close button.

Choose the Bookmark element   Click here to see all of your bookmarks

Click here to jump to the bookmark

FIGURE 13.20

You can use the Find and Replace dialog box to navigate the document using bookmarks.

 TIP You can also use the Go To tab in the Find and Replace dialog box to navigate to other designated elements in your documents, including footnotes, endnotes, and headings.

Word 2013 also bookmarks the last place you were working in a document when you last saved and closed your file, and it offers to jump you right back there when you reopen the file. A bookmark prompt icon appears, as shown in Figure 13.21, which you can click to return to the spot. If you don't want to pick up where you left off, just ignore the icon.

 NOTE Bookmarks are a part of the document, so if you hand off your document to another user, just remember everyone who reads your document reads your bookmarks as well. For that reason, you might want to remove them from a document first, or simply make sure they're acceptable for all audiences.

Word bookmarks the last spot you
were working on and displays this icon.

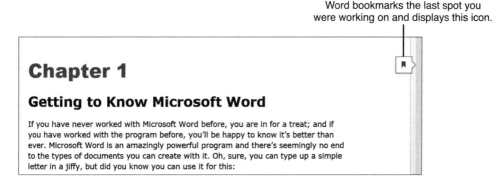

FIGURE 13.21

Word 2013 automatically bookmarks your last editing location in a document and offers to take you there.

Navigating Long Documents with the Navigation Pane

The longer your document grows, the more important it is to learn how to move around in it. Word has just the tool for you to zip back and forth to the places you want to view—the Navigation pane. This pane, shown in Figure 13.23, displays your document headings as a list, or shows each page as a thumbnail image (small image), and also doubles as a search function. To turn on the Navigation pane, click the Navigation Pane check box on the View tab. (A check mark means the pane is turned on; no check mark means the pane is off.) You can also press Ctrl+F to open the pane.

Click the Headings link at the top of the pane to view all the headings listed in the pane, as demonstrated in Figure 13.22. To jump to a heading, click it in the pane.

Click the Pages link to view your pages as thumbnail images. To jump to a page, click it in the list.

To use the pane as a search tool, click the Results link and then click in the Search box and type in your keyword or phrase. Press Enter or click the Search button. Any matching results are listed in the pane, similar to Figure 13.23. Click a result to jump to that spot in the document. You can also use the pane to find objects, like drawings, among the text, or figure references and section numbers and the like. You might also use the Navigation pane to scan through pages to spot errors.

Click here to turn on the Navigation pane

Navigation pane

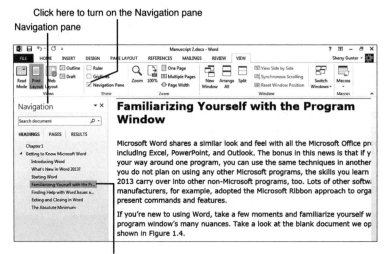

Click a heading to jump right to it in the document

FIGURE 13.22

You can use the Navigation pane to view all the headings in a document and navigate to a particular one.

Type a keyword or term here

Click the Results link

Word highlights the search term in the document

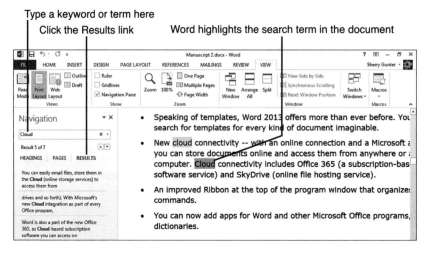

FIGURE 13.23

You can use the Navigation pane to search for words or phrases in the document.

To close the pane, click its Close button (the X button in the upper-right corner), or deselect the Navigation Pane check box on the View tab.

 TIP The Navigation pane is moveable—just click and drag its title bar to turn it into a free-floating box. To dock it again to the side of the window, double-click its title bar.

THE ABSOLUTE MINIMUM

Here are the key points to remember from this chapter:

- Use Outline view any time you want to plan out a document as a hierarchical structure, using headings and levels. Find the Outline view on the View tab.

- Word makes inserting footnotes and endnotes to cite sources, add explanations, and reference other information super easy. Look for these tools on the References tab.

- You can assign captions to figures and tables you insert to help clarify and explain. Look for the captioning tool on—you guessed it—the References tab.

- You can insert cross-references to other parts of your document, but the catch is you have to use reference "types" throughout your document, such as figures or headings, so you have something to reference to. Click the Cross-Reference button on the References tab to get started.

- Add an index at the back of your document that refers the reader to the locations of all the important terminology you use in the text. Look for the indexing tools in the Index group on the References tab.

- Dress up the front of your document with a table of contents that lets everyone know what content you cover and where to find it. The table of contents tools appear on the left end of the References tab.

- Insert bookmarks in places you want to revisit in a flash, such as a heading or the last paragraph you were typing in when you stepped away from your document (after saving and closing the file, of course). Display the Insert tab to find the bookmarking tool.

- Word has a special pane you can use to quickly jump to parts of your document or even conduct a search. Find the Navigation Pane feature on the View tab.

14

COLLABORATING, REVIEWING, AND SHARING DOCUMENTS

Word processing doesn't have to be a lonely activity. You can share your documents with other users. Word has lots of tools that enable you to track and check revisions, insert comments for others, compare documents, and go over each edit with a fine-toothed comb. Well, maybe not a comb, really more like a digital brush, but you get the general idea. You can easily collaborate with others, and this chapter shows you how to do it.

Tracking and Reviewing Documents

If you share your documents with other users in an editorial-like environment—such as swapping files for feedback in which everyone adds their commentary to a document—you can turn on Word's Track Changes feature and keep track of who makes what changes to the text. For example, if your department is working on a project that involves input from everyone on the team, you can pass the document around and collect everyone's changes, then review the changes, accepting or discarding each one as needed. The Track Changes tool enables you to track comments, insertions, deletions, formatting changes, and more. Figure 14.1 shows an example of a document being edited by several users. The Review tab has a group of tools for noting everyone's edits under the group name Tracking. If you have a document ready for sharing, you can turn on tracking and send it forth. When you get the document back with everyone's input, you can review it change by change using the tools found in the Changes group (also located on the Review tab, right next to the Tracking group).

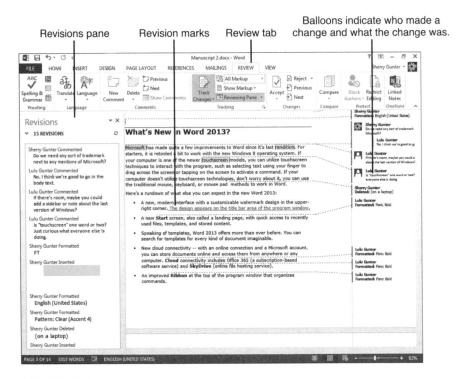

FIGURE 14.1

Here's an example of a document with changes being tracked.

You can also control how the changes appear in the document as you add your input. You can choose to view changes in full as you make them, or hide them so you can concentrate on the text and not all the editing marks. Hiding the edits doesn't mean they're not still there and being saved with the document, because they are. The only way to remove the tracked changes is to accept or reject them.

Turning on Tracking

The Track Changes tool toggles on and off. You can also lock it so it's sure to stay on for the next person who uses the file.

 TIP To display the track changes indicator on the status bar, right-click the bar and select Track Changes from the menu. This quickly lets you know whether you're tracking changes or not.

To turn on Word's tracking feature, click the Track Changes drop-down arrow on the Review tab (see Figure 14.2) and select Track Changes from the menu.

FIGURE 14.2

The Track Changes button.

The button now appears activated on the tab, shown in Figure 14.3.

FIGURE 14.3

The Track Changes button now appears active.

If you want to make sure the tracking feature stays on at all times, or at least until it's review time, you can assign a password. This way, no one can accidentally (or on purpose) turn the feature off, thus ensuring all the edits stay put. To lock tracking, follow these steps:

1. On the Review tab, click the Track Changes drop-down arrow.

2. Select Lock Tracking.

3. The Lock Tracking dialog box opens, as shown in Figure 14.4. Type a password.

FIGURE 14.4

The Lock Tracking dialog box.

4. Retype the password to confirm.

5. Click OK.

To unlock it, repeat steps 1 and 2 again, this time opening the Unlock Tracking dialog box. Type the password and click OK.

 TIP You can open the Advanced Track Changes Options dialog box to control markup for different authors. Click the dialog box launcher located in the lower-right corner of the Tracking group to display the Track Changes Options dialog box, and then click the Advanced button to open the Advanced Track Changes Options dialog box.

Changing the Markup Display

As you start working with a document with the tracking feature turned on, Word keeps track of the edits you make, from big ones to small ones. You can decide how much of these changes you want to see while they happen. For example, you might want to see every deleted line or every formatting change that occurs. Or maybe you're the exact opposite and don't want to see crossed-out lines while you concentrate on your work. You might prefer to see everything organized in the Revisions pane, or all the comments off to the side. It's your view, so it's your choice.

Use the Display for Review drop-down menu, shown in Figure 14.5, to choose a display mode. Here are your choices:

- **Simple Markup**—Changes are noted only with a vertical line in the left margin next to the line of text containing the change. Comments are indicated by an icon in the right margin.

- **All Markup**—This view shows all the changes to a document, including red lines through deleted text, underlining for inserted text, and color coding for each different user's input comments.

- **No Markup**—This view shows the changes incorporated into the document without any markup details or notes.

- **Original**—This view displays the document in its original state, before any edits.

FIGURE 14.5

The Display for Review menu.

In addition to your display of revisions, you can also customize which types of revisions appear onscreen. Click the Show Markup drop-down arrow, shown in Figure 14.6, to turn the display of individual types of revisions on or off, such as comments people add, insertions and deletions, and formatting changes. Many of these markup items are displayed already, but you can turn each one on or off as needed—a check mark next to the name means the item is displayed; no check mark means the item is not displayed.

FIGURE 14.6

Control which revisions appear using the Show Markup menu.

Depending on the settings you have turned on, you can view revisions in balloons or inline. The *inline* choice shows edits in the document only, whereas the *balloon* choice lets you see not only the revisions in the text, but also the details about who made the changes. It does this by displaying the user's name or initials along with the revision off to the right side of the document, as shown in Figure 14.7. In previous versions of Word, the revision details appeared in actual comic book balloon-like boxes. Those balloon boxes are gone now, but the concept remains.

To change the view of balloons, click the Balloons command in the Show Markup menu and make your selection.

Balloons

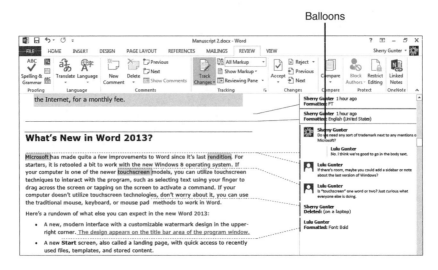

FIGURE 14.7

Balloons display details about the revision and the initials of who made the revision.

There's one more way you can review revisions—use the Revisions pane, shown in Figure 14.8. This pane lists all the revisions in order. To display the pane, click the Reviewing Pane button on the Review tab. You can choose to view the pane vertically (as shown in Figure 14.8) or horizontally. To jump to an edit in the actual document, click the revision in the list.

To turn the pane off, click the pane's Close button or click the Reviewing Pane button on the Review tab again.

 TIP You can open the Track Changes Options dialog box to control which revisions appear in the document, too. Click the dialog box launcher located in the lower-right corner of the Tracking group to display the dialog box.

Revisions pane

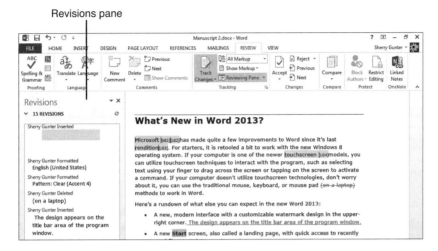

FIGURE 14.8

You can use the Revisions pane to view each revision in a document.

Working with Comments

You can use Word's commenting feature to add comments to documents as part of your reviewing tasks. For example, you might want to add a note that everyone else sees, querying a sentence or word choice. Other reviewers can respond to the comment. If you are viewing revision marks using balloons (see the previous section to learn more), comments appear off to the right. To respond to someone's comment, look for a comment icon, as shown in Figure 14.9. Click the icon to add your own reply, as shown in Figure 14.10.

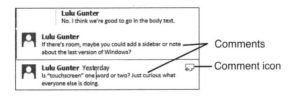

FIGURE 14.9

Find Word's commenting tools among the Comments group on the Review tab.

FIGURE 14.10

Type a response to a comment and it appears below the original comment.

To add a new comment, click in the document where the comment applies or select the text. Click the New Comment button on the Review tab (see Figure 14.11). Word adds a new comment balloon off to the right if you're using the markup balloons, similar to what you see in Figure 14.11. If you're using the Revisions pane, it appears there, as demonstrated in Figure 14.12. In either case, you can start typing your comment text immediately. Click outside the comment area when you're finished.

New Comment button

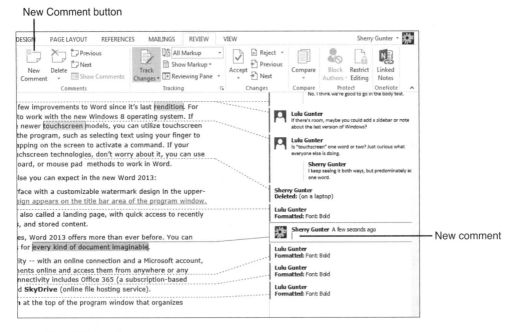

FIGURE 14.11

You can use the New Comment button to insert a new comment.

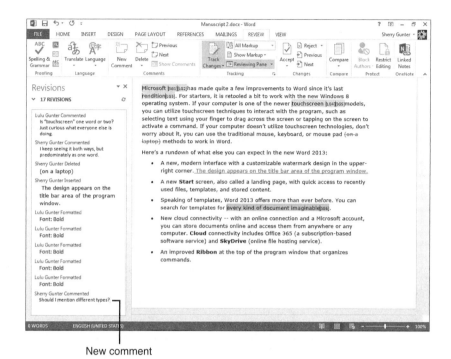

New comment

FIGURE 14.12

You can also use the Revisions pane to insert comments.

To remove a comment, click the comment tag in the text (see Figure 14.13), click the Delete button on the Review tab, and click Delete. The drop-down menu also has commands for removing all the comments.

Delete button for comments

Comment tag

FIGURE 14.13

One way to remove a comment is to click its tag and click the Delete button.

Another option is the shortcut menu, which offers a super-fast way to work with comments. Right-click a comment to view the pop-up menu, which now includes a set of commands for comments. (Because you right-clicked a comment, the comment commands appear; right-click menus are always task-related.) You can edit a comment, reply to it, delete it, or mark it as done. When you mark a comment as completed, it appears grayed out if you're viewing comment balloons.

 TIP You can use the Previous and Next buttons in the Comments group on the Review tab to navigate your document comment by comment for review.

Reviewing Changes

When you get your document back, you can start reviewing it and deciding which changes to keep and which to dismiss. You find tools for doing all this located in the Changes group on the Review tab, as shown in Figure 14.14. Starting at the top of the document, you can progress from one revision to another. You might prefer to turn on the revision balloons to see who made what change, or display the Revisions pane (see the previous section to learn more about each).

FIGURE 14.14

Look for the reviewing tools right next to the tracking tools on the Review tab.

Here's how to utilize the reviewing tools:

- Click the Next button to move to the next revision in the document.
- Click the Previous button to move back to the previous revision.
- Click the Accept button's drop-down arrow to display a menu of choices for accepting the change.
- To accept the change and move to the next revision directly, click the Accept button (not the drop-down arrow).
- Click the Reject button's drop-down arrow to display a menu of choices for rejecting the change.
- To reject the change and move to the next revision directly, click the Reject button (not the drop-down arrow).

- To accept all the changes in the document, click the Accept button's drop-down arrow and click Accept All Changes.

- To reject all the changes in the document, click the Reject button's drop-down arrow and click Reject All Changes.

- To accept or reject all and turn off the tracking feature, opt for the last choice listed in the Accept or Reject drop-down menus.

To turn off the Track Changes tool when finished with the document review, click the Track Changes button on the Review tab. Be sure to save your cleaned-up version of the document, or you have to repeat the process of reviewing and accepting/deleting everyone's changes.

Comparing Documents

If a Word document wasn't reviewed with change tracking turned on, you still can compare the edited version with the original version automatically to see what changes were made. You compare an original document with an updated version by creating a third document that displays all the differences between the two documents. Changes are marked in the same way that tracked changes are marked with multiple authors, and you use the same reviewing principles to check each change in the comparison document.

To compare documents, open the original document in Word and follow these steps:

1. On the Review tab, click the Compare button (see Figure 14.15).

2. Click Compare.

FIGURE 14.15

Use the Compare button to launch Word's document-comparing feature.

3. In the Compare Documents dialog box, shown in Figure 14.16, click the Original document drop-down arrow and choose the original document file. (You can also navigate to the file using the Browse option.)

Select the original document here.

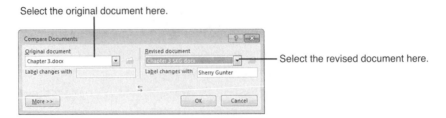

Select the revised document here.

FIGURE 14.16

Specify which two documents you want to compare.

4. Click the Revised document drop-down arrow and choose the revised version of the file (or click the Browse option to navigate to the file).

5. Click OK.

Word opens a new document comparing both versions, along with the original and revised documents and the Revisions pane (see Figure 14.17). Just like the tracking changes feature, Word shows revisions in the document as well as in the Revisions pane. You can use the tools on the Review tab to change how markup is displayed, and review the document, accepting and rejecting changes as needed. When you're finished, remember to save your revised document!

New document merging change

Revisions pane

Original document

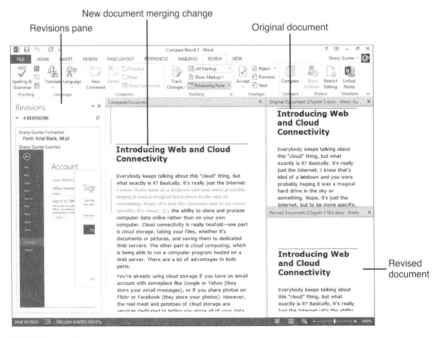

Revised document

FIGURE 14.17

The screen is filled with the two documents you're comparing, a third showing the differences, and the Revisions pane.

TIP You can click the More button in the Compare Documents dialog box and choose what elements you want to compare, such as comments and formatting.

Editing Portable Document Format (PDF) Files

New to Word 2013, you can now edit PDF files as documents. Although you could certainly view PDFs in Word in previous versions of the program, and save documents to the PDF file format, you could not edit a PDF file directly. Instead, you had to rely on a separate PDF editor to make changes to a PDF file. The PDF format, which stands for Portable Document Format, is an open document format that enables users with differing programs to read the file. PDF files are quite common these days, and now you can open and edit them within Word, after doing a little conversion first.

 NOTE See Chapter 2, "Working with Office Applications," for more information about saving Word documents as PDFs.

When you attempt to open a PDF file, a prompt box appears warning you you're about to convert the file. Click OK and it's off and running. Within seconds (usually), the file is converted and the document opens onscreen just like any other text file. You can now work with the document, making changes as needed. You can even save it back to its PDF file format. (Click the File tab, choose Save As, and choose the PDF file format when naming the file.)

You can also open a PDF file from the Explorer window and designate Word as the program to edit PDFs. Right-click the PDF file, click Open with, and click Word (desktop). The prompt box appears and you can convert the file.

Sharing Documents with Others

There are lots of ways you can share your documents with other users, especially for collaborating and reviewing. You can

- Save a document to a Universal Serial Bus flash drive (those portable stick things that plug into your laptop or computer's USB port) and share it that way.

- Send your document as a file attachment in an email message. (More on that option in the next chapter.)

- Save your document on your SkyDrive account and invite people to access the file. See Chapter 2 for more information about sharing files in Microsoft applications.

- Share files using a Microsoft SharePoint or Microsoft Office 365 account. SharePoint is Microsoft's web-based collaboration portal for businesses; it enables team members to view and share documents. These tools are beyond the scope of this book.

 NOTE Microsoft SharePoint and Microsoft Office 365 are beyond the scope of this book. See *SharePoint 2013 On Demand* by Steve Johnson and *Office 365 In Depth* by Paul Sanna for more information, both from Que Publishing.

THE ABSOLUTE MINIMUM

Here are the key points to remember from this chapter:

- The first step to collaborating on a document is to turn on Word's Track Changes tool, found on the Review tab.

- You can use the Compare tool to compare an original document with its revised version.

- You can edit PDF files in Word—after you perform a little conversion process, that is.

- You can share a document on your SkyDrive account by inviting others to see it. This technique requires that you first store your file on the cloud and then invite people using their email addresses.

EXCEL 2013 BASICS

Excel is a full-featured spreadsheet application that's part of Microsoft Office 2013. With Excel, you can perform calculations, create charts, and analyze numerical data. An Excel file is called a workbook and each workbook can contain one or more sheets.

After exploring the Excel interface and its unique terminology, this chapter shows you how to create workbooks from scratch or from templates. It also shows you how to add, delete, and move sheets within a workbook or between workbooks.

Even a well-planned sheet layout might be missing something, such as a date column. Or you might change your mind in the middle of the design, deciding that you want a table elsewhere on a sheet. Instead of starting over, you learn how to insert rows or columns and move your tables to a new location on your sheet.

Exploring the Excel Window

When you open Excel 2013 for the first time, you see the Start screen, shown in Figure 15.1. This screen includes a list of Excel starter templates. (See "Using Templates to Quickly Create New Workbooks" later in this chapter for more details about templates.) For now, click the Blank Workbook item in the upper-left corner to open a blank spreadsheet, as shown in Figure 15.2.

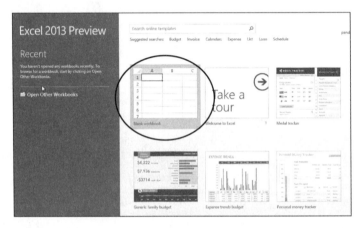

FIGURE 15.1

Select the Blank Workbook item (circled) to open a blank spreadsheet.

Quick Access Toolbar (QAT)

Name Box   Formula Bar   Ribbon   Column Header

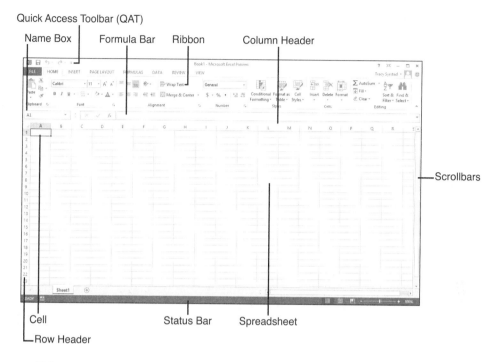

Scrollbars

Cell   Status Bar   Spreadsheet

Row Header

FIGURE 15.2

The Excel window is made up of many components that you use when working on a spreadsheet.

TIP To create a new workbook if you are already have another workbook open, click the File tab, select New, and then select Blank Workbook. Alternatively, you can press Ctrl+N on the keyboard. For more information about opening, closing, and saving files, see Chapter 2, "Working with Office Applications."

The big grid taking up most of the Excel window is the spreadsheet, also known as a worksheet or, simply, a sheet. Each little box is a cell. Multiple cells selected together are commonly known as a range.

Right above the grid are letters known as column headers. Down the left side of the grid are numbers, also known as row headers. The intersection of a single column and a single row is a cell. Each cell has an address made up of the column letter and the row number. Figure 15.3 shows cell C8 selected. Note the C in the column header is highlighted as is the 8 in the row header.

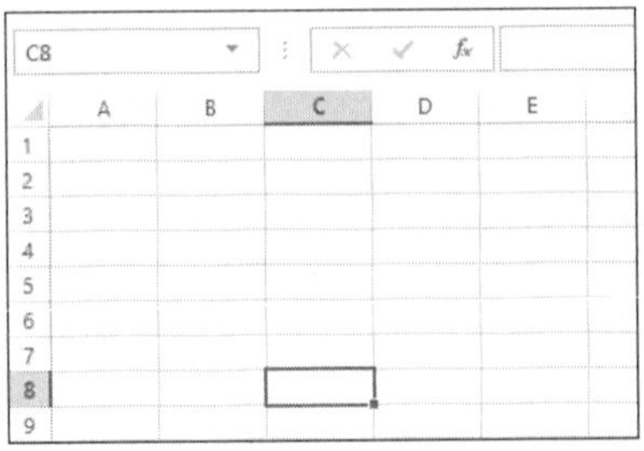

FIGURE 15.3

The intersection of a column and a row is a cell. The cell gets its name from the column and row headers, in this case C8.

Above the headers and to the left is the Name box. This box shows you what you have selected on the sheet. This can be a cell address, a named range, a table, a chart, or some other object on the sheet. When you first open Excel, the Name box likely shows A1. If you select another cell on the sheet, the address changes to show that cell's address, such as C8. Later in this chapter, you find out how you can use the Name box to quickly move to another area of the sheet.

To the right of the Name box is the formula bar, which is a slight misnomer. Although that is probably the most common use of this field, the formula bar actually reflects anything that's been typed into a cell, not just formulas.

At the top of the Excel window, you find the Ribbon and the Quick Access Toolbar, which is covered in Chapter 1, "Getting Started with Microsoft Office 2013."

Below and to the right of the grid are scrollbars, which you can use to move around the sheet. You can either click and drag a bar or use the arrows at either end of the scroll area.

The status bar is along the bottom of the Excel window. Not only does it show the status of Excel, such as Ready or Calculating, on the left side, but it also includes buttons for changing the page view or zoom. In the right corner of the status bar is the Zoom slider. You can use the slider or the – and + buttons to change the zoom of the active sheet.

To the left of the Zoom slider are three buttons for changing how you view the active sheet:

- **Normal**—This is the default view, showing just the sheet.

- **Page Break Preview**—Displays where columns and rows break to print onto other pages. Dashed lines signify automatic breaks that Excel places based on settings, such as margins. Solid lines are manually set breaks. See Chapter 22,

"Preparing Workbooks for Distribution and Printing," for more information on setting and moving page breaks.

- **Page Layout**—This view is similar to an editable Print Preview—you can see what your page looks like when it prints out, but you can still enter data and make other changes. Columns and rows move between pages as you adjust their widths or the margins of the page. You can also enter information directly into the header and footer of a page. See Chapter 22 for information on adding headers and footers.

Moving Around and Making Selections on a Sheet

You can move around on a sheet using the mouse or the keyboard, depending on which method is most comfortable for you. To select a cell using the mouse, click it. To select a cell using the keyboard, use the navigation arrows on the keyboard. You can also use the number keypad arrows if the NumLock feature is turned off.

Keyboard Shortcuts for Quicker Navigation

Using the navigation arrows on the keyboard can be a little slow, especially if you have a lot of cells between your currently selected cells and the one you want to select. Even using the mouse can take some time to navigate from the top of your data to the bottom. The following list details a few keyboard shortcuts to make navigation a little easier:

- Ctrl+Home jumps to cell A1, located at the upper-left corner of the sheet.

- Ctrl+End jumps to the last row and column in use.

- Ctrl+Left Arrow jumps to the first column with data to the left of the currently selected cell. If there is no data to the left then it selects a cell in the first column, A.

- Ctrl+Right Arrow jumps to the first column with data to the right of the currently selected cell. If there is no data to the right then it selects a cell in the last column, XFD.

- Ctrl+Down Arrow jumps to the first row with data below the currently selected cell. If there is no data below the selected cell then it selects a cell in the last row.

- Ctrl+Up Arrow jumps to the first row with data above the currently selected cell. If there is no data above the selected cell then it selects a cell in row 1.

Selecting a Range of Cells

You'll often find yourself needing to select more than a single cell. For example, if you have text on a sheet you want to apply a new font to, instead of selecting one cell at a time and applying the font, you can select all the cells and then apply the font, as shown in Figure 15.4.

FIGURE 15.4

The ability to select a range is an important skill to have when working on a sheet.

 TIP   When selecting a range, it doesn't matter if you start at the top or bottom or far left or far right of the range.

To select a range using the mouse, follow these steps:

1. Click in a cell in the corner of your selection.

2. Hold down the mouse button as you drag the mouse to cover the desired cells.

3. When you get to the last cell, let go of the mouse button. Excel selects a range similar to what is shown in Figure 15.4. As long as you don't click elsewhere on the sheet, the range remains selected.

To select a range using the keyboard, follow these steps:

1. Click in a cell in the corner of your selection.

2. Press F8 on the keyboard.

3. Use the arrow keys to navigate to the end of the desired range.

4. Press F8 on the keyboard to stop the selection from extending. As long as you don't select another cell on the sheet, the range remains selected.

 NOTE   Pressing F8 on the keyboard activates the Extend Selection option in Excel. If you look at the left side of the status bar, you see Extend Selection. As long as the option is on, selecting different cells extends the selection.

Using Templates to Quickly Create New Workbooks

Templates are a great way for keeping data in a uniform design. You could simply design your workbook and reuse it as needed, but if you accidentally save data before you have renamed the file, your blank workbook is no longer clean. When using a template, there's no risk of saving data in the template because you are working with a copy of the original workbook, not the workbook itself.

Using Microsoft's Online Templates

Microsoft offers a variety of templates—such as budgets, invoices, and calendars— which can help you start a project. You can search for templates to fit your needs either from the Start screen or by clicking the File tab and selecting New to open the New screen, which displays a selection of templates. Alternatively, you can enter your own keywords in the Search field at the top of the New screen. A search returns matches, which you can filter from a list on the right.

TIP When you place your cursor over a template preview, a pushpin appears in its lower-right corner, giving you the option to pin it so that it always appears in the list. If you found your template by searching for it, this is a way to make it easily accessible the next time you need it.

When you select a template, a preview window opens, as shown in Figure 15.5. The preview shows a larger example of the template, a brief explanation of its purpose, and how the template has been rated by other users. If you click Create, the template is downloaded (for first-time use) and opened.

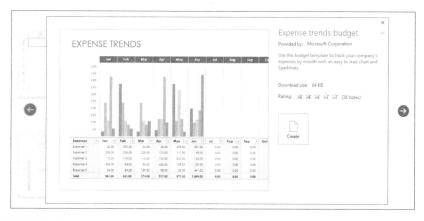

FIGURE 15.5

Use the left and right arrows in the template preview window to scroll through other available templates before opening one.

Saving a Template

 NOTE You do not have to save templates to the configured templates location if you plan to double-click or right-click to open a copy of the file.

Before you can use your own template or one provided to you and not downloaded from the Office Store, you have to configure where to store your templates. This is a folder where you place all the templates you want to access through the New screen. To set up the location, click the File tab, select Options, and select the Save tab on the Excel Options dialog box. Next, enter the path in the Default Personal Templates Location field. After you have a location configured, the Personal link appears to the right of the Featured link on the New screen. Featured shows Microsoft's online templates; Personal shows templates in the locally configured location.

 CAUTION The location must exist before you enter it in the field. To make sure you get the path correct, navigate to it in File Explorer, copy the full path from the address bar, and then paste it in the Excel field.

Opening a Locally Saved Template to Enter Data

There are multiple ways to open a template to enter data, and you can use the method that is most convenient to you. To open a template to create a new workbook, use one of the following methods:

- Double-click the file from its saved location.

- From its saved location, right-click the file and select New.

- Click the File tab, select New, and select the template from the list of online templates.

- Click the File tab, select New, click the Personal link, and select from the list of templates saved locally. See the previous "Saving a Template" section for details on how to configure the location. The Personal option doesn't appear unless you set up the location in the Excel Options dialog box.

 NOTE If you need to make changes to the design of a template, the previous methods for opening a copy of the template don't work. Instead, to open the original template to make changes, right-click the file and select Open.

Working with Sheets and Tabs

A sheet, also known as a spreadsheet or worksheet, is where you enter your data in Excel. A workbook can have multiple sheets—the number is limited only by the power of the computer opening the workbook.

Each sheet has a tab, visible above the status bar, as shown in Figure 15.6. The sheet with data that you're looking at is considered the active sheet. To select another sheet, click its tab.

FIGURE 15.6

The font of the sheet tab you are working on, Sheet1, is bold compared with the other sheet tabs.

Inserting a New Sheet

The quickest way to add a new sheet to a workbook is to click the circle with a plus sign that appears to the right of the rightmost sheet tab. This inserts a new sheet to the right of the active sheet.

To insert a new sheet to the left of a specific sheet, select the sheet (refer to the "Activating Another Sheet" section), click the Insert button on the Home tab, and select Insert Sheet from the menu.

A third method is to right-click the tab to the right of where you want the new sheet to appear. From the menu, select Insert, select Worksheet, and click OK. The new sheet appears to the left of the tab you right-clicked, as shown in Figure 15.7.

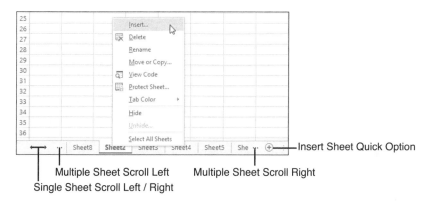

FIGURE 15.7

You can control where a new sheet is inserted by right-clicking a tab and selecting Insert.

Activating Another Sheet

To activate another sheet, click its tab along the bottom of the Excel window. You can also navigate sheet to sheet using the keyboard. Ctrl+Page Up selects the sheet to the left; Ctrl+Page Down selects the sheet to the right.

If you have more sheets than can fit in the tab area, three small dots appear on the left and right side of the area, to show there are more sheets available to view, as shown in Figure 15.7. Clicking the three dots quickly scrolls through multiple sheets. If instead, you need to scroll one sheet at a time, click the left and right arrows located to the left of the sheet tab area.

If you right-click the left and right arrows instead, a list of all sheets in the workbook appears. You can then select a sheet, click OK, and go straight to that sheet.

Selecting Multiple Sheets

You can select multiple sheets at one time. This doesn't activate them all at once. It groups them together so that an action on one, such as changing the tab color, affects all of them.

To select multiple sheets, select the first one and then, while holding down the Ctrl key, select the tabs for the others. As you select each sheet tab, the sheet name becomes bold.

To ungroup the sheets, you can either select any sheet other than the active sheet or right-click any tab and select Ungroup Sheets.

Deleting a Sheet

If you no longer need a sheet, you can delete it, getting it out of your way and reducing the size of your workbook. To delete a sheet, right-click the sheet's tab and select Delete. You can also delete a sheet by making it your active sheet, clicking the Delete button on the Home tab, and selecting Delete Sheet from the drop-down. If there is data on the sheet, a prompt appears to verify that you want to delete the sheet.

 CAUTION Deleting a sheet cannot be undone.

Moving or Copying Sheets Within the Same Workbook

You might want to reorganize sheets within the current workbook to group similar sheets together. Or you might need to copy a sheet to run tests on the data but don't want to change the original. To move a sheet within a workbook, click the Format button on the Home tab and select Move or Copy Sheet from the menu. You can also access the Move or Copy dialog box by right-clicking a sheet tab and selecting Move or Copy.

In the Move or Copy dialog box, shown in Figure 15.8, make sure the To Book field is the current workbook. If you're making a copy of the sheet, select the Create a Copy box. Then, in the Before Sheet dialog box, select the sheet you want the active sheet to be placed in front of (to the left of). You can also reorganize the sheets in a workbook by clicking, holding the mouse button down, and dragging the sheet's tab to a new location. If you want to copy the sheet then hold down the Ctrl key as you move the sheet tab.

FIGURE 15.8

The Move or Copy dialog box enables you to copy or move sheets within a workbook or between two different workbooks.

Moving or Copying Sheets Between Workbooks

Many database programs export data to an Excel workbook or compatible file, but they might not let you choose an existing workbook to export to. If you have a report workbook designed in which you need the new data, you can copy or move the exported data from its workbook to your report workbook. To move a sheet to a new workbook, click the Format button on the Home tab and select Move or Copy Sheet from the menu. Alternatively, right-click a sheet tab and select Move or Copy.

To move or copy a sheet to another workbook, the second workbook must already be open. Make sure the sheet you want to move or copy is the active sheet. Then, using the Move or Copy dialog box, shown in Figure 15.8, select from the To Book field the workbook to move or copy the sheet to. If you're making a copy of the sheet, select the Create a Copy box. In the Before Sheet dialog box, select the sheet you want the active sheet to be placed in front of (to the left of).

 CAUTION When you move or copy a sheet from one workbook to another, any formulas on that sheet linked to another sheet in the original workbook remain linked to the sheet in the original workbook unless you also include the linked sheet(s) in the move or copy procedure.

Renaming a Sheet

Excel's sheet names, Sheet1, Sheet2, and so on, aren't very descriptive. Also, when you copy a sheet in a workbook that already has a sheet by that name, Excel copies the sheet name, appending a number to the end of it. For example, if you copy Sheet1 within the same workbook, Excel renames it to Sheet1 (2). To give a sheet a more meaningful name, click the Format button on the Home tab and select Rename Sheet from the menu. Excel selects the current sheet name in the sheet's tab, and you can type in the new name. You can also rename a sheet by right-clicking the sheet's tab and selecting Rename.

Coloring a Sheet Tab

If you have several sheets you want to visually group together, you can color their tabs. For example, if you have some sheets that are for data input and others for reports, you could color your data input sheet tabs a light yellow and the report tabs a light blue.

To change the color of a tab, click the Format button on the Home tab, and select Tab Color from the menu. A selection of colors appears from which you can select the desired color. The tab color of the active sheet appears as a gradient but fills the entire tab for the other sheets. You can also change the tab color by right-clicking the tab and selecting Tab Color.

Working with Rows and Columns

It's hard to create the perfect data table the first time around. There's always something you've forgotten, such as the date column. Or maybe you did remember the date column but put it in the wrong place. Thankfully, you don't have to start over. You can insert, delete, and move entire columns and rows with a few clicks of the mouse.

Selecting an Entire Row or Column

When you select an entire row or column on a sheet, you are selecting beyond what you can see on the sheet. You really do select the entire row or column and whatever you do to the part you can see affects the entire selection.

To select an entire row, place your cursor on the header until it turns into a single black arrow and then click the header for the row. For example, to select row 5, as shown in Figure 15.9, click the header 5. To select an entire column, click the header for the column.

3	2008	2000	123	42	21	0	TRUE	1
4	2008	2000	233	42	26	9	TRUE	1
5	2008	2000	258	30	11	0	TRUE	1
6	2008	2000	264	23	4	0	TRUE	1
7	2008	2000	310	21	12	0	TRUE	1

FIGURE 15.9

Click the headers to quickly select an entire row or column.

If you need to select multiple, contiguous rows (or columns), click the first header and then, as you hold down the mouse button, drag the mouse down (or up) until you have selected all the rows you need. Let go of the mouse button and perform your desired action on the selection.

If you need to select multiple, noncontiguous rows (or columns), click the first header and then, as you hold down the Ctrl key, carefully click the headers of the other rows. When you're done selecting, release the Ctrl key and perform your desired action on the selection.

Inserting an Entire Row and Column

You might want to insert a row if your data table is missing titles over the data. Or, you might need to insert a column if the data table is missing a column of information and you don't want to enter the information at the end (right side) of the table. When you insert a row, Excel shifts the existing data down. When you insert a column, Excel shifts the existing data to the right.

TIP If you select multiple rows or columns, Excel inserts that many rows or columns. For example, if you need to insert five new rows in your data, instead of highlighting one row, right-clicking and selecting Insert and then repeating this four more times, select five rows, right-click, and select Insert and—voila!—you have five blank rows. Note that the selection doesn't have to be contiguous. For example, if you've selected several noncontiguous rows, Excel inserts one row beneath each selected row.

To insert a new row or column within an existing data set, select a cell in the row or column where you want the inserted row or column to go. For example, if you need to insert a new row 10, select a cell in row 10. On the Home tab, click the Insert button and select Insert Sheet Rows or Insert Sheet Columns. For a shortcut, you can right-click the row or column header and select Insert.

Deleting an Entire Row and Column

When you import data from another source, you might need to clean it up by deleting rows or columns of data you don't need. When deleting a row, Excel shifts the data below the row up. For example, after deleting row 5, what was in row 6 now appears in row 5. If deleting a column, Excel shifts the data that was to the right of the deleted column to the left.

To delete a row or column, select a cell in the row or column to delete, click the Delete button on the Home tab, and select Delete Sheet Rows or Delete Sheet Columns. For a shortcut, you can right-click the row or column header and select Delete.

 TIP Your selection of rows or columns does not have to be contiguous. Excel deletes what you have selected.

Moving Entire Rows and Columns

You have to be careful when moving rows and columns. Depending on the method you use, you could end up overwriting other cells. To move rows or columns when you aren't worried about overwriting existing data, follow these steps:

1. Select the row or column you want to move.

2. The selection is surrounded by a thick line. Place your cursor over the line until it turns into a four-headed arrow, as shown in Figure 15.10.

3. Click on the line and hold the mouse button down.

4. Drag the selection to a new location and let go.

5. If there is any data in the new location, Excel asks if you want to overwrite it. If you say No, the move is canceled. The original row or column is still there, but it's empty.

FIGURE 15.10

When the cursor changes to a four-headed arrow, you can click and drag the column to a new location.

If you need to keep data in the new location intact, you could insert a row or column in the new location, copy the data to be moved, paste it in the inserted rows or columns and then go back to the original location, select it again, and delete it. Or, you could get it done more quickly by selecting and cutting the row or column, right-clicking the new location, and selecting Insert Cut Cells. Excel moves the data in the new location, inserting the cut data and also deleting the data in the old location.

To perform these actions using the Ribbon, after selecting and cutting the row or column, select a cell in the new location, click the Insert button on the Home tab, and select Insert Cut Cells from the menu.

 TIP With one small addition, you can use both of the previous methods to copy a row to a new location. If you're using the drag method, hold down the Ctrl key as you drag the row to the other location. If you're using the menu method, copy the row instead of cutting it and select Insert Copied Cells from the menu.

Working with Cells

Just like you can insert, move, and delete entire rows and columns, you can also insert, move, and delete cells. This section shows you how to quickly jump to a cell you can't currently see on your sheet, select noncontiguous ranges, and insert, move, and delete cells.

Selecting a Cell Using the Name Box

Earlier in this chapter, you learned how each cell has an address made up of the column and row it resides in. You also explored navigation basics—either click a cell or use the keyboard to select a cell.

You can also jump to a cell by typing the cell address in the Name box, located above the sheet in the left corner. This is a great way of traveling quickly to a specific location on a large sheet.

To use this method, you must enter the cell address properly—that is, the column and then the row. For example, if you want to jump to cell AA33, you must type in AA33; you can't type in 33AA. After typing the address, press Enter and the currently selected cell moves to cell AA33.

Selecting Noncontiguous Cells and Ranges

In the section "Selecting a Range of Cells" earlier in this chapter, you read about the basics of cell and range selection. In this section, you find out how to select multiple, noncontiguous ranges, as shown in Figure 15.11.

FIGURE 15.11

You can select noncontiguous cells by holding down the Ctrl key as you select each range.

You don't always want to select cells right next to each other. For example, you might want to select only the cells with negative values and make them bold. You could select each cell one at a time and apply the bold format. Or, you could hold down the Ctrl key and select each cell. After you have selected all the cells, you let go of the Ctrl key and select your desired format (or other action).

 CAUTION When you select a cell using the Ctrl key method, you cannot deselect it. If you make a mistake in your cell selection, you have to start over.

Inserting Cells and Ranges

When you insert or delete rows and columns, Excel shifts all the data on the sheet. If you don't want all the data shifted, select a specific range and then either right-click over the selection and choose Insert or click the Insert button on the Home tab and select Insert Cells from the menu. A prompt appears, asking you in which direction you want to shift your existing data, as shown in Figure 15.12. If you want to insert rows, choose Shift Cells Down. If you want to insert columns, choose Shift Cells Right.

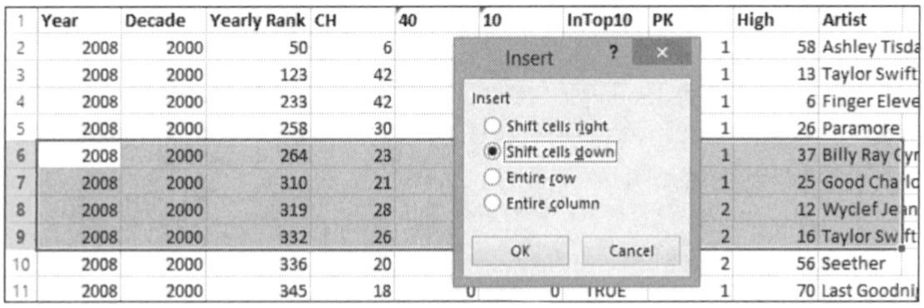

	Year	Decade	Yearly Rank	CH	40	10	InTop10	PK	High	Artist
1	Year	Decade	Yearly Rank	CH	40	10	InTop10	PK	High	Artist
2	2008	2000	50	6				1	58	Ashley Tisda
3	2008	2000	123	42				1	13	Taylor Swift
4	2008	2000	233	42				1	6	Finger Eleve
5	2008	2000	258	30				1	26	Paramore
6	2008	2000	264	23				1	37	Billy Ray Cyr
7	2008	2000	310	21				1	25	Good Cha
8	2008	2000	319	28				2	12	Wyclef Jean
9	2008	2000	332	26				2	16	Taylor Swift
10	2008	2000	336	20				2	56	Seether
11	2008	2000	345	18	0	0	TRUE	1	70	Last Goodni

Insert dialog box:

Insert
- Shift cells right
- ● Shift cells down
- Entire row
- Entire column

OK   Cancel

FIGURE 15.12

You can control how much of a row or column is inserted by selecting a specific range beforehand.

Deleting Cells and Ranges

When you delete a range, you remove the cells from the sheet, shifting other data over to fill in the empty space. If you aren't careful, you can ruin the careful layout of your sheet—for example, moving data from the credit column to the debit column. If what you really want is to delete the data in the cells, leaving the cells intact, Excel calls this *clearing the contents*. For specifics on clearing contents, see the section "Clearing the Contents of a Cell," in Chapter 16, "Entering Sheet Data."

To delete a range from a sheet, select the range and on the Home tab, click the Delete button and select Delete Cells from the menu. From the Delete dialog box that opens, choose whether you want to Shift Cells Left or Shift Cells Up. You can also open the dialog box by right-clicking the selected range and choosing Delete from the menu.

Moving Cells and Ranges

You have to be careful when moving a range—you could end up overwriting other cells. If you need to move rows or columns and aren't worried about overwriting existing data, use the following method. If you don't want to overwrite existing data in the new location, you need to use the Insert Cells method explained in the section "Inserting Cells and Ranges." To move rows or columns when you aren't worried about overwriting existing data, follow these steps:

1. Select the range you want to move.

2. The selection is surrounded by a thick line. Place your cursor over the line until it turns into a four-headed arrow, as shown in Figure 15.13.

3. Select the line and hold the mouse button down.

4. Drag the selection to a new location and let go.

5. If there is any data in the new location, Excel asks if you want to overwrite it. If you select No, Excel cancels the move. Select Yes to complete the move and clear the contents of the original range.

FIGURE 15.13

Be careful when dragging your selection to a new area as it overwrites anything there.

THE ABSOLUTE MINIMUM

Here are the key points to remember from this chapter:

- When you open Excel 2013 for the first time, the Start screen greets you.

- You can navigate Excel sheets using the mouse or the keyboard, depending on which method is most comfortable for you. Keyboard shortcuts are also available to speed up navigating a large sheet.

- Starting from scratch isn't the only option for creating a workbook—you can download an online template from Microsoft's vast collection or use your own template.

- A sheet, also known as a spreadsheet or worksheet, is where you enter all your data in Excel. You can insert, delete, move, copy, rename, or color sheets.

- Excel sheets include multiple rows and columns that you can insert, move, copy, and delete.

- Just like you can insert, move, and delete entire rows and columns, you can also insert, move, and delete cells.

16

ENTERING SHEET DATA

Data entry is one of the most important functions in Excel—and one of the most tedious, especially when the data is repetitive. This chapter shows you tricks for copying down data, fixing entered data, and helping your users enter data correctly by providing a predefined list of entries.

Understanding Excel Data Types

It's important to differentiate types of data because Excel treats each differently. You tell Excel what kind of data is in a cell by how you type it into the cell or by how you format the cell. Data in Excel can fall into one of four categories:

- **Numbers**—Numeric data that can be used for calculation purposes.

- **Text**—Alphabetic *or* numeric data that is not used for calculation purposes. Examples of numeric text are phone numbers or Social Security numbers.

- **Dates and Times**—Although dates and times may be considered alphanumeric, there are occasions where you might want to perform calculations on the values, so it is important to identify the data correctly to Excel.

- **Formulas and Functions**—A powerful part of Excel, it's important that Excel knows you're entering a formula or it will treat what you enter like text. This topic is covered in detail in Chapter 18, "Using Formulas."

You can't combine types of data in a cell. You can type "5 oranges"—but Excel sees that as text. It won't separate the "5" as a number and the "oranges" as text. If you want to deal with the 5 as a number then you need to enter it into its own cell.

Entering Data

Excel offers several ways to enter data. The easiest method is to simply type data into a cell. You can also use copy, cut, paste, and paste special to enter data or use a series to quickly fill a range.

Entering Different Types of Data into a Cell

How you initially type data into a cell affects how Excel interprets it. You can save yourself some time if you let Excel format your data, but it will only do so properly if it can understand what you want. The following sections explain how you help Excel understand what you want.

Typing Numbers into a Cell

Numbers are the simplest thing to type into a cell. You select a cell, type in a number, press Enter or Tab, and you're done.

TIP Although Enter and Tab are commonly used to exit out of a cell, you can also use the navigation keys on the keyboard.

Typing Text into a Cell

If you simply select a cell and start typing without any forethought, you might get unexpected results. For example, select a cell and type the ZIP Code for Chester, MA, which is 01011, and press Enter or Tab. The beginning 0 disappears and all you see is 1011, as shown in Figure 16.1.

FIGURE 16.1

Excel tries its best to decipher the data you enter, but sometimes you have to help it out.

The reason this happens is because Excel assumes you are typing in a number, and numbers do not start with zeros. Although ZIP Codes are numeric, they aren't numbers—that is, you don't do any math with them. You need to plan ahead—recognize that you are entering numeric data that should be treated like text and let Excel know this. To let Excel know that you are entering a number that should be treated like text, type an apostrophe before you type the number (such as '01011).

Typing Dates and Times into a Cell

Dates and times are another category in which it's important for Excel to know what you are typing in. But in this case, the important thing to remember is to *not* put an apostrophe or other character before your date or time. Excel is very smart about date and time entry, and if you simply type it in, it does a very good job of deciphering your data.

Excel uses the system-configured date format. For example, in the United States, when entering numeric dates, the month comes first: May 14, 2013 is written as 5/14/13.

When entering times, you must enter it using a 24-hour clock, also known as military time, or include the a.m. or p.m.

 NOTE If you need to enter a symbol that isn't available on the keyboard, click the Symbol button or Equation button on the Insert tab to find more options.

Using Copy, Cut, Paste, Paste Special to Enter Data

You can copy or cut data from different sources, such as other workbooks, Word documents, or web pages, and paste the information onto a sheet. Depending on how the data appeared in the original source, you might have to modify it after you paste it in Excel.

One of the ways you can clean up data copied or cut from another source is to use the Paste Special command instead of just Paste. To access this special command, click the arrow on the Paste button on the Home tab or right-click on a cell. Various Paste Special options display. If you place your cursor over one of the icons, a tip appears, as shown in Figure 16.2. You can access more options by clicking Paste Special at the bottom of the drop-down.

FIGURE 16.2

The Paste Special drop-down provides quick access to the more commonly used options.

Using Paste Special with Ranges

Figure 16.2 shows the Paste Special options available if you're pasting a range copied or cut from within Excel. The Paste area of the dialog box has different paste options you can choose from. For example, if you select Values then you only paste the value of what you copied. The formatting and formulas will not be pasted. If you do want the original formatting and also the values then select Values and Number Formats. If you want a combination of values and comments then you need to use Paste Special twice, selecting Values once and then Comments the second time.

The Operation area enables you to perform simple math on the selected range. For example, if you have a list of prices that need to go up by 1.5%, type .015 in a cell and copy the cell. Select your range of prices and bring up the Paste Special dialog box. From the dialog box, select Values (so you don't lose any formatting you have on your prices) from the Paste area and Multiply from the Operation area. Click OK. The resulting prices will have increased by 1.5%.

Using Paste Special with Text

If you copy or cut data within a cell (versus the entire cell) or from a non-Excel source, such as a Word document or web page, the Paste Special options are limited. Depending on the source, text, or graphic, you might get the options shown in Figure 16.3.

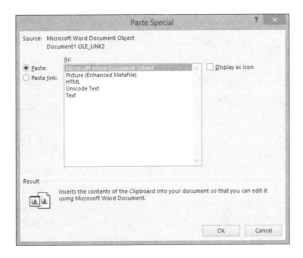

FIGURE 16.3

When doing a Paste Special with text, there are fewer options available.

NOTE The options available depend on the original source. For example, if you copied text from within a cell (versus the entire cell) then you only see pasting options for Unicode Text and Text. You don't have the option of pasting the text as a Word document object because it didn't originate from Word.

As you select an option in the As list box, an explanation appears in the Result area at the bottom of the dialog box. If you select the Paste Link option to the left of the list, you're also able to link the pasted data to its original source.

Using Paste Special with Images and Charts

When pasting images and charts, the dialog box is similar to that shown in Figure 16.3, but the As list box options differ, listing various image types. The different types can affect image resolution and workbook size.

Using Paste to Merge a Noncontiguous Selection in a Row or Column

If you try to copy/paste a noncontiguous selection from different rows and columns, an error message appears. But if the selection is in the same row or column, Excel enables you to copy and paste the data. When the data is pasted, though, it is no longer separated by other cells, as shown in Figure 16.4. You can use this method to create a table of specific values copied from another table.

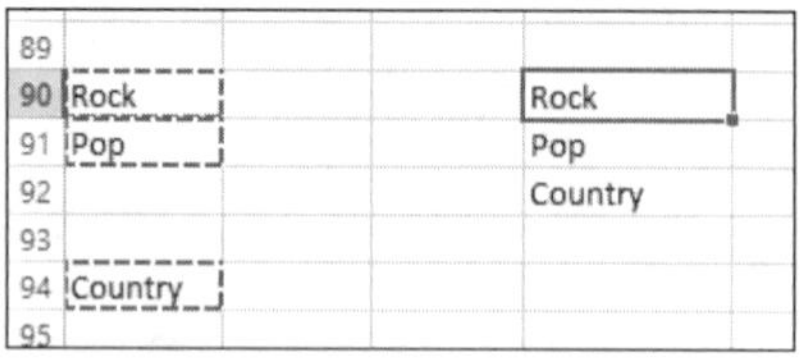

FIGURE 16.4

Data from rows 90, 91, and 94 was copied from the table on the left to create the list on the right using the method explained in this section.

Using Text to Columns to Separate Data in a Single Column

You can use the Text to Columns button on the Data tab to separate data in a single column into multiple columns—for example, if you have full names in one column and need a column with first names and a column with last names. When you select the command, a wizard dialog box opens to help you through the process. In step 1 of the wizard, select whether the text is Delimited or Fixed Width (see the next sections for definitions of Delimited and Fixed Width). In step 2, you provide more details on how you want the text separated. In step 3, you tell Excel the basic formatting to apply to each column.

If you have data in the columns to the right of the column you are separating, Excel overwrites the data. Be sure to insert enough blank columns to not overwrite your existing data before beginning Text to Columns. See the section "Inserting an Entire Row and Column" in Chapter 15, "Excel 2013 Basics," for instructions on how to insert columns.

Working with Delimited Text

Delimited text is text that has some character, such as a comma, tab, or space, separating each group of words that you want placed into its own column. To separate delimited text into multiple columns, follow these steps:

1. Highlight the range of text to be separated.

2. On the Data tab, click the Text to Columns button. The Convert Text to Columns Wizard opens.

3. Select Delimited from step 1 of the wizard, as shown in Figure 16.5, and click Next.

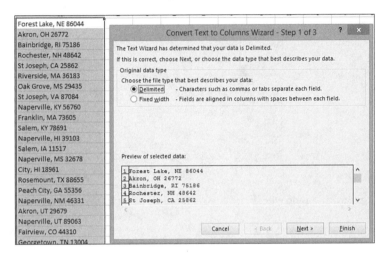

FIGURE 16.5

Select the Delimited option to separate text joined by delimiters, such as commas, spaces, or tabs.

4. Select one or more delimiters used by the grouped text, as in Figure 16.6, and click Next.

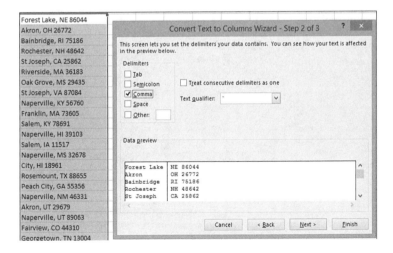

FIGURE 16.6

Select the Delimited option to use the comma as a delimiter between the city, the state, and ZIP Code.

5. For each column of data, select the data format. For example, if you have a column of ZIP Codes you need to set the format as Text so any leading zeros are not lost. But be warned—setting a column to Text prevents Excel from properly identifying formulas entered into that column.

6. Click Finish. The text is separated, as shown in Figure 16.7.

Forest Lake	NE 86044
Akron	OH 26772
Bainbridge	RI 75186
Rochester	NH 48642
St Joseph	CA 25862
Riverside	MA 36183
Oak Grove	MS 29435

FIGURE 16.7

Using Text to Columns with a comma delimiter separated the city from the state and ZIP Code.

Working with Fixed-Width Text

Fixed-width text describes text where each group is a set number of characters. You can draw a line down all the records to separate all the groups, as shown in Figure 16.8. If your text doesn't look like it's fixed width, try changing the font to a fixed-width font, such as Courier. It's possible that it's fixed-width text in disguise.

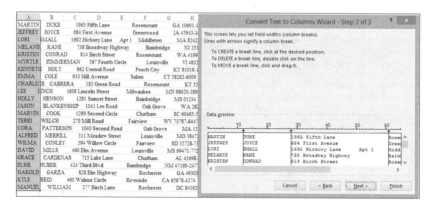

FIGURE 16.8

Use the Fixed Width option when each group in the data has a fixed number of characters.

To separate fixed-width text into multiple columns, follow these steps:

1. Highlight the range of cells that includes text to be separated.

2. On the Data tab, click the Text to Columns button.

3. Select Fixed Width from step 1 of the wizard and click Next.

4. Excel guesses at where the column breaks should go (refer to Figure 16.8). You can move a break by clicking and dragging it to where you want it, insert a new break by clicking where it should be, or remove a break by double-clicking it. Click Next.

5. For each column of data, select the data format. For example, if you have a column of ZIP Codes, you need to set the format as Text so any leading zeros are not lost, as shown in Figure 16.9.

6. Click Finish.

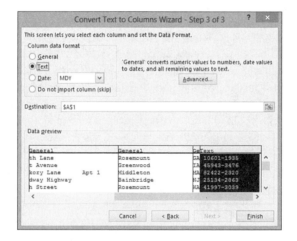

FIGURE 16.9

In step 3 of the wizard, set the format of each column.

Using Series to Quickly Fill a Range

The fill handle, shown in Figure 16.10, can speed up data entry by completing a series for you. Excel comes with several preconfigured series, such as months, days of the week, and quarters. You can also add your own series, as described in the "Creating Your Own Series" section later in this chapter.

——Fill Handle

FIGURE 16.10

Use the fill handle to quickly fill in a series.

Extending a Series Containing Text

To extend a series containing text, enter the text you want the series to start with and press Ctrl+Enter to exit the cell, but keep it selected. Place your cursor over the lower-right corner of the cell until a black cross appears. Click the mouse button and as you hold it down, drag the fill handle.

You don't need to start at the beginning of the series. You can start anywhere in the series and Excel continues it, starting over if you drag the handle long enough. For example, if you begin a series in A1 with Sunday and drag the fill handle to A8, Sunday appears again, repeating the series.

 **CAUTION** If the text series contains a numerical value, Excel instead copies the text and extends the numerical portion. For example, if you try to extend Monday 1, you get Monday 2, not Tuesday 2. But if you type in Jan 1 and extend that text, Excel extends the numerical portion until Jan 31, then switches to Feb 1. It does this because dates are actually numbers. Seeing the date as Jan 1 is a matter of formatting.

Editing and Managing Data

Excel offers many options for editing and managing sheet data. You can edit multiple sheets at one time, create tables, fix numbers stored as text, search for and find data, and use data validation to limit data entry in specific cells.

Editing Data

Now that you know how to enter data into a blank cell—how do you edit data already in a cell? If you select a cell and start typing, you'll overwrite what was originally in the cell. You have three methods to choose from:

- **Double-click**—When you place your cursor over a cell and it's a big white cross, double-click and the cursor appears wherever you double-clicked, so you can go directly to a word or between numbers.

- **Formula bar**—Select the cell and then click where you want to edit in the formula bar.
- **F2**—Select the cell and press F2. The cursor appears at the right end of data in the cell.

When you're done making changes, press Enter or whatever method you prefer to exit out of the cell and save your changes. If you change your mind about the changes while you're still in the cell, press Esc and you exit the cell without saving your changes.

Editing Multiple Sheets at One Time

You can change the exact same range on multiple sheets at a time by grouping the sheets and making the change to one of the sheets. For example, you can enter the word *Sales* in cell A1 of all the selected sheets. Or you can apply a bold format to cell C2 in a group of sheets.

To make a change to multiple sheets by just changing one sheet, follow these steps:

1. Go to one of the sheets you need to change.

2. While holding down the Ctrl key, select the tabs of the other sheets you want to make the same change to. This groups the sheets together.

3. Make the changes to the active sheet.

4. To ungroup the sheets, select another sheet, or right-click a sheet tab and select Ungroup Sheets.

Clearing the Contents of a Cell

To clear the data from a range—leaving the cells otherwise intact, such as the formatting—select the range and press the Delete key or right-click over the selection and choose Clear Contents.

 CAUTION You might be tempted to use the spacebar to clear a cell. DON'T! Although you can't see the space in the cell, Excel can. That space can throw off Excel's functions because to Excel, that space is a character.

Clearing an Entire Sheet

To clear a sheet of all data, but leave any formatting intact, click the intersection between the headers, shown in Figure 16.11, and press Delete or right-click and choose Clear Contents.

To clear a sheet of all data and formatting, select the entire sheet using the intersection between the headers, right-click and select Delete, or click the Delete button on the Home tab.

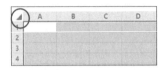

FIGURE 16.11

Clicking the intersection of the row and column headers selects all the cells on the sheet.

Working with Tables

When you enter information in multiple columns on a sheet, it is often referred to as a table, as in a table of data. But Excel also has a special term for a setting you can apply to a data table, imbuing it with special abilities and rules. This term is also *Table*. When your data table is defined as a Table, additional functionality in Excel is made available. For example, with Excel's intelligent Tables, the following additional functionality becomes available:

- AutoFilter drop-downs are automatically added to the headings.

- You can apply predesigned formats, such as banded rows or borders.

- You can remove duplicates based on the values in one or more columns.

- You can toggle the total row on and off.

- Adding new rows or columns automatically extends the table.

- You can take advantage of automatically created range names.

 NOTE Throughout this book, in references to this special kind of Table the T is capitalized. A normal table that does not have the additional functionality has a lowercase t.

Defining a Table

For your data to convert to a Table, it must be set up properly. This means that, except for the headings row (row 1 in Figure 16.12), each row must be one complete record of the data set—for example, a customer or inventory item. Column headers are not required, but if they are included then they must be at the top of the data. If your data does not include headers, Excel inserts some for you.

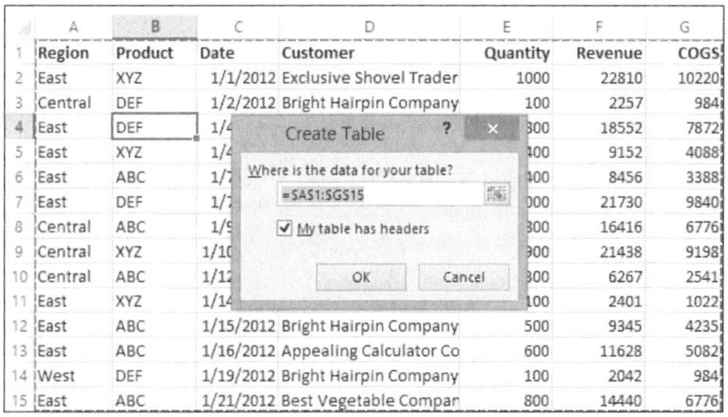

FIGURE 16.12

Set up your data properly to define it as a Table.

After your data is set up properly, select a cell in the data set and define the Table with one of the following methods:

- On the Insert tab, click the Table button.
- On the Home tab, click the Format as Table button, and select a style to apply to the data.
- Press Ctrl+T.
- Press Ctrl+L.

When you use any one of the preceding methods, Excel determines the range of your data by looking for a completely empty row and column. The Create Table dialog box opens, showing the range Excel has defined. You can accept this range or modify it as needed. To modify it, you can click the sheet and, holding the mouse button down, drag to create a box enveloping your entire data set. You can also modify it by editing the cell addresses in the Create Table dialog box.

If Excel was able to identify headers, the My Table Has Headers dialog box is selected, so make sure that Excel has correctly identified whether your data has headers and click OK. If there are no headers then make sure the box is unselected and click OK. Your table is formatted with AutoFilter drop-downs in the headers, as shown in Figure 16.13.

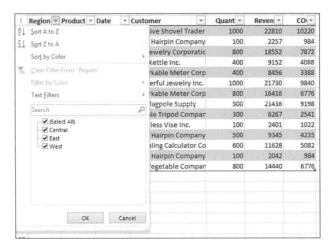

FIGURE 16.13

A Table automatically has AutoFilter drop-downs in the headers.

 NOTE With the creation of the Table, the Table Tools – Design displays in the ribbon. Whenever you select a cell in a Table, this tab appears. It contains functionality and options specific to tables.

Expanding a Table

After your data is defined as a Table, the Table automatically expands as you add adjacent rows and columns. If you don't want the new entry to be part of the Table, you can tell Excel by clicking the lightning bolt icon that appears and then selecting either Undo Table AutoExpansion or Stop Automatically Expanding Tables, as shown in Figure 16.14.

FIGURE 16.14

If you don't want a new row or column to be part of the Table then instruct Excel to undo or stop the autoexpansion.

CAUTION When adding new rows to the bottom of a Table, make sure the total row is turned off; otherwise, Excel cannot identify the new row as belonging with the existing data. The exception is when you tab from the last data row; Excel inserts a new row and moves the total row down.

To manually resize a Table, click and drag the angle bracket icon in the lower-right corner of the Table. You can also select a cell in the Table and click the Resize Table button on the Table Tools – Design tab. Specify the new range in the Resize Table dialog box that opens.

Adding a Total Row to a Table

When you select the Total Row check box on the Table Tools – Design tab, Excel adds a total row to the bottom of the active Table. By default, Excel adds the word Total to the first column of the Table and sums the data in the rightmost column, as shown in Figure 16.15. If the rightmost column contains text, Excel returns a count instead of a sum.

Total						73006
						None
						Average
						Count
						Count Number
						Max
						Min
						Sum
						StdDev
						Var
						More Function

FIGURE 16.15

Selecting the Total Row check box adds a total row to the bottom of the Table.

Each cell in the total row has a drop-down of functions that can be used to calculate the data above it. For example, instead of the sum, you can calculate the average, max, min, and more. Just make a selection from the drop-down and Excel inserts the formula in the cell.

 TIP The functions listed in the drop-down are calculated using variations of the SUBTOTAL function. For more information on this function, see Chapter 23, "Creating Subtotals and Grouping Data."

Fixing Numbers Stored as Text

Sometimes when you import data or receive data from another source, the numbers might be converted to text. When you try to sum them, nothing works. That is because Excel does not sum numbers stored as text.

When numbers in a sheet are being stored as text, Excel lets you know by placing a green triangle in the cell. When you select the cell and click the warning sign that appears, Excel informs you that the number is being stored as text, as shown in Figure 16.16. It then gives you options for handling the number, such as Convert to Number or Ignore Error.

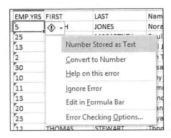

FIGURE 16.16

With Background Error Checking enabled, Excel informs you if a number is being stored as text.

If you have a worksheet with thousands of cells, it takes a long time to convert them all to numbers. Three options for doing a larger-scale conversion are covered in the next sections.

Using Convert to Number on a Range

One option for converting multiple cells into numbers is to use the information drop-down that Excel has provided:

1. Select the range consisting of all the cells you need to convert (making sure that the first cell in the range needs to be converted). The range can include text and other numerical values, as long as it doesn't include cells you do not want to be converted to numbers.

2. Click the warning symbol in the first cell.

3. From the drop-down, select Convert to Number, and all cells in the selected range are modified, turning the numbers to true numbers.

Using Paste Special to Force a Number

If you have the Background Error Checking disabled and don't see the green warning triangle, try this method for converting cells to numbers:

1. Enter a 1 in a blank cell and copy it.

2. Select the cells containing the numbers, right-click, and select Paste Special, Paste Special.

3. From the dialog box that opens, select Multiply, and click OK.

The act of multiplying the values by 1 forces the contents of the cells to become their numerical values.

TIP You can also copy a blank cell and use the Add option instead of Multiply.

Using Text to Columns to Convert Text to Numbers

In step 3 of the Text to Columns wizard, you select the data type of a column. You can use this functionality to also correct numbers being stored as text. To convert a column of numbers stored as text to just numbers, follow these steps:

1. Highlight the range of text to be converted.

2. On the Data tab, click the Text to Columns button.

3. Click Finish. The numbers are no longer considered numbers stored as text.

NOTE For more information on the Text to Columns wizard, refer to the section "Working with Delimited Text" earlier in this chapter.

Finding Data on Your Sheet

If you press Ctrl+F or select Find from the Find & Select drop-down list on the Home tab, the Find and Replace dialog box opens. Through this dialog box, you can find data anywhere on the sheet or in the workbook. Click the Replace tab and you can quickly replace the found data.

Click the Options button and the Find dialog box opens, showing several options to aid in your search, as shown in Figure 16.17:

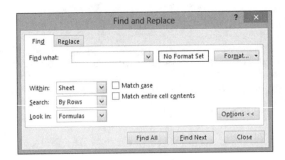

FIGURE 16.17

Click the Options button to open the full search potential of the Find and Replace dialog box.

- **Within**—You can search just the active Sheet or the entire Workbook. You can also narrow Excel's search by selecting the range before bringing up the dialog box.

- **Search**—To have the search go down all the rows of one column before going on to the next column, set this to By Rows. To have the search go across all columns in a row before going on to the next row, select By Columns.

- **Look In**—By default, Excel looks in Formulas, that is, the true value of the data in a cell. When you've applied formulas or formatting to a sheet, what you see in a cell might not be what is actually in the cell. Look at Figure 16.18. The value 22.81 is obviously at the top of the column, but a search in Excel does not find it because the value in the cell was calculated. To search for the value, change the drop-down to Values. You can also choose to search in Comments.

FIGURE 16.18

If Excel can't find the number you know is on the sheet, check your settings. If set to Formulas, change to Values and vice versa.

CAUTION The settings in the Find and Replace dialog box are stored throughout an Excel session. This means that if you change them in the morning for a search and then try a search again later in the afternoon without having closed Excel at all during the day, the settings changes you've made are still active, even if you're searching a different workbook.

Performing a Wildcard Search

What if you don't know the exact text you're looking for? For example, you're doing a search for Jon Smith, but don't know if Jon was entered correctly. To do a wildcard search, you can use an asterisk (*) to tell Excel there might or might not be additional characters between the n, like this: Jo*n Smith. In this case, Excel returns John Smith, Jon Smith, and Jonathan Smith.

Using Data Validation to Limit Data Entry in a Cell

Data validation enables you to limit what a user can type in a cell. For example, you can limit users to whole numbers, dates, a list of selections, or a specific range of values. Custom input and error messages can be configured to guide the user entry.

The available validation criteria are as follows:

- **Any Value**—The default value allowing unrestricted entry.

- **Whole Number**—Requires a whole number be entered. You can select a comparison value (Between, Not Between, Equal To, and so on) and set the Minimum and Maximum value.

- **Decimal**—Requires a decimal value be entered. You can select a comparison value (Between, Not Between, Equal To, and so on) and set the Minimum and Maximum value.

- **List**—Requires user to select from a predefined list, as shown in Figure 16.19. The source can be within the Data Validation dialog box or can be a vertical or horizontal range on any sheet.

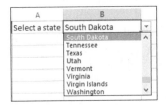

FIGURE 16.19

Provide users with a list of entries to choose from.

- **Date**—Requires a date be entered. You can select a comparison value (between, not between, equal to, and so on) and set the minimum and maximum value.

- **Time**—Requires a time be entered. You can select a comparison value (between, not between, equal to, and so on) and set the minimum and maximum value.

- **Text Length**—Requires a text value be entered. You can select a comparison value (between, not between, equal to, and so on) and set the minimum and maximum number of characters.

- **Custom**—Uses a formula to calculate TRUE for valid entries or FALSE for invalid entries.

Limiting User Entry to a Selection from a List

Data validation enables you to create a drop-down in a cell, restricting the user to selecting from a predefined list of values (refer to Figure 16.19).

To set up the source range and configure the data validation cell, follow these steps:

1. Create a vertical or horizontal list of the values to appear in the drop-down. You can place these values in a sheet different from where the drop-down will actually be placed and then hide the sheet, preventing the user from changing the list.

2. Select the cell you want the drop-down to appear in.

3. On the Data tab, click the Data Validation button. The Data Validation dialog box opens.

4. From the Allow field of the Settings tab, select List.

5. Place your cursor in the Source field.

6. Select the list you created in step 1, as shown in Figure 16.20. If your list is short, instead of the separate list you created in step 1, you can enter the values separated by commas directly in the Source field. For example, you could enter Yes, No in the source field (no quotes, no equal sign).

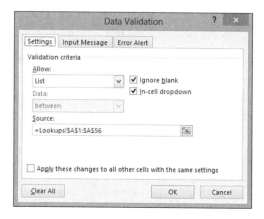

FIGURE 16.20

The source for the validation list can be a different sheet. You can then hide the sheet from users.

7. If you want to provide the user with an input prompt, go to the Input Message tab and fill in the Title and Input Message fields.

8. If you want to provide the user with an error message, go to the Error Alert tab and fill in the Style, Title and Error Message fields.

9. Click OK.

 NOTE The font and font size of the text in the drop-down is controlled by your Windows settings, not Excel.

THE ABSOLUTE MINIMUM

Here are the key points to remember from this chapter:

- Excel data falls into one of several categories: numbers, text, dates, times, formulas, and functions.

- Although the easiest way to enter data in Excel is to simply type it, Excel offers other options as well. You can also use clipboard functions to enter data or use a series to quickly fill a range.

- Excel offers many options for editing and managing sheet data. You can edit multiple sheets at one time, create tables, fix numbers stored as text, search for and find data, and use data validation to limit data entry in specific cells.

IN THIS CHAPTER

- Adjusting Row Heights and Column Widths
- Aligning Text in a Cell
- Formatting Numbers
- Creating Hyperlinks
- Applying Conditional Formatting
- Using Cell Styles to Quickly Apply Formatting
- Using Themes to Ensure Uniformity in Design

FORMATTING SHEETS AND CELLS

Now that you have your data on a sheet, you need to format it so that it's easy to decipher and readers can quickly make sense of it. From simple font formatting, wrapping text, and merging cells to placing icons in cells so it's obvious how one number compares with another, Excel has the tools you need to make reports visually interesting.

NOTE See Chapter 3, "Working with Text," to learn about the cell formatting options in the Font group on the Home tab.

Adjusting Row Heights and Column Widths

If you can't see all the data you enter in a cell or the data in a column doesn't use up very much of the column width, you can adjust the column width as needed. Several methods are available for adjusting column widths on a sheet. Each method described here also works for adjusting row heights:

- **Click and drag the border between the column headings**—Place your cursor on the border between two column headings, as shown in Figure 17.1. When the cursor turns into two arrows, you can click and drag to the right to make the column to the left wider or drag to the left to make the column narrower. The advantage of this method is you have full control of the width of the column. The disadvantage is that it affects only one column.

FIGURE 17.1

The border between columns is the key to quickly adjusting the column width.

- **Double-click the border between the column headings**—Excel automatically adjusts the left column to fit the widest value in that column. The advantage of this method is that the column is now wide enough to display all the contents. The disadvantage is if you have a cell with a very long entry, the new width might be impractical.

- **Select multiple columns and drag the border for one column**—The width of all the columns in the selection adjusts to the same width as the one you just adjusted.

- **Select multiple columns and double-click the border for one column**—Each column in the selection adjusts to accommodate its widest value.

- **Apply one column's width to other columns**—If you have a column with a width you want other columns to have, you can copy that column and paste its width over the other columns by using the Column Widths option of the Paste Special dialog box.

- **Use the controls on the ribbon**—Select the column(s) to adjust, click the Format button on the Home tab, select Column Width, enter a width, and click OK.

- **AutoFit a column to fit all the data below a title row**—If you have a long title and need to fit the column to all the data below the title, double-clicking the border between column headings won't work as this adjusts the column width based on the title. Instead, select the data in the column, without the title, and use the AutoFit Column Width option under Home, Cells, Format.

TIP You can also use the Font Size drop-down list (found in the Font group on the Home tab) to adjust row height automatically. The default row height is based on the largest font size in the row. For example, if cell F2 has a font size of 26, even if there is no other text in the row, the row automatically adjusts to approximately 33. You can take advantage of this to set the height of a row, instead of manually setting the row height. The advantage is that when a user tries autofitting the row height, your setting won't change.

Aligning Text in a Cell

The Alignment group on the Home tab consists of tools that affect how a value is situated in a cell or range. You can also access these controls from the Alignment tab of the Format Cells dialog box.

There are six alignment buttons in the Alignment group, representing the most popular settings for how a value is situated in a cell. Top Align, Middle Align, and Bottom Align describe the vertical placement of the value in the cell. Align Text Left, Center, and Align Text Right describe the horizontal placement of the value in the cell. More options are available in the Format Cells dialog box on the Alignment tab. The Mini toolbar has only one button for horizontal alignment, which centers the text of the selected cell.

Merging Two or More Cells

Merging cells takes two or more adjacent cells and combines them to make one cell. For example, if you are designing a form with many data entry cells and need space for a large comment area, resizing the column might not be practical as it also affects the size of the cells above it. Instead, select the range you want the comments to be entered in and merge the cells. Any text other than that found in the upper-left cell of the selection is deleted as the newly combined cell takes on the identity of this first cell.

On the Alignment tab in the Format Cells dialog box, there is a check box for Merge Cells. In the upper-right corner of the Mini toolbar is a toggle button (Merge/Unmerge) to merge and center the text of the selected range.

The Merge & Center drop-down in the Alignment group on the Home tab offers several options to merge cells in different ways:

- **Merge & Center**—This is the default action of the drop-down button. The selected cells will be merged and the text will be centered.

- **Merge Across**—If you have several rows where you want to merge the adjacent cells in the same row, you can select all the rows (and their adjacent columns to merge) and select Merge Across (see Figure 17.2).

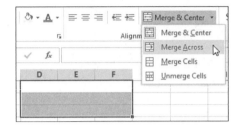

FIGURE 17.2

Notice that although several rows are selected, using Merge Across kept the separate rows intact.

- **Merge Cells**—Equivalent to the check box in the Format Cells dialog box, the selected range will be merged, retaining the alignment of the upper-left cell in the selection.

- **Unmerge Cells**—Use this option to unmerge the selected cells.

Use caution when merging cells because it can lead to potential issues:

- Users will be unable to sort if there are merged cells within the data.

- Users will be unable to cut and paste unless the same cells are merged in the pasted location.

- Column and row AutoFit won't work.

- Lookup type formulas return a match only for the first matching row or column.

 TIP For an alternative to merging to get a title centered over a table, refer to the section "Centering Text Across a Selection."

Centering Text Across a Selection

As noted in the preceding section, "Merging Two or More Cells," merging cells can cause problems in Excel, limiting what you can do with a table. If you need to center text over several columns, instead of merging the cells, center the text across the multiple columns. To center a title across the top of a table without merging the cells, as shown in Figure 17.3, follow these steps:

1. Type your title in the leftmost cell to the table.

2. Select the title cell and extend the range to include all cells you want the title centered over.

3. Press Ctrl+1 or click the Format button on the Home tab and select Format Cells to open the Format Cells dialog box.

4. Select the Alignment tab.

5. From the Horizontal drop-down, select Center Across Selection.

6. Click OK.

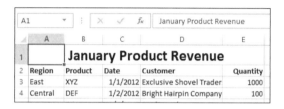

FIGURE 17.3

Use Center Across Selection instead of merging cells to center a title on a report.

Wrapping Text in a Cell to the Next Line

When you type a lot of text in a cell, it continues to extend to the right beyond the right border of the cell if there is nothing in the adjacent cell. You can widen the column to fit the text, but sometimes that might be impractical. If that's the case, you can set the cell to wrap text, moving any text that extends past the edge of the column to a new line in the cell.

Normally, when you wrap a cell, the row height automatically adjusts to fit the text. If it doesn't, make sure you don't have the cell merged with another; Excel does not autofit merged cells. If there are merged cells, unmerge them and manually force an autofit (see the "Adjusting Row Heights and Column Widths" section). The row height begins to automatically adjust again.

To turn on text wrapping, select the cell and click the Wrap Text button on the Home tab or select Wrap Text on the Alignment tab of the Format Cells dialog box. There is no option on the Mini toolbar.

CAUTION If you manually adjust the row height any time before pasting, the height won't adjust automatically. To reset the row so it adjusts automatically again, double-click the border between the desired row and the one beneath.

Indenting Cell Contents

By default, text entered in a cell is flush with the left side of the cell whereas numbers are flush to the right. To move a value away from the edge, you might be tempted to add spaces before or after the value. If you change your mind about this formatting at a later time, it can be quite tedious to remove the extraneous spaces.

Instead, use the Increase Indent and Decrease Indent buttons to move the value about two character lengths over. Increase Indent moves the value away from the edge it is aligned with. Decrease Indent moves the value back toward its edge.

 TIP If you use the Increase Indent and Decrease Indent buttons with a right-aligned number, the number becomes left-aligned and adjusts from the left margin. This does not occur with right-aligned text. To correct this, select the Alignment tab of the Format Cells dialog box, set the Horizontal alignment to Right, and then set the Indent value.

When adjusting the Indent from the Format Cells dialog box, the Alignment tab uses a single Indent field with a number to indicate the number of indentations. The Mini toolbar does not offer options for indenting.

Changing Text Orientation

Vertical text can be difficult to read, but sometimes limited space makes it a requirement. The Orientation button, which looks like ab written at a 45-degree angle, has multiple variations of Vertical Text, Angle Counterclockwise, Angle Clockwise, Vertical Text, Rotate Text Up, and Rotate Text Down. The Orientation section in Format Cells, Alignment offers more precise control (see Figure 17.4). There is no option on the Mini toolbar.

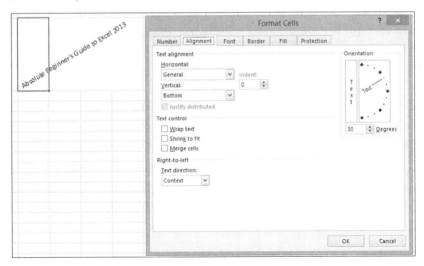

FIGURE 17.4

Use the Orientation settings to rotate the contents of a cell.

Formatting Numbers

The Number Format drop-down in the Number group of the Home tab has 11 formatting options available (General is the default). Figure 17.5 shows an example of each format.

FIGURE 17.5

The Number Format drop-down offers many quick formatting options.

Below the Number Format drop-down is a drop-down button with a dollar sign ($) on it—the **Accounting Number** format. This button applies the accounting format to the selected range. From the drop-down, you can select different currency symbols.

Also beneath the drop-down are buttons for applying the **Percent Style (%)** and **Comma Style (,)** formats to a selection.

Use the Increase Decimal and Decrease Decimal buttons on the Home tab in the Number group (see Figure 17.6) to quickly increase and decrease the number of decimal places shown in number formats that use decimals. The Increase Decimal button has an arrow pointing left, whereas the Decrease Decimal button has an arrow pointing right.

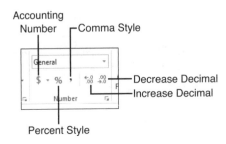

FIGURE 17.6

You can increase or decrease decimals easily in Excel.

Applying Number Formats with the Format Cells Dialog Box

The way you see number data in Excel is controlled by the format applied to the cell. For example, you might see the date as August 21, 2012, but what is actually in the cell is 41142. Or you might see 10.5%, but the actual value in the cell is 0.105. This is important because when doing calculations, Excel doesn't care what you see. It deals only with the actual values.

There are only a few formatting options on the Home tab in the Number group. This section reviews the formatting options available on the Numbers tab of the Format Cells dialog box. (Click the dialog box launcher in the lower-right corner of the Number group to open.)

The Number tab includes a variety of number formatting options, described in this section. To apply a number format, select the range, select the desired format from the dialog box, and click OK.

General

General is the default format used by all cells on a sheet when you first open a workbook. Decimal places and the negative symbol are shown if needed. Thousand separators are not.

Number

By default, the **Number** format uses two decimal places but does not use the thousands separator. You can change the number of decimal places, turn on the thousands separator, and choose how to format negative numbers, as shown in Figure 17.7.

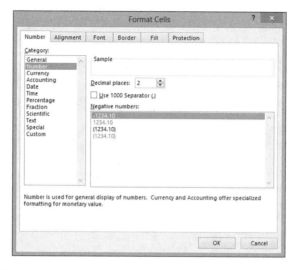

FIGURE 17.7

Additional options might be available when you select a format to apply.

Currency

The default **Currency** format displays the system's currency symbol, two decimal places, and a thousands separator. You can change the number of decimal places, change the currency symbol, and select a format for negative numbers.

Accounting

Accounting is similar to Currency but automatically lines up the currency symbols on the left side of the cell and decimal points to the right side of the cell. The default Accounting format displays the system's currency symbol, two decimal places, and a thousands separator. You can change the number of decimal places and the currency symbol.

Date

There is no default **Date** format. Sometimes Excel reformats the date you enter; sometimes it keeps it the way you entered it. You can select a date format from the list in the Type box, which also contains date and time formats.

The date formats vary from short dates, such as 4/5, to long dates, such as Monday, April 5, 2010. When selecting a date format, look at the sample above the Type list. It helps you differentiate between the format 14-Mar, which is March 14, and the format Mar-01, which is March 2001, not March 1.

Time

There is no default **Time** format. You can select a time format from the list in the Type box, which also contains two date and time formats.

Excel sees times on a 24-hour clock. That is, if you enter 1:30, Excel assumes you mean 1:30 a.m. But if you enter 13:30, Excel knows you mean 1:30 p.m.

If you need to display times beyond 24 hours, such as if you're working on a timesheet adding up hours worked, use the time format 37:30:55, as shown in Figure 17.8.

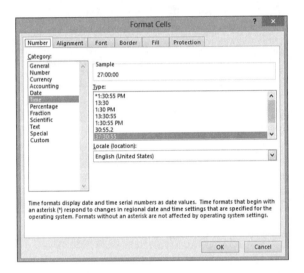

FIGURE 17.8

There are various time formats available.

Percentage

The default **Percentage** format includes two decimal places. When you apply this format, Excel takes the value in the cell, multiplies it by 100, and adds a % at the end. When you use the cell in a calculation, the actual (decimal) value is used. For example, if you have a cell showing 90% and multiply it by 1,000, the result is (in General format) 900 (0.9*1,000).

If you include the % when you type the value in the cell, in the background Excel converts the value to its decimal equivalent, but the Percentage format is applied to the cell.

Fraction

The **Fraction** category rounds decimal numbers up to the nearest fraction. You can select to round the decimal to one, two, or three digits, or to round to the nearest half, quarter, eighth, sixteenth, tenth, or hundredth.

Scientific

The default **Scientific** category displays the value in scientific notation accurate to two decimal places. You can change the number of decimal places.

Text

There are no controls for the **Text** category. Setting this format to a cell forces Excel to treat the numbers in the cell as text, and you view exactly what is in the cell. If you set this format before typing in a number, the number becomes a number stored as text and might not work in some calculations.

Special

The **Special** category provides formats for numbers that do not fall in any of the preceding categories because the values are not actually numbers. That is, they aren't used for any mathematical operations and instead are treated more like words.

The four special types are specific to U.S. formatting:

- **ZIP Code**—Ensures that East Coast cities do not lose the leading zeros in their ZIP Codes.
- **ZIP Code + 4**—Ensures that East Coast cities do not lose the leading zeros in their ZIP Codes and formats the +4 in ZIP codes.
- **Phone Number**—Formats a telephone number with parentheses around the area code and a dash after the exchange.
- **Social Security Number**—Uses hyphens to separate the digits into groups of three, two, and four numbers.

Custom Format

A custom format enables you to create a format specific to your situation and can contain up to four different formats, each separated by a semicolon.

You should keep several things in mind when creating a custom format:

- Use semicolons to separate the code sections.
- If there is only one format, it applies to all numbers.

- If there are two formats, the first section applies to positive and zero values. The second section applies to negative values.

- If there are three formats, the first section applies to positive values, the second section applies to negative values, and the third section applies to zero values.

- If all four sections are used, they apply to positive, negative, zero, and text values, respectively.

Figure 17.9 shows a custom number format using all four sections. The table in C9:D13 displays how the formats would be applied to different values. The \M in in the first and second section adds an M to the numerical values. The @ in the fourth section is a placeholder for any text the user types into the cell. Note the value in cell D11 is red and a zero, not a blank, must be entered in cell C12 for "No Sales" to appear.

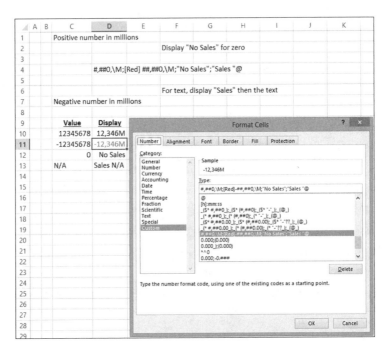

FIGURE 17.9

Use the four sections of a custom format to design formatting for positive, negative, zero, and text values.

TIP If you see ### in a cell, try increasing the size of the column. Sometimes Excel doesn't automatically adjust the column width for an entered number.

Creating Hyperlinks

Hyperlinks enable you to open web pages in your browser, create emails, and jump to a specific cell on a specific sheet in a specific workbook. For web and email addresses, Excel automatically recognizes what you've typed and applies the format accordingly, turning the cell into a clickable link.

If you want to link to a sheet, you have to go through the Insert Hyperlink dialog box, shown in Figure 17.10. You can open the dialog box by right-clicking on a cell and selecting Hyperlink or clicking the Hyperlink button on the Insert tab.

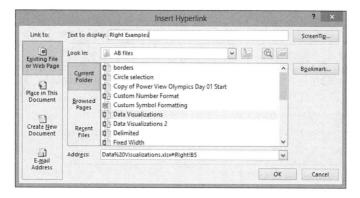

FIGURE 17.10

Use hyperlinks to help users quickly jump to sheets and specific ranges.

Being able to create a hyperlink to a sheet can be useful if you want to create a table of contents for a large workbook or a series of workbooks.

If you select just a sheet, Excel defaults to cell A1 on the sheet, but you can link to any specified cell. To create a hyperlink to a specific sheet, follow these steps:

1. Select the cell where you want the link.

2. On the Insert tab, click the Hyperlink button to open the Hyperlinks dialog box.

3. Browse to the workbook you want to link to. If you want to link to a cell in the current workbook, click the Place in This Document button.

4. If linking to an external workbook, click the Bookmark button to open the Select Place in Document dialog box. If linking to the active workbook, continue to step 5.

5. Select the sheet from the Cell Reference list. If you have a specific cell address you want the link to go to, enter it in the Type the Cell Reference field. Or, if you have a name assigned to the cell, select it from the Defined Names list. In that case, you don't have to enter a cell reference.

6. Click OK.

7. If the cell selected in step 1 is blank, the Text to Display field at the top of the dialog box shows the destination for the hyperlink. You can type in new text if desired.

8. Click OK. The next time you click on the cell, you follow the link.

Applying Conditional Formatting

An unformatted sheet of just numbers isn't going to grab your audience's attention. But sometimes you don't have time to create a colorful report—or do you? Conditional formatting enables you to quickly apply color and icons to data. The quick formatting options consist of the following:

- **Data Bars**—A data bar is a gradient or solid fill of color that starts at the left edge of the cell. The length of the bar represents the value in the cell compared with other values in the range the format is applied to. The smallest numbers have just a tiny amount of color and the largest numbers in the range fill the cell.

- **Color Scales**—A color scale is a color that fills the entire cell. Two or three different colors are used to relay the relative size of each cell to other cells in the range the format is applied to.

- **Icon Sets**—An icon set is a group of three to five images that provide a graphic representation of how the number in a cell compares with the other cells in the range the format is applied to.

The quickest way to apply one of the conditional formats is to select all the cells you want to apply it to, click the Conditional Formatting button on the Home tab and select one of the formatting options from the submenu that appears, as shown in Figure 17.11. As you move your cursor over the options, your range changes to reflect the connection. When you find the formatting you want, click it, and it is applied to your range.

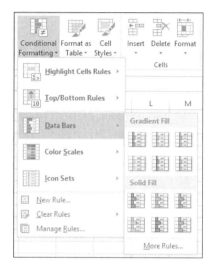

FIGURE 17.11

Quickly apply formatting to your data by selecting one of the prebuilt options in the Conditional Formatting drop-down.

 TIP When you select a range of numbers, in the lower-right corner of the very last cell Excel's Quick Analysis tool displays with several preset conditional formatting options to choose from.

Using Cell Styles to Quickly Apply Formatting

You're probably used to using styles in Word but never realized that styles are also available in Excel. Select a range in Excel and click the Cell Styles button on the Home tab. Move your cursor over the predefined styles and watch your range update to reflect the styles.

You aren't limited to these predefined styles. You can create and save your own style for use throughout the workbook it's saved in. To quickly create a custom style in the active workbook, follow these steps:

1. Select a cell with all the formatting styles needed.

2. On the Home tab, click the Cell Styles button, and select New Cell Style.

3. If there is any type of formatting you do not want as part of the style, such as the alignment, unselect that style option.

4. Enter a name for the style in the Style Name field and click OK.

Using Themes to Ensure Uniformity in Design

Themes are collections of fonts, colors, and graphic effects that can be applied to a workbook. This can be useful if you have a series of company reports that need to have the same color and fonts. Only one theme can affect a workbook at a time.

Excel includes several built-in themes, which you can access from the Themes drop-down under Page Layout, Themes. You can also create and share themes you design.

A theme has the following components, which you can apply individually, instead of applying an entire Theme package:

- **Fonts**—A theme includes a font for headings and a font for body text.
- **Colors**—There are 12 colors in a theme: 4 for text, 6 for accents, and 2 for hyperlinks.
- **Graphic effects**—Graphic effects include lines, fills, bevels, shadows, and so on.

Applying a New Theme

The Themes group on the Page Layout tab has four buttons:

- **Themes**—Enables you to switch themes or save a new one
- **Colors**—Enables you to select a new color palette from the available built-in themes
- **Fonts**—Enables you to select a new font palette from the available built-in themes
- **Effects**—Enables you to select a new effect from the available built-in themes

Before applying a theme, arrange the sheet so you can see any themed elements such as charts or SmartArt. Then click the Themes button on the Page Layout tab and watch the elements update as you move your cursor over the various themes in the Themes drop-down. When you find the one you like, click it, and it will be applied to the workbook.

If you just want to change a theme component, make a selection from the component's drop-down in the same way you would a theme.

Creating a New Theme

To create a new theme, you need to specify the colors and fonts and select an effect from the respective component's drop-down. Then, under the Themes drop-down, choose Save Current Theme to save the theme.

To create a new theme, follow these steps:

1. On the Page Layout tab, click the Colors button, and select Customize Colors.

2. To change an item's color, such as Accent 5 in Figure 17.12, choose its drop-down to open the color chooser.

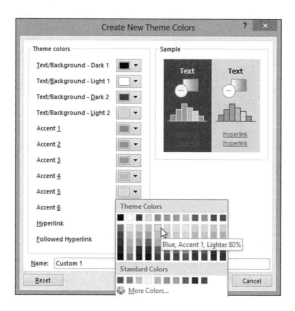

FIGURE 17.12

You can customize different aspects of a theme.

3. When you find the desired color, click it to apply it to your theme.

4. Repeat steps 2 and 3 for each color you want to change.

5. In the Name field at the bottom, type a name for your color theme.

6. Click Save.

7. On the Page Layout tab, click the Fonts button, and select Customize Fonts.

8. To change the Heading font, choose its drop-down to open the font list.

9. When you find the desired font, click it to apply it to your theme. The Sample box on the right updates to reflect your selection.

10. Repeat steps 8 and 9 for the Body font.

11. In the Name field at the bottom, type a name for your font theme.

12. Click Save.

13. On the Page Layout tab, click the Effects button.

14. Select an effect from the gallery of built-in effects.

15. On the Page Layout tab, click the Themes button, and select Save Current Theme.

16. Browse to where you want to save the theme, type a name for it, and click Save.

Sharing a Theme

To share a theme with other people, you must send them the *.thmx file you saved when you created the theme.

When they receive the file, they should save it to either their equivalent theme folder or some other location by clicking the Themes button on the Page Layout tab and selecting Browse for Themes.

THE ABSOLUTE MINIMUM

Here are the key points to remember from this chapter:

- If you can't see all the data you enter in a cell or the data in a column doesn't use up very much of the column width, you can adjust the column width as needed.

- The Number group on the Home tab has several quick formatting options. You can also apply more advanced number formatting in the Format Cells dialog box.

- Hyperlinks enable you to open web pages in your browser, create emails, and jump to a specific cell on a specific sheet in a specific workbook.

- With conditional formatting, you can quickly apply color and icons to data.

- Apply colors to titles, headings, and selected cells using cell styles.

- Themes are collections of fonts, colors, and graphic effects that you can apply

18

USING FORMULAS

Excel is great for simple data entry, but its real strength is its capability to perform calculations. After you design a sheet to perform calculations, you can easily change the data and watch Excel instantly recalculate.

This chapter not only shows you how to enter a formula, but also teaches you fundamental basics, such as the difference between absolute and relative referencing, which is important when you want to copy a formula to multiple cells, and how to use a Name to refer to a cell instead of having to memorize a cell address. You'll take the formula basics you learn here and apply them later in Chapter 19, "Using Functions," to really crank up the calculating power of your workbook.

Entering a Formula into a Cell

Entering a basic formula is straightforward. Select the cell, enter an equal sign, type in the formula, and press Enter. Typing the formula is very similar to entering an equation on a calculator, with one exception. If one of the terms in your formula is already stored in a cell, you can point to that cell instead of typing in the number stored in the cell. The advantage of this is that if the other cell's value ever changes, your formula automatically updates.

To enter a formula that includes a pointer to another cell, follow these steps:

1. Select the cell you want the formula to be in.

2. Type an equal sign. This tells Excel you are entering a formula.

3. Type the first number and an operator, as you would on a calculator. There's no need to include spaces in the formula.

 NOTE See the section "Using Mathematical Operators" for more information on the operators you can use.

4. Select the cell you want to include in the formula. The cell can even be on another sheet or in another workbook.

5. Press Enter. Excel calculates the formula in the cell.

 TIP If you select the wrong cell, as long as you haven't typed anything else, such as a +, you can select another cell right away and Excel replaces the previous cell address with a new one. If you have typed something else, you need to highlight the incorrect cell address before you select the correct one.

Of course, there's no need to have any numbers in a formula. It can consist entirely of cell addresses, as shown in Figure 18.1. The table in the figure calculates the total value of inventory by multiplying the cost (column B) by the quantity (column C). To enter the formula, after typing the equal sign, select the first cell, type an operator, and then select the second cell. After pressing Enter, copy the formula down to the other rows using the fill handle.

| D2 | ▼ | : | ✕ | ✓ | fx | =B2*C2 |

◢	A	B	C	D
1	SKU	Cost	Qty	Total
2	J41	40.76	23	937.48
3	A20	88.37	45	3976.65

FIGURE 18.1

Using cell addresses in formulas, instead of values, means the value in cell D2 automatically updates when those other cells, B2 and C2, are updated.

 NOTE For information on using the fill handle to extend a series, see Chapter 16, "Entering Sheet Data," or refer to the section "Copying a Formula Using the Fill Handle" later in this chapter.

Three Ways of Entering a Formula's Cell References

After typing the equal sign to start a formula, you have three options for entering the rest of the formula:

- Type the complete formula.
- Type numbers and operator keys, but use the mouse to select cell references.
- Type numbers and operator keys, but use the arrow keys to select cell references.

 NOTE See the section "Using Mathematical Operators" for more information on the operators you can use.

The method you use depends on what you find most comfortable. Some users consider the first method the quickest because they never have to move their fingers off the main section of the keyboard. For others, using the mouse makes more sense, especially when selecting a large range for use in the formula.

Relative Versus Absolute Formulas

When you copy a formula, such as =B2*C2, down a column, the formula automatically changes to =B3*C3, then =B4*C4, and so on. Excel's capability to change cell B2 to B3 to B4 and so on is called *relative referencing*. This is Excel's default behavior when dealing with formulas, but it might not always be what you want to happen. If the cell address must remain static as the formula is copied, you need to use *absolute referencing*. This is achieved through the strategic placement of dollar signs ($) before the row or column reference, as shown in Table 18.1.

TABLE 18.1 Relative Versus Absolute Reference Behavior

Format	Copied Down	Copied Across
A1	A2—the row reference updates	B1—the column reference updates
$A$1	$A$1—neither reference updates	$A$1—neither reference updates
$A1	$A2—the row reference updates	$A1—neither reference updates
A$1	A$1—neither reference updates	B$1—the column reference updates

Using a Cell on Another Sheet in a Formula

When writing a formula, not all the cells you need to use have to be on the same sheet. As a matter of fact, it might be a better design to have different types of information on different sheets and then pull them together on one sheet using formulas. For example, if you have to periodically import data from another source, instead of possibly messing up the layout of your calculation table by sharing the sheet with the imported data, import the table to a separate sheet and use linked formulas to reference the required cells. Another use could be a lookup table that you allow users to update, but the sheet with the calculations is protected, allowing users to only view that information, not edit it.

To reference a cell on another sheet, navigate to the sheet and then select the cell, as you would if the cell were on the same sheet as the formula. If you have more cells to select, enter your operator and continue to select cells, returning to the formula sheet if needed. If the last cell you need is on a different sheet, press Enter when you are done and Excel returns you to the sheet with the formula.

Figure 18.2 shows a sales sheet that calculates the tax for each record (row). Instead of placing the tax rate in the formula itself, it is placed in another cell on a sheet named Lookups. The tax formula uses an absolute reference to the tax rate cell (Lookups!$B$1), but a relative reference to the cost of the item (D2), as shown in Figure 18.6. When the formula is copied down, all records reference the tax rate cell, but their own item cost. And, if the tax rate needs to be modified, you only have to change it in the one cell (Lookups!$B$1) to update all the records.

| E2 | | ⌄ | ⠇ | ✕ | ✓ | *fx* | =D2*Lookups!$B$1 | |

⠘	A	B	C	D	E
1	Date	QuotelD	Description	Amount	Tax
2	9/17/2012	3622	Fund Management System	$2,000.00	$ 120.00
3	9/1/2012	3623	SI Summary Rollup	$1,000.00	$ 60.00
4	5/3/2012	3624	Automated Chart Report	$1,200.00	$ 72.00
5	7/13/2012	3625	Card Transaction Records	$1,000.00	$ 60.00
6	7/1/2012	3626	Service Contracts Analysis	$ 600.00	$ 36.00

FIGURE 18.2

A separate sheet is often used to store lookup values, like the Lookups sheet in this formula. This is a good idea because it makes layout changes to the data sheet easier.

Using F4 to Change the Cell Referencing

When you type in a formula and select a cell or range, Excel uses the relative reference. If you need the absolute reference, you will probably either type in the address manually or go back and change the address after you are done with the whole formula. Another option is to change the reference to what you need while typing in the formula. You can do this by pressing the F4 key right after selecting the cell or range. Each time you press the F4 key, it changes the cell address to another reference variation, as shown in Figure 18.3.

When you enter the formula:	
	=B2
Press F4 once:	
	=$B$2
Press F4 again:	
	=B$2
Press F4 again:	
	=$B2

FIGURE 18.3

Use F4 to toggle through the variations of relative to absolute referencing.

 TIP If you need to change a reference after you've already entered the formula, you can still place your cursor in the cell address and use the F4 key to toggle through the references.

For example, to change the cell address in a formula to a column fixed reference as you type it in, follow these steps:

1. Select the cell you want the formula to be in.

2. Type an equal sign.

3. Type the first number and operator, as you would on a calculator.

4. Select the cell you want to include in the formula.

5. Press F4 once and the address changes to absolute referencing. Press F4 again and it becomes a Row Fixed Reference. Press F4 a third time and it becomes a Column Fixed Reference.

 TIP If you miss the reference you need to use the first time, continue pressing F4 until it comes up again.

6. Press Enter. Excel calculates the formula in the cell.

Using Mathematical Operators

Excel offers the mathematical operators listed in Table 18.2.

TABLE 18.2 Mathematical Operators

Operator	Description
+	Addition
-	Subtraction
/	Division
*	Multiplication
^	Exponents
()	Override the usual order of operations
-	Unary minus (for negative numbers)
=	Equal to
>	Greater than
<	Less than
>=	Greater than or equal to
<=	Less than or equal to
<>	Not equal to
&	Join two values to produce a single value
,	Union operator
:	Range operator
(space)	Intersection operator

Understanding the Order of Operations

Excel evaluates a formula in a particular order if it contains many calculations. Instead of calculating from left to right like a calculator, Excel performs certain types of calculations, such as multiplication, before other calculations, such as addition.

You can override this default order of operations using parentheses. If you don't, Excel applies the following order of operations:

1. Unary minus

2. Exponents

3. Multiplication and division, left to right

4. Addition and subtraction, left to right

For example, if you have the formula

=6+3*2

Excel returns 12, because first it does 3*2, then adds the result (6) to 6. But, if you use parentheses, you can change the order:

=(6+3)*2

produces 18 because now Excel does the addition first (6+3) and multiplies the result (9) by 2.

Using Names to Simplify References

It can be difficult to remember what cell you have a specific entry in, such as a tax rate, when you're writing a formula. And if the cell you need to reference is on another sheet, you have to be very careful writing out the reference properly, or you must use the mouse to go to the sheet and select the cell.

It would be much simpler if you could just use the word TaxRate in your formula— and you can, by applying a Name to the cell. After a name is applied to a cell, you can create any references to the cell or range by using the name instead of the cell address. For example, where you once had =B2*$H$1, you could now have =B2*TaxRate, assuming H1 is the cell containing the tax rate.

There are only a few limitations to remember when creating a name:

- The name must be one word. You can use an underscore (_), backslash (\), or period (.) as spacers.

- The name cannot be a word that might also be a cell address. This was a real problem when people converted workbooks from legacy Excel to Excel 2007 or newer because some names, such as TAX2009, weren't cell addresses before. Now in Excel 2007 and newer, such names cause problems when opening a legacy workbook. So name carefully!

- The name cannot include any invalid characters, such as a question mark (?), exclamation point (!), or hyphen (-). The only valid special characters are the underscore (_), backslash (\), and period (.).

- Names are not case sensitive. Excel sees "sales" and "Sales" as the same name.

- You should not use any of the reserved words in Excel. These are Print_Area, Print_Titles, Criteria, Database, and Extract.

Applying and Using a Name in a Formula

To apply a Name to a cell, select the cell, type the Name in the Name box, and press Enter. As long as the Name has not been applied to another cell in the workbook, it replaces the cell address of the selected cell. But if the Name has been applied elsewhere in the workbook, Excel takes you to that cell.

To apply a name to a cell and then use the name in a formula, follow these steps:

1. Select the cell or range you want to apply the name to.

2. In the Name field, type in the name, as shown in Figure 18.4.

3. Press Enter for Excel to accept the name.

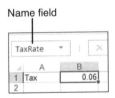

FIGURE 18.4

After you select a cell or range, you can type a name for it in the Name field.

4. Select the cell containing the formula that should reference the name.

5. Replace the cell or range address with the name you just created, or type in a new formula from scratch using the name where you would use the cell or range address, as shown in Figure 18.5.

| E2 | ▼ | : | × | ✓ | fx | =D2*TaxRate | |

	A	B	C	D	E
1	Date	QuoteID	Description	Amount	Tax
2	9/17/2012	3622	Fund Management System	$2,000.00	$ 120.00
3	9/1/2012	3623	SI Summary Rollup	$1,000.00	$ 60.00
4	5/3/2012	3624	Automated Chart Report	$1,200.00	$ 72.00
5	7/13/2012	3625	Card Transaction Records	$1,000.00	$ 60.00
6	7/1/2012	3626	Service Contracts Analysis	$ 600.00	$ 36.00
7	5/26/2012	3627	FTD Upload	$ 175.00	$ 10.50

FIGURE 18.5

Using Names can simplify entering formulas.

If you can't remember the name assigned to a range, you can look it up by clicking the drop-down in the Name field or by selecting Formulas, Defined Names, Use in Formula, which opens up a drop-down of available names. You can also click the Name Manager button on the Formulas tab, which not only lists the defined names, but shows the range they apply to.

Global Versus Local Names

Names can be *global*, which means they are available anywhere in the workbook. Names can also be *local*, which means they are available only on a specific sheet. With local names, you can have multiple references in the workbook with the same name. Global names must be unique to the workbook.

The Name Manager dialog box (shown in Figure 18.6 and found in the Defined Names group on the Formulas tab), lists all the names in a workbook, even a name that has been assigned to both the global and local levels. The Scope column lists the scope of the name, whether it is the workbook or a specific sheet such as Sheet1. When you create a Name, by default it is global. To make the Name local, you have to include the sheet name followed by an exclamation point (!) before typing the Name. If the sheet name is more than one word then you have to wrap the sheet name in single quotes. For example, if the sheet name is "SD Sales" and you're creating the TaxRate name to use just on that sheet then the name you type would be 'SD Sales'!TaxRate.

CAUTION If you have both a local and global reference with the same Name, when you create a formula on the sheet with the local reference, a tip box will appear, letting you choose which reference you want to use.

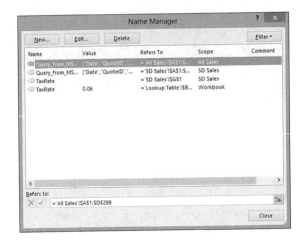

FIGURE 18.6

The Name Manager dialog box lists all local and global names.

Inserting Formulas into Tables

NOTE See the "Defining a Table" section in Chapter 16 for information on defining a table.

When your data has been defined as a Table, Excel automatically copies new formulas created in adjacent columns down to the last row in the Table.

To add a new calculated column to a Table, follow these steps:

1. Type a field header in row 1 of the column adjacent to the rightmost column of the Table. Excel extends any Table formatting to the new column.

2. Select the first data cell in the column. This is cell H2 in Figure 18.7.

3. Type your formula for the selected cell.

4. Press Enter and Excel copies the formula down the column.

Customer	Quantit	Reven	COGS	Profit
Alluring Shoe Company	500	11240	5110	=F2-G2
Alluring Shoe Company	400	9204	4088	
Alluring Shoe Company	900	21465	9198	
Alluring Shoe Company	400	9144	4088	
Alluring Shoe Company	500	10445	4235	

FIGURE 18.7

Type a formula in the first cell of a Table column and Excel copies it down the rest of the column. Note that if you select the columns instead of typing in the cell references, your resulting formula will look quite different.

After entering the formula, a lightning bolt drop-down appears by the cell. If you don't want the automated formula copied, select Undo Calculated Column or Stop Automatically Creating Calculated Columns.

 NOTE If you select the cells instead of typing the cell address, you see Names in the formula instead of the cell address. Refer to the next section "Using Table Names in Table Formulas" to understand why.

Using Table Names in Table Formulas

Names are automatically created when you define a Table. A name, or a specifier, for each column and the entire Table is created. Just like you can use names to simplify references in your standard formulas, you can use these names to simplify references to the data in your Table formulas. A formula using [@Quantity] is easier to understand than E2.

To create a Table formula using column specifiers instead of cell addresses, you can type in the column name preceded by @ and surrounded by square brackets, or you can use the mouse or keyboard to select the desired cell in the Table. To add a new calculated column to a Table, follow these steps:

1. Type a field header in row 1 of the column adjacent to the rightmost column of the Table. Excel extends any Table formatting to the new column.

2. Select the first data cell. This is cell H2 in Figure 18.8.

3. Enter your formula. Instead of typing in cell addresses, use the keyboard or mouse to select the cells. You will notice that column specifiers appear instead of cell addresses.

 NOTE If you select a cell in a different row than that of the formula cell, you see a cell address. Excel expects formulas in a Table to reference the same row or an entire column or Table.

4. Press Enter and Excel copies the formula down the column.

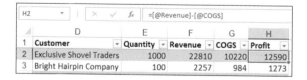

FIGURE 18.8

The use of specifiers in Table formulas makes it much easier to interpret what fields are used in the calculation.

After entering the formula, a lightning bolt drop-down appears by the cell. If you don't want the automated formula copied, select Undo Calculated Column or Stop Automatically Creating Calculated Columns.

In Figure 18.8, look at the formula in the formula bar. Notice the column specifiers are preceded by @. This is to specify that the formula is referring to the value of the specifier in that column. If the @ is dropped, then the formula would be referring to the entire column.

Converting Formulas to Values

Formulas take up a lot of memory, and the recalculation time can make working in a large workbook a hassle. At times, you need a formula only temporarily; you just want to calculate the value once and won't ever need to calculate it again. You could manually type the value over the formula cell, but if the result is a long number, or if you have a lot of calculation cells, this isn't convenient. You could copy the range and then use Paste Special, Values, but there's a faster option you can access from a special right-click menu. To access the menu and quickly convert formula to their values, follow these steps:

1. Select the range of formulas.

2. Place your cursor on the right edge of the dark border around the range so that it turns from the white plus sign to four black arrows, as if you were going to move the range to a new location.

3. While holding your right mouse button down, drag the range to the next column and then back to the original column.

 CAUTION Be very careful that you place the range exactly where it was originally. Excel allows you to use this method to place the range in a new location.

4. Let go of the right mouse button.

5. From the context menu that appears, shown in Figure 18.9, select Copy Here as Values Only.

	E	F	G	H
	Tax			
	$ 120.00			
	$ 60.00			
	$ 72.00	Move Here		
	$ 60.00	Copy Here		
	$ 36.00			
	$ 10.50	Copy Here as Values Only		
	$ 6.60	Copy Here as Formats Only		
	$ 96.00			
	$ 14.40	Link Here		
	$ 12.00			
	$ 12.00	Create Hyperlink Here		
	$ 4.50	Shift Down and Copy		
	$ 6.00			
	$ 4.50	Shift Right and Copy		
	$ 12.00	Shift Down and Move		
	$ 14.40			
	$ 12.00	Shift Right and Move		
	$ 7.20	Cancel		

FIGURE 18.9

By placing the cursor on the range's border, holding down the right mouse button and dragging to and fro, a hidden menu appears with various options to apply to the range.

Copying a Formula to Another Cell

You can use four ways to enter the same formula in multiple cells:

- Copy the entire cell and paste it to the new location.

- Enter the formula in the first cell and then use the fill handle to copy the formula.

- Preselect the entire range for the formula. Enter the formula in the first cell and press Ctrl+Enter to simultaneously enter the formula in the entire selection.

- Define the range as a Table. Excel automatically copies new formulas entered in a Table. See the section "Inserting Formulas into Tables" for more information.

Copying a Formula Using the Fill Handle

This method is useful if you need to copy your formula across a row or down a column. To copy a formula by dragging the fill handle, follow these steps:

1. Select the cell you want the formula to be in.

2. Type the formula in the first cell.

3. Press Ctrl+Enter to accept the formula and keep the cell as your active cell. If you press Enter instead, that's fine—just reselect the cell.

4. Click and hold the fill handle, which looks like a little black square in the lower-right corner of the selected cell. When the cursor is positioned correctly, it turns into a black cross, as shown in Figure 18.10.

5. Drag the fill handle to the last cell that needs to hold a copy of the formula.

6. Release the mouse button. The first cell is copied to all the cells in the selected range.

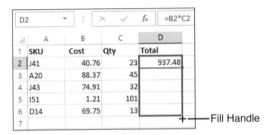

FIGURE 18.10

Clicking and dragging the fill handle is a quick way to copy a formula a short distance.

Copying a Formula by Using Ctrl+Enter

If you have a large range to copy a formula into, and the range isn't a single column or single row, using Ctrl+Enter might be useful. This method copies the formula into the columns and/or rows of the selection, such as a rectangle or even a selection of noncontiguous cells. To copy a formula using Ctrl+Enter, follow these steps:

1. Select the range, or noncontiguous cells, you want the formula to be in.

2. Type the formula in the first cell, ensuring your cell referencing is correct.

3. Press Ctrl+Enter. Excel copies the formula to all cells in the selected range.

Copying Formulas Rapidly Down a Column

If you need to copy a formula into just a few rows, using the fill handle is fine. But if you have several hundred rows to update, you could zoom right past the last row. And if you have thousands of rows, using the fill handle can take quite some time.

One solution is to copy the formula, select the range, and paste the formula into the range. But it can still be a bit tricky to select the entire range you need to paste to.

If you have a data set without any completely blank rows, you can double-click the fill handle and have it quickly fill the formula down the column to the last row of the data set.

To quickly fill the formula down the column to the last row of the data set, follow these steps:

1. Enter your formula in the first cell of the column.

2. Verify that your data set is contiguous without any blank rows or columns. To do this, select the cell from step 1 and press Ctrl+A. Excel selects all the cells of the data set until it runs into a blank row and column. If you see any blank columns or rows interfering with the desired selection, add some temporary text and then try the selection again.

3. After you've verified that the data set is contiguous, place your cursor on the fill handle until it turns into a black plus sign, as shown in Figure 18.10.

4. Double-click and the formula is copied down the sheet until it reaches the end of the data set (a fully blank row).

 TIP If you don't see the fill handle, it's possible you have the option turned off. On the File tab, select Options, go to the Advanced tab of the Excel Options dialog box, and ensure the Enable Fill Handle and Cell Drag-and-Drop check box is selected.

THE ABSOLUTE MINIMUM

Here are the key points to remember from this chapter:

- Although Excel is a great tool for organizing data, creating formulas is where the real power within the program starts.

- Excel offers three ways to enter a formula's cell reference: typing, using the mouse, or using the arrow keys.

- Copying a formula to another cell is a great time-saving technique, particularly if you have a lot of calculations to make.

- Excel offers several tools to help you resolve formula problems.

19

USING FUNCTIONS

A function is like a shortcut for using a long or complex formula. If you've ever summed cells by adding them individually (as in =A1+A2+A3+A4+A5), you could have instead used a SUM function like this: =SUM(A1:A5). Excel offers more than 400 functions. These include logical functions, lookup functions, statistical functions, financial functions, and more.

This chapter shows you how to look up functions available in Excel and reviews some functions helpful for everyday use.

TIP Only a handful of Excel's functions are reviewed here. For a more in-depth review of functions and possible scenarios you'd use them in, see *Excel 2013 In Depth*, by Bill Jelen (Que Publishing, ISBN 978-0-7897-4857-7).

Understanding Functions

Before you get started using functions, take a few minutes to learn how Excel uses these important calculation tools.

Exploring a Function

A function consists of the name used to call it and might or might not include arguments, which are variables used in the calculation. In the formula =SUM(A1:A5), SUM is the function and A1:A5 is the argument.

Normally, the syntax of a function is like this:

FunctionName(Argument1, Argument2, ...)

But there are some functions that have no arguments or the argument is optional. There are a few rules to keep in mind when using functions:

- Arguments must be entered in the order required by the function.
- Arguments must be separated by commas.
- Arguments can be cell references, numbers, logicals, or text.
- Some arguments are optional. Optional arguments are placed after the required ones.
- If you skip an optional argument to use one after it, you still have to place a comma for the one you skipped.
- Some functions, such as NOW(), do not require arguments, but the parentheses must still be included in the formula.

Finding Functions

You can always search Excel's Help to find a function, but you might get more than just the function information you're looking for. Instead, narrow down the results by using tools provided specifically for searching functions.

The Formulas tab has a Function Library group with drop-downs grouped by function type. Selecting any function listed in a drop-down opens it up in the Formula Wizard.

If you aren't sure which function you need, or if you need more help in using a function, there are several ways to open the Insert Function dialog box, which helps you find the required function:

- On the Home tab or Formulas tab, click the arrow below the AutoSum button and select More Functions from the menu.

- On the Formulas tab, click another button in the Function Library group and select Insert Function from the menu.

- On the Formulas tab, click the Insert Function button in the Function Library group.

- Click the fx button by the formula bar.

When you click Insert Function, the dialog box shown in Figure 19.1 opens. You can enter a search term in the Search for a Function field or select a category from the drop-down. Results appear in the list box. When you select a function from the list box, the arguments and a brief description of the function appear. When you find the function you want to use, highlight it and click OK. The function appears in the active cell and the Function Arguments dialog box opens, ready to help you fill in the rest of the arguments.

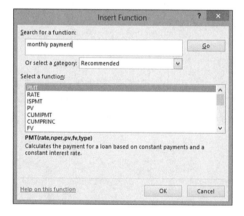

FIGURE 19.1

The Insert Function dialog box helps search through Excel's more than 400 available functions.

Entering Functions Using the Function Arguments Dialog Box

After you enter a function in a cell, the Function Arguments dialog box shown in Figure 19.2 opens. It enables you to enter the arguments for the selected function. Other than beginning with the Insert Function dialog box as explained in the previous section, you can also open the Function Arguments dialog box by selecting a cell with a function already in it and using any of the methods listed in the "Finding Functions" section.

A field exists for each argument. If the function has a variable number of arguments, like the SUM function, a new field is automatically added when needed. The following list identifies the parts of the Function Arguments dialog box shown in Figure 19.2:

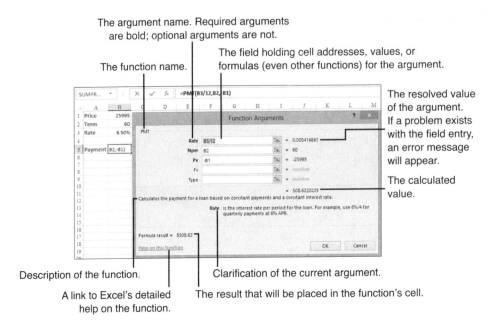

FIGURE 19.2

The Function Arguments dialog box helps with the arguments of the selected function.

Figure 19.2 shows the PMT function being using to calculate the monthly payment for a loan. The loan amount is in cell B1, the number of months in cell B2, the APR in cell B3. The function is in cell B5. To insert the function and select its arguments, follow these steps:

1. Select the cell that holds the formula (cell B5).

2. On the Formulas tab, click the Insert Function button. In the Search field, type PMT and click Go.

3. PMT displays in the list of functions. Highlight it and click OK. The Function Arguments dialog box opens. If the dialog box is covering the values on the sheet (B1:B3), then click the title of the dialog box and drag it out of the way.

4. The first argument is Rate, the interest rate. When you click in the field and look at the description, notice it says this is the interest rate per period. Because your value is the annual rate, you need to divide it by 12. But first, you need to select

it on the sheet. Click cell B3 and the cell address appears in the Rate field with the cursor blinking at the end of it. Enter /12 to get the monthly rate.

5. The second argument is the Nper, number of payments for the loan. First click the field in the dialog box and then select cell B2 on the sheet.

6. Click in the Pv field (present value of the loan) in the dialog box. Before selecting the cell on the sheet, enter a - (a minus sign) so that when you do click the cell on the sheet, you are making the value negative. You do this because of the way the function works. If you didn't make this value negative, the payment itself would be negative.

7. Fv (future value after the last payment is made) and Type (–1 when the payment is made at the beginning of the period, 0 when it's made at the end of the period) are both optional arguments and can be left blank.

8. If you do not see any error messages in the calculated value in the dialog box, click OK to have the cell accept the formula.

Entering Functions Using In-Cell Tips

If you are already familiar with the function you need, you can begin typing it in the cell or formula bar directly. After you enter an equal sign and select the first letter of the function, Excel drops down a list of possible functions, narrowing the list with each letter entered. You can also select from the list using the arrow and Tab keys.

After you select the function, an in-cell tip appears, as shown in Figure 19.3. The current argument is bold. Optional arguments appear in square brackets. If you want to use the Function Arguments dialog box, press Ctrl+A after typing the function name in the cell. For more help with the function, click the function name in the tip, and Excel's detailed Help file for the function appears.

FIGURE 19.3

If you're already familiar with the function, you can use the in-cell help to guide you in filling out the arguments.

TIP If the in-cell help is in the way, place your cursor on the tip until it turns into a four-headed arrow and then click and drag it out of your way.

To type a function, such as SUM, directly into a cell, follow these steps:

1. Select the cell where you want to place the formula.

2. Type an equal sign.

3. Begin typing the name of the function. When the drop-down list appears, you can continue typing or scroll the list to highlight the function and press Tab.

4. Enter the first argument. The argument can be a cell address (you can type it or select it on the sheet), a value, or a formula.

5. If there is another argument, type a comma and then enter the next argument. Repeat this step for each argument. As you enter each argument, notice that the argument becomes bold in the in-cell tip, showing you your position in the function.

6. When you're finished entering all the arguments, type the closing parenthesis and press Enter or Tab for the cell to accept the formula.

TIP You don't always have to enter the closing parenthesis; sometimes Excel does it for you. But because the location and need is a guess by Excel, it's best to be in the habit of doing it yourself.

Using the AutoSum Button

Excel provides one-click access to the SUM function through the AutoSum button on the Home tab. You can apply the AutoSum function to a range of cells in a variety of ways:

- Select a cell adjacent to the range and click the AutoSum button.

- Highlight the range including the adjacent cell where you want the formula placed, and then click the AutoSum button.

- If you need to sum multiple ranges, select the entire table, including the adjacent row or column where you want results to appear, and then click the AutoSum button.

Unless you select the range you want to calculate, Excel guesses which cells you are trying to sum and highlights them. If the selection is correct, press Enter to accept the solution. If the selection is incorrect, make the required changes and then press Enter to accept the solution.

 TIP   If you can catch Excel's incorrect selection before you accept the formula, the range Excel wants to use should still be highlighted. If it is, then you can select your desired range right away. If the selection is not highlighted, you have to highlight it first.

You should keep an eye out for a couple of things when using the AutoSum function:

- Be careful of numeric headings (such as years) when letting Excel select the range for you. Excel cannot tell that the heading isn't part of the calculation range, and you need to correct the selection before accepting the formula.

- Excel looks for a column to sum before summing a row. In Figure 19.4, the default selection by Excel is the numbers above the selected cell, instead of the adjacent row of numbers.

	Q1	Q2	Q3	Q4	Total	
East	2396	3239	4765	2181	12581	
Central	4338	2008	2558	2959	11863	
West	3026	4174	4956	1613	=SUM(F9:F10)	
Total					SUM(number1, [number2], ...)	

FIGURE 19.4

Excel defaults to calculating columns before rows. Instead of summing the West data, Excel selects the totals from East and Central instead.

SUM Rows and Columns at the Same Time

You can SUM multiple ranges at the same time, including rows and columns. In Figure 19.5, the totals in column F and row 6 were calculated at the same time. This was done by selecting the entire table, including the Total row and column, before clicking the AutoSum button. You could also have a single row and column selection, for example, just Q1 (column B) and East (row 3) data. To do so, follow these steps:

1. Select B3:B6.

2. While holding down the Ctrl key, select B3:F3.

3. Click the AutoSum button.

4. Excel calculates and inserts the corresponding totals in the total cells.

	Q1	Q2	Q3	Q4	Total
East	2396	3239	4765	2181	12581
Central	4338	2008	2558	2959	11863
West	3026	4174	4956	1613	13769
Total	9760	9421	12279	6753	38213

FIGURE 19.5

Excel is smart enough to determine that you want to sum each individual row and column.

Other Auto Functions

The default action of the AutoSum button is the SUM function, but several other functions are available. To access these other functions, click the drop-down arrow:

- **Sum**—Adds the values in the selected range (the default action)
- **Average**—Averages the values in the selected range
- **Count Numbers**—Returns the number of cells containing numbers
- **Max**—Returns the largest value in the selected range
- **Min**—Returns the smallest value in the selected range

These other options work on a range in the same way as the SUM function, but you have to select them from the drop-down, whereas with SUM, you can just click the button.

Using the Status Bar for Quick Calculation Results

If you just need to see the results of a calculation and not include the information on a sheet, Excel offers six quick calculations, listed in Figure 19.6, that appear in the status bar when the data is selected.

 CAUTION Changes to the status bar affect the application, not just the active workbook or sheet.

To see the list of functions and be able to edit the values shown in the status bar, you must first select some data on a sheet. Next, right-click the status bar and the Customize Status Bar menu, shown in Figure 19.6, appears. You can toggle the check mark next to the functions you want to show or hide in the status bar. After you select the functions you want, whenever you select data, the resulting calculations appear in the status bar.

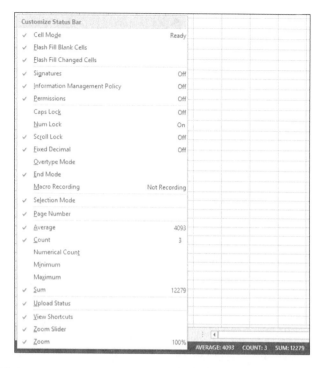

FIGURE 19.6

You can modify the status bar to show the results of calculations done to selected data.

  TIP Use the status bar to quickly verify all numbers in a range are indeed numbers. Select the range and if the resulting sum isn't correct, then at least one cell holds a number as text.

Using Quick Analysis for Column Totals

When you select multiple adjacent cells, the Quick Analysis icon, shown in Figure 19.7, appears in the lower-right corner of the selection. Click the icon, select TOTALS and various quick calculations appear. You can use the arrows on the left and right side of the icons to scroll through the list. After you find the calculation you want, click it. Excel places the calculated values at the bottom of each column in your range.

  TIP This tool does not calculate across the row. If you try, it overwrites any information in the row beneath your selection.

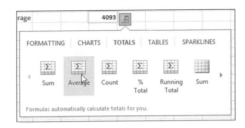

FIGURE 19.7

You can use the Quick Analysis tool to calculate a column, but not a row.

THE ABSOLUTE MINIMUM

Here are the key points to remember from this chapter:

- A function consists of the name used to call it and might or might not include arguments, which are variables used in the calculation. In the formula =SUM(A1:A5), SUM is the function and A1:A5 is the argument.

- The Function Arguments dialog box, which opens after you enter a function in a cell, assists in entering the arguments for the selected function.

- If you are already familiar with the function you need, you can begin typing it in the cell or formula bar directly.

- Excel provides one-click access to the SUM function through the AutoSum button on the Home tab.

20

SORTING DATA

This chapter shows you the various ways you can sort your data, even by color. Sorting data is a significant capability in Excel, enabling you to view data from least to greatest, greatest to least, by color, or even by your own customized sort listing.

Sorting Excel Data

Excel lets you sort your cell data in a variety of ways: by value, cell color, font color, or conditional formatting.

Preparing Data

Your data should adhere to a few basic formatting guidelines to make the most of Excel's sorting capabilities:

- There should be no blank rows or columns. The occasional blank cell is acceptable.
- Every column should have a header.
- Headers should be in only one row.

If these guidelines aren't followed, Excel can get confused and is unable to find the entire table or header row on its own. Also, Excel can only work with one header row—any rows after the first header row get treated like data.

Opening the Sort Dialog Box

The Sort dialog box allows up to 64 sort levels. Through the dialog box, you can sort multiple columns by values, cell color, font color, or by conditional formatting cell icons. The sort order can be ascending, descending, or by a custom list. If your data has headers, they are listed in the Sort By drop-down list; otherwise, the column headings (A, B, C, and so on) are used.

There are four ways to access the Sort dialog box:

- On the Home tab, select Custom Sort from the Sort & Filter drop-down list.
- On the Data tab, select Sort from the Sort & Filter drop-down list.
- Right-click any cell and select Sort, Custom Sort.
- From a filter or Table drop-down list, select Sort by Color, Custom Sort.

Sorting by Values

When you use the Sort dialog box, Excel applies each sort in the order it appears in the list. In Figure 20.1, the Region column is sorted first. The Customer column is sorted second, as outlined in the following steps:

1. Ensure that the data has no blank rows or columns and that each column has a one-row header.

2. Select a cell in the data. Excel uses this cell to determine the location and size of the data table.

3. On the Home tab, select Custom Sort from the Sort & Filter drop-down list to open the Sort dialog box.

4. Make sure the My Data Has Headers check box is selected. Excel does not select the headers themselves, only the data.

5. Make sure all the data's columns and rows are selected. If they are not all selected, a blank column or row exists, confusing Excel as to the size of your table. Exit from the Sort dialog box, delete the blank columns and rows, and start the process again.

 NOTE If for some reason you can't delete the blank columns or rows, then preselect the entire table before opening the Sort dialog box.

6. From the Sort By drop-down list, select the first column header, Region, to sort by.

7. From the Sort On drop-down list, select Values.

8. From the Order drop-down list, select the order by which the column's data should be sorted, A to Z.

9. To add another sort column, this time for Customer, click Add Level and repeat steps 6 to 8. Repeat these steps until all the columns to sort by are configured, as shown in Figure 20.1.

10. If you realize that a field is in the wrong position, use the up or down arrows at the top of the dialog box to move the field to the correct location.

11. Click OK to sort the data.

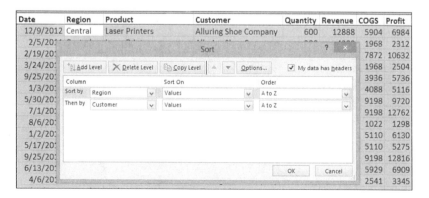

FIGURE 20.1

Use the Sort dialog box to sort data by multiple levels.

When you look at the data after it is sorted, notice the regions are grouped together; for example, Central is at the top of the list. Within Central, the customer names are alphabetized. If you scroll down to the next region, East, the customer names are alphabetized within that region. If the data should have listed the customers and then the regions, the two sort fields need to be switched so that Excel sorts the Customer field first and the Region field second.

Sorting by Color or Icon

Although sorting by values is the most typical use of sorting, Excel can also sort data by fill color, font color, or an icon set from conditional formatting. You can apply fill and font colors through conditional formatting or the cell format icons.

In addition to sorting colors and icons through the Sort dialog box, the following options are also available when you right-click a cell and select Sort from the context menu:

- Put Selected Cell Color on Top
- Put Selected Font Color on Top
- Put Selected Cell Icon on Top

If you use one of the preceding options to sort more than one color or icon, the most recent selection is placed above the previous selection. So, if yellow rows should be placed before the red rows, sort the red rows first, and then sort the yellow rows.

In Figure 20.2, conditional formatting was used to highlight in red the top 10 profit record and yellow was used to highlight the ones in the bottom 10%.

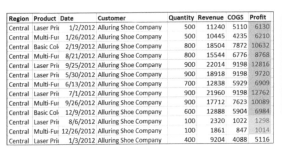

FIGURE 20.2

You can use the Sort dialog box to sort cells by more than just their values, such as the cell color.

The data was then sorted using the following steps so that the red cells are at the top and the yellow directly beneath:

1. Ensure that the data has no blank rows or columns and that each column has a one-row header.

2. Select a cell in the data. Excel uses this cell to determine the location and size of the data and highlights what it sees as the data table.

3. Right-click the cell and select Sort, Custom Sort.

4. Make sure the My Data Has Headers check box in the upper-right corner is selected. Excel does not select the headers themselves.

5. Make sure all the data's columns are selected. If they are not all selected, a blank column exists, confusing Excel as to the size of your table.

6. From the Sort By drop-down list, select the first column header to sort by, Profit.

7. From the Sort On drop-down list, select Cell Color.

8. From the first Order drop-down list, select the color by which the column's data should be sorted.

9. From the second Order drop-down list, select whether the color should be sorted to the top or bottom of the data. If you select multiple colors to sort at the top of the data, the colors still appear in the order chosen.

10. Click Add Level to include the yellow Profit cells in the sort and repeat steps 6 to 9. Repeat these steps until all the columns to sort by are configured.

11. If you realize a field is in the wrong order, use the up or down arrows to move it to the correct location.

12. Click OK to sort the data.

 TIP If your data is formatted as a Table (Insert, Tables, Table), you don't have to go through the Custom Sort dialog box. Instead, click the arrow in the header, go to Sort by Color and select the color you want sorted to the top of the table.

Performing a Quick Sort

If your sorting needs are simple, you can perform a quick sort on one or more columns.

Using the Quick Sort Buttons

CAUTION Sort options are retained for a sheet during a session. So if you set up a custom sort with the Case Sensitive option turned on and then do a quick sort, the quick sort is case sensitive.

The quick sort buttons offer one-click access to sorting cell values. They do not work with colors or icons. There are four ways to get to the quick sort buttons:

- On the Home tab, select Sort A to Z or Sort Z to A from the Sort & Filter drop-down list.
- On the Data tab, select AZ or ZA from the Sort & Filter drop-down list.
- Right-click any cell and select Sort, Sort A to Z, or Sort Z to A.
- From a filter drop-down list, select Sort A to Z or Sort Z to A.

The quick sort buttons are very useful when sorting a single column. When sorting just one column, make sure you select just one cell in the column. If you select more than one cell, Excel sorts the selection, not the column. It prompts to verify that this is the action you want taken before doing it. Also ensure there are no adjacent columns or Excel will want to include them in the sort. If there are adjacent columns, select the entire column before sorting.

If you use the quick sort buttons to sort a table of more than one column, Excel sorts the entire table automatically. Because there is no dialog box, it's very important that every column have a header. If just one header is missing, Excel does not treat the header row as such and includes it in the sorted data.

TIP If you have filters turned on for the table, Excel automatically treats the row where the filter arrows are as the header row.

CAUTION The actual button text might change depending on the type of data in the cell. For example, if the column contains values, the text is Sort Smallest to Largest. If the column contains text, it is Sort A to Z.

Quick Sorting Multiple Columns

If you keep in mind that Excel keeps previously organized columns in order as new columns are sorted, you can use this to sort multiple columns. For example, if the Customer column is organized, Excel doesn't randomize the data in that column when the Region column is sorted. Instead, Customer retains its order to the degree it falls within the Region sort. The trick is to apply the sorts in reverse to how they would be set up in the Sort dialog box.

To manually perform the "Sort by Values" example shown in Figure 20.2, follow these steps:

1. Make sure all columns have headers. If even one column header is missing, Excel does not sort the data properly.

2. Select a cell in the column that should be sorted last, the Customer column.

3. Click the desired quick sort button in the Sort & Filter group on the Data tab.

4. Select a cell in the next column, Region, to be sorted.

5. Click the desired quick sort button in the Sort & Filter group on the Data tab.

6. The table is now sorted by Region and then Customers within each region.

Fixing Sort Problems

If it looks like the data did not sort properly, refer to the following list of possibilities:

- Make sure no hidden rows or columns exist.

- Use a single row for headers. If you need a multiline header, either wrap the text in the cell or use Alt+Enter to force line breaks in the cell.

- If the headers were sorted into the data, there was probably at least one column without a header.

- Column data should be of the same type. This might not be obvious in a column of ZIP Codes where some, such as 57057 are numbers, but others that start with 0 are actually text. To solve this problem, convert the entire column to text.

- If sorting by a column containing a formula, Excel recalculates the column after the sort. If the values change after the recalculation, such as with RAND, it might appear that the sort did not work properly, but it did.

THE ABSOLUTE MINIMUM

Here are the key points to remember from this chapter:

- Excel lets you sort your cell data in a variety of ways: by value, cell color, font color, or conditional formatting.

- Quick sort is a useful option if your sorting needs are simple.

- Excel provides several ways to fix sort problems.

FILTERING AND CONSOLIDATING DATA

This chapter shows you how to use Excel's filtering functionality to look at just the desired records. It also shows you how to create a list of unique items, delete duplicates, and consolidate data.

Filtering and consolidating data are important tools in Excel, especially when you are dealing with large amounts of data. The filtering tools can quickly reduce the data to the specific records you need to concentrate on. The consolidation tool can bring together information spread between multiple sheets or workbooks.

Filtering Data

To make the most out of Excel's filtering capabilities, your data should adhere to a few basic formatting guidelines:

- There should be no blank rows or columns. The occasional blank cell is acceptable.

- There should be a header above every column.

- Headers should be in only one row.

If you don't follow these guidelines, Excel can get confused and is unable to find the entire table or header row on its own. Also, Excel can only work with one header row—any rows after the first header row get treated like data.

Applying a Filter to a Data Set

Filtering enables you to view only the data you want to see by hiding the other data. You can apply a filter to multiple columns, narrowing the data. As you filter the data and rows are hidden, the row headers (1, 2, 3, and so on) become blue. Anytime you see blue row headers, you know the data has been filtered. An icon that looks like a funnel replaces the arrow on the column headings that have a filter applied, as shown in the Customer heading in Figure 21.1.

Region	Product	Date	Customer	Quantit
Central	Laser Printers	1/2/2012	Bright Hairpin Company	100
Central	Laser Printers	9/9/2012	Bright Hairpin Company	700
Central	Laser Printers	11/23/2012	Bright Hairpin Company	300
Central	Laser Printers	5/19/2011	Bright Hairpin Company	700
Central	Laser Printers	7/29/2011	Bright Hairpin Company	300
East	Laser Printers	6/30/2011	Bright Hairpin Company	100
East	Laser Printers	7/22/2011	Bright Hairpin Company	300
East	Laser Printers	12/12/2011	Bright Hairpin Company	500

FIGURE 21.1

You can tell which column(s) are filtered by the filter icon where the drop-down arrow used to be.

The Filter button is a toggle button. Click it once to turn filtering on and click it again to turn filtering off. To activate the filtering option, select a single cell in the data set and use one of the following:

- On the Home tab, click the Sort & Filter button and select Filter.

- On the Data tab, click the Filter button.

NOTE When a data set is turned into a Table, the headers automatically become filter headers.

CAUTION It is very important to select only a single cell because it is possible to turn on filtering in the middle of a data set if you have more than one cell selected.

When a filter is applied to a data set, drop-down arrows appear in the column headers. Click an arrow to open up the Filter dialog box, which remains open until you click OK, Cancel, or outside the dialog box. One or more selections can be made from each drop-down, filtering the data below the headers. Filters are additive, which means that each time a filter selection is made, it works with the previous selection to further filter the data.

TIP If you have a long list of items or need to widen the dialog box to see the full text of a line, place your cursor over the three dots in the lower-right corner of the dialog box, and click and drag to resize. The change in size will not be saved—you need to do it again next time you open the dialog box.

Managing Filters

After applying a filter, you can modify, reapply, or clear it in a variety of ways.

Turning Filtering On for One Column

You can turn on filtering for a single column or for two or more adjacent columns. Even though you can only select a filter item in select columns, the filter is applied to the entire table. This can be useful if you want to limit the filtering users can apply. If the sheet is then protected, users cannot turn on filtering for the other columns. (See "Allowing Filtering on a Protected Sheet" for more information.)

To control what column has filtering, select the header and the first cell directly beneath the header. Then do one of the following:

- On the Home tab, click the Sort & Filter button and select Filter.
- On the Data tab, click the Filter button.

Filtering for Listed Items

The filter listing, shown in Figure 21.2, is probably the most obvious filter tool when you open the drop-down. For text, numbers, and ungrouped dates, a listing of all unique items in the column appears. (See the "Filtering the Grouped Dates Listing" section if dates appear grouped by year and month.) All items will be checked because they are all visible the first time you open the drop-down, but you can select just the items that should appear in the data. Any item that no longer bears a check mark will be hidden.

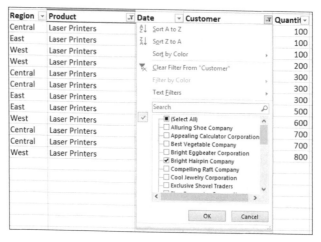

FIGURE 21.2

Filter a column by selecting the item(s) you want to see from the dialog box.

We have a table of the sales of various printers in 2011 and 2012. We want to narrow the table down to Laser Printers sold to Bright Hairpin Company. To filter columns for specific items, follow these steps (if filtering a Table [Insert, Tables, Table], skip to step 3):

1. Select a single cell in the data set to apply filtering to.

2. On the Data tab, click the Filter button.

3. Open the drop-down of the Product column.

4. Unselect the Select All item to clear all the check marks in the list.

5. Select Laser Printers and click OK. Now only Laser Printers are shown in the table.

6. Repeat steps 3–5 for the Customer column and Bright Hairpin Company.

7. Click OK. The sheet updates, showing only the items selected.

Filtering the Grouped Dates Listing

NOTE This section applies to dates that are grouped, as shown in Figure 21.3. The grouping is controlled by the Group Dates in the AutoFilter Menu check box on the Advanced tab of the Excel Options dialog box. (Select File, Options to open this dialog box.) By default, this option is selected. If unselected, the dates appear in a list like the filter for number and text items. You can refer to the section "Filtering for Listed Items" for more information on that type of filter listing.

Dates in the filter listing are grouped by year, month, and day. All items are checked because they are all visible the first time you open the drop-down, but you can select just the items that should appear in the data. Any item that no longer bears a check mark will be hidden.

If you click the + icon by a year, it opens up, showing the months. Click the + icon by a month, and that month opens to show the days of the month. An entire year or month can be selected or unselected by clicking the desired year or month. For example, to deselect 2011 and January 2012 in Figure 21.3, deselect the 2011 group, and then deselect the January group under 2012. The data filters to show only February through December 2012.

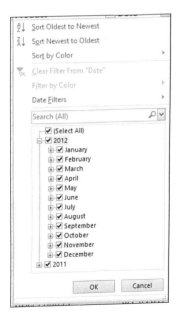

FIGURE 21.3

By default, dates are grouped by year and month in the Filter dialog box.

To filter for only June 12–14, 2012, follow these steps (if filtering an existing Table, skip to step 3):

1. Select a single cell in the data set to apply filtering to.

2. On the Data tab, click the Filter button. Click OK to continue.

3. Open the drop-down of the Date column to filter.

4. Deselect the Select All item to clear all the check marks in the list.

5. Click the + icon to the left of 2012.

6. Click the + icon to the left of June.

7. Select 12, 13, and 14.

8. Click OK. The sheet updates, showing only the dates selected.

Using Text, Number, and Date Special Filters

With careful planning or additional columns, you can filter for all types of reports such as top 10, quarterly reports, and ranges of values. But not all filtering is easy or quick. The filter listing has options to make it easier. Special filters are available in the filter drop-down depending on which data type (text, numbers, or dates) appears most often in a column. All the special filters, except for ones that take action immediately, open the Custom AutoFilter dialog box, allowing two conditions to be combined using AND or OR.

If the column contains mostly text, Text Filters is available from the filtering listing. Choosing Text Filters opens a list with the following options: Equals, Does Not Equal, Begins With, Ends With, Contains, and Does Not Contain. Selecting one of these options opens a Custom AutoFilter dialog box, in which you can enter text to filter by.

 TIP When entering the text you want to filter by, you can use wildcards. Use an asterisk (*) to replace multiple characters or a question mark (?) to replace a single character.

If the column contains mostly numbers, Number Filters is available with the following options: Equals, Does Not Equal, Greater Than, Greater Than or Equal To, Less Than, Less Than or Equal To, Between Top 10, Above Average, and Below Average. Selecting Top 10, Above Average, or Below Average automatically updates the filter to reflect the selection.

If Top 10 is selected, you can specify the top or bottom items or percent to view. For example, you could choose to view the bottom 15% or the top seven items.

For columns with dates, the special filter, Date Filters, offers a wide selection of options, including additional options under All Dates in the Period. The options dealing with quarters refer to the traditional quarter of a year, January through March being the first quarter, April through June being the second quarter, and so on. When using the Custom AutoFilter option, the dialog box for dates includes calendars to aid in data entry.

To create the bottom 25% report for the previous quarter shown in Figure 21.4, follow these steps:

1. Open the drop-down of the Date column.

2. Select Date Filters, All Dates in the Period, Quarter 2. The data automatically filters to the 2nd quarter, April–June.

3. Open the drop-down of the numeric column, Quantity, to filter.

4. Select Number Filters, Top 10. The Top 10 AutoFilter appears.

5. Select Bottom from the leftmost drop-down.

6. Enter 25 in the middle field.

7. Select Percent from the rightmost drop-down.

8. Click OK; the table filters show the bottom 25%.

FIGURE 21.4

The special filters make it easier to create quarterly reports reflecting records that fall within specific parameters.

Filtering by Color or Icon

Data can be filtered by font color, color (set by cell fill or conditional formatting), or icon by going to the Filter by Color option in the filter listing. There, colors and/or icons used in the column are listed, as shown in Figure 21.5.

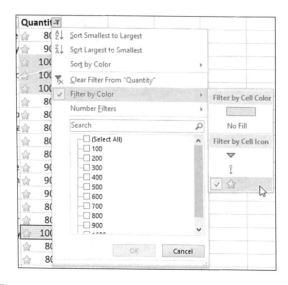

FIGURE 21.5

You can filter by the colors and icons in the table.

The data table in Figure 21.5 uses conditional formatting icons to denote which record quantities are below average (arrow), average (exclamation mark), or above average (star). Also, quantities greater than or equal to 1,000 have a green cell fill. To filter to show only the above average items, open the drop-down filter for the Quantity column. Select Filter by Color and then from the icons listed, select the star. The list automatically updates to show only the star records.

NOTE Refer to the section "Applying Conditional Formatting" in Chapter 17, "Formatting Sheets and Cells," for steps on how to apply your own custom icon formatting.

Filtering by Selection

Even without the filter turned on, you can right-click any cell in a column, go to Filter, and choose to filter by the cell's value, color, font color, or icon. Doing so turns on the AutoFilter and configures the filter for the selected cell's property.

This filtering is additive. If you filter a cell by one value and then go to a cell in another column and filter by its value, the result is those rows that satisfy both filter criteria. You cannot filter by a property more than once within the same column, but you can filter a column by multiple properties—for example, filter by icon and then value.

To use filter selection to filter records meeting a specific value and icon, such as the below average East records in Figure 21.6, follow these steps:

1. Right-click a cell in the Region column containing the value (East) to filter by.

2. Select Filter, Filter by Selected Cell's Value. The AutoFilter drop-downs appear in the column header and the table updates to show only East records.

3. Right-click a cell in the Quantity column containing the icon (a down arrow) to filter by.

4. Select Filter, Filter by Selected Cell's Icon. The table now shows all below average records from the East region.

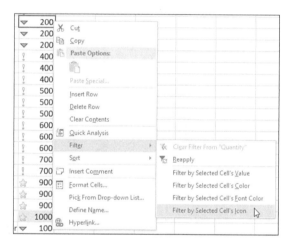

FIGURE 21.6

Right-clicking a specific cell enables you to quickly filter by that cell's value, cell color, font color, or icon.

Allowing Filtering on a Protected Sheet

Normally, if you set up filters on a sheet, protect the sheet, and then send it out to other users, the recipients won't be able to filter the data. If you want others to be able to filter your protected sheet, follow these steps:

1. Select a single cell in the data set to apply filtering to.

2. On the Home tab, click the Sort & Filter button and select Filter from the menu. The filter is turned on for the data set.

3. On the Review tab, click the Protect Sheet button.

4. In the listing for Allow All Users of This Worksheet To, scroll down and select Use AutoFilter.

5. Optionally, enter a password in the Password to Unprotect Sheet field if you want to apply a password to the sheet.

6. Click OK.

7. If you entered a password in step 5, Excel prompts you to reenter the password. Do so and click OK.

Users won't be able to modify the data you've protected, but they can use Excel's various AutoFilter tools to filter the data as needed.

 NOTE For more information on protecting your data, see "Protecting the Data on a Sheet" in Chapter 22, "Preparing Workbooks for Distribution and Printing."

Clearing a Filter

You can clear a filter from a specific column or for the entire data set. To clear all the filters applied to a data set, use one of the following methods:

- On the Home tab, click the Sort & Filter button and select Clear.
- On the Data tab, click the Clear button.
- Turn off the filter entirely using one of the following methods:
  - On the Home tab, click the Sort & Filter button and select Filter.
  - On the Data tab, click the Filter button.

To clear all the filters applied to a specific column, use one of the following methods:

- Click the filter drop-down arrow and select Clear Filter from Column Header.
- Click the filter drop-down arrow and select Select All from the filtering list.
- Right-click a cell in the column to clear and select Filter, Clear Filter from Column Header.

Reapplying a Filter

If data is added to a filtered range, Excel does not automatically update the view to hide any new rows that don't fit the filter settings. You can refresh the filter's settings so they include the new rows through one of the following methods:

- On the Home tab, click the Sort & Filter button and select Reapply.
- On the Data tab, click the Reapply button.
- Right-click a cell in the filtered data set and select Filter, Reapply.

Removing Duplicates from a Data Set

You've received a report where a user duplicated data by importing twice. You could try sorting the data and creating a formula in another column that compares rows, but with more than 700,000 rows, it could take a while for the formula to calculate, and you aren't even sure if the process is foolproof. Instead, use the Remove Duplicates option to ensure the process. You can remove duplicates by clicking the Remove Duplicates button on the Data tab. If the data set is a Table, click the Remove Duplicates button on the Table Tools – Design tab.

 CAUTION The tool permanently deletes data from a table based on the selected columns in the Remove Duplicates dialog box. Unlike other filters, it does not just hide the rows. Because of this, you might want to copy the data before deleting the duplicates.

To remove duplicates based on the Region, Product, Date, and Customer, follow these steps:

1. Select a cell in the data set.

2. On the Data tab, click the Remove Duplicates button.

3. Excel highlights the data set. If columns are missing in the selection, go back and make sure there are no blank separating columns.

4. From the Remove Duplicates dialog box, make sure My Data Has Headers is selected if the data set has headers.

5. By default, all the columns are selected. A selected column means the tool uses the columns when looking for duplicates. Duplicates in an unselected column are ignored. In the Columns list box, select the columns to use in the search for duplicates, as shown in Figure 21.7.

6. Click OK. The data set updates, deleting any duplicate rows. A message box appears informing you of the number of rows deleted and the number remaining in the data set.

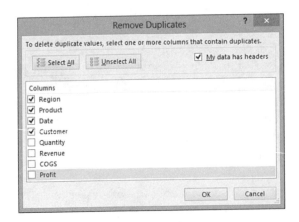

FIGURE 21.7

Remove Duplicates enables you to specify which columns you want to use to verify duplicate records.

Consolidating Data

The Remove Duplicates tool is great for completely removing duplicates, but what if you wanted to remove duplicates based on some fields and, at the same time, combine the data of other fields? For example, you have a sheet with 2011 data and a sheet with 2012 data. You need to create a quantity sold report combining the data based on the company name but separating the different years. You could create a pivot table or use the Consolidate tool. The Consolidate tool, found under Data Tools on the Data tab, helps you create a report of unique records with combined data. It even combines data from different sheets and workbooks. You can do this in one of three ways:

- **By Position**—Sum data found on different sheets or in different workbooks based on their positions in the data sets. For example, if the ranges are A1:A10 and C220:C230, the results are A1+C220, A2+C221, A3+C222, and so on. Do not select either of the options under Use Labels In.

- **By Category**—Sum data found on different sheets or in different workbooks based on matching row and column labels, similar to a pivot table report. The references must include the labels in the leftmost column of the ranges. Select either or both of the options under Use Labels In to have the labels appear in the final data.

- **By Column**—Combine the data to a new sheet, with each data set in its own column. Select the Top Row option under Use Labels In.

The Reference field is where the data sets are entered. Click Add to add the selection to the All References list. If the data set is in a closed workbook, you can reference it only by using a range name. Click the Browse button to find and select the workbook. After the exclamation point (!) at the end of the path, enter the range name assigned to the data set.

 NOTE See "Using Names to Simplify References" in Chapter 18, "Using Formulas," for details on how to create a range name.

If Create Links to Source Data is selected, the consolidated data updates automatically when the source is changed. Also, the consolidated data is grouped, as shown in Figure 21.8. Click the + icon to the left of the data to open the group and see the data used in the summary. Column B of the report shows the name of the workbook in the first instance of its data.

	A	B	C	D
1			Quantity	Revenue
1118		Remarkable Notebook Suppl	6000	125488
1119		2012 Sales	200	4158
1120			200	4158
1121			600	13962
1122			600	13962
1123			500	11220
1124			500	11220
1125		2011 Sales	100	2029
1126			100	2029
1127		Supreme Eggbeater Corporat	2800	62738
1136		Vivid Yardstick Inc.	4800	102480
1145		Paramount Wax Inc.	4000	78500
1154		Fine Barometer Corporation	4600	100060

FIGURE 21.8

When Create Links to Source Data is selected, the final report includes the individual values of the selected references.

A few things to keep in mind when using this tool:

• The range selected must be adjacent columns.

• If your reference field consists of multiple sheets, as you go from sheet to sheet, Excel automatically selects the same range as the previous sheet.

• If you select Left column, data is combined based on the leftmost column of the selection and the selected function is used on all other columns in the range.

• If doing a consolidation by position or by column, you have to select a specific range, versus clicking the column headers to select the entire column.

• The range on which the function is applied must be numerical.

You have two reports, sales from 2011 and sales from 2012, on separate sheets. To combine the customers and the quantity sold onto a single report, follow these steps:

1. Select the top leftmost cell where the consolidated report should be placed, such as cell A1. If other data is on the sheet, make sure there is enough room for the new data.

2. On the Data tab, click the Consolidate button.

3. Select the desired function, SUM, from the Function drop-down.

4. Place the cursor in the Reference field.

5. Go to the sheet with the desired data set.

6. Select the data set, making sure the labels to be combined are in the leftmost column and that the column headers are included in the selection.

7. Click the Add button.

8. Repeat steps 4 to 7 for each additional data set.

9. To include the top and/or left column labels, select the corresponding option. If combining text fields, as we are here, Left Column must be selected.

10. Click OK.

THE ABSOLUTE MINIMUM

Here are the key points to remember from this chapter:

- The AutoFilter tool provides many options for filtering your data, making it easier to focus on just the data that's important at the moment.

- You aren't limited to just filtering values. The AutoFilter tool includes options for filtering by icon, font color, or cell color. If you need to completely remove duplicates, then the Remove Duplicates tool might be the one you need, especially with its ability to choose which columns you want to base the duplicates on.

- For combining data into a single report, even between workbooks, use the Consolidate tool and select Create Links to Source Data to ensure your report updates automatically.

PREPARING WORKBOOKS FOR DISTRIBUTION AND PRINTING

When you're done designing your workbook, you probably want to share it with others. But first, you might want to do a little cleanup, such as adding comments so users can understand what goes in specific fields, hiding sheets you don't want users to see, or protecting certain cells so users cannot accidently erase your formulas. You can also protect the file so the wrong eyes can't pry into it.

 NOTE This chapter focuses on Excel-specific customizations for printing and distributing workbooks. For more information about printing and sharing content in Office 2013, see Chapter 2, "Working with Office Applications."

Preparing to Print or Share Your Workbook

There are several things you might want to do before printing or sharing a workbook, such as adding cell comments, enabling multiple users, hiding sheets, locking rows and columns, or protecting sheet data.

Using Cell Comments to Add Notes to Cells

Cell comments are comments or images you can attach to a cell that appear when a cursor is placed over the cell. By default, the cell comment looks like a yellow sticky note. You can tell if a cell has a comment by the red triangle in the upper-right corner of the cell, as shown in cell A2 of Figure 22.1. Use cell comments to explain to the user what type of data to enter into the cell, explain what the data in the cell is used for, show the user an image of the product being referenced, or any other information you want to convey.

FIGURE 22.1

Use cell comments to convey additional information to a user without using valuable sheet space.

Inserting and Editing a Cell Comment

To insert a comment, click New Comment on the Review tab or right-click the cell where the comment should be placed and select Insert Comment. A yellow comment box appears, with the Excel user-defined name already entered to indicate who is entering the comment. If you want, you can delete this text. Otherwise, type the text you want into the comment box. When you're done, click any cell on the sheet to exit from the comment.

To edit a hidden comment, select the cell and click the Edit Comment button on the Review tab or right-click the comment's cell and select Edit Comment to make it visible. Your cursor is automatically placed within the comment box. If the comment is already visible, you can click in the comment box and make changes to the text.

Formatting a Cell Comment

After you've inserted a cell comment, you can format the text and the box or insert an image as the background fill. There are two dialog boxes available when you right-click a comment and select Format Comment. The first, which you open by right-clicking the *inside* of the comment box, only enables you to format the text in the comment. The other opens when you right-click on the comment box while your cursor is a four-headed arrow, as shown in Figure 22.2. It enables you to format the text or box.

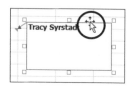

FIGURE 22.2

When your cursor changes to a four-headed arrow (shown here), right-click and select Format Comment to format the text or box.

Inserting an Image into a Cell Comment

You can insert an image into a cell comment as a background fill, as shown in Figure 22.3. The image takes up the entire box and resizes as you resize the box. You can still type text in the comment; the text displays on top of the image.

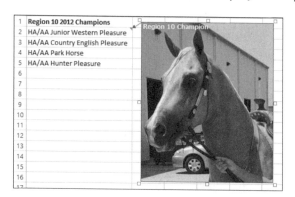

FIGURE 22.3

Insert an image into a cell comment to give the users a visual reference to a label.

To insert an image in a cell comment and change the color of the text so that it shows up over the image, follow these steps:

1. Right-click the cell to which you want to add the comment and select Insert Comment. A cell comment appears with the cursor inside.

2. Place your cursor along any edge of the comment until it turns into a four-headed arrow and then right-click and choose Format Comment. If the Format Comment dialog box that opens only has one tab—Font—close the dialog box and try again. The dialog box that appears should have multiple tabs.

3. Select the Colors and Lines tab of the Format Comment dialog box.

4. From the Color drop-down in the Fill section, select Fill Effects to open the Fill Effects dialog box.

5. Select the Picture tab and click the Select Picture button.

6. The Insert Pictures dialog box opens, enabling you to browse for a picture on the computer, at Office.com, anywhere online, or from your SkyDrive. When you find the image, click Insert and you return to the Fill Effects dialog box.

7. Select Lock Picture Aspect Ratio to lock the image ratio. Click OK twice to return to Excel.

8. Resize the comment box if necessary to see the entire image.

9. Highlight the text in the comment box.

10. Right-click within the comment box and select Format Comment.

11. From the Color drop-down of the Font tab, select a new color for the font. Click OK.

Showing and Hiding Cell Comments

A cell comment becomes visible when the cursor passes over the cell and then hides again when the cursor is past. If you need the comment to stay open, select the cell and click the Show/Hide Comment button on the Review tab or right-click over the cell and select Show/Hide Comment. If you want to see all the comments on the sheet, click the Show All Comments button on the Review tab. Select the option again to hide the comment(s).

Deleting a Cell Comment

To delete a comment, select the cell and click the Delete button on the Review tab or right-click over the cell's comment and select Delete Comment.

Allowing Multiple Users to Edit a Workbook at the Same Time

Excel workbooks are not designed to be accessed by multiple users at the same time. But Microsoft understands that sometimes there is a need for more than one person to edit a workbook at the same time and has provided a limited option. To enable multiple users, follow these steps:

1. On the Review tab, click the Share Workbook button to open the Share Workbook dialog box.

2. Select Allow Changes by More Than One User at the Same Time.

3. Select the Advanced tab to configure how long the change history should be kept, how copies are updated, and how conflicts should be handled.

4. Click OK.

5. Excel prompts you to save the workbook. Click OK to share the workbook.

Hiding and Unhiding Sheets

There might be sheets in your workbook that you do not want others to see, such as calculation sheets, data sheets, or sheets with lookup tables. You can hide sheets from users by navigating to the sheet you want to hide and then selecting Home, Format, Hide & Unhide, Hide Sheet. This hides the active sheet—the one you were looking at. You can also hide a sheet by right-clicking the sheet's tab and selecting Hide.

 CAUTION A workbook must have at least one sheet visible.

To unhide a sheet, click the Format button on the Home tab and select Hide & Unhide, Unhide Sheet from the menu. A dialog box listing all hidden sheets opens. Select the sheet you want to unhide and click Unhide. If you have multiple sheets to unhide, you must repeat these steps for each sheet.

Locking Rows or Columns in Place

If you've set up your data in a Table, Excel places the Table headers into the column headings when you scroll down the sheet, as shown in Figure 22.4. But normally, when you scroll through a sheet and your data isn't formatted as a Table, your row and column headers disappear. This can be inconvenient when you have a lot of data and need the identifying headers. With the Freeze Panes options, you can force the top rows, leftmost columns, or both to remain visible as you scroll around the sheet.

TIP If you have your data formatted as a Table and the headers do not appear in the column headings when scrolling, ensure that you don't have the Freeze Panes option turned on and ensure that you do have a cell in the Table selected.

Region	Product	Date	Customer	Quantity	Revenue	COGS	Profit	
East	Laser Printe	1/9/2011	Alluring Shoe Company	900	21465	9198	12267	
West	Laser Printe	1/11/2011	Alluring Shoe Company	400	9144	4088	5056	
Central	Multi-Funct	1/26/2011	Alluring Shoe Company	500	10445	4235	6210	
Central	Basic ColorJ	2/5/2011	Alluring Shoe Company	200	4280	1968	2312	

FIGURE 22.4

Table column headers become part of the column headings so that they are always visible when you scroll down the sheet.

Three options are available under View, Window, Freeze Panes:

- **Freeze Panes**—Freezes rows and/or columns depending on the cell you have selected at the time. This option changes to Unfreeze Panes if any rows or columns are already frozen.

- **Freeze Top Row**—Freezes the first visible row of the sheet.

- **Freeze First Column**—Freezes the first visible column of the sheet.

CAUTION When using the Freeze Top Row or Freeze First Column options, the selection of one automatically undoes the selection of the other. So, if you want to freeze both the top row and first column, you must use the Freeze Panes option.

Freezing Multiple Rows and Columns

The Freeze Top Row and Freeze First Column options enable you to freeze the first row or first column on the sheet; however, if you need to freeze multiple rows and/or columns, you need to use the Freeze Panes option. This option freezes the sheet based on the cell selected when the option is selected. It freezes any rows above and any columns to the left of the selected cell. For example, to freeze row 1 and columns A and B at the same time, select cell C2 and then select View, Window, Freeze Panes, Freeze Panes. Now, when you scroll around the sheet, you always see row 1 and columns A and B.

Clearing Freeze Panes

To turn off the Freeze Panes option, click the Freeze Panes button on the View tab, and select Unfreeze Panes. If you have rows and columns frozen, you can't choose to unfreeze one or the other. You must unfreeze it all and then refreeze the part you want to keep frozen.

Protecting the Data on a Sheet

Protecting a sheet prevents users from changing the content of locked cells. By default, all cells have the locked option selected and you purposefully unlock them. (See the following section "Unlocking Cells.") Sheet protection must be applied to each sheet individually.

To protect a sheet, click the Protect Sheet button on the Review tab. The Protect Sheet dialog box opens, from which you can select what actions a user can do to the sheet. You can also enter a password. You have to enter it twice.

Unlocking Cells

While a sheet is still unprotected, you can unlock specific cells so that when the sheet is protected, users can still enter information in the cells you want. To change the protection of selected cells, click the Format button on the Home tab and select Format Cells, or right-click on the selection and choose Format Cells. In the Format Cells dialog box, select the Protection tab and unselect the Locked option. When you've unlocked the desired cells, protect the sheet to protect the other cells.

Allowing Users to Edit Specific Ranges

Unlocking cells and protecting the sheet is an all-or-none solution. That is, none of your users will be able to modify the protected cells unless they can unprotect the sheet first. Suppose you have a form where traveling employees fill in the top half and accounting fills in the bottom half. You want to protect the sheet, so that travelers can't accidentally fill in the bottom half, but you don't want to provide the sheet password to accounting so they can fill in the bottom half. On the Review tab, click the Allow Users to Edit Ranges button to assign a password to specific ranges, allowing authorized users to edit those ranges.

Configuring Page Setup

Page setup refers to settings that control how a sheet looks when it's printed. These settings include page orientation (portrait or landscape), paper size, page margins, row and column repeats, and printing headings, gridlines, and comments.

Some of these options are available directly on the Page Layout tab. To access all these sheet options, click the Print Titles button on the Page Layout tab. The Page Setup dialog box opens directly to the Sheet tab, shown in Figure 22.5.

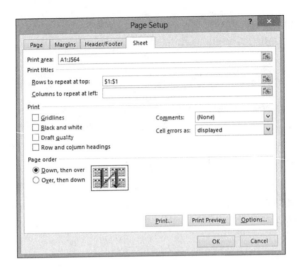

FIGURE 22.5

Instead of breaking up your table and repeating the header so that it prints on each page, use the Print Titles option to have Excel automatically copy the row onto each page.

Repeating Rows or Columns on Each Printed Page

When you have a report that spans several pages, you probably want to repeat your row or column headers on all the pages. Follow these steps to have your header row repeat at the top of each printed page:

1. On the Page Layout tab, click the Print Titles button. The Page Setup dialog box opens to the Sheet tab (refer to Figure 22.5).

2. Click the Collapse Dialog button on the far-right side of the Rows to Repeat at Top field. This minimizes the dialog box and allows you to more easily interact with the sheet.

3. Select the row(s) you want to repeat by clicking the numbered row header(s). You can only select the entire row, not just a few columns of it.

4. Click the button on the far-right side of the Rows to Repeat at Top field to return to the dialog box.

5. Click OK. The selected row(s) now repeat at the top of each printed page.

Scaling Your Data to Fit a Printed Page

You might find your data is a few rows too long or a few columns too wide to print on a single page. Using Scale to Fit on the Page Layout tab, you can adjust the scaling options available to get your data to print as you see fit. These options are also available in the Page Setup dialog box on the Page tab, though the labels are slightly different.

The Width drop-down is useful if you have a few columns going to the next page. From the drop-down, you can choose how many pages you want to force the table to print to. For example, if your report is printing on two pages because you have a column going to the second page, choose 1 page from the drop-down to have Excel adjust the settings, forcing that last column to stay with the others. Similarly, the Height drop-down is used when you have a few too many rows going to another page.

 NOTE When you customize the Width and Height, you cannot adjust the Scale. To adjust the Scale, the Width and Height must be set to Automatic.

Scale enables you to configure how a sheet will print by setting the percentage of the normal size at which you want it. 100% is the normal size of the table. Set the percentage to 50% and Excel reduces the size of the table by 50%, allowing for more of it to appear on a sheet, and shrinking the text. Set the percentage to 150% and Excel increases the size of the table and the text.

 TIP Sometimes you need to increase the font size of a printed report. Instead of increasing the font on the sheet, adjust the scale when printing.

Creating a Custom Header or Footer

There are two ways you can customize the header or footer. One method is through the Header/Footer tab of the Page Setup dialog box, which you can open using the Page Setup shortcut. When you're on the tab, click Custom Header or Custom Footer to design the header or footer. The other method is available when you are viewing your sheet in Page Layout view and you click in the header or footer area, opening the Header & Footer Tools – Design tab. Both provide the same design options, just in a different manner.

 NOTE See the "Exploring the Excel Window" section in Chapter 15, "Excel 2013 Basics," for more information on Page Layout view.

The header and footer are unique to each sheet. Each header and footer is broken into three sections: left section, center section, and right section. You can customize each of these three sections in numerous ways. For example, you can add page numbering, the current date, the sheet name, and so forth.

To add one of the options to a section of a header or footer, first select the section and then click the corresponding button. You can then select the text or image and apply formatting to it.

Adding an Image to the Header and Footer

You can add a company logo to a header so that it appears when printed, instead of taking up space on the computer screen. It's an easy way to give a report a more professional look. To insert a logo in the header's left section, as shown in Figure 22.6, follow these steps:

								1 of 12
Region	Product	Date	Customer	Quantity	Revenue	COGS	Profit	
Central	Laser Printe	1/2/2011	Alluring Shoe Company	500	11240	5110	6130	
Central	Laser Printe	1/3/2011	Alluring Shoe Company	400	9204	4088	5116	
East	Laser Printe	1/9/2011	Alluring Shoe Company	900	21465	9198	12267	

FIGURE 22.6

Use the header to add a company logo to a printed sheet.

CAUTION You can only insert one image per section of a header or footer.

1. On the View tab, click the Page Layout button.

2. As you move your cursor over the area that says Click to Add Header, the three sections of the header appear highlighted. Click the leftmost section. This places your cursor in that section.

3. On the Header & Footer Tools – Design tab, click the Picture button.

4. From the Insert Pictures dialog box, browse or search for the image to import. You can look for images on your local drive, online at Office.com, on the Web (you can search through Bing), or on your SkyDrive.

5. When you find the desired image, select it and click Insert.

NOTE At this time, you won't see the image in the header. Instead, you will see the code for the image: &[Picture]. Anytime you're in Edit mode—your cursor is in a section—you see the code. When you are no longer editing the header or footer, the image appears.

6. On the Header & Footer Tools – Design tab, click the Format Picture button. Adjust the size on the Size tab. Select the Picture tab if you need to change the color of the image or crop it. Click OK.

TIP If you know the needed height for the image to fit in the header but not the width, make sure Lock Aspect Ratio is selected before you adjust the height. The width automatically adjusts, preserving the ratio of the image.

7. Click anywhere outside the header and the image appears. If you need to modify the image even more, click in the section and repeat step 6.

Adding Page Numbering to the Header and Footer

Page numbering is set up in the header or footer of a sheet. You can show just the page number (1, 2, 3, and so on) or you can show the page number out of the total number of pages, as shown in the right header section in Figure 22.6. If you select multiple sheets when printing, the page numbering is consecutive for all the sheets in the order they appear in the workbook.

To insert page numbering based on the total number of pages, follow these steps:

1. On the View tab, click the Page Layout button.

2. As you move your cursor over the area that says Click to Add Header, the three sections of the header appear highlighted. Click the rightmost section. This places your cursor in that section.

3. On the Header & Footer Tools – Design tab, click the Page Number button. This places the code for page numbering, &[Page], in the section.

4. You might not see it, but after placing the code, your cursor was placed at the end of the text. So begin typing the following right away: Type a space and then the word of followed by another space. Note that you might not see the second space appear.

5. Click Number of Pages. You should now see the following in the section: &[Page] of &[Pages]. Click anywhere outside the footer and you see the current page number and the total number of pages.

Using Page Break Preview to Set Page Breaks

When in the Page Break Preview viewing mode, you can see where columns and rows will break to print onto other pages. Blue dashed lines signify automatic breaks that Excel places based on settings, such as margins. Blue solid lines are manually set breaks. You can move these lines to set the page breaks where you want by clicking and dragging them to a new location. Follow these steps to change the location of a column break:

1. Select Page Break Preview from the View tab.

2. Place your cursor over the blue column line you want to move until it becomes a double-headed arrow. The line can be solid or dashed.

3. Hold down the mouse button and drag the blue line to where you want the column break to be.

4. Release the mouse button. The dashed blue line becomes a solid blue line, as shown in Figure 22.7.

E	F	G	Pr
Quantity	Revenue	COGS	
500	11240	5110	
400	9204	4088	
900	21465	9198	
400	9144	4088	

FIGURE 22.7

After you've moved an automatically set column break, it changes from a dashed line to the solid line of a manually set break.

You can also insert additional (row) page breaks by selecting a cell in the row you want to be first on the next printed page, clicking the Breaks button on the Page Layout tab, and selecting Insert Page Break. A solid blue line appears above the selected cell. To remove a manually inserted page break, select a cell directly beneath the solid blue line, click the Breaks button on the Page Layout tab, and select Remove Page Break.

THE ABSOLUTE MINIMUM

Here are the key points to remember from this chapter:

- Cell comments, freeze panes, and hidden sheets are just a few of the finishing touches you can make to your workbook before presenting it to other users. You might also want to protect your work, especially at the sheet level, so that users don't accidentally overwrite your formulas.

- If you're going to print out your sheet for distribution through your company or as an invoice to a client, a logo in the header can give the sheet a nice but subtle touch of professionalism. If, instead, you're going to distribute the workbook electronically, you might want to remove any personal information.

CREATING SUBTOTALS
AND GROUPING DATA

This chapter shows you how you can summarize and group together data using Excel's Subtotal and grouping tools. The ability to group and subtotal data enables you to summarize a long sheet of data to fewer rows. The individual records are still there so that you can unhide them if you need to investigate a subtotal in detail.

Creating Subtotals

The easiest way to create subtotals in Excel is using the SUBTOTAL function. If you need more power or flexibility, Excel also offers a Subtotal tool. After creating your totals, you can format and sort them based on your specific requirements.

Using the SUBTOTAL Function

The SUBTOTAL function calculates a column of numbers based on the code used in the function. With the correct code, SUBTOTAL can calculate averages, counts, sums, and eight other functions listed in Table 23.1. It can also ignore hidden rows when the 100 version (101, 102, and so on) of the code is used.

TABLE 23.1 SUBTOTAL Function Numbers

Function_num (Includes Hidden Values)	Function_num (Ignores Hidden Values)	Function	Function Description
1	101	AVERAGE	Averages the numbers in the range
2	102	COUNT	Counts the number of cells containing numbers in the range
3	103	COUNTA	Counts the number of cells that are not empty in the range
4	104	MAX	Returns the largest value in the range
5	105	MIN	Returns the smallest value in the range
6	106	PRODUCT	Multiplies together all the numbers in the range
7	107	STDEV	Calculates the standard deviation of the range based on a sample
8	108	STDEVP	Calculates the standard deviation based on the entire range
9	109	SUM	Adds up all the numbers in the range
10	110	VAR	Estimates the variance based on a sample
11	111	VARP	Calculates the variance based on the entire range

The syntax of the SUBTOTAL function is as follows:

SUBTOTAL(function_num, ref1,[ref2],...)

Figure 23.1 shows the SUBTOTAL function in action versus the SUM function. The SUBTOTAL function with a code of 109 ignores any cells in the range that include SUBTOTAL functions themselves, as shown in the Grand Total. Column E uses the SUM function instead of SUBTOTAL and does not ignore the hidden rows or previous SUM formulas in the Grand Total.

	A	B	C	D	E
			Quantity with		Quantity with
1	Region	Product	SUBTOT		SUM
2	Central	Laser Printers	500		500
3	Central	Laser Printers	400		400
4	Central	Multi-Function	400		400
5	Central	Multi-Function	100		100
6	Central	Laser Printers	900		900
7	Central	Multi-Function	900		900
8	Central	Multi-Function	500		500
9	Central	Laser Printers	400		400
10	Central Total		4100	=SUBTOTAL(109,C2:C9)	4100
11					
12	East	Multi-Function	500		500
13	East	Laser Printers	900		900
14	East	Laser Printers	900		900
15	East	Basic ColorJet P	300		300
16	East	Multi-Function	400		400
17	East	Basic ColorJet P	300		300
18	East	Multi-Function	800		800
19	East	Basic ColorJet P	200		200
20	East	Basic ColorJet P	600		600
21	East Total		4900	=SUBTOTAL(109,C12:C20)	4900
22					
23	West	Laser Printers	600		600
24	West	Laser Printers	400		400
25	West	Multi-Function	1000		1000
26	West	Basic ColorJet P	300		300
27	West	Basic ColorJet P	300		300
28	West	Multi-Function	300		300
29	West	Multi-Function	1000		1000
30	West Total		3900	=SUBTOTAL(109,C23:C29)	3900
31					
32	Grand Total		12900	=SUBTOTAL(109,C2:C29)	25800

FIGURE 23.1

SUBTOTAL can ignore hidden rows and other SUBTOTAL calculations, as shown in the Grand Total. The SUM function adds all data in its range.

Summarizing Data Using the Subtotal Tool

The SUBTOTAL function is very useful, but if you have a large data set, it can be time consuming to insert all the Total rows. When your data set is large, use the Subtotal tool from the Data tab in the Outline group. This tool groups the sorted data, applying the selected function.

CAUTION You cannot use the Subtotal tool on a data set that has been converted to a Table (Insert, Tables, Table).

From the Subtotal dialog box, shown in Figure 23.2, you can select the column to group the data by, the function to subtotal by, and which columns to apply the subtotal to.

FIGURE 23.2

Use the Subtotal tool to group data and apply subtotals to specific columns.

Figure 23.3 shows a report where the quantity sold was summarized by region. When data is subtotaled with this method, group/ungroup buttons are added along the row headers. You can use the (–) buttons to group the data rows together, showing only the Total, as was done for the Central region. Click a (+) button to expand the data.

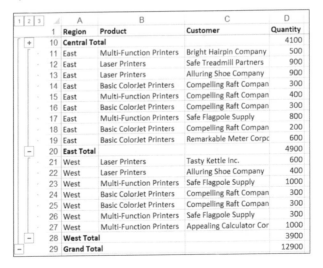

	Region	Product	Customer	Quantity
10	Central Total			4100
11	East	Multi-Function Printers	Bright Hairpin Company	500
12	East	Laser Printers	Safe Treadmill Partners	900
13	East	Laser Printers	Alluring Shoe Company	900
14	East	Basic ColorJet Printers	Compelling Raft Compan	300
15	East	Multi-Function Printers	Compelling Raft Compan	400
16	East	Basic ColorJet Printers	Compelling Raft Compan	300
17	East	Multi-Function Printers	Safe Flagpole Supply	800
18	East	Basic ColorJet Printers	Compelling Raft Compan	200
19	East	Basic ColorJet Printers	Remarkable Meter Corpc	600
20	East Total			4900
21	West	Laser Printers	Tasty Kettle Inc.	600
22	West	Laser Printers	Alluring Shoe Company	400
23	West	Multi-Function Printers	Safe Flagpole Supply	1000
24	West	Basic ColorJet Printers	Compelling Raft Compan	300
25	West	Basic ColorJet Printers	Compelling Raft Compan	300
26	West	Multi-Function Printers	Safe Flagpole Supply	300
27	West	Multi-Function Printers	Appealing Calculator Cor	1000
28	West Total			3900
29	Grand Total			12900

FIGURE 23.3

Use the Subtotal tool to quickly summarize the quantity by region. You can then group the data, showing only the Total rows, like the Central Total.

To create the report shown in Figure 23.3, follow these steps:

1. Sort the data by the column the summary should be based on, the Region column.

 NOTE   See Chapter 20, "Sorting Data," for more information about sorting by columns.

2. Select a cell in the data set.

3. On the Data tab, click the Subtotal button. The Subtotal dialog box, shown in Figure 23.2, opens.

4. From the At Each Change In field, select the column by which to summarize the data, Region.

5. From the Use Function field, select the function to calculate the totals by. Because you want to sum the quantities, choose SUM, but there are many functions to choose from.

6. From the Add Subtotal To field, select the column(s) the totals should be added to, Quantity. Notice that, by default, the last column is already selected.

7. Click OK. The data is grouped and subtotaled, with a grand total at the very bottom.

Placing Subtotals Above the Data

By default, subtotals appear below the data being summarized. If the subtotals need to appear above the data instead, deselect Summary Below Data in the Subtotal dialog box. This also places the Grand Total row at the top of the data, directly below the headings.

Expanding and Collapsing Subtotals

When data is grouped and subtotaled, outline symbols appear to the left of the row headings, as shown in Figure 23.3. Click the numbered icons at the top (1, 2, 3 in Figure 23.3) to hide and unhide the data in the sheet. For example, clicking the 2 hides the data rows, showing only the Total and Grand Total rows. Clicking the 1 hides the Total rows, showing only the Grand Total. Clicking the 3 unhides all the rows.

Below the numbered icons, next to each Total and Grand Total, are the expand (+) and collapse (–) icons. These expand or collapse the selected group.

Removing Subtotals or Groups

To remove all the subtotals and groups, click the Remove All button in the Subtotal dialog box. To remove only the group and outline buttons, leaving the subtotal row intact, select Data, Outline, Ungroup, Clear Outline. You can also use Ctrl+8 to toggle the visibility of the outline buttons.

CAUTION You cannot undo Clear Outline. If you accidentally select the option, click a cell in the table, bring up the Subtotal dialog box and click OK. The symbols will be replaced.

Copying the Subtotals to a New Location

If you hide the data rows, copy all the Subtotal rows, and paste them to another sheet, all the data, including the hidden data rows, appear in the new sheet. To copy and paste only the subtotals, follow these steps to select only the visible cells:

1. Click the Outline icon so that only the rows to copy are visible.

2. Select the entire data set. If the headers are to be included, you can do this quickly by selecting a single cell in the data set and pressing Ctrl+A.

3. On the Home tab, select Go to Special from the Find & Select drop-down list, and then select Visible Cells Only, as shown in Figure 23.4. (The dashed lines in the figure are shown for emphasis only. They appear in the next step.)

4. On the Home tab, click the Copy button.

5. Select the cell where the data is to be pasted.

6. On the Home tab, click the Paste button. The SUBTOTAL formulas are converted to values automatically.

TIP A shortcut for step 3 is to press Alt+; (semicolon).

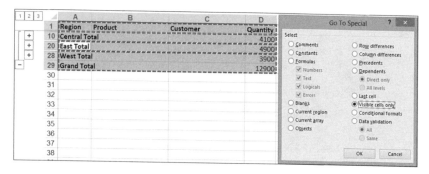

FIGURE 23.4

Select Visible Cells Only to copy and paste only the Total rows.

Formatting the Subtotals

If you hide the data rows, select the subtotal rows, and apply formatting to them, all the data, including the hidden data rows, reflect the new formatting. To format just the subtotals, follow these steps to select only the visible cells:

1. Click the Outline icon so that only the rows to copy are visible.

2. Select the entire data set. If the headers are to be included, you can quickly do this by selecting a single cell in the data set and pressing Ctrl+A.

3. On the Home tab, select Go to Special from the Find & Select drop-down list, and select Visible Cells Only, as shown in Figure 23.4.

4. Apply the desired formatting.

   TIP   A shortcut for step 3 is to press Alt+; (semicolon).

Subtotaling by Multiple Columns

Figure 23.5 shows a report in which the Revenue, COGS, and Profit columns are summed by Region and Product. To subtotal by multiple columns, sort the data set by the desired columns and then apply the subtotals, making sure Replace Current Subtotals is not selected. The subtotals should be applied in order of greatest to least.

	Region	Product	Quantity	Revenue	COGS	Profit
1	Region	Product	Quantity	Revenue	COGS	Profit
2	Central	Laser Printers	500	11240	5110	6130
3	Central	Laser Printers	400	9204	4088	5116
4	Central	Laser Printers	900	21888	9198	12690
5	Central	Laser Printers	400	10044	4088	5956
6		**Laser Printers Total**		52376	22484	29892
7	Central	Multi-Function Printers	400	6860	3388	3472
8	Central	Multi-Function Printers	100	1740	847	893
9	Central	Multi-Function Printers	900	17505	7623	9882
10	Central	Multi-Function Printers	500	10445	4235	6210
11		**Multi-Function Printers Total**		36550	16093	20457
12	**Central Total**			88926	38577	50349

FIGURE 23.5

Apply subtotals to both Region (the major column) and then Product (the minor column) to get subtotals of both.

For example, if the data is sorted by Region, with the products within each region sorted, apply the subtotal to the Region column and then the Product column, like this:

1. Sort the data by the columns the summary should be based on. Because the report is to be by Region and then Product, sort by Region first, and then sort by Product.

2. Select a cell in the data set.

3. On the Data tab, click the Subtotal button.

4. From the At Each Change In field, select the major column, Region, by which to summarize the data.

5. From the Use Function field, select the function, SUM, to calculate the totals by.

6. From the Add Subtotal To field, select the columns the totals should be added to—Revenue, COGS, Profit.

7. Click OK.

8. Repeat steps 3 to 7 for the secondary column, selecting the minor column, Product, and unselecting Replace Current Subtotals.

Sorting Subtotals

If you try to sort a subtotaled data set while viewing all the data, Excel informs you that doing so removes all the subtotals. Although the data itself cannot be sorted, the subtotal rows can be, and the grouped data remains intact. To do this, collapse the data so that only the subtotals are being viewed, and then apply the desired sort.

Adding Space Between Subtotaled Groups

When you insert subtotals into a data set, only subtotal rows are added between the groups. The report might appear crunched together for some reviewers (see Figure 23.6), and they might request that rows be inserted, separating the subtotaled groups from each other. You can insert extra space into a subtotaled report in two ways.

Region	Product	Customer	Quantity	Revenue	COGS	Profit
Central	Laser Printers	Alluring Shoe Company	500	11240	5110	6130
Central	Laser Printers	Alluring Shoe Company	400	9204	4088	5116
East	Laser Printers	Alluring Shoe Company	900	21465	9198	12267
West	Laser Printers	Alluring Shoe Company	400	9144	4088	5056
Central	Multi-Function Printers	Alluring Shoe Company	500	10445	4235	6210
		Alluring Shoe Company Total		61498	26719	34779
Central	Multi-Function Printers	Appealing Calculator Corporation	900	17505	7623	9882
West	Multi-Function Printers	Appealing Calculator Corporation	1000	19250	8470	10780
		Appealing Calculator Corporation Total		36755	16093	20662
East	Multi-Function Printers	Bright Hairpin Company	500	10245	4235	6010
		Bright Hairpin Company Total		10245	4235	6010
East	Basic ColorJet Printers	Compelling Raft Company	300	5961	2952	3009
West	Basic ColorJet Printers	Compelling Raft Company	300	7032	2952	4080
West	Basic ColorJet Printers	Compelling Raft Company	300	6735	2952	3783
East	Multi-Function Printers	Compelling Raft Company	400	8164	3388	4776
East	Basic ColorJet Printers	Compelling Raft Company	300	6240	2952	3288
East	Basic ColorJet Printers	Compelling Raft Company	200	4740	1968	2772
		Compelling Raft Company Total		38872	17164	21708

FIGURE 23.6

The close rows in this report can make it difficult to see the different groups.

If the report is going to be printed, you probably don't need to insert blank rows. You just need to create the illusion because the actual need is for more space between the subtotal and the next group. You can create the illusion by adjusting the row height of the subtotal rows. To increase the amount of space when the subtotal is placed below the data, follow these steps:

1. Collapse the data set so that only the subtotals are in view.

2. Select the entire data set, except for the header row.

3. Press Alt+; (semicolon) to select the visible cells only.

4. On the Home tab, click the Format button, and select Row Height.

5. Enter a new value in the Row Height dialog box.

6. Click OK.

7. On the Home tab, click the Top Align button.

8. Spacing now appears between each group, as shown in Figure 23.7.

Region	Product	Customer	Quantity	Revenue	COGS	Profit
Central	Laser Printers	Alluring Shoe Company	500	11240	5110	6130
Central	Laser Printers	Alluring Shoe Company	400	9204	4088	5116
East	Laser Printers	Alluring Shoe Company	900	21465	9198	12267
West	Laser Printers	Alluring Shoe Company	400	9144	4088	5056
Central	Multi-Function Printers	Alluring Shoe Company	500	10445	4235	6210
		Alluring Shoe Company Total		61498	26719	34779
Central	Multi-Function Printers	Appealing Calculator Corporation	900	17505	7623	9882
West	Multi-Function Printers	Appealing Calculator Corporation	1000	19250	8470	10780
		Appealing Calculator Corporation Total		36755	16093	20662
East	Multi-Function Printers	Bright Hairpin Company	500	10245	4235	6010
		Bright Hairpin Company Total		10245	4235	6010
East	Basic ColorJet Printers	Compelling Raft Company	300	5961	2952	3009
West	Basic ColorJet Printers	Compelling Raft Company	300	7032	2952	4080
West	Basic ColorJet Printers	Compelling Raft Company	300	6735	2952	3783
East	Multi-Function Printers	Compelling Raft Company	400	8164	3388	4776
East	Basic ColorJet Printers	Compelling Raft Company	300	6240	2952	3288
East	Basic ColorJet Printers	Compelling Raft Company	200	4740	1968	2772
		Compelling Raft Company Total		38872	17164	21708

FIGURE 23.7

Adjust the row height and text alignment of the subtotal rows to separate the groups.

 TIP If the subtotal row is above the data then skip step 7 as, by default, alignment is set to Bottom Align.

Grouping and Outlining Rows and Columns

You can manually group selected rows and columns by clicking the Group button on the Data tab. This is helpful if you have a sheet designed for multiple users and you want to only show them rows and/or columns specific to the user. After the data is grouped, an Expand/Collapse button is placed below the last row in the selection or to the right of the last column in the selection.

 CAUTION An outline can only have up to eight levels.

If the data to be grouped includes a calculated Total row or column between the groups, you can use the Auto Outline option found in the Group drop-down. This option creates groups based on the location of the rows or columns containing formulas. If the data set contains formulas in both rows and columns, though, the option creates groups for both rows and columns. This tool works best if there are no formulas within the data set itself, unless you do want the groups to be created based off those calculations.

Use the Group option for absolute control of how the rows or columns are grouped. For example, if you have a catalog with products grouped together, users can expand or collapse each group to view the products, as shown in Figure 23.8. By default, the Expand/Collapse buttons appear below the data. To get them to appear above the grouped data, first apply a subtotal to the data set with Summary Below Data deselected. Then undo the change and apply the desired groupings.

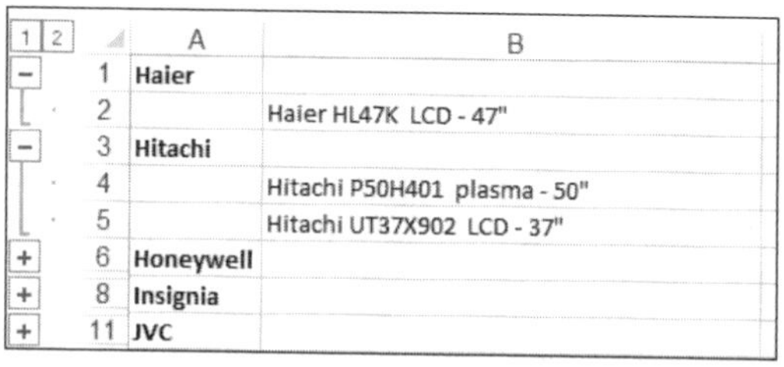

FIGURE 23.8

Group items together to make it easier for users to view only the desired items.

To manually group rows with the Expand/Collapse button above the grouped data set, follow these steps:

1. Select a cell in the data set.

2. On the Data tab, click the Subtotal button.

3. A message might appear telling you that Excel cannot determine which row has column labels. Click OK.

4. In the Subtotal dialog box, deselect Summary Below Data and click OK.

5. Excel inserts subtotal rows in the data. Click the Undo button in the Quick Access toolbar to remove the rows. Although it might appear that you've just undone all the previous steps, these steps were required to configure where the outline icon would appear.

6. Select the first set of rows to group together. Do not include the header. For example, to create the Hitachi grouping in Figure 23.8, select rows 4 and 5 to group. To create the Haier group, select only row 2.

7. On the Data tab, click the Group button.

8. Repeat steps 6 and 7 for each group of rows.

TIP Press the F4 key to repeat the last command performed in Excel. So, after grouping one set of rows, select the next group and press F4, select another group and press F4, and so on. As long as you don't perform another command, pressing F4 groups the selected rows.

You can clear groups using one of two ways from the Data, Outline, Ungroup drop-down:

- **Ungroup**—Ungroups the selected data. This method ungroups a single row from a larger group if that is all that is selected.
- **Clear Outline**—Clears all groups on a sheet unless more than one cell is selected, in which case the selected item is ungrouped. If used on data that was subtotaled using the Subtotal button, the subtotals remain; only the groupings are removed.

THE ABSOLUTE MINIMUM

Here are the key points to remember from this chapter:

- Excel simplifies subtotaling data with its SUBTOTAL function, but you can also use the Subtotal tool if you need more power or flexibility.
- Excel also enables you to create groups of rows and columns.

24

CREATING CHARTS AND SPARKLINES

Charts are a great way to graphically portray data. They're a quick and simple way to emphasize trends in data. Some people prefer to look at them instead of trying to make sense of rows and columns of numbers. Excel offers two methods of charting data—charts and sparklines. Charts, which you are most likely familiar with, are large graphics with a title and numbers and/or text along the left and bottom. Sparklines are miniature charts in cells with only markers to represent the data. This chapter provides you with the tools to create simple, but useful, charts. For further information, refer to *Charts & Graphs: Microsoft Excel 2013* (ISBN 978-0-7897-4862-1) by Bill Jelen.

Creating a Chart

Excel provides numerous charting possibilities. Before creating a chart, however, it's worth spending a few minutes exploring chart types and elements.

Preparing Data

The first step in creating a chart is ensuring that the data is set up properly. Although the following rules aren't going to prevent a chart from being created, heeding these rules allows Excel to help you create a chart by identifying the chart components:

- Ensure that there are no blank rows or columns.

- Ensure that headers along the left column and top row identify each series.

- If your row or column headers include numbers, leave the upper-left corner of the chart blank. (See cell A1 in Figure 24.1.) If the cell isn't blank, Excel might be confused when it tries to help you create the chart, and it might assume there are no category labels and chart the header as data.

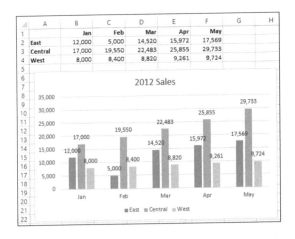

FIGURE 24.1

A basic chart and its source data. A chart consists of many components that you can configure.

Elements of a Chart

A chart is a graphical representation of numerical data. Behind every chart is a data range on a sheet, like the table shown in A1:F4 in Figure 24.1. This range is called the *source data*.

A *series* is a row or column from the source data represented on the chart as a line, a bar, or other marker used to portray the data. A typical series consists of the following:

- **Series name**—The cell with the name of the series that will appear in the legend

- **Series values**—The row or column containing the data to be charted

- **Category labels**—The range containing the label that will appear along the axis, identifying the series value

In Figure 24.1, the series names are East, Central, and West. The series values are presented by the thick-shaded vertical columns. The category labels are the months, Jan through May, along the horizontal axis, also known as the x-axis.

 NOTE If you use the Quick Analysis tool or Recommended Charts options, Excel helps you create a chart by trying to ascertain whether the rows or columns in the source data are to be used as a series. Normally, the row or column set consisting of fewer items defaults to the series, but Excel might switch this depending on the chart type. If the number of rows and columns are equal, Excel might offer a chart of each type. In Figure 24.1, Excel correctly determined that East, Central, and West were the series for the chart because the source data had fewer rows (three) than columns (five).

 CAUTION The following chart elements are the most common. Not all may appear depending on the selected chart's type.

Gridlines are horizontal or vertical lines in the chart that help make it easier to read the values of the markers.

The *axes* consist of major and minor gridlines that usually go below and to the left of the charted data (except for pie charts), labeling or marking intervals of the data. An axis might also have an Axis Title or Display Units Label. The horizontal axis, the one that goes left to right, is also known as the x-axis. The vertical axis, the one that goes up and down, is also known as the y-axis.

The *legend* is the color code for the chart series, identifying each series by the name assigned to it. In Figure 24.1, the legend is placed along the bottom of the chart.

Data labels are text that appears in the chart by the series marker, identifying the value of the points being charted, as shown in Figure 24.1.

The *chart title* is located at the top of the chart. By default, it isn't linked to a cell on the sheet—you must manually type it in.

 TIP See the section "Editing and Formatting a Chart Title" for a tip on linking a chart title to a cell.

Error bars are markers on a chart that look like the capital letter I. They're used to see margins of error in the data.

A *trendline* is a line on a chart that shows data trends, including future values. You can add trendlines to only the following nonstacked, 2D charts: bar, column, line, area, stock, and scatter.

Put together, a chart has two areas:

- **Plot area**—Consists of the series and inner gridlines
- **Chart area**—Consists of the area surrounding the plot area, including the frame of the chart

Types of Charts

There are ten chart groups, each with several types you can select from, in Excel. Further manual changes, such as mixing chart types, provide even more variations. The ten charts groups are:

 TIP In the Charts group on the Insert tab, there are eight buttons, with the Radar drop-down button listing Stock, Surface, and Radar.

- **Column**—Includes 2D Column and 3D Column chart types that feature markers relating the vertical height to size. They are useful for showing data changes over a period of time or comparing items. 3D Cylinder, 3D Cone, and 3D Pyramid charts can be created by modifying a 3D Column chart.
- **Line**—Includes 2D Line and 3D Line chart types. They are useful for displaying continuous data over time against a common scale.
- **Pie**—Includes 2D Pie, 3D Pie, and Doughnut chart types. Pie charts are most suitable for single-series data sets. They are useful for showing how an item is proportional to the sum of all items. A doughnut chart is similar to a pie chart in that it shows how an item is proportional to the whole, but unlike a pie chart, it can include more than one series.

- **Bar**—Includes 2D Bar and 3D Bar chart types that feature markers relating the horizontal width to size. They are useful for comparing items. 3D Cylinder, 3D Cone, and 3D Pyramid charts can be created by modifying a 3D Column chart.

- **Area**—Includes 2D Area and 3D Area chart types. They are similar to line charts except that the area underneath the line is filled with color. Area charts emphasize the magnitude of change over time.

- **Scatter (XY)**—Includes Scatter chart types of just markers, just lines, or combined markers and lines. They show the relationships among numeric values in several data series or can be used to plot two groups of numbers as one series of x,y coordinate. Also includes 2D Bubble and 3D Bubble chart types used to plot data points with the size of a bubble suggesting its relationship to the other bubbles.

- **Stock**—Illustrates the fluctuation of the data, such as stocks or temperatures.

- **Surface**—Finds the optimum combinations between two sets of data.

- **Radar**—Compares the total values of several data series.

- **Combo**—Helps you combine multiple chart types.

Column, Line, Bar, and Area chart types have three basic patterns available:

- **Clustered**—In a clustered chart, the markers are plotted side by side, making it easier to compare markers. The downside is that it is more difficult to tell if the data is increasing or decreasing in comparison with the next cluster. When viewing the chart types, clustered chart types show a light marker next to a dark marker.

- **Stacked**—In a stacked chart, the markers are plotted on top of each other, making it easier to see how the sum of data changes, but making it more difficult to see how a specific series changes over time. When viewing the chart types, stacked charts show a dark marker on top of or to the right of a light marker. The stacks are of differing heights.

- **100% stacked**—In a 100% stacked chart, the markers are plotted on top of each other. All stacks are scaled to have a height of 100%, enabling you to see which data points make the largest percentage of each stack. When viewing the chart types, stacked charts show a dark marker on top of or to the right of a light marker. The stacks are of the same heights.

CAUTION With the variety of charts available and the settings to make them eye catching, you might be tempted to choose a chart type based on its visual appeal—but keep in mind that not all chart designs will properly convey a true interpretation of the data.

Adding a Chart to a Sheet

There are three ways to add a chart to a sheet. You can use the chart buttons in the Charts group on the Insert tab, the Quick Analysis tool, or the Recommended Charts tool.

With two of the methods—Quick Analysis tool and Recommended Charts—you pick from a group of charts Excel has selected for you. You can still customize the chart after it's placed on the sheet—Excel just offers a place to start. The third method enables you to choose from all available charts.

After you've added a chart to a sheet, you can select it by clicking anywhere in the chart area. No matter which method you choose, you'll have to add a chart title after the chart is inserted. See the section "Editing and Formatting a Chart Title" for instructions on how to do this. You can also change the color and apply a chart style. (See the section "Applying Chart Styles and Colors.")

Using the Quick Analysis Tool

The Quick Analysis tool is a quick way to insert a chart on a sheet. When you select data on the sheet, the Quick Analysis tool appears in the lower-right corner of the selection, as shown in Figure 24.2. When you click the icon and select Charts, Excel suggests different chart types based on its analysis of the selected data.

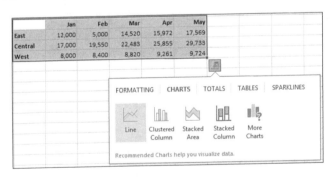

FIGURE 24.2

Use the Quick Analysis tool to bring up a list of suggested chart types.

As you move your cursor over the suggestions, a preview image appears, so you can see what your data would look like in the selected chart type. When you've decided which chart you want, click the icon and Excel inserts the chart on the sheet. If you don't see a chart type you like, selecting More Charts opens a list of the Recommended Charts. See the following section "Viewing Recommended Charts."

Viewing Recommended Charts

You don't have to select your data range before viewing Excel's recommended charts, but it does ensure that Excel properly interprets the range. You must have at least one cell in the source data selected; click the Recommended Charts button on the Insert tab to open the Insert Chart dialog box, shown in Figure 24.3.

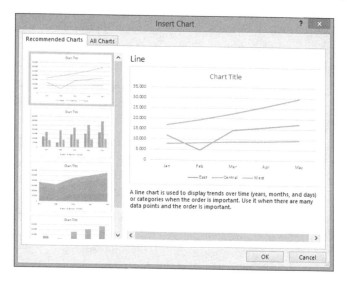

FIGURE 24.3

Excel recommends charts based on its interpretation of your data.

On the left side of the dialog box are Excel's recommended charts. Click a chart and a larger version appears on the right side of the dialog box. When you see one you like, select it and then click OK. It is added to the active sheet. If you don't see a chart type you like, select the All Charts tab to see all the charts available in Excel. See the following section "Viewing All Available Charts" for more information.

Viewing All Available Charts

For access to all available charts—not just the ones Excel thinks you might find useful—select at least one cell in your source data and then select one of the chart type drop-downs in the Charts group of the Insert tab or click on the See All Charts dialog launcher in the lower-right corner of the Charts group.

If you open a drop-down from the Charts group, you can move your cursor over the individual charts and a preview appears on the sheet. If you see the chart you want, click its icon and the chart is added to the sheet.

If you don't see the chart you want, select the More [chart type] Charts text at the bottom of the drop-down to open the Insert Chart dialog box to the chart group you were looking at previously. If you click the ribbon shortcut instead, it opens the Insert Chart dialog box to the Recommended Charts tab. Click the All Charts tab to view all charts.

The left side of the Insert Chart – All Charts dialog box lists all the chart groups available. When you select a group, the available types are shown along the upper-right side of the dialog box. If you select a type, a preview appears below the types. Depending on the source data setup, you might get two or more previews, reflecting possible data series configurations. If Excel cannot interpret the source data, you don't get a preview image. For example, an Open-High-Low-Close Stock chart requires a very specific setup of opening price, high price, low price, and closing price.

When you place your cursor over a preview, a larger version appears. After you find the chart you want, select it, and then click OK; it is added to the sheet.

Modifying Charts

Excel charts offer a multitude of formatting options. You can change chart colors, styles, and layouts; modify chart elements; resize a chart; switch rows and columns, and much more.

Adding, Removing, and Formatting Chart Elements

When you select a chart, three icons appear on the right side of it. The first, which looks like a plus sign, is for Chart Elements, the items reviewed in the section "Elements of a Chart."

 NOTE You can also access a list of elements by clicking the Add Chart Element button on the Chart Tools – Design tab. This list doesn't offer the ability to turn elements on/off by just selecting the element. Instead, you must open the element's submenu and make a selection.

Select an element to have it appear in the chart. Deselect it to hide it. For additional options concerning the element, such as its location in the chart, click the arrow that appears to the right of the element. A list of options displays, as shown in Figure 24.4. Selecting More Options opens a task pane on the right side of Excel. Depending on the selected element, the options shown change, but it is from this task pane that you can make more changes to the element's formatting, such as the color, 3D design, and alignment.

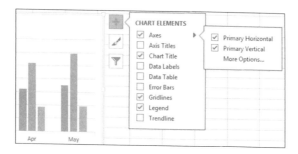

FIGURE 24.4

The Chart Elements list allows you to turn an element on or off and adjust its settings.

Editing and Formatting a Chart Title

Unless you have a single data series with a row header, when you insert a chart, Excel places a "Chart Title" placeholder at the top of the chart. To change the text, click in the text box and replace the generic "Chart Title." You can also apply formatting to the title. If you select the entire text box, the formatting applies to the entire title. Otherwise, you can select a single character or word to format.

 CAUTION The selection frame around the text box changes depending on the mode the selection is in. When the frame is selected and the frame is solid, any formatting applies to the entire frame and its contents. If the frame is dashed then the selection is inside the frame.

 TIP To move the text box to a custom location, place your cursor along the box edge until it turns into a four-headed arrow. At this point, hold down the mouse button and drag the box to a new location.

Excel doesn't have the built-in ability to link a dynamic chart title to a cell, but you can do it with a little work. To do this, select the title text box, ensuring the selection frame is solid, not dashed. Next, place your cursor in the formula bar, type an equal sign (=), and then click on the cell containing the title text. Press Enter and the title updates to reflect the cell's text. As the text in the cell changes, the chart title also updates.

If you decide to make the title static again, right-click the title and select Edit Text. You can also toggle the chart title on and off to reset the title.

Changing the Display Units in an Axis

Excel bases the units shown in an axis off the data. Excel displays units in millions or billions if that is what your data contains, taking up quite a bit of room. You can change the display units, reducing the amount of space used and making the axis easier to read. To do this, right-click the axis and select Format Axis. From the task pane, select Axis Options, the last icon that looks like a chart. Near the bottom of the Axis Options section is a section for Display Units, as shown in Figure 24.5. Open the drop-down and select how you want the units to be abbreviated. If you don't want abbreviation text appearing by the axis, deselect Show Display Units Label on Chart. Instead, you can customize the chart title.

FIGURE 24.5

Change the display units of a numerical axis to reduce the amount of space used.

Applying Chart Styles and Colors

After you've inserted a chart, you might want to move the chart title, move the legend, add a background, change the color of the series, or apply any number of changes to make the chart more attention getting. You can apply each change yourself, or you can see what chart styles Excel has available.

When you select a chart, three icons appear along the right side of it. Clicking the second icon with the paintbrush opens up a Style dialog box, in which you can scroll and view various styles, as shown in Figure 24.6. As you place your cursor over each one, your chart updates and provides a preview of the style. When you find a style you like, click it and your chart updates.

 NOTE You can also access this list of styles by selecting your chart and viewing the options in the Chart Styles group on the Chart Tools – Design tab.

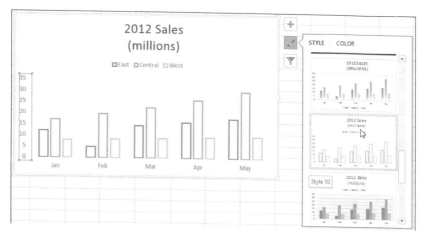

FIGURE 24.6

Apply one of Excel's existing chart styles to create an eye-catching chart.

If you click the Color tab of the Styles dialog box (or click the Change Colors button on the Chart Tools – Design tab), various color combinations are shown. If you place your cursor over a color sample, the data series in the chart updates. When you find a color scheme you like, click it and your chart updates.

 TIP If you click once on a single series in the chart so that only the series is selected, you can change the color of the selected series by clicking the Shape Fill button on the Chart Tools – Format tab. If you click twice (two single clicks, not a double-click) on a specific data point in a series so that only it, not the entire series, is selected, you can apply a color to just that data point.

Applying Chart Layouts

Chart layouts are predefined layouts offering combinations of the chart elements: legend, chart title, axis title, data labels, and data table. From Chart Tools, Design, Chart Layouts, Quick Layout, up to 12 layouts are available, depending on the type of chart selected. If you place your cursor over a layout sample, the chart updates and provides a preview. When you find a layout you like, click it and your chart updates. If none of the predefined combinations is what you want, you can manually modify each element.

Moving or Resizing a Chart

The default location for a chart is the same sheet as the data. If you create your chart using the Quick Analysis tool or the Recommended Charts options, you have no control on where the chart is initially placed. But a chart can be moved to another location on the same sheet, to a new sheet, or to its own chart sheet.

To move a chart elsewhere on the same sheet, click anywhere in the chart area and drag the chart to the new location. Be careful not to click in the plot area or you'll move the actual chart itself within the frame.

To relocate the chart to another sheet, first make sure the new sheet exists. Then, select the chart and click the Move Chart button on the Chart Tools – Design tab. From the Move Chart dialog box that opens, select the new sheet from the Object In drop-down.

To resize a selected chart, place the cursor at any of the four corners or midway along any of the edges of the frame. When the cursor changes to a double-headed arrow, click and drag the chart to the desired size.

Switching Rows and Columns

If, after inserting a chart, you want to switch the row/column setup being used for the data series, select the chart and then click the Switch Row/Column button found on the Chart Tools – Design tab in the Data group. Excel switches the range used for the series and the range used for the category labels.

Changing an Existing Chart's Type

You don't have to re-create a chart from scratch if you want to change the chart type. Just select the chart, and then select a new chart type from the Charts group on the Insert tab. Any formatting that can transfer over will be included in the new chart type. You can also click the Change Chart Type button on the Chart Tools – Design tab. See the section "Viewing All Available Charts" for instructions on using the dialog box.

Updating Chart Data

Unless the source data is a Table, the chart won't automatically update as new data is added to the data set. To manually update the data source of a chart, do one of the following:

- On the Chart Tools – Design tab, click the Select Data button. Alternatively, right-click the chart and choose Select Data. Update the Chart data range in the Select Data Source dialog box, shown in Figure 24.7.

- When the chart is selected, the data source is highlighted with a colored border. The borders can be manually modified, changing the source range, by clicking and dragging to include the new rows. Make sure you place your cursor in the corner of the range and get a double-headed arrow, not a four-headed arrow. If using this method, be careful to not move the range when trying to expand it.

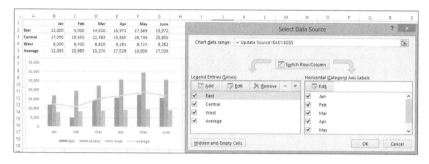

FIGURE 24.7

The original data range was A1:F5. After adding the June data, the source data range is updated to include the new data in the chart.

In addition to the two previous methods, the existing series on a chart can be updated by copying the new data and pasting it into the chart. To do this, follow these steps:

1. Ensure that the new data has a header similar to the existing data. It is especially important that a heading entered as a Date is still a Date and not Text.

2. Select the new data, including the header.

3. Right-click over the selection and choose Copy.

4. Select the chart.

5. On the Home tab, click the Paste button. The chart updates with the new data.

Adding Sparklines to Data

A *sparkline* is a chart inside of a single cell based on a single row or column of data. It can be placed right next to the data it's charting or on another sheet. Because the sparkline is in the background of the cell, you can still enter text in that cell.

There are three types of sparklines available: Line, Column, and Win/Loss. Different colors can be applied to them and various settings in the Show group of the Sparkline Tools – Design tab affect how the sparkline will be designed.

To add a sparkline to your data, select either the cell where you want the sparkline to go or the data set (not including the headers) and select one of the options in the Sparklines group on the Insert tab. Fill in the fields of the Create Sparklines dialog box and the sparklines are added to the selected location.

 TIP   As long as Excel can tell you have the same number of sparkline cells and corresponding ranges, you can create adjacent sparklines based on adjacent data sets. Just select the multiple sparkline cells or data sets at the same time. If you create sparklines together using this method, they are grouped and changes to the settings affect them all.

Adding Points to a Sparkline

After you've created a sparkline, you can choose to show the High Point, Low Point, Negative Points, First Point, Last Point, and Markers (line charts only), as shown in the first three examples in Figure 24.8. To add points to a sparkline, select the sparkline and on the Sparkline Tools – Design tab, select the desired points in the Show group. Each point can be assigned its own color by going to the Marker Color drop-down in the Style group of the tab.

	A	B	C	D	E	F	G	H
1	Column Chart with High Point Indicators (Dark Columns)							
2		Q1	Q2	Q3	Q4			
3	East	9,853	7,141	2,339	634			
4	Central	6,826	6,599	7,594	1,839			
5	West	6,411	260	755	2,074			
6								
7	Line Chart with Markers							
8		Jan-12	Feb-12	Mar-12	Apr-12	May-12	Jun-12	
9	East	2,689	1,332	3,233	1,369	2,970	21	
10	Central	1,028	1,931	1,894	2,089	1,279	1,388	
11	West	121	3,181	3,415	4,887	3,545	1,313	
12								
13	Win/Loss Chart with Negative Points Highlighted							
14		Jan	Feb	Mar	Apr	May	Jun	
15	East	84	67	-26	43	3	-97	
16	Central	96	-70	-14	-26	-4	88	
17	West	42	-45	15	-28	-50	90	
18								
19	Column Chart with Date Axis							
20		1/1/2012	1/4/2012	1/5/2012	1/6/2012	1/7/2012	1/8/2012	
21	East	9,853	7,141	2,339	634	2,689	2,970	
22	Central	6,826	6,599	7,594	1,839	1,028	1,279	
23	West	6,411	260	755	2,074	121	3,545	

FIGURE 24.8

Use Sparklines to add in-cell charts to your data.

For example, to create the first set of sparklines in Figure 24.8, follow these steps:

1. Select F3:F5, the cells where the sparklines will be placed.

2. On the Insert tab, click the Column button in the Sparklines group.

3. Place your cursor in the Data Range field and then select range B3:E5 on the sheet.

4. Verify the Location Range is correct and then click OK.

5. From the Show group on the Sparkline Tools – Design tab, select High Point. Excel colors the high point in each sparkline a different color.

6. To change the color of the high point, go to the Marker Color drop-down in the Style group. From the drop-down, select High Point, and then select a new color for the marker.

Spacing Markers in a Sparkline

The fourth set of charts in Figure 24.8 uses the Date Axis Type option to space the columns in respect to the date of the data set. Note the space in the sparkline between the first and second columns. This is parallel to the date difference between the first two columns of data. The setting is available in the sparklines Axis drop-down in the Group group.

 CAUTION   The date range must include real dates. For example, Jan, Feb, Mar, and the like don't work because they are not actual dates, but if the actual dates are 1/1/12, 2/1/12, 3/1/12, and they are simply formatted to just show the month then they work to spread out the data in the sparkline.

To space sparklines based on the dates in the data set, as shown in Figure 24.8 where there are two days (1/2/12 and 1/3/12) missing between the first and second dates, follow these steps:

1. Select a cell in the sparkline group.

2. On the Sparkline Tools – Design tab, click the Axis button, and select Date Axis Type from the drop-down list.

3. The Sparkline Date Range dialog box opens. Select the date range, B20:G20 in Figure 24.8, to apply to the sparklines.

4. Click OK. The sparklines update to accommodate the spacing in the selected date range.

Deleting Sparklines

You cannot simply highlight a sparkline and delete it. Instead, to delete a sparkline, on the Sparkline Tools – Design tab, click the Clear button, and choose either Clear Selected Sparklines to clear just the selected sparkline or select Clear Selected Sparkline Groups to clear a set of sparklines grouped together.

THE ABSOLUTE MINIMUM

Here are the key points to remember from this chapter:

- You can create a variety of chart types with Excel data, including bar, pie, column, line, and area charts.

- Excel charts offer a multitude of formatting options. You can change chart colors, styles, and layouts; modify chart elements; resize a chart; switch rows and columns, and much more.

- A sparkline is a chart inside a single cell based on a single row or column of data. You can place sparklines next to the data they're charting or on another sheet.

25

CREATING PIVOT TABLES AND SLICERS

Pivot tables can summarize one million rows with five clicks of the mouse button. For example, if you have sales data broken up by company and product then you can quickly summarize the sales by company then product or, with a few clicks, reverse the report and summarize by product then company. Or if you're in charge of all the local kids' soccer leagues then you can create a report showing the number of boys versus girls, grouped by age. A pivot table can do all this and more. Another option is a slicer, which allows you to filter a pivot table, but in a much more user-friendly way.

NOTE Pivot tables are so powerful with so many options that this chapter cannot cover it all. This chapter provides you with the tools to create straightforward, but useful, pivot tables. For even more details, refer to *Pivot Table Data Crunching: Microsoft Excel 2013* (ISBN 978-0-7897-4875-1) by Bill Jelen and Michael Alexander.

Creating a Pivot Table

There are three ways to create a pivot table: by scratch or using one of two automated tools. With two of the methods—Quick Analysis tool and Recommended Pivot Tables—you pick from a group of pivot tables Excel has selected for you. You can still customize the report after it's placed on the sheet—Excel just offers a place to start. The third method enables you to design a report from scratch. First, however, it's important to learn more about pivot tables before you create one.

Preparing Data for Use in a Pivot Table

To take full advantage of a pivot table's capabilities, your data should adhere to a few basic formatting guidelines:

- There should be no blank rows or columns.

- If a column contains numeric data, don't allow blank cells in the column. Use zeros instead of blanks.

- Each row should be a complete record.

- There shouldn't be any Total rows.

- There should be a unique header above every column.

- Headers should be in only one row; otherwise, Excel gets confused because it's unable to find the header row on its own.

Figure 25.1 shows a data set properly formatted for working with pivot tables. Figure 25.2 shows a data set not suitable for pivot tables. Instead, the dates should all be in one column. And although a person might understand that all the data shown is relevant to the West region, Excel does not.

Region	Product	Date	Customer	Quantity	Revenue	COGS	Profit
Central	Laser Printe	1/2/2011	Alluring Shoe Company	500	11240	5110	6130
Central	Laser Printe	1/3/2011	Alluring Shoe Company	400	9204	4088	5116
East	Laser Printe	1/9/2011	Alluring Shoe Company	900	21465	9198	12267
West	Laser Printe	1/11/2011	Alluring Shoe Company	400	9144	4088	5056
Central	Multi-Funct	1/26/2011	Alluring Shoe Company	500	10445	4235	6210
Central	Basic ColorJ	2/5/2011	Alluring Shoe Company	200	4280	1968	2312
Central	Basic ColorJ	2/19/2011	Alluring Shoe Company	800	18504	7872	10632
East	Laser Printe	2/23/2011	Alluring Shoe Company	1000	20940	10220	10720
East	Laser Printe	3/2/2011	Alluring Shoe Company	400	8620	4088	4532

FIGURE 25.1

This data is great for pivot tables.

Region	Customer	Product	1/1/2011	1/2/2011	1/3/2011	1/4/2011	1/6/2011
Central	Alluring Shoe Company	Laser Printers		6130	5116		
		Basic ColorJet Printers	5290		3723		
		Multi-Function Printers					
	Appealing Calculator Corporat	Laser Printers					
		Basic ColorJet Printers					
		Multi-Function Printers	9882		3472	4293	
	Best Vegetable Company	Basic ColorJet Printers					
	Bright Eggbeater Corporation	Basic ColorJet Printers					
		Multi-Function Printers					
	Bright Hairpin Company	Laser Printers		12690			
		Basic ColorJet Printers					5890

FIGURE 25.2

This data set is not suitable for a pivot table.

Pivot Table Compatibility

Pivot table compatibility between Excel 2013 and the legacy versions is a bit tricky:

- If you open an .xlsx file with a converter in a legacy version, the pivot tables do not work.

- If you create pivot tables in an .xlsx file (file type used by Excel 2007 and newer) and then save the file as an .xls file (file type used by legacy Excel), the pivot tables do not work. The Compatibility Checker dialog box opens when you save the file, warning of the incompatibilities, such as Show Values As.

- To get a pivot table created in 2013 to work in legacy Excel, save the file as an .xls file before creating the pivot table. Close and reopen the file, and then create the pivot table. Any options not compatible with older versions of Excel, such as slicers (which you can read more about later in this chapter), are not available. Strangely enough, you can apply Show Values As and save the file. Excel does not warn of compatibility issues and the pivot table opens fine in legacy versions.

Pivot Table Field List

There are two parts to a pivot table report—the pivot table itself and the PivotTable Field List, which appears only when a cell in the pivot table is selected. The PivotTable Field List consists of a list of the column headers in the data set (the fields) and the four areas of a pivot table.

Figure 25.3 shows a basic pivot table, using all four areas of a pivot table to summarize product profit by year and quarter on a regional basis. The four areas are as follows:

- **Filters**—Limits the report to a specific criteria; in this case, you are looking at only the Central region's revenue. Instead of creating a separate report for each region, use the Report filter to view the desired region.

- **Columns**—The headers going across the top of the pivot table—in this case, the breakdown by year and quarter.

- **Rows**—The headers going down the left side of the pivot table—in this case, the Products. If there is more than one field, the fields display in a hierarchical view, with the second field under the first field.

- **Values**—The data being summarized—in this case, Profit. The data can be summed, counted, and many other calculation types.

Not all four areas must be used. Each area can have more than one field.

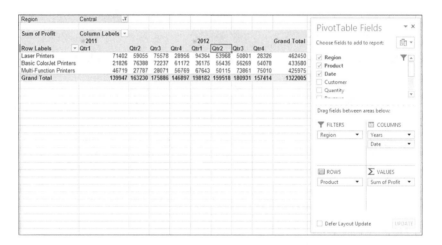

FIGURE 25.3

A basic pivot table using all fields to summarize 2011 and 2012 quarterly product sales for the Central region.

Using the Quick Analysis Tool

The Quick Analysis tool is a quick way to create a pivot table. When you select data on the sheet, the Quick Analysis tool appears in the lower-right corner of the selection. When you click on the icon and select Tables, Excel suggests different pivot tables based on its analysis of the selected data. Placing your cursor over a PivotTa... icon opens a preview window, as shown in Figure 25.4. If you click the icon, Excel creates the pivot table on a new sheet. If none of the previews show what you want, select the More icon to open the Recommended PivotTables dialog box.

TIP You don't have to select the entire data set. As long as your data is set up properly, Excel will be able to extrapolate the table from the selection of two cells.

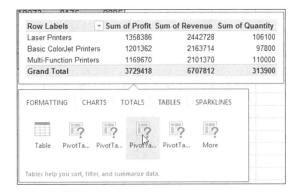

FIGURE 25.4

Use the Quick Analysis tool to bring up a list of suggested pivot tables.

Viewing Recommended Pivot Tables

As long as your data is set up properly, you don't have to select the entire table before viewing Excel's recommendations. Select at least one cell in the source data and then click the Recommended PivotTables button on the Insert tab to open the Recommended PivotTables dialog box shown in Figure 25.5.

On the left side of the dialog box are Excel's recommended pivot tables. Click a pivot table and a larger version appears on the right side of the dialog box. When you see one you like, select it and then click OK. The pivot table is created on a new sheet.

If you don't see a pivot table you like, click the Blank PivotTable button to create your own pivot table. See the following section, "Creating a Pivot Table from Scratch," for more information.

FIGURE 25.5

Excel recommends pivot tables based on its interpretation of your data.

Creating a Pivot Table from Scratch

Creating a pivot table is simple if the data set is suitable for pivot tables. After you've told Excel what the data source is, it can be quickly created by selecting the desired fields in the field list. Based on the data in a field, Excel places the selected field in the area it thinks it should go. Text fields are placed in the Rows area. Numeric fields are placed in the Values area and summed.

When you select fields in the field list and add them to an area that already contains fields, the new fields are placed below the existing fields. The up/down layout in the area corresponds to a left/right layout of the fields in the pivot table, except for the Filters area, which also goes up/down.

The order of the fields and the area in which they're located can be changed by clicking the field and dragging it to a new location. You can also drag fields from the field list to an area, instead of selecting them and letting Excel choose their locations.

Region	(All)					
Column Labels						
	Laser Printers		Basic ColorJet Printers		Multi-Function Printers	
Row Labels	Sum of Quantity	Sum of Profit	Sum of Quantity	Sum of Profit	Sum of Quantity	Sum of Profit
Alluring Shoe Company	8900	109978	8500	106893	9200	99458
Appealing Calculator Corporation	9000			111738	10700	112893
Best Vegetable Company	1500			12300	800	7664
Bright Eggbeater Corporation	7000			75937	5900	63990
Bright Hairpin Company	7600			54536	6300	71106
Compelling Raft Company	9700			102630	15300	164547
Cool Jewelry Corporation	900			10680	200	1858
Exclusive Shovel Traders	10600			102035	9800	108622
Fine Barometer Corporation	200			17312	800	8536
Leading Utensil Corporation	1000			2314	500	4705
Matchless Vise Inc.	7400			101083	7400	79734
Paramount Wax Inc.	800			2412	1000	8780
Reliable Tripod Company	6500			98550	5100	56347
Remarkable Meter Corporation	10200			130115	15000	153917
Remarkable Notebook Supply	1300			7609	1000	8720
Safe Flagpole Supply	12200			170374	14600	153185
Safe Treadmill Partners	1100			6630	1000	9370
Secure Toothpick Corporation	1000			1374	300	3318
Stunning Furnace Partners	1200			8901	700	6545
Succulent Jewelry Inc.	1600			8912	300	2991
Superior Vegetable Corporation	1800			11110	500	5400
Supreme Eggbeater Corporation	600			7345	200	2464
Tasty Kettle Inc.	1000			2302	400	3748
Unsurpassed Banister Corporation	1100			11648	100	972
Unusual Quilt Inc.	300			11754	1400	14548
Vivid Yardstick Inc.	800		9696	600	10192	800	8328

PivotTable Fields panel overlay:

PivotTable Fields

Choose fields to add to report:

☑ Region
☑ Product
☐ Date
☑ Customer

Drag fields between areas below:

▼ FILTERS — Region
▦ COLUMNS — Product / ∑ Values
▦ ROWS — Customer
∑ VALUES — Sum of Quant... / Sum of Profit

☐ Defer Layout Update   UPDATE

FIGURE 25.6

You aren't limited to pivot table reports Excel thinks would be useful. Design your own or customize one from Excel's suggestions.

The pivot table in Figure 25.6 summarizes product quantity and profit by customer. It also enables users to filter by region. To create this report, follow these steps:

1. Make sure the data set is set up properly, as explained in the section "Preparing Data for Use in a Pivot Table."

2. Select a cell in the data set.

3. On the Insert tab, click the PivotTable button (not the drop-down arrow).

4. The Create PivotTable dialog box, shown in Figure 25.7, opens and Excel selects the data set. The address is shown in the Table/Range field. If the selection is correct, continue to step 5. If the selection is not correct, return to step 1.

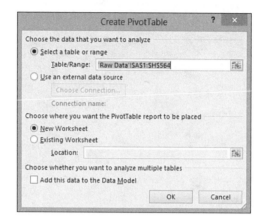

FIGURE 25.7

Use the Create PivotTable dialog box to identify the source data and where the pivot table should be created.

 CAUTION You could correct Excel's selection, but if Excel didn't select the data set properly then there is likely something wrong with its layout, which could affect the pivot table created.

5. Select the location where the pivot table is to be placed. The default location is always a new sheet. If using an existing sheet, ensure there is enough room on the sheet for the pivot table's rows and columns.

6. Click OK. The pivot table template and field list appear on a new sheet (or on an existing sheet, if that is what you selected), as shown in Figure 25.8.

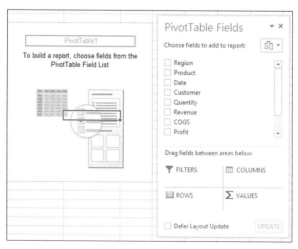

FIGURE 25.8

After the pivot table template and field list appear, you can start designing the report.

7. Select the fields that should be the row labels, Customer. If there needs to be more than one field for the row labels, select them in the order they need to appear in, left to right, on the report.

8. Select the fields the report should summarize, Quantity and Profit. Notice that when you select two or more fields to summarize, Excel adds a Values field to the Columns area.

9. Add a column label, Product, by clicking and dragging the field from the list to the Columns area.

10. Click and drag the Region field from the list to the Filters area.

Modifying a Pivot Table

After you create a pivot table, you can modify its content, sort it, or change its appearance.

Removing a Field

To remove a field from a pivot table, deselect it from the field list or click it in the area and select Remove Field. You can also click and drag the field from the area to the sheet until an X appears by the cursor. When the X appears, release the mouse button.

Renaming a Field

You can rename a field as it appears in the pivot table by typing a new name directly in the cell. The name must be unique and cannot be the same as the field's original name before it was placed in the pivot table.

Changing the Calculation Type of a Field Value

When Excel identifies a field as numeric, it automatically sums the data. If it cannot identify the field as numeric, it counts the data. No matter which calculation type Excel appoints to a value field, you can change it by selecting the field in the pivot table, clicking the Field Settings button on the PivotTable Tools – Analyze tab, and selecting an option from the Summarize Values By list in the Value Field Settings dialog box. You can also open the Value Field Settings dialog box by right-clicking a value in the pivot table and selecting Value Field Settings.

Changing How a Pivot Table Appears on a Sheet

There are three ways the pivot table report will appear, as shown in Figure 25.9. You can change the view by clicking the Report Layout button on the PivotTable Tools – Design tab, and selecting the desired layout from the drop-down:

- **Compact**—This is the default configuration for .xlsx, .xlsm, and .xlsb files. All the fields in the row labels area share the same column. The Total, such as the West Total, appears in the same row as the field.
- **Outline**—The fields in the row labels area each have their own column. The Total, such as the West Total, appears in the same row as the field.
- **Tabular**—This is the default configuration for an .xls file. The fields in the row labels area each have their own column. The Total, such as the West Total, appears in its own row beneath its group.

Compact		Outline			Tabular		
Row Labels	Sum of Revenue	Region	Product	Sum of Revenue	Region	Product	Sum of Revenue
Central	2375879	Central		2375879	Central	Laser Printers	832414
Laser Printers	832414		Laser Printers	832414		Basic ColorJet	776996
Basic ColorJet	776996		Basic ColorJet	776996		Multi-Function	766469
Multi-Function	766469		Multi-Function	766469	Central Total		2375879
East	2493003	East		2493003	East	Laser Printers	897949
Laser Printers	897949		Laser Printers	897949		Basic ColorJet	891799
Basic ColorJet	891799		Basic ColorJet	891799		Multi-Function	703255
Multi-Function	703255		Multi-Function	703255	East Total		2493003
West	1838930	West		1838930	West	Laser Printers	712365
Laser Printers	712365		Laser Printers	712365		Basic ColorJet	494919
Basic ColorJet	494919		Basic ColorJet	494919		Multi-Function	631646
Multi-Function	631646		Multi-Function	631646	West Total		1838930
Grand Total	6707812	Grand Total		6707812	Grand Total		6707812

FIGURE 25.9

Excel offers three ways of viewing and working with a pivot table report.

If you have either Outline or Tabular applied, you can choose to repeat the item labels by selecting Repeat All Item Labels from the Report Layout drop-down.

Sorting Pivot Tables

Excel automatically sorts text data alphabetically when building a pivot table. You can drag any row label, column label, or record to a new location. To reset the table back to its default state, remove the affected field from the area, refresh the table, then put the field back.

Another option is to sort using one of the methods in the following sections. When a sort is applied in a pivot table, it remembers the settings, so as you pivot the table, the sort sticks.

The quick sort buttons offer one-click access to sorting cell values. There are four entry points to the quick sort buttons:

- On the Home tab, click the Sort & Filter button, and then select either Sort A to Z or Sort Z to A.

- On the Data tab, select either the AZ or ZA quick sort buttons to sort the active field.

- Right-click a cell in the pivot table, select Sort, and choose from Sort A to Z or Sort Z to A.

- From a pivot label drop-down, select Sort A to Z or Sort Z to A.

 NOTE The actual button text might change depending on the type of data in the cell. For example, if the column contains only values, the text is Sort Smallest to Largest. If the column contains text, it is Sort Z to A.

Unlike sorting outside pivot tables, it doesn't matter if you have more than one cell selected during the sort. Excel automatically sorts the entire pivot table. If multiple columns are selected, Excel sorts by the leftmost column in the selection.

To quickly sort a field, select a cell in the field you want to sort by or a label to sort by labels. Apply the desired quick sort method outlined previously. The data re-sorts based on the selection. The Sort dialog box updates for the selected field.

 CAUTION A downside of using the quick sort buttons on the Home and Data tabs is that if you continue to pivot the table, Excel forgets the sort settings. However, if you use the pivot table sort options, Excel remembers the sort settings.

Creating Slicers

Slicers enable you to filter a pivot table, but in a much more user-friendly way. Unlike the filter drop-downs, slicers are always visible and you can change their dimensions to better fit your sheet design, as shown in Figure 25.10. There are three filters—Region, Product, and Customer—in the figure.

To insert a slicer, click the Insert Slicer button on the PivotTable Tools – Analyze tab. The Insert Slicers dialog box opens, listing all fields except calculation fields. The field for which a slicer is added does not need to be visible in the pivot table. Slicers can be sized and placed as needed. Use the Slicer Tools tab, available when you select a slicer, to modify many settings, such as changing the look of the slicers and attaching the slicer to multiple pivot tables.

Row Labels	Sum of Revenue	Sum of Profit
⊞ Alluring Shoe Company	223540	125088
⊞ Appealing Calculator Corporation	209326	116562
⊞ Best Vegetable Company	22140	12300
⊞ Bright Eggbeater Corporation	109320	61901
⊞ Bright Hairpin Company	100748	55143
⊞ Compelling Raft Company	315631	175744
⊞ Cool Jewelry Corporation	2484	1462
⊞ Exclusive Shovel Traders	288393	159689
⊞ Fine Barometer Corporation	19926	11106
⊞ Leading Utensil Corporation	8876	4788
⊞ Matchless Vise Inc.	151310	83867
⊞ Paramount Wax Inc.	9064	4976
⊞ Reliable Tripod Company	157637	88840
⊞ Remarkable Meter Corporation	294033	158716

Region
- Central
- East
- West

Product
- Laser Printers
- Basic ColorJet Printers
- Multi-Function Printers

Customer
- Alluring Shoe Company
- Appealing Calculator Corporation
- Best Vegetable Company
- Bright Eggbeater Corporation
- Bright Hairpin Company
- Compelling Raft Company
- Cool Jewelry Corporation
- Exclusive Shovel Traders

FIGURE 25.10

Slicers offer a more visually pleasing and user-friendly way of filtering pivot tables.

THE ABSOLUTE MINIMUM

Here are the key points to remember from this chapter:

- A pivot table is a table that summarizes and analyzes Excel data.

- You can modify a pivot table's content, appearance, or sort order.

- If you need to share the pivot table with others, add slicers to make it easier for them to filter and view the data important to them.

26

POWERPOINT 2013 BASICS

PowerPoint is a powerful, easy-to-use presentation design application that is part of the Microsoft Office suite of products. You can use PowerPoint to create presentations for a variety of audiences and for a variety of purposes. A presentation communicates information, and a good presentation can truly convince, motivate, inspire, and educate its audience. PowerPoint offers the tools both to create a basic presentation and to enhance and customize your presentation slides to meet your goals. In this chapter, you explore the many features and benefits of using PowerPoint—including the new features introduced in PowerPoint 2013—and learn to create a basic presentation.

Exploring PowerPoint

One of PowerPoint's strengths is its flexibility. Using themes, templates, and other presentation building blocks, you can quickly create a basic presentation even if you have little or no design skills. If you are a designer, PowerPoint's advanced features and customization options give you complete creative control. With PowerPoint, you can do the following:

- Create a presentation using a color-coordinated theme or a template, or you can create a blank presentation. You can also import a presentation outline from another application such as Microsoft Word.

- Add text and tables to your presentation slides to convey basic information.

- Add visual content with charts, pictures, clip art, SmartArt graphics, and other shapes or objects.

- Bring multimedia into the picture using sound, video, and animation.

- Add interactivity with hyperlinks and action buttons.

- Create and print notes and handouts for you and your audience.

- Share and collaborate on presentations with others in your organization.

- Access PowerPoint using the PowerPoint web app or a mobile device.

- Deliver a presentation onscreen using a computer, broadcast it online, or create a presentation video that you can post on the Web.

Exploring New PowerPoint 2013 Features

PowerPoint 2013 includes many new features that users of previous versions will enjoy, including the following:

- **Start screen**—Get started with PowerPoint by opening a recent presentation or selecting a theme to create a new presentation.

- **Theme variants**—Apply a variant to a theme. This feature is useful if you like a particular theme, but your branding requires different colors or styles.

- **Alignment guides**—Align objects and text automatically.

- **Merge shapes**—Combine two or more selected shapes by using a union, fragment, intersect, or other effect.

- **Enhanced Presenter view**—Enhance the Presenter view with slide zoom and a navigation grid.

- **Reply comments**—Enrich the collaborative process by adding replies to presentation comments.

- **Full screen mode**—Click the Full Screen Mode button in the upper-right corner of the PowerPoint screen to display Normal view in full screen.

- **Online video**—Search for and insert videos from YouTube or your SkyDrive account. Also search Bing for relevant videos or use a video embed code to insert online videos.

- **Online audio**—Search for and insert royalty-free audio clips from Office.com.

- **Online pictures**—Search for and insert pictures from Office.com, your SkyDrive account, and Flickr. Also search Bing for relevant pictures licensed under Creative Commons.

- **Enhanced Sharing**—Share your presentations online on SharePoint or SkyDrive by default.

- **MP4 video creation**—Create MP4 videos from your PowerPoint presentations.

- **Account window**—Update your user information and connect to other accounts.

- **Widescreen support**—Provide built-in widescreen (16:9) support. Optionally, switch to standard slide size (4:3).

Understanding PowerPoint Presentations

Before you start creating your first PowerPoint presentation, you need to understand *themes, templates,* and *slide layouts,* which are the presentation building blocks.

A theme and a template are not too different. Whereas a theme has built-in styles for fonts, colors, effects, backgrounds, and layouts, a template may have a collection of sample slides that you can use to create your slide content rather than starting from scratch. All themes and templates contain one or more Slide Masters, which you can access within the Slide Master view. Finally, each Slide Master has a set of child layouts that cater to different slide uses, such as a title slide, a title and content slide, a picture slide, and so on. The individual location of different placeholders on these slides is controlled by Slide Layouts. In the next few paragraphs, you discover more about how these individual building blocks work together.

Understanding Themes

A *theme* is a standalone file with colors, fonts, and effects to use in a single presentation. Other Microsoft Office 2013 applications, such as Word and Excel, also support themes. This enables you to create a consistent look and feel between your Office documents. A theme also stores information about backgrounds and layouts other than colors, fonts, and effects.

Each theme contains the following:

- **Fonts**—A theme contains two fonts: one for headings and one for body text.

- **Colors**—PowerPoint color schemes include a set of coordinated colors for text, backgrounds, accents, and hyperlinks. Each theme provides multiple color *variants* that give you more options for customizing a theme you like with the colors you require.

- **Effects**—Office themes apply graphic effects to tables, text, charts, diagrams, shapes, and pictures.

Every presentation has a theme—even a blank presentation, which uses the Office theme. You can apply a theme when you first create your presentation or apply one at any time to an existing presentation. See Chapter 27, "Customizing Themes and Backgrounds," for more information about themes.

Understanding Templates

A *template* is a starter document that you apply when you create a new presentation. Templates can include slide layouts; theme colors, fonts, and effects; background styles; and content for a specific type of presentation, such as for a project status meeting or training seminar.

Understanding Slide Layouts

In addition to themes and templates, the other important design feature you need to consider is the *slide layout*. A *slide layout* helps you add specific types of content to your slides, such as text, tables, charts, and pictures.

By default, PowerPoint offers multiple choices of layout (see Figure 26.1), but you can create your own layouts as well. If the predefined layouts don't suit your needs, you can modify a blank slide or modify one of the existing layouts by adding, moving, or deleting objects.

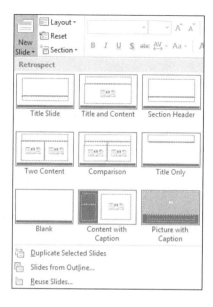

FIGURE 26.1

Choose an existing layout or start from scratch.

The default layouts are as follows:

- **Title Slide**—Include placeholders for a title and subtitle.

- **Title and Content**—Include placeholders for a title and one content item, such as a table, chart, SmartArt graphic, picture, or media file.

- **Section Header**—Introduce a new presentation section. See "Adding Sections to Your Presentation" later in this chapter for more information.

- **Two Content**—Include placeholders for a title and two content items.

- **Comparison**—Include placeholders for a title and two content items, each with a text heading.

- **Title Only**—Include a placeholder for a title only.

- **Blank**—Include a completely blank slide.

- **Content with Caption**—Include placeholders for a brief title, text, and content item.

- **Picture with Caption**—Include placeholders for a large picture, title, and text.

Depending on the theme you apply, some or all of the following additional slide layouts might also be available (for example, the Facets and Slice themes both include additional slide layouts):

- Panoramic Picture with Caption
- Title and Caption
- Quote with Caption
- Name Card

- Quote Name Card
- True or False
- 3 Column
- 3 Picture Column

The Title and Content, Two Content, Comparison, and Content with Caption layouts include a content palette as a placeholder. This content palette includes six buttons, as shown in Figure 26.2:

- Insert Table
- Insert Chart
- Insert a SmartArt Graphic

- Pictures
- Online Pictures
- Insert Video

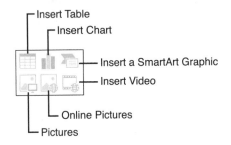

FIGURE 26.2

The content palette makes it easy to add tables, charts, pictures, and more.

 NOTE   See Chapter 3, "Working with Text," for more information about inserting text in placeholders.

On any slide that contains the content palette, you can also enter a bullet list using the starter bullet that displays in the upper-left corner of the slide area. If you click one of the buttons on the palette, this bullet disappears. Future chapters cover each of these options in more detail.

Understanding PowerPoint Views

PowerPoint includes several different *views*, which are arrangements of slides and tools on the screen that you use to work with and look at your presentation. Which view you use depends on what you're doing. The View tab, shown in Figure 26.3, includes numerous view buttons in the Presentation Views group and the Master Views group.

FIGURE 26.3

Select a view option on the View tab.

 TIP You can also click one of the view buttons in the lower-right portion of the PowerPoint window to display the Normal, Slide Sorter, Reading, and Slide Show views.

PowerPoint's views include the following:

- **Normal view**—This is the default view, as shown in Figure 26.4. Normal view displays your current slide in the middle of the page, a Slides pane that displays thumbnails of all the slides in your presentation, and a Notes pane that includes space for you to write speaker's notes or notes to yourself about your presentation.

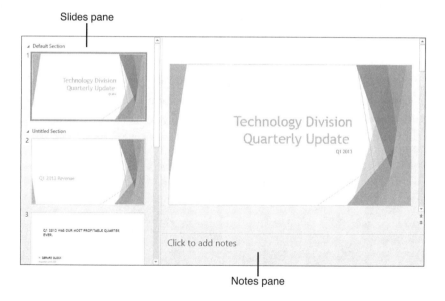

FIGURE 26.4

Normal view is PowerPoint's default viewing option.

 TIP Use the scrollbar on the right side of the Slides pane to navigate between presentation slides. You can also use the Page Up and Page Down keys to move among slides.

NOTE PowerPoint's default view for a new presentation is Normal view. If you want to change this, click the File tab, select Options, and go to the Advanced tab in the Options dialog box, where you can specify your default view in the Display section.

- **Outline view**—This view displays an outline of your presentation, including the text in the title and text placeholders.

- **Slide Sorter view**—This view displays miniature previews of all the slides in your presentation, making it easier for you to organize them. See Chapter 30, "Outlining Presentations," for more information.

- **Notes page view**—This view displays your notes in a full-page format, making it easier to view the content you enter on the Notes pane.

- **Reading view**—Reading view displays your slides as they would appear in a slide show, full screen, but with navigation buttons and menus in the lower-right corner.

- **Master views**—PowerPoint's three master views include the Slide Master, Handout Master, and Notes Master views. You use these views only when you customize your masters, including the placeholders, backgrounds, and colors that appear on your slide layouts. See Chapter 35, "Working with Slide Masters," for more information.

Exploring PowerPoint File Formats

PowerPoint enables you to save your presentation in a variety of file formats. In addition to saving as a standard presentation, you can also save as a PDF, XPS document, template, theme, show, image, or video.

CAUTION Be aware that if you save a PowerPoint 2013 presentation in an older format, you could lose some presentation features if they aren't compatible with the older version.

Creating a Presentation

You can create a presentation in several different ways, depending on the amount of content and design assistance you need. You can create the following:

- **Presentation using a theme**—Creating a new presentation using a PowerPoint theme provides an initial design with coordinated colors, fonts, and effects.

- **Presentation using a template**—Use one of PowerPoint's existing templates, a template you create yourself, or a template from Office.com's collection of templates.

- **Blank presentation**—A blank presentation contains black text on a white background with no content suggestions. Create a blank presentation only when you are experienced with PowerPoint and want to create a custom design. Even if you want to create a custom presentation, it often saves you time to start with a similar existing design and then customize it.

 TIP If you're going to create a complex presentation, it's often beneficial to create a storyboard before actually working in PowerPoint. A *storyboard* is a visual roadmap for your presentation. Begin by mapping out your complete presentation flow. By determining up front the order of your content and the best way to communicate your message (text, tables, charts, audio, video, or pictures), you can design your presentation faster and more effectively.

Creating a Presentation with a Theme

Using a coordinated PowerPoint theme as a starting point is a good way to create a presentation.

To create a presentation with a theme, follow these steps:

1. Click the File tab and then click New to open the New window in Backstage view (see Figure 26.5).

FIGURE 26.5

Create a coordinated design using a theme.

NOTE Step 1 assumes you already have PowerPoint open and the Ribbon is available. If you're just opening PowerPoint, you don't need to click the File tab to view the theme thumbnails.

2. Review the theme thumbnails that display on the New window and select the theme you want to apply to your presentation. PowerPoint opens a dialog box with more options (see Figure 26.6).

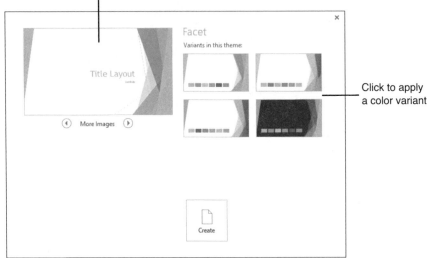

View sample slide layouts for this theme

Click to apply a color variant

FIGURE 26.6

Customize your selected theme with a variant.

3. Select a color variant to apply to your theme.

4. Click the Create button. PowerPoint opens a new presentation with a Title Slide layout. Figure 26.7 shows a sample new presentation.

FIGURE 26.7

Get started with your new presentation by adding slides and content.

Creating a Presentation from an Online Template or Theme

In addition to the default themes that come with PowerPoint, you can search an online collection of thousands of templates and themes, one of which is sure to be a great match for your presentation.

To create a presentation from an online template or theme, follow these steps:

1. Click the File tab and then click New to open the New window in Backstage view (refer to Figure 26.7).

 NOTE Step 1 assumes you already have PowerPoint open and the Ribbon is available. If you're just opening PowerPoint, you don't need to click the File tab to view the Search Online Templates and Themes box.

2. In the Search Online Templates and Themes box, enter keywords related to the type of template or theme you're looking for and then click the Search button. PowerPoint offers a few suggestions below the search box that you can click. PowerPoint displays options that match your search criteria (see Figure 26.8).

Scroll for more options   Filter by category

FIGURE 26.8

PowerPoint offers a vast collection of online templates and themes from which to choose.

 TIP Optionally, you can further filter your results by selecting one of the categories that display on the right side of the window.

3. Select the template or theme that you want to apply to your presentation. PowerPoint opens a dialog box with more information about your choice (see Figure 26.9).

FIGURE 26.9

Learn more about your selected template.

4. Click the Create button. PowerPoint opens a new presentation based on your selected template or theme.

Creating a Presentation from Scratch

If you have your own vision for your presentation and want to start with a blank slate, you can create a presentation from scratch.

To create a blank presentation, follow these steps:

1. Click the File tab and then click New to open the New window (refer to Figure 26.7).

2. Click the Blank Presentation thumbnail to open a blank slide in Title Slide layout.

3. From here, you can adjust the design and formatting to suit your needs.

 NOTE See Chapter 2, "Working with Office Applications," for more information about managing your presentations (and other Office documents), including opening, closing, renaming, deleting, and saving files.

Adding Slides to Your Presentation

To add a new slide to an open presentation, on the Home tab, click the lower portion of the New Slide button. From here, you can take one of the following actions:

- Select a layout from the gallery that appears (refer to Figure 26.2). See "Understanding Slide Layouts," earlier in this chapter, for more information about layout options.

- Select Duplicate Selected Slides to insert duplicates of the slides selected on the Slides tab.

- Select Slides from Outline to create slides from an outline you created in another application, such as Microsoft Word. See Chapter 30 for more information.

- Select Reuse Slides to open the Reuse Slides pane, as shown in Figure 26.10. You can reuse slides from another PowerPoint presentation or from a slide library.

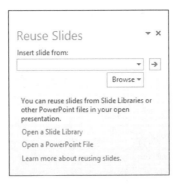

FIGURE 26.10

Reuse slides from a presentation on your computer or in a slide library.

 TIP Alternatively, click the top portion of the New Slide button to add a slide using the layout of the active slide automatically without opening the gallery. Pressing Ctrl+M also performs this same task.

Adding Sections to Your Presentation

PowerPoint enables you to add sections to your presentations. These are particularly useful for large presentations where it's easy to get lost in a sea of slides. You can use sections to define presentation topics or distinguish between speakers, for example.

You can also use the Section Header slide layout to further define presentation sections. See the "Understanding Slide Layouts" section, earlier in this chapter, for more information.

To add a section to your presentation, follow these steps:

1. In either Normal view or Slide Sorter view, select the slide that starts the section you want to insert.

2. On the Home tab, click the Section button and then select Add Section from the menu (see Figure 26.11). PowerPoint inserts an untitled section.

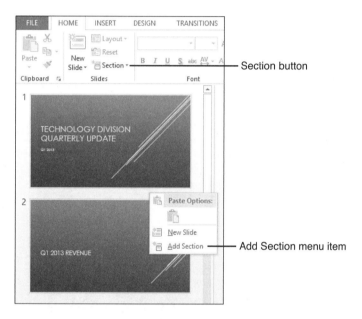

FIGURE 26.11

Add sections to better manage large presentations.

 TIP Alternatively, right-click between two slides on the Slides pane where you want to insert a section and from the menu that displays click Add Section.

3. Select the untitled section, click the Section button again, and select Rename Section. The Rename Section dialog box displays. You can also right-click the section to open this dialog box.

4. Enter a Section Name setting and then click the Rename button.

You can follow this procedure to enter as many sections as you need in your presentation.

Collapsing and Expanding Sections

If you have a lot of slides and sections, you might want to collapse them for easier viewing on the Slides tab. To do so, click the Section button on the Home tab and then select Collapse All from the menu. You can also collapse sections by right-clicking a section and selecting Collapse All from the menu. Expand collapsed sections by selecting Expand All from these same menus.

Removing Sections

To remove a section, select it, click the Section button on the Home tab, and select Remove Section from the menu. To remove all sections, select Remove All Sections. You can also remove a section by right-clicking it and selecting Remove Section from the menu that appears.

When you remove a section, PowerPoint deletes the section marker but not the slides in that section. If you want to remove a section and its slides, right-click the section and select Remove Sections & Slides from the menu.

 CAUTION PowerPoint doesn't ask for confirmation when you delete sections, so think carefully before proceeding.

THE ABSOLUTE MINIMUM

Here are the key points to remember from this chapter:

- Before you start creating your first PowerPoint presentation, you need to understand themes, templates, and slide layouts, which are the presentation building blocks.

- You can create a presentation using a theme or template, or create your own design from scratch.

- Adding slides to your presentation is easy with PowerPoint's collection of ready-made slide layouts.

- Using sections is a great way to break up large presentations where it's easy to get lost in a sea of slides.

27

CUSTOMIZING THEMES AND BACKGROUNDS

PowerPoint offers numerous tools to help you create presentations quickly and easily. There are times, however, when you might not like your initial choices or need to go beyond existing designs to create a truly unique presentation. Fortunately, PowerPoint makes it easy to switch to a new theme, apply multiple themes, change your theme's color variant, or format a presentation background.

Applying a New Theme to Your Presentation

When you create a presentation, PowerPoint prompts you to choose a theme, which is a coordinated set of colors, fonts, and effects. However, you can easily change the theme originally applied to your presentation in a matter of seconds.

 NOTE See Chapter 26, "PowerPoint 2013 Basics," for a reminder about the components of a theme.

To apply a new theme to your existing presentation, follow these steps:

1. Click the Design tab to view the Themes group (see Figure 27.1), which displays several potential themes. Your presentation's current theme displays to the far left.

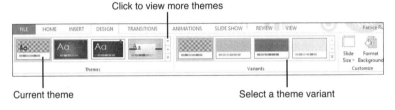

FIGURE 27.1

Select a new theme in the Themes group.

2. If none of these themes suits your needs, click the down arrow on the right side of the Themes box to display a gallery of additional themes, as shown in Figure 27.2.

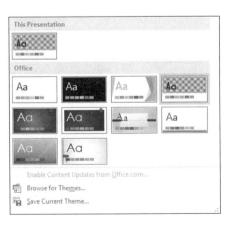

FIGURE 27.2

Choose a theme that best matches your presentation.

3. Pause your mouse over each theme to preview it in your active slide.

4. Select the theme you want to use.

5. Optionally, select a color variant in the Variants group on the Design tab. PowerPoint applies this new theme and its selected variant to your presentation.

Applying Multiple Themes to a Single Presentation

PowerPoint enables you to use more than one theme in a presentation. Multiple themes might be appropriate if you want to use one theme for your title slide and another for the rest of your presentation. Or if your presentation is divided into several distinct sections, you might want to use a separate theme for each. Figure 27.3 shows an example of a presentation with multiple themes.

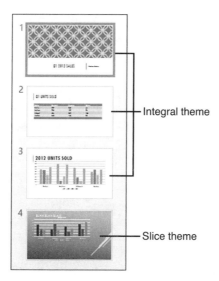

FIGURE 27.3

Use different themes to distinguish parts of a presentation.

 CAUTION Although it's easy to apply multiple themes, you should carefully consider whether it's a good idea. Too many contrasting styles and designs can make your presentation confusing and difficult to follow.

To apply a different theme to a group of slides, select the slides whose theme you want to change (in Normal view or Slide Sorter view). On the Design tab, select the new theme in the Themes group. PowerPoint applies the new theme only to the selected slides. The unselected slides retain the original theme.

 CAUTION If you select only a single slide, PowerPoint applies the theme to the entire presentation. To apply a theme to a single slide, right-click the theme in the Themes group and then select Apply to Selected Slides from the menu.

 TIP You can also apply a new variant to selected slides by right-clicking a variant in the Variants group and selecting Apply to Selected Slides from the menu.

Applying a New Theme Variant

When you created your presentation, PowerPoint prompted you to select a new variant without changing your presentation's theme. To do so, select a new variant in the Variants group on the Design tab (refer to Figure 27.1).

Formatting Presentation Backgrounds

You can further customize your presentation by formatting its background. In addition to applying specific background colors, you can also apply gradient or texture fills, hide background graphics, apply artistic effects, and modify pictures.

Formatting Your Presentation's Background

Formatting a background is an easy way to change the appearance of your presentation and its theme.

To format a background, follow these steps:

1. On the Design tab, click the Format Background button. The Format Background pane opens (see Figure 27.4).

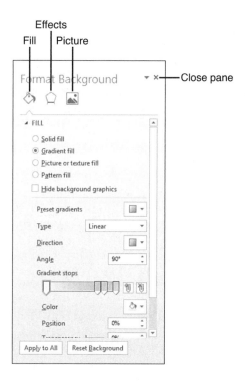

FIGURE 27.4

The Format Background pane enables you to make many changes in one place.

2. Click one of the following buttons to display related content on the pane: Fill, Effects, or Picture.

3. After specifying your background preferences in this pane, click the Apply to All button. The new background displays on your presentation slides, overriding the theme's background.

The tools available on the Format Background pane are very similar to those found on the Format Shape pane. See Chapter 5, "Working with Shapes and SmartArt," for more information about this pane.

 TIP Another option is to apply a background style. On the Design tab, click the down arrow in the lower-right corner of the Variants group and select Background Styles. A gallery opens with several background style options to choose from.

Omitting Background Graphics

If you want to omit the background graphics included with the template you applied to your presentation, click the Fill button on the Format Background pane and then select the Hide Background Graphics check box. For example, selecting this check box on a presentation whose theme includes pictures or shapes removes these objects but retains the original colors.

Resetting a Background

If you customize your background and decide you prefer the original, you can easily reset it. To reset the background to the theme default, click the Format Background button on the Design tab and click the Reset Background button on the Format Background pane.

Customizing Themes

If PowerPoint's built-in themes don't suit your needs, you can customize the fonts, colors, and effects in a theme and create your own theme.

Customizing Theme Color Schemes

Every PowerPoint theme includes a color scheme, a set of 12 coordinated colors used in the following parts of your presentation:

- Text and background (two light and two dark)
- Accents (six colors for graphs, charts, and other objects)
- Hyperlinks
- Followed hyperlinks

Applying a New Slide Color Scheme

If you don't like the colors in a particular theme, you can apply another color scheme.

To apply a new scheme, follow these steps:

1. On the Design tab, click the down arrow in the lower-right corner of the Variants group and select Colors. A gallery of color schemes displays, as shown in Figure 27.5.

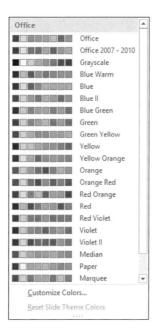

FIGURE 27.5

You can modify your presentation's color scheme.

2. Pause your mouse over each scheme to preview it on your presentation.

3. Click the scheme you prefer to apply it to your presentation.

Applying Multiple Color Schemes to a Single Presentation

PowerPoint also enables you to apply multiple color schemes within a single presentation. As with applying multiple themes, think carefully before applying many different colors to your presentation. To apply multiple color schemes to your presentation, follow these steps:

1. Select the slides to which you want to apply a separate color scheme. You can do this on the Slides panes on the left side of your screen or in Slide Sorter view.

2. On the Design tab, click the down arrow in the lower-right corner of the Variants group and select Colors. The theme colors gallery displays.

3. In the gallery, right-click the new color scheme, and choose Apply to Selected Slides. PowerPoint applies the color scheme to only the selected slides. The unselected slides retain the original color scheme.

To return to a single color scheme, select that scheme from the gallery.

CAUTION Although the capability to apply multiple color schemes to your presentation adds flexibility and creativity, be sure not to overdo it. Consider carefully before applying more than one color scheme to verify that your presentation is still consistent and readable.

Creating a Custom Color Scheme

Occasionally, you might want to customize the individual colors in a color scheme. For example, you might like a particular scheme but want to modify one of the text/background colors. Or you might want to use colors that match your company's logo or other design elements.

To create a custom color scheme, follow these steps:

1. On the Design tab, click the down arrow in the lower-right corner of the Variants group and select Colors to open the colors gallery.

2. In the gallery, select Customize Colors to open the Create New Theme Colors dialog box (see Figure 27.6).

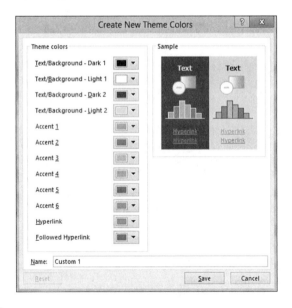

FIGURE 27.6

Change the color of certain areas of your presentation to customize it.

3. In the dialog box, select theme colors for text, backgrounds, accents, and hyperlinks from the drop-down lists. The Sample box previews your selections.

4. Enter a name for your new color scheme.

5. When you're happy with your choices, click the Save button. Your new color scheme now displays as a custom color scheme, available for selection from the gallery.

To edit custom color schemes, right-click the appropriate color scheme in the gallery, and select Edit from the shortcut menu. Make your changes in the Edit Theme Colors dialog box, and click Save.

To delete a custom color scheme, right-click the appropriate color scheme in the gallery, and select Delete from the shortcut menu. Click Yes to confirm the deletion. The custom scheme no longer displays in the gallery.

Customizing Theme Fonts

Although each theme comes with coordinating fonts, you can apply new fonts to your presentation—or create your own.

Applying New Theme Fonts

To apply new theme fonts, follow these steps:

1. On the Design tab, click the down arrow in the lower-right corner of the Variants group and select Fonts. The font gallery displays, as shown in Figure 27.7.

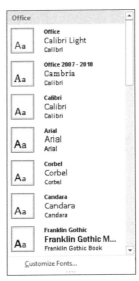

FIGURE 27.7

Select the fonts you want to use in your presentation.

2. Pause your mouse over each font pair to preview on your presentation. The font gallery shows two fonts in each pair. The first is for headings (both titles and subtitles) and the second is for body text, which includes all text other than title text such as text in tables, charts, and so on.

3. Choose the font pair you prefer from the font gallery.

Creating New Theme Fonts

To create new theme fonts, follow these steps:

1. On the Design tab, click the down arrow in the lower-right corner of the Variants group and select Fonts.

2. In the font gallery, click Customize Fonts to open the Create New Theme Fonts dialog box (see Figure 27.8). If you enable multiple language support, this dialog box might contain additional options.

FIGURE 27.8

Select your own heading and body text fonts.

3. Select a new Heading Font and a new Body Font from the drop-down lists. The Sample box previews your selections.

4. Enter a name for your custom font pair.

5. Click the Save button. Your new custom font pair now displays in the font gallery.

 TIP Be sure that any new fonts you apply are readable on your slides. Theme fonts are designed to be easy to read with all theme color schemes.

Editing Custom Fonts

To edit custom fonts, follow these steps:

1. Right-click the custom font pair you want to edit in the font gallery and choose Edit from the shortcut menu. The Edit Theme Fonts dialog box displays, which is nearly identical to the Create New Theme Fonts dialog box.

2. Make your changes in the Edit Theme Fonts dialog box.

3. Click the Save button.

 TIP   To delete custom fonts, right-click the custom font pair in the font gallery, and choose Delete from the shortcut menu. Click Yes when prompted to confirm. Your custom fonts no longer display in the font gallery.

Customizing Theme Effects

In addition to colors and fonts, you can also apply new effects that coordinate with your theme. These effects affect the look of tables, text, charts, diagrams, shapes, and pictures. Theme effects play a particularly important role with objects to which you've applied shape styles.

On the Design tab, click the down arrow in the lower-right corner of the Variants group and select Effects. A gallery of theme effects displays, as shown in Figure 27.9.

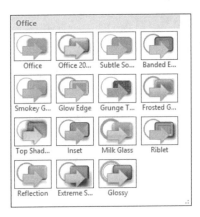

FIGURE 27.9

Select a theme effect to apply to your presentation.

Pause your mouse over each effect to preview it on your presentation. Note that changes display only if your slide content is affected by theme effects. Click the effect you prefer to apply it to your presentation.

Working with Custom Themes

If you modify the fonts, colors, and effects of a theme, you might want to save it to apply to future presentations. For example, you might want to create a custom theme to use throughout your company.

Creating and Saving a Custom Theme

To create a custom theme, follow these steps:

1. Make any theme changes such as changes to your theme's colors, fonts, and effects.

2. On the Design tab, click the down arrow in the lower-right corner of the Themes group.

3. Select Save Current Theme from the gallery. The Save Current Theme dialog box opens.

4. Enter a filename for your new theme.

5. Click the Save button to save your theme as an Office Theme file type stored in the Document Themes folder. Your theme is now available to select from the gallery.

THE ABSOLUTE MINIMUM

Here are the key points to remember from this chapter:

- If you don't like the theme you applied to your presentation, you can switch to another in a matter of seconds.

- PowerPoint enables you to use more than one theme in a presentation, but think about clarity and consistency before using this feature.

- Applying a new color variant is another way to change your presentation's appearance quickly.

- You can further customize your presentation by formatting its background, including fills, artistic effects, and pictures.

- For more creative control, you can customize theme colors, fonts, and effects.

FORMATTING AND ORGANIZING OBJECTS, SLIDES, AND PRESENTATIONS

After you create a presentation, you most likely will want to modify its appearance. Fortunately, it's easy to modify slides, objects, and entire presentations in PowerPoint.

PowerPoint offers numerous ways to manage and format slide objects, including several automatic formatting options and the optional use of gridlines and guides. You can also organize entire presentations using tools such as Slide Sorter view.

Manipulating Objects

In PowerPoint, an *object* refers to any of the components you include on your slides, such as shapes, pictures, text boxes, placeholders, SmartArt, charts, WordArt, and so forth.

You can easily cut, copy, paste, move, and resize PowerPoint objects.

Cutting an Object

To cut a selected object, click the Cut button in the Clipboard group on the Home tab or press Ctrl+X. To cut more than one object, hold down the Shift key while selecting objects, or drag a selection box around all the objects with the mouse.

 TIP If you cut something by mistake, click the Undo button to retrieve it.

Copying an Object

To copy a selected object, click the Copy button on the Home tab or press Ctrl+C.

 TIP To copy the attributes of one object and apply them to another object, use the Format Painter button on the Home tab. For example, if you select an object with 3-D effects, click the Format Painter button and then select another object so that the new object gets the same 3-D effects.

 NOTE When you copy an object, it displays on PowerPoint's Clipboard. To view the Clipboard, click the down arrow to the right of the Clipboard group on the Home tab to open the Clipboard pane. You can also select which item to paste on this pane.

Pasting an Object

To paste a cut or copied object, follow these steps:

1. Click the down arrow below the Paste button to open the Paste Options box, as shown in Figure 28.1, where you can preview the appearance of the pasted object on your slide. If you don't want to preview, click the Paste button directly (or press Ctrl+V) and skip to step 4.

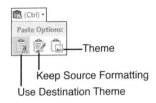

Theme

Keep Source Formatting

Use Destination Theme

FIGURE 28.1

Preview an object before pasting it.

2. Pause your mouse over each option button to preview what the pasted object would look like on your slide before actually pasting it into your presentation. Depending on what you paste and the context in which you paste it, any of the following option buttons could display in the Paste Options box:

-   **Keep Source Formatting**—Format the object as it was formatted in the location from which you copied it. This displays only when your destination slide has a different theme than the source.

-   **Use Destination Theme**—Apply the current theme formatting to the object. This is the default when you paste the object directly.

-   **Picture**—Convert the pasted item to a picture. To select a specific picture format, click the Paste Special link in the Paste Options box and choose a format from the Paste Special dialog box.

-   **Keep Text Only**—Remove all formatting from pasted text. This displays only when you paste text without having a text placeholder open first. PowerPoint creates a placeholder for the text as it pastes it.

3. Click a button in the Paste Options box to paste using the selected paste option.

4. After you paste an object, the Paste Options button displays to its lower-right. If you aren't satisfied with the initial paste option you selected, you can click this button and select another option.

  TIP If the Paste Options button doesn't display below a pasted object, verify that this feature is active. To do so, click the File tab, select Options, and go to the Advanced tab on the PowerPoint Options dialog box. Select the Show Paste Options Button When Content Is Pasted check box and click OK.

Moving and Resizing an Object

To move an object, select it and drag to a new location.

You can resize an object using resizing handles, which display around an object's edges when you select it. Figure 28.2 illustrates these handles.

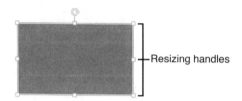

Resizing handles

FIGURE 28.2

Resizing handles make it easier to adjust the size and shape of your object.

Drag the handles with the mouse to make the object smaller, larger, or a different shape. Notice that depending on which sizing handle you select—a corner or interior handle—you can either enlarge the entire object or change its shape. To resize the object proportionately so that it keeps its shape, press the Shift key and drag a corner handle.

Arranging Objects

If your presentation includes multiple objects, you might need to order, group, align, or rotate them to achieve your desired effect. Using the tools available when you click the Arrange button on the Home tab, you can maintain complete control over the appearance of your presentation objects.

These tools are also available on the contextual Drawing Tools – Format tab that displays when you select an object.

Layering Objects

When you place two or more objects on a slide, you might want part of one to display on top of part of another. This is called *layering* the objects. You can do this for pure visual effect or to indicate that the overlapping objects have a relationship to each other. PowerPoint lets you control each object's layering, so if two objects are layered and you want the one below to display on top, you can change it.

To specify an object's layer order in relation to the other objects on a slide, follow these steps:

1. Select the object whose order you want to arrange. If the object you want to select is hidden from view, press the Tab key to cycle through all objects to find the one you want.

2. On the Home tab, click the Arrange button and choose one of the following options: Bring to Front, Send to Back, Bring Forward (one layer) , or Send Backward (one layer).

3. Click the order option you prefer from the menu. PowerPoint applies it to your selected object.

Figure 28.3 shows two sets of layered objects.

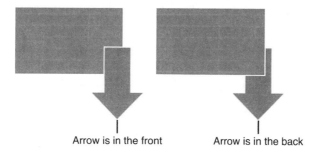

Arrow is in the front   Arrow is in the back

FIGURE 28.3

You can layer objects for a special effect.

TIP You can also access these layering options if you select an object, right-click, and choose from the submenu options that display.

Grouping Objects

It's difficult to move several objects on your slide and keep them positioned in proportion to each other. Fortunately, you can group two or more objects so that PowerPoint treats them as one object. For example, if you combine WordArt with a clip art image to create a logo, you can group these objects so that they stay together when you move them. A grouped set of objects moves in unison, always remaining in the same relative positions.

When you format grouped objects, the formatting applies to all the objects. For example, let's say you have two grouped objects that were originally different colors. If you now recolor them, the new color applies to both objects, not just one. To make individual changes, you have to ungroup the objects.

To group multiple objects on a slide, follow these steps:

1. Select the objects you want to group by pressing the Shift key and clicking individual objects.

2. On the Home tab, click the Arrange button.

3. Select the Group option on the menu that displays.

The object handles now treat the objects as one, as shown in Figure 28.4.

FIGURE 28.4

Group objects to treat them as one.

If you don't like the way you grouped objects and want to remove this grouping, click the Arrange button and select Ungroup from the menu. To revert back to the grouping, click the Arrange button and select Regroup.

Aligning Objects

To align and distribute objects relative to each other or to the slide, follow these steps:

1. Select the objects you want to align by pressing the Shift key and clicking individual objects.

2. On the Home tab, click the Arrange button, and choose Align. A submenu displays.

3. If you want to align or distribute relative to the slide itself, select Align to Slide. If you want to align or distribute relative to the objects, select Align Selected Objects. For example, let's say you select several objects and want to align them to the left. If you choose Align to Slide, all the objects move to the leftmost edge of the slide. If you choose Align Selected Objects, they align to the left side of the leftmost object.

4. Specify how you want to align the selected objects. You can align to the left, right, center, top, middle, or bottom. Optionally, you can also distribute objects horizontally or vertically, spacing them evenly. PowerPoint aligns your objects based on the direction you specify.

TIP Alternatively, you can also select an object and use the arrow keys to nudge the object in the direction of the arrow.

Rotating and Flipping Objects

Many times when you add a shape or clip art image, it ends up facing the wrong direction. For example, you might add a callout to draw attention to specific text, but the callout is pointing the wrong way.

 TIP To rotate or flip a single object in a group, you need to ungroup the objects first and then regroup the objects when you finish.

To quickly rotate an object, follow these steps:

1. Select the object you want to rotate.

2. Place the mouse pointer over the green rotation handle that displays at the top of the object, as shown in Figure 28.5.

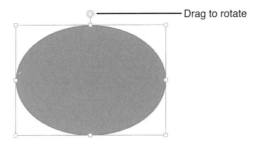

FIGURE 28.5

Use the rotation handle to quickly rotate an object.

3. Drag this handle to rotate the object. Pressing the Ctrl key while rotating changes the rotation angle 15° at a time.

You can also select rotation options by clicking the Arrange button on the Home tab and selecting Rotate from the menu. From here, you can choose to rotate right or left 90°, flip vertically or horizontally, or open the Format Shape dialog box.

Using the Selection Pane

Using the Selection pane, you can reorder slide objects and specify their visibility. Choosing to hide a specific object is temporary. This action doesn't delete it from the slide, and you can choose to make it visible again at any time.

To open this pane, click the Selection Pane button on the Drawing Tools – Format tab. Figure 28.6 shows the Selection pane.

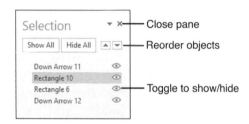

FIGURE 28.6

Temporarily hide objects in your presentation.

Working with Gridlines and Guides

Another way to align slide objects is to use gridlines and guides. These useful tools help you align objects on the slide or place objects in a precise location.

Gridlines display on your slides as small squares. Select the Gridlines check box on the View tab to display gridlines.

Guides divide your slide into quarters. Select the Guides check box on the View tab to display guides.

You can drag a guide to reposition it up, down, left, or right.

If you want to add another guide, right-click your slide and select either Add Vertical Guide or Add Horizontal Guide from the menu.

 NOTE Gridlines and guides are invisible during a slide show and don't display on a printed presentation.

Using Smart Guides

By default, PowerPoint uses smart guides to help you align objects. When you start to reposition an object in relation to another object, PowerPoint recognizes this and displays temporary guides to help you align correctly. To deactivate—or activate—this feature, right-click your slide and select Grid and Guides, Smart Guides from the menu.

Using the Grid and Guides Dialog Box

Using the Grid and Guides dialog box offers several advanced alignment features. To open this dialog box, shown in Figure 28.7, right-click your slide and select Grid and Guides from the menu.

FIGURE 28.7

You can snap objects to a grid.

In the Grid and Guides dialog box, you can snap objects to a grid, specify grid spacing, activate gridlines, display smart guides, and more.

Organizing Slides

In addition to organizing and formatting slide objects, you can also organize slides. Organizing slides is easy in PowerPoint: Select the slide you want to move and drag it to a new location.

You can organize and rearrange slides using three different PowerPoint views:

- **Normal view**—A good choice if you know exactly what you want to move and want to do it quickly.

- **Slide Sorter view**—Suited to major slide reorganizations, this view enables you to see thumbnails of multiple slides on a single page.

- **Outline view**—Read the content of your slides as you reorganize.

See Chapter 26, " PowerPoint 2013 Basics," to learn more about PowerPoint views.

Using Slide Sorter View

To open Slide Sorter view, click the Slide Sorter icon on the lower-right corner of the PowerPoint window, or click the Slide Sorter button on the View tab. Figure 28.8 displays Slide Sorter view.

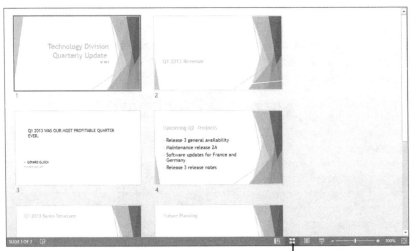

Open Slide Sorter view

FIGURE 28.8

Analyze and organize slides in Slide Sorter view.

In this view, you see smaller versions of your slides in several rows and columns. By viewing the basic content of each slide, you can more easily rearrange their order.

To move a slide in the Slide Sorter, select it and drag it to a new location. To view a particular slide in more detail, double-click it. To delete a slide in Slide Sorter view, select it and press the Delete key. To select multiple slides to delete, press Ctrl, select the slides, and then press the Delete key.

Copying and Moving Slides from One Presentation to Another

Using the Slide Sorter view, you can copy or move slides from one presentation to another. To do so, follow these steps:

1. Open both the source and destination presentations in Slide Sorter view.

2. On the View tab, click the Arrange All button. PowerPoint displays both presentations in different window panes in Slide Sorter view, as shown in Figure 28.9.

Maximize window   Close window

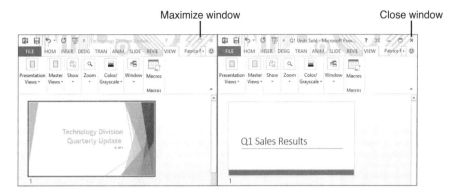

FIGURE 28.9

By splitting panes between two presentations, you can copy or move slides between them.

3. To copy a slide, select it and then drag it to the desired location in the other presentation. PowerPoint places the slide in the destination presentation, but it also remains in the source.

4. To move a slide, select it, press Ctrl+X, position the mouse in the new destination location, and press Ctrl+V. The slide is removed from the source presentation and inserted in the destination presentation.

5. To move or copy more than one slide at a time, press Ctrl as you drag slides from the source presentation.

6. If each presentation uses a different theme, the slide changes to the formatting of the new presentation, and the Paste Options button displays. If you want to retain the formatting of the source presentation, click the down arrow to the right of the Paste Options button and choose Keep Source Formatting. To go back to the formatting of the target presentation, choose Use Destination Theme.

 CAUTION Although you can combine multiple themes in a single presentation, think carefully before doing so. Combining can make your presentation confusing.

7. To remove the dual-window view, click the Close button in the upper-right corner of the presentation you no longer want to view.

8. Click the Maximize button in the upper-right corner of the presentation you want to keep active.

TIP If more than one presentation is open at a time and each is in a maximized window, you can press Ctrl+F6 to cycle through them. This helps when you want the full-screen view and want to copy/move from one presentation to the next without having to use the Window menu.

Deleting Slides

If you no longer need a slide or make a mistake and want to start again, you can delete it. You can delete slides in Normal view, Outline view, or Slide Sorter view.

To delete a slide, select the slide or slides you want to remove and press the Delete key. To delete multiple consecutive slides, press the Shift key and then select the slides. To delete multiple nonconsecutive slides, hold down the Ctrl key and then select the slides.

Changing Slide Size

In addition to rearranging slides, you can also change slide size. In PowerPoint 2013, the default slide size is widescreen (16:9) to match the dimensions of most computers and projectors. If you prefer, you can change your slide size to the former default (4:3) by clicking the Slide Size button on the Design tab.

THE ABSOLUTE MINIMUM

Here are the key points to remember from this chapter:

- You can cut, copy, and paste PowerPoint objects with the click of a button.

- PowerPoint offers a multitude of ways to manage and format slide objects, including aligning, layering, grouping, rotating, and flipping objects to meet your presentation needs.

- Gridlines, guides, and smart guides help you align slide objects and place objects in a precise location.

- You can organize your presentation and move slides from one presentation to another using Slide Sorter view.

29

ADDING TABLES TO A PRESENTATION

Tables offer a great option for presenting and structuring related data on a PowerPoint slide in ways that are easy to read and aesthetically pleasing.

Understanding PowerPoint Tables

A *table* is an object that conveys related information in columns and rows. If you've created tables in other applications, such as Word, you know how valuable they are for communicating information. Tables are also efficient and flexible. For example, rather than creating three separate bullet list slides, each listing the five most important features of your three main products, you can summarize all this information in a table on a single slide. Alternatively, you can present information on individual slides and then summarize everything in a table at the end of the presentation.

You can include a table in a PowerPoint presentation in several ways:

- **Insert a table from the content palette**—PowerPoint's basic table-insertion feature places a table into a slide, based on the number of rows and columns you specify. You can then format, customize, and add data to the table.

- **Draw a table**—When you need to create a complex table, one that the basic table feature can't make, you can draw it right on your slide. It takes longer to draw your own table, though.

- **Insert an Excel table**—Insert a table that takes advantage of the table formatting and calculation options available only in Excel.

Inserting a Table

One of the easiest ways to insert a table in a PowerPoint presentation is to start with a slide layout that includes the content palette.

To add a new slide that contains a table, follow these steps:

1. On the Home tab, click the down arrow below the New Slide button. A gallery of slide layouts displays.

2. Select one of the layouts that includes a content palette, such as the Title and Content, Two Content, Comparison, or Content with Caption layout from the gallery. A new slide displays.

3. On the content palette, click the Insert Table button to open the Insert Table dialog box, illustrated in Figure 29.1.

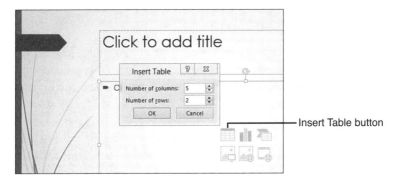

Insert Table button

FIGURE 29.1

Choose the number of rows and columns you want to include.

 TIP You can also open the Insert Table dialog box by clicking the Table button on the Insert tab. This option works best if you want to insert a table on a blank slide.

4. Choose the number of columns and rows to display and click the OK button. A blank table displays in your slide, as shown in Figure 29.2.

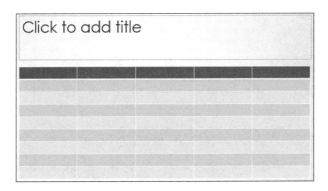

FIGURE 29.2

Enter table text to complete your table.

5. Click the **title placeholder** to remove the placeholder text and then enter a title for the slide.

6. Add the text you want in each cell of the table, clicking inside the table and then either tabbing to the cell or clicking in the cell.

You can format this text as you would any other text. For example, you might want to make the first row or column bold, or add other special formatting.

Drawing Custom Tables

If the default table options don't give you what you need, create a custom table. Drawing your own table lets you make columns and rows of varying widths, for example. For some people, drawing a table is faster than customizing a table created from a table placeholder.

To draw a table, follow these steps:

1. On the Insert tab, click the Table button and select Draw Table from the menu that displays. The mouse pointer becomes a pencil.

2. Drag the mouse diagonally across the slide to create a box about the size you think the table should be.

3. On the Table Tools – Design tab, click the Draw Table button in the Draw Borders group. The mouse pointer becomes a pencil again.

4. Select the type of lines you want to draw from the Pen Style, Pen Weight, and Pen Color drop-down buttons.

5. Use the pen to draw lines inside the box to make columns and rows.

If you make a mistake or want to imitate the Merge Cell feature, select the line you want to delete and then click the Eraser button on the Table Tools – Design tab. Use this eraser to remove the lines between rows and cells as necessary.

 TIP To make it easier to create rows and columns, on the View tab, click Gridlines.

Inserting Excel Spreadsheets

If you want to take advantage of Excel's formatting and calculation features in your table, you can insert an Excel table in your PowerPoint presentation. You can insert an Excel table on any PowerPoint slide, but this works best on blank slides or slides with the Title Only layout.

To insert a table you can format as an Excel spreadsheet, follow these steps:

1. On the Insert tab, click the Table button and choose Excel Spreadsheet. An Excel table displays on your slide.

2. Using the table handles, resize your table to fit your slide.

3. Enter your table data as you would in an Excel spreadsheet. The Ribbon now presents many Excel options, including the Formulas and Data tabs. Figure 29.3 shows a sample Excel table.

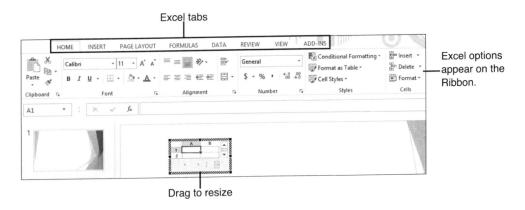

FIGURE 29.3

An Excel table enables you to use Excel's formatting and calculation features in PowerPoint.

4. Click anywhere outside the Excel table to return to the normal PowerPoint interface.

Formatting Tables

When you click in a table cell, a contextual tab displays called the Table Tools tab. This tab includes two contextual tabs: Design and Layout. These tabs are contextual in that they display only in context with a table. If you're not working on a table, they don't display on the Ribbon.

TIP   The Table Tools tab doesn't display when you click a table formatted as an Excel spreadsheet. Instead, double-click the Excel table to display Excel Ribbon tabs you can use for formatting.

Figure 29.4 illustrates the Table Tools – Design tab. Figure 29.5 illustrates the Table Tools – Layout tab. Combined, they contain the majority of the tools you need to format tables.

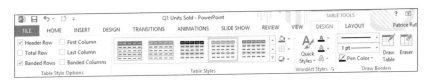

FIGURE 29.4

Choose formatting options for your table, including styles and borders.

FIGURE 29.5

Manipulate table rows and columns as well as set alignment.

PowerPoint lets you format tables in a number of ways, including the following:

- Applying different border styles, widths, and colors
- Inserting and deleting rows and columns
- Merging and splitting cells
- Applying table effects, including gradients, textures, background, and 3-D effects
- Aligning cell text to the top, bottom, or center

Setting Table Style Options

The Table Style Options group on the Table Tools – Design tab offers the following options for formatting the rows and columns in your table:

- **Header Row**—Apply a different color to the top row in a table and make its text bold.
- **Total Row**—Apply a different color to the bottom row in a table and make its text bold.
- **Banded Rows**—Highlight every other row in a table, using alternating colors, for easier viewing.
- **First Column**—Bold the text in the first column.
- **Last Column**—Bold the text in the last column.
- **Banded Columns**—Highlight every other column in a table, using alternating colors, for easier viewing.

Figure 29.6 shows a table with a header row and a total row.

Q1 Units Sold			
Region	Standard	Premium	Deluxe
Eastern	561	498	46
Southern	786	129	78
Midwest	654	267	126
Western	598	468	75
TOTAL	2,599	1362	325

FIGURE 29.6

Applying row and column formatting makes your table easier to read and understand.

Applying a Table Style

The Table Styles group on the Table Tools – Design tab displays suggested table style options. To view other options, click the down arrow on the right side of this group, as illustrated in Figure 29.7. If you want to remove formatting, click Clear Table.

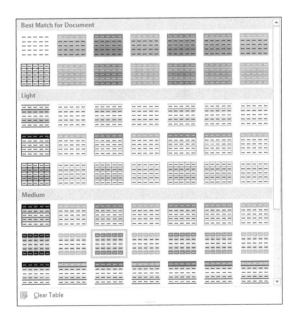

FIGURE 29.7

Apply any of a variety of formatting options to your table, or clear all formatting.

Creating a Border

Use borders to draw attention to your table or even to specific information in your table. New tables get a black, solid line border by default, but you can change this. To format the border, select the table and use the Table Tools tab to change the border style, width, and color and to set where borders display.

Setting the Border Style

To set the border style, click the Pen Style drop-down list on the Table Tools – Design tab, which is located in the Draw Borders group. Choose the border style you prefer from the list, which includes the option to apply no border, a solid line, or a variety of dashed line styles.

Setting the Border Width

To set the border width, on the Table Tools – Design tab, click the Pen Weight drop-down list and choose the width you prefer. Options include point sizes from 1/4 point (a thin line) to 6 points (a thick line).

Setting the Border Colors

To set the border color, click the Pen Color button. The gallery that displays offers several possible colors, based on the presentation's theme colors. For more color choices, click More Border Colors to open the Colors dialog box. Learn more in Chapter 5, "Working with Shapes and SmartArt."

Creating Borders

You can specify which parts of your table contain borders: the whole table or only specific outside or inside areas. Applying creative borders such as diagonals is another option.

To set borders, on the Table Tools – Design tab, click the down arrow to the right of the Borders button. Select the border you prefer from the available options.

Setting Table Fill Color

You can change the color that fills one or more cells in your table.

 CAUTION Be sure that your table text is still readable if you change a cell's fill color. For example, if your text is black, don't fill cells with dark blue.

To change table fill color, follow these steps:

1. Select the cells whose fill color you want to change.

2. On the Table Tools – Design tab, click the down arrow next to the Shading button.

3. From the palette that displays, you can perform the following actions:

    • Choose from the colors on the palette. You can choose colors that complement your theme or any of a variety of standard colors.

    • Click More Fill Colors to open the Colors dialog box. You can either choose from a large number of colors in this dialog box or create a custom color.

    • Apply pictures, gradients, textures, and table backgrounds. See Chapter 5 for more information about these options.

To remove a fill you no longer want, select No Fill from the palette.

Applying Table Effects

The Table Tools – Design tab also offers the option to apply formatting effects such as bevel, shadow, and reflection to your table. Click the down arrow next to the Effects button to view available formatting effects. You can also select table text and choose any of the formatting options in the WordArt Styles group. Learn more in Chapter 3, "Working with Text."

Working with Columns and Rows

It never fails: As soon as you create a table and format it just so, you find that you need to add or remove information.

To insert a row into your table, click in the row above or below where you want to insert the row. Then, from the Table Tools – Layout tab, choose Insert Above or Insert Below, as appropriate. PowerPoint inserts the row, as shown in Figure 29.8.

Q1 Units Sold			
Region	Standard	Premium	Deluxe
Eastern	561	498	46
Southern	786	129	78
				←New row
Midwest	654	267	126
Western	598	468	75
TOTAL	2,599	1362	325

FIGURE 29.8

Add rows if you didn't create enough during the initial table creation.

When you add or delete rows and columns, your table might no longer fit well on the slide. You then need to resize the table by dragging a corner. Be careful, however, that you don't hide existing text by making the cells too small during resizing. If you want to insert multiple rows, select that number of rows before selecting the Insert command. For example, if you select two rows and then choose Insert Above in the Table Tools – Layout tab, PowerPoint inserts two rows above the selected rows.

To add a new column to your table, click in the column to the left or right of where you want to insert the column. Then choose Insert Left or Insert Right from the Table Tools – Layout tab.

Merging and Splitting Cells

One way PowerPoint makes tables flexible is by enabling you to *merge* and *split* table cells. For example, if you want a table to have a title centered at the top, you can merge all the cells across the top row. If you need to show two separate bits of information in one location, you can split one cell into two.

To merge cells, select the cells you want to merge. Then, on the Table Tools – Layout tab, click the Merge Cells button. Figure 29.9 illustrates five cells that were merged into one.

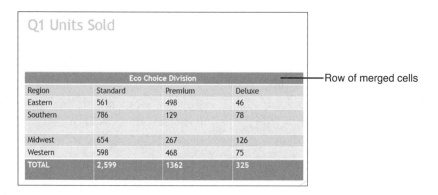

FIGURE 29.9

Merged and split cells have a variety of applications within a table.

 NOTE If you already have text in each of the cells you merge, each cell's text becomes a line of text in the new single cell.

To split a cell, select the cell you want to split, and then click the Split Cells button on the Table Tools – Layout tab. The Split Cells dialog box displays, where you can specify the number of rows and columns you want to insert in this particular cell.

Specifying Other Layout Options

The Table Tools – Layout tab offers other formatting options to explore. In the Cell Size group, you can set cell size options, such as the following:

- **Table Row Height**—Apply the specified height to table rows you select.
- **Table Column Width**—Apply the specified width to the table columns you select.
- **Distribute Rows**—Resize the rows you select so that they're the same width.
- **Distribute Columns**—Resize the columns you select so that they're the same height.

In the Alignment group, you can specify alignment, text direction, margins, and table size:

- **Align Text Left**—Align selected text to the left.
- **Center**—Center selected text.
- **Align Text Right**—Align selected text to the right.
- **Align Top**—Align text to the top of the cell.
- **Center Vertically**—Align text to the vertical center of the cell.
- **Align Bottom**—Align text to the bottom of the cell.
- **Text Direction**—Set the text direction as horizontal, rotated 270°, rotated 90°, or stacked.
- **Cell Margins**—Set text margins in a normal, narrow, or wide format, changing how far your text is from the cell's edges. You can also remove all margins.

In the Table Size group, specify the exact height and width of the table. Optionally, you can also lock the aspect ratio as you make changes (to prevent the table from getting formatted out of perspective).

In the Arrange group, perform advanced multiple-object formatting, such as bringing objects to the front or sending them to the back.

Adding Bulleted and Numbered Lists Within Tables

To create a bulleted list within a table cell, select the cell. Then, on the Home tab, click the Bullets button. To create a numbered list within a table cell, select the cell. Then, on the Home tab, click the Numbering button.

Deleting Tables and Table Contents

If you no longer need your table or want to start over creating a table, you can delete an existing table in your PowerPoint presentation. You can also delete rows, columns, or selected table text.

To delete an entire table, on the Table Tools – Layout tab, click the Delete button and then click Delete Table from the menu that displays.

 TIP Another way to delete a table is to click the outside border of the table to select the entire table and then press the Delete key.

To delete rows or columns, select the rows or columns you want to delete. Then, on the Table Tools – Layout tab, click the Delete button. Select either Delete Rows or Delete Columns from the menu that displays. PowerPoint deletes the selected content. To delete text in a cell, select the text (not just the cell) and press the Delete key.

THE ABSOLUTE MINIMUM

Here are the key points to remember from this chapter:

- Tables provide an easy and efficient way to summarize data on your PowerPoint slides.

- Drawing a custom table offers the most flexibility but the least automation.

- Insert an Excel spreadsheet to take advantage of that application's features and functionality.

- PowerPoint gives you a multitude of table formatting options, including borders, colors, shading, merging, and more.

- If you make a mistake, you can delete a table row or column, or even an entire table.

30

OUTLINING PRESENTATIONS

A solid, well-organized outline helps you achieve the goals of your presentation. Fortunately, PowerPoint offers features that simplify the outlining process. You can use Outline view to display and organize your outline in PowerPoint or create an outline in Microsoft Word or another application and insert it into a presentation.

Creating an Effective Presentation Outline

Before you actually create a presentation, you need to determine its purpose, organize your ideas, and establish the flow of what you're going to say. In other words, you need to create an outline, or storyboard.

You can outline your presentation in a few ways: on paper, in another application such as Microsoft Word, and directly in PowerPoint. Which one is best depends on the type of presentation you're delivering, its length and complexity, and—most important—your personal preferences.

Using Outline View

No matter which method you use to create your outline, you might want to use PowerPoint's Outline view to organize this information at some point.

 TIP You can change the size of any pane in PowerPoint by dragging its border to a new location. To do this, move the mouse over the border and, when the cursor changes to a double-headed arrow, click and drag.

To open Outline view, click the Outline View button on the View tab. Your presentation's outline displays in a pane on the left side of the window, replacing the Slides pane, and shares the interface with the slide itself and related notes. Figure 30.1 shows Outline view.

1 ☐ **Technology Division Quarterly Update**
    Q1 2013

2 ☐ **Q1 2013 Revenue**

3 ☐ **Q1 2013 was our most profitable quarter ever.**
    1 President and CEO
    2 Gerard Glock

4 ☐ **Upcoming Q2 Projects**
    • Release 3 general availability
    • Maintenance release 2A
    • Software updates for France and Germany
    • Release 3 release notes

FIGURE 30.1

Outline view offers a flexible approach to creating an outline.

Each slide is numbered and followed by a slide icon and the title text. The body text is listed under each slide title. This body text includes bulleted and indented lists and other text information. The title text is also referred to as the *outline heading*, and each individual point in the body text is referred to as a *subheading*. Clip art, tables, charts, and other objects don't display in the outline.

Adding new outline information is simple. Enter the content and then press the Enter key to move to the next point. To delete a point you no longer need, select it and press the Delete key.

Modifying Your Outline

When you right-click the content of any slide in Outline view, a contextual menu displays, as shown in Figure 30.2.

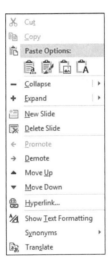

FIGURE 30.2

Right-click to view this menu of outlining options.

Although some of the options on this menu are generic—such as Cut, Copy, and Paste—most focus on editing and formatting slide content in Outline view. Table 30.1 lists the options found on this menu.

TABLE 30.1 Outline Menu Options

Menu Option	Description
Collapse	Hide all body text for the selected slides. Select Collapse All to hide all body text in the entire outline.
Expand	Display all body text for the selected slides. Select Expand All to display all body text in the entire outline.
New Slide	Insert a new slide after the selected slide.
Delete Slide	Delete the selected slides.
Promote	Change the selected text's outline level to the previous level, applying that level's style and formatting. Pressing Shift+Tab also promotes selected text.
Demote	Change the selected text's outline level to the next level, applying that level's style and formatting. Pressing the Tab key also demotes selected text.
Move Up	Move the selected text so that it displays before the previous item in the outline.
Move Down	Move the selected text so that it displays after the next item in the outline.
Hyperlink	Add a hyperlink to the selected text.
Show Text Formatting	Show the actual presentation font formatting in Outline view.

 NOTE Most of these menu options work best for slides that contain a lot of text, such as bulleted lists. If your slides emphasize other types of content, such as graphics and charts, you'll find it to be more convenient to rearrange content directly on your slides.

Promoting and Demoting Outline Points

You can demote outline headings and promote and demote subheadings to reorganize and rearrange your presentation. Promoting a first-level subheading makes it a heading (slide title) in a new slide. Promoting a second-level subheading (such as indented text or lower-level bullet) moves it up to the next level. On the other hand, promoting indented text outdents it.

For example, if you right-click the text of a second-level bullet in the outline (see Figure 30.3) and select Promote from the menu, the bullet becomes a first-level bullet (see Figure 30.4).

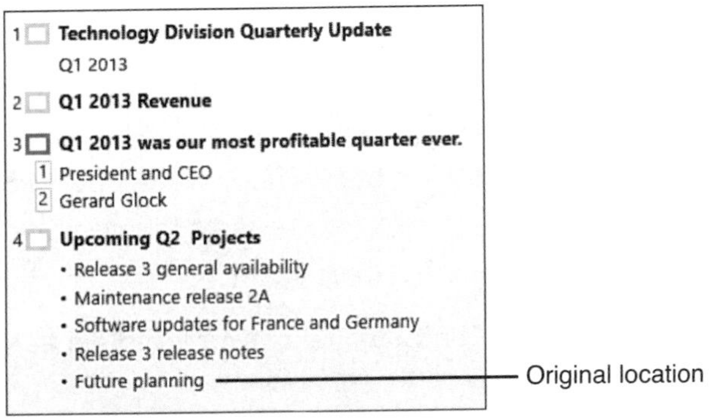

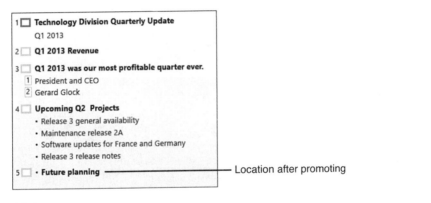

Original location

FIGURE 30.3

If a list item is at the wrong level, you can promote it.

Location after promoting

FIGURE 30.4

Promoting the list item moves it up one level but doesn't change its location.

If you promote a first-level bullet, it becomes a slide title, and PowerPoint inserts a new slide into the presentation. Demoting works in much the same way as promoting. Demoting a slide title makes it a first-level item and adds the slide's contents to the end of the previous slide. Demoting other text indents the text to the next outline level.

When you demote a slide, the text content remains and carries over to the previous slide, but any graphics or notes are deleted. To keep the notes and graphics, copy them to their destination using the Clipboard and then demote the slide.

Moving Outline Points Up and Down

You can also move each outline item up or down in the outline. To move an item up, right-click it and select Move Up from the menu. If you want to move an item down the outline, as you might expect, select Move Down from the menu.

Collapsing and Expanding Outline Points

To make it easier to read a long outline, collapse and expand slides and their body text.

To collapse the body text of slides in Outline view, follow these steps:

1. Right-click in Outline view to display a menu of options.

2. From the menu, pause your mouse over the Collapse option to display a submenu.

3. Select Collapse All from the submenu. On the outline, the slide numbers and titles remain, but the related body text is hidden from view.

To display your outline's detail again, right-click and select Expand and then Expand All from the menus.

 TIP To collapse the body text of an individual slide, right-click it and select Collapse from the menu. Right-click again and then select Expand to display the hidden text. If you want to collapse and expand more than one slide, but not all slides, press Shift, choose the consecutive slides, and then select Collapse or Expand. The slides you select must be consecutive.

Collapsing and expanding your outline makes it easier to print. You can print an entire outline in detail, only certain sections in detail, or only a collapsed summary outline. Learn more in Chapter 36, "Creating and Printing Presentation Materials."

Showing Slide Formatting

By default, Outline view displays each heading and subheading in the same font, bolding the headings for emphasis. If you want the outline to display using the actual fonts and formatting of the presentation, right-click the slide content and select Show Formatting from the menu.

Each item's specific font and attributes—such as size, bold, italic, underlining, and shadow—now display on the outline. The text's color is always black, though, regardless of the color formatting you've applied.

Inserting an Outline from Another Application

If you create an outline in another application, you can insert this file directly into PowerPoint, which can work with outlines in many different formats, such as Word documents (.doc and .docx), Rich Text Format (.rtf), Text files (.txt), or HTML (.htm).

You can insert an outline into a blank presentation or into a presentation that already includes slide content. In the latter case, PowerPoint inserts the outline after the current slide.

To insert an outline from another application, follow these steps:

 CAUTION   Be sure the file you want to insert is closed. If it's open in another application, PowerPoint gives you an error message.

1. On the Home tab, click the down arrow below the New Slide button.

2. At the bottom of the gallery, click Slides from Outline. Figure 30.5 shows the Insert Outline dialog box that displays.

FIGURE 30.5

Insert an outline you created in another application.

 TIP   The Insert Outline dialog box offers many of the same advanced options found in the Open dialog box. Learn more in Chapter 26, "PowerPoint 2013 Basics."

3. Navigate to the file you want to import and then click the Insert button. PowerPoint creates new slides and inserts the outline content onto these slides.

If your outline doesn't insert as you anticipated, review your source document for any possible formatting problems. You can also use Outline view to revise your inserted content. Another option is to simply cut and paste your content onto your PowerPoint slides.

THE ABSOLUTE MINIMUM

Here are the key points to remember from this chapter:

- A solid, well-organized outline can make a big difference in the success of your presentation.

- Use Outline view to organize your slides, including promoting and demoting slide content.

- If you already have an existing outline in another application (such as Microsoft Word), you can import it into PowerPoint without retyping.

31

REVIEWING PRESENTATIONS

Providing feedback on PowerPoint presentations is an important part of the presentation design process in many organizations. Fortunately, PowerPoint simplifies this process with several powerful but flexible reviewing tools. Using the Review tab and Comments pane, you can add and manage presentation comments easily. If reviewers work on their own copies of a presentation, you can use the Compare feature to compare review copies to your master and incorporate any changes.

Understanding PowerPoint Reviewing Tools

If you're a longtime PowerPoint user, you're probably familiar with PowerPoint's commenting tools. In version 2010, PowerPoint introduced the capability to compare two presentations and collaboration through co-authoring—features that are new to many PowerPoint 2013 users as well.

This chapter focuses specifically on the reviewing tools you find on the Review tab.

 NOTE In addition to enabling you to manage comments and compare presentations, the Review tab also offers numerous proofing and language tools. See Chapter 3, "Working with Text," for more information about these tools.

Working with Comments

Using comments—the electronic version of Post-it® Notes—is key to a successful presentation review. The Comments group on the Review tab offers five buttons that provide all the features you need to review and comment on a PowerPoint presentation (see Figure 31.1).

FIGURE 31.1

Use the buttons on the Review tab to add and manage presentation comments.

These buttons include the following:

- **New Comment**—Insert a comment about a slide or slide object.
- **Delete**—Delete a selected comment. Alternatively, click the down arrow to delete all comments on the current slide or all comments in the current presentation.
- **Previous**—Move to the previous comment in a presentation.
- **Next**—Move to the next comment in a presentation.
- **Show Comments**—Display the Comments pane or show markups.

Adding Comments to Slides

The best way to communicate your suggested changes to a presentation's author is to add a comment. You must use Normal view to add comments; Slide Sorter view doesn't support this feature.

To add a comment to a slide, follow these steps:

1. Select the slide object to which you want to add a comment, such as a text box, chart, or picture. If you want to comment on the slide as a whole, don't select anything.

2. On the Review tab, click the New Comment button. The Comments pane (see Figure 31.2) opens, displaying a comment box with your name and image.

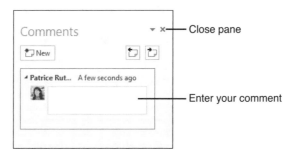

FIGURE 31.2

Comments are a great way to provide feedback on a presentation.

3. Enter your comment in the box.

4. Optionally, click the New button on the Comments pane to add another comment. If you want to comment on a specific slide object, select it before clicking the New button.

5. When you finish entering comments, click the Close button (x) to close the Comments pane.

PowerPoint displays comment markers for each comment you enter. PowerPoint places all general comment markers in the upper-left corner of the slide. If you add more than one general comment, the markers are stacked. If your comment relates to a specific slide object, the marker displays next to that object. Figure 31.3 shows a sample slide with two general comments, a comment about the slide title, and a comment about a chart.

Comments about the slide   Comment about the slide title

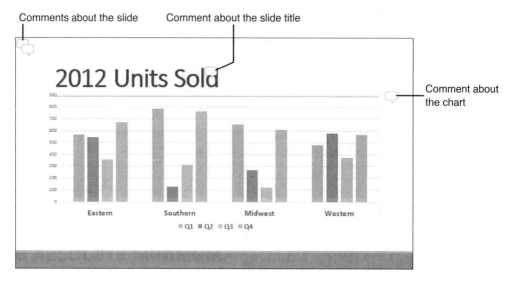

Comment about
the chart

FIGURE 31.3

Add comments about overall slide content or about a specific slide object.

 NOTE Optionally, you can move a comment marker from its default location by selecting it and dragging it with the mouse. This makes it more difficult to determine the focus of the comment, however.

Reviewing Comments

Use the Next and Previous buttons in the Comments group on the Review tab to move from comment to comment, evaluating each one on the Comments pane and making any needed presentation changes. When you reach the end of a presentation, clicking the Next button brings you back to the presentation's first comment.

 TIP You can also use the Next and Previous buttons on the Comments pane (located just below the Close button) to move through comments.

Editing and Replying to Comments

To edit a comment, follow these steps:

1. Click the comment marker for the comment you want to edit; the Comments pane opens.

2. In the Comments pane, click the comment box to edit its contents (see Figure 31.4).

FIGURE 31.4

Edit comments on the Comments pane.

3. Make the appropriate changes and then click outside the comment box to close it.

 TIP If comment markers don't display in your presentation, click the down arrow below the Show Comments button and select Show Markup from the menu.

To reply to a comment, select it on the Comments pane and enter your comment in the Reply box (refer to Figure 31.4).

Deleting Comments

After you read a comment and make any required presentation changes, you'll probably want to delete that comment. PowerPoint offers two ways to do this:

- Select a comment on the Comments pane and click the Delete button in its upper-right corner (refer to Figure 31.4).
- Select a comment marker on a slide and click the Delete button on the Review tab. (The Comments pane also opens by default.)

To delete all comments on the current slide, click the down arrow below the Delete button and then choose Delete All Comments and Ink on This Slide from the menu.

To delete all the comments in your entire presentation, click the down arrow below the Delete button and choose Delete All Comments and Ink in This Presentation.

Hiding Comments

If you don't want to delete comments, an alternative is to hide them so that they don't display on your presentation slides. To do so, click the down arrow below the Show Comments button and select Show Markup from the menu to remove its check mark.

Be aware that comments don't display in a slide show, so it isn't necessary to hide or delete them before presenting a show.

Comparing Presentations

Although it's best if all reviewers comment on and edit the same version of a presentation, such as one stored in a central location, there are times when they will enter comments in a separate version of your presentation. Fortunately, the Compare group on the Review tab (see Figure 31.5) offers several options for comparing presentations and accepting or rejecting potential changes.

FIGURE 31.5

The buttons on the Compare group simplify the consolidation of multiple presentation versions.

 NOTE Until you click the Compare button and select another presentation to compare, none of the other buttons in this group are available.

To compare an open PowerPoint presentation with another presentation, follow these steps:

1. On the Review tab, click the Compare button. The Choose File to Merge with Current Presentation dialog box opens, as shown in Figure 31.6.

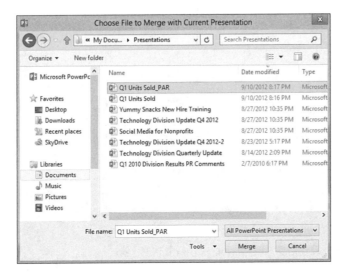

FIGURE 31.6

Select a presentation to compare.

2. Navigate to the presentation you want to compare and then click the Merge button. PowerPoint merges the two presentations and enables you to review, accept, and reject changes.

3. Manage your changes in one of the following ways:

   - Use the Revisions pane.

   - Use the Next and Previous buttons in the Compare group to scroll through changes.

   - Click the Accept button to accept all changes.

Which option is best for you depends on your personal preferences and the number of suggested changes. The rest of this section covers the many ways you can view, edit, accept, and reject changes in a compared presentation.

Working with the Revisions Pane

When you click the Compare button, the Revisions pane opens with the Details tab selected by default (see Figure 31.7).

FIGURE 31.7

Quickly see presentation differences on the Revisions pane.

On the Details tab, you can view slide changes, such as comments or text replacements, and presentation changes, such as the application of a new theme.

On the Slides tab, shown in Figure 31.8, you can view slide changes by reviewer.

FIGURE 31.8

Click the down arrow in the Revisions pane for more slide review options.

To accept all the changes for a specific reviewer, select the check box to the left of that person's name. You can also click the down arrow to the right of each slide to do the following:

- Accept changes by this reviewer (for this slide).
- Reject changes by this reviewer (for this slide).
- Preview any animations added to the comparison presentation.

To close the Revisions pane, click the Close button (x) in the upper-right corner. Alternatively, on the Review tab, click the Reviewing Pane button, which serves as a toggle for this pane.

Viewing Revisions

You can also view and manage changes with buttons on the Review tab. Click the Next button in the Compare group to view each suggested change sequentially. PowerPoint highlights the change on the Revisions pane, letting you know what the suggested change is and who suggested it.

To accept the change, select the check box that precedes the change information. Continue to click the Next button until you finish cycling through all the changes. To go back, click the Previous button to return to the previous change.

Accepting Changes

If you want to accept an active change, click the Accept button. For more options, click the down arrow below the Accept button. From the menu that displays, you can do the following:

- Accept the current change (the same as clicking the Accept button).
- Accept all changes to the current slide.
- Accept all changes to the current presentation.

 TIP   You can also accept changes on the Revisions pane or by clicking the check box to the left of any change that displays on a slide.

Rejecting Changes

After you accept a change, the Reject button on the Review tab becomes available. If you want to reject the active change, click the upper part of the Reject button. For more options, click the down arrow below the Reject button. From the menu that displays, you can do the following:

- Reject the current change (the same as clicking the Reject button).
- Reject all changes to the current slide.
- Reject all changes to the current presentation.

Ending the Review

When you finish comparing presentations, click the End Review button. PowerPoint opens a dialog box confirming that you want to proceed. All your accepted changes are applied to your original presentation; changes you didn't accept are discarded. Note that you can't undo this action.

THE ABSOLUTE MINIMUM

Here are the key points to remember from this chapter:

- PowerPoint offers a collection of reviewing tools that help you manage presentation feedback, an important part of the presentation design process in many organizations.

- The Comments group on the Review tab and the Comments pane offer everything you need to enter, edit, manage, reply to, and delete presentation comments.

- PowerPoint's Compare feature simplifies the process of comparing and consolidating feedback from multiple versions of your presentation.

32

WORKING WITH CHARTS

Charts enliven your presentation with visual impact and convey routine data in a way that your audience can easily understand and analyze. PowerPoint offers a variety of chart types, including the popular column, pie, and bar charts as well as more creative options such as line, stock, surface, radar, and combo charts.

You can create charts directly in PowerPoint or import charts from Excel. From there, use PowerPoint's plentiful chart formatting, design, and style tools to enhance and customize charts to meet your presentation needs.

Understanding Charts

Charts enable you to display, analyze, and compare numerical data in a graphical format. For example, you could use a column chart to compare sales revenue by region over a period of time (see Figure 32.1). Or you could create a pie chart that illustrates the percentage of revenue each of your product lines contributes to your total company revenue (see Figure 32.2).

FIGURE 32.1

Compare data with a column chart.

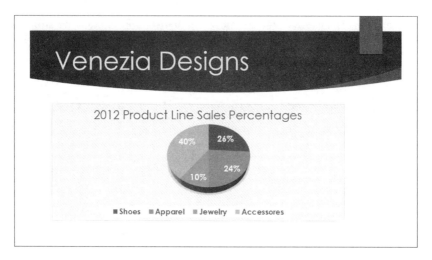

FIGURE 32.2

Analyze percentages with a pie chart.

PowerPoint also offers a vast array of design and formatting options to make your charts as aesthetically pleasing as they are informational, enhancing the presentation's appearance. You can use the default worksheet in PowerPoint to enter your chart data or take advantage of the formatting and charting tools available in Excel to create charts. You can also insert an existing Excel chart into your presentation.

Understanding Chart Terminology

Before creating a chart, it's a good idea to learn—or refresh your memory about—basic chart terminology. Table 32.1 lists the basic concepts you need to understand to make the most of PowerPoint chart functionality.

TABLE 32.1 Chart Terminology

Term	Definition
Axis	A line defining the chart area. PowerPoint charts have two axes: a vertical axis that displays data (the y-axis) and a horizontal axis that displays categories (the x-axis).
Chart area	The entire chart and all its components.
Data label	A label that provides information about a data marker.
Data points	Values that display on a chart in the form of columns, bars, or pie slices, for example. A *data marker* represents each individual data point.
Data series	A group of related data points on a chart, identified by a specific color or pattern.
Legend	A small box that describes the patterns or colors used to distinguish chart data series or categories.
Plot area	The area of the chart included inside the axes.

Understanding Chart Types

PowerPoint offers multiple chart types, each with several variations to choose from. For example, if you want to create a column chart, PowerPoint offers several variations of the basic column chart, including options for creating stacked, clustered, and 3-D column charts.

 CAUTION The number of available chart options can become overwhelming. To choose the right chart type, think carefully about the information you want to present and the message you want to convey with this data, and then select a chart type suited to your data.

Table 32.2 lists PowerPoint chart types.

TABLE 32.2 PowerPoint Chart Types

Chart Type	Description
Column	Compare data in two or more vertical columns. This chart type works well if you want to compare categories or data across a specific time span.
Line	Display data across a line with markers for each value.
Pie	Display a round pie-shaped chart with percentages of a total.
Bar	Compare data in two or more horizontal bars.
Area	Display value trends in a single area.
X Y (Scatter)	Compare data with points.
Stock	Display stock data (or other scientific data) in terms of volume and open, high, low, and close value.
Surface	Display numeric data in 3-D columns and rows.
Radar	Compare the value of several series of data.
Combo	Combine two different chart types, such as a column and line chart.

Inserting Charts

The fastest way to add a chart to your presentation is to apply a slide layout that contains the content palette. See Chapter 26, "PowerPoint 2013 Basics," for more information about PowerPoint slide layouts.

To insert a chart, follow these steps:

1. Click the down arrow below the New Slide button on the Home tab and then choose an appropriate layout from the gallery that displays. For example, you could choose the Title and Content, Two Content, Comparison, or Content with Caption layout.

2. On your new slide, click the Insert Chart button on the content palette, as shown in Figure 32.3. The Insert Chart dialog box opens (see Figure 32.4).

Insert Chart button

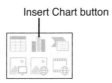

FIGURE 32.3

Click the Insert Chart button to get started.

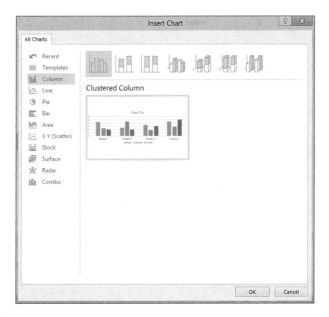

FIGURE 32.4

Choose from a variety of chart types.

TIP Another way to insert a chart is to click the Chart button on the Insert tab.

3. In the Insert Chart dialog box, select the button for the chart type you want to insert. See "Understanding Chart Types," earlier in this chapter, for an explanation of each chart type.

NOTE You can also view any chart templates you've saved by clicking the Templates button. See "Saving Your Chart as a Template," later in this chapter, for more information about creating chart templates. On the Templates tab of the Insert Chart dialog box, you can also click the Manage Templates button to rename and delete your saved charts.

4. Select the icon for the specific chart type you want to insert and then click the OK button. PowerPoint displays the chart on your slide and opens a worksheet with sample data in the format needed for the selected chart type (see Figure 32.5).

Edit data in Excel   Close worksheet

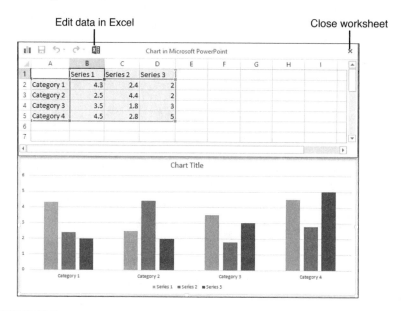

FIGURE 32.5

Enter your chart data in the worksheet.

5. Replace the sample data that displays in the worksheet with your actual data. The format of the sample data varies based on the chart type you selected in the Insert Chart dialog box.

 TIP Click the Edit Data in Microsoft Excel button to open Excel, which offers more formatting options.

6. When you're done entering data, click the Close (x) button in the upper-right corner of the worksheet.

7. PowerPoint displays the chart on your slide. From here, you can add a chart title and format your chart as needed.

Inserting a Chart from Excel

If you want to reuse an existing chart you created in Excel, you can quickly copy and paste it into PowerPoint.

To insert a chart from Excel, follow these steps:

1. Open the Excel worksheet that contains the chart you want to use in PowerPoint.

2. Select and copy (Ctrl+C) the chart you want to use.

3. Open your PowerPoint presentation and paste (Ctrl+V) the chart on the slide where you want to insert it.

4. Click the Paste Options button below the lower-right corner of the chart and select one of the following buttons, as shown in Figure 32.6:

   - **Use Destination Theme & Embed Workbook**—Embed the chart in your presentation and apply formatting from your presentation theme. You can modify the chart in PowerPoint, but any changes you make to the source in Excel aren't carried over.

   - **Keep Source Formatting & Embed Workbook**—Embed the chart in your presentation and retain the formatting applied in Excel. You can modify the chart in PowerPoint, but any changes you make to the source in Excel aren't carried over.

   - **Use Destination Theme & Link Data**—Insert the chart in your presentation (with a link to the source in Excel) and apply formatting from your presentation theme. Any changes you make to the source chart in Excel are carried over to PowerPoint.

   - **Keep Source Formatting & Link Data**—Insert the chart in your presentation (with a link to the source in Excel) and retain the formatting applied in Excel. Any changes you make to the source chart in Excel are carried over to PowerPoint.

   - **Picture**—Insert the chart as a picture. You can format your chart as you would any other picture in PowerPoint, but you can't change or update the chart data.

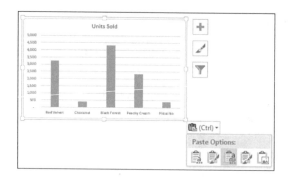

FIGURE 32.6

Specify how to paste Excel charts in PowerPoint.

You can then format and modify your chart based on the constraints of your Paste Options selection.

Modifying and Formatting Charts

PowerPoint offers a variety of ways to modify and format your charts, which you explore in this section. New to PowerPoint 2013 are three buttons that display to the right of a selected chart: Chart Elements, Chart Styles, and Chart Filters.

PowerPoint also includes two contextual tabs that enable you to modify the design and format of your charts. These are appropriately named the Chart Tools – Design tab and the Chart Tools – Format tab. These tabs are nearly identical to the Chart Tools tabs in Excel.

NOTE Contextual tabs display only when a chart is selected. If they disappear, select your chart again to view them. Also be aware that depending on your choice of chart type, not all options are available on the Chart Tools tabs.

TIP You can also apply animation effects to your charts, such as having each series fly in separately. See Chapter 34, "Working with Animation and Transitions," for more information about chart animations.

Displaying, Hiding, and Modifying Chart Elements

PowerPoint charts include a variety of titles and labels that you can display, hide, and modify using the Chart Elements menu.

Select a chart and click the Chart Elements button to display this menu (see Figure 32.7). Here you can specify whether you want to show or hide each element by selecting or deselecting its check box and, optionally, choosing additional options from the menus that display. You can also specify your preferred formatting options.

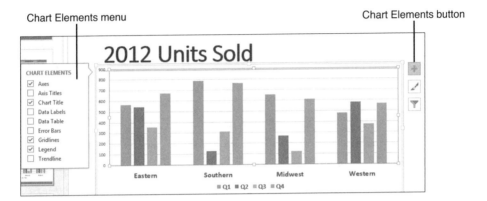

Chart Elements menu   Chart Elements button

FIGURE 32.7

Specify the chart elements you want to display on your chart.

The available menu options vary by chart type and could include the following:

- **Axes**—Display the primary horizontal axis or the primary vertical axis.

- **Axis Titles**—Display the primary horizontal axis title or the primary vertical axis title.

- **Chart Title**—Display your chart title above the chart or as a centered overlay.

- **Data Labels**—Display data labels in one of five ways in relation to the data point (centered, inside the end, inside the base, outside the end, or as a data callout).

- **Data Table**—Display a data table with or without a legend key.

- **Error Bars**—Display error bars using standard error, by percentage, or with standard deviation.

- **Gridlines**—Display any or all of the following gridlines: primary major horizontal, primary major vertical, primary minor horizontal, or primary minor vertical.

- **Legend**—Display the legend at the right, top, left, or bottom.

- **Lines**—Display drop lines or high-low lines.

- **Trendline**—Display a linear, exponential, linear forecast, or two-period moving average trendline based on a specific series in your chart.
- **Up/Down Bar**—Display up/down bars.

 TIP   It's sometimes hard to imagine how all these label options will actually look on your chart, so you might need to experiment a bit to find the format that works best.

Select the More Options link at the end of each menu to open the Format pane where you can select from additional options.

Modifying Chart Design

The Chart Tools – Design tab, as shown in Figure 32.8, enables you to change your chart type, edit chart data, and apply chart layouts and styles.

FIGURE 32.8

The Chart Tools – Design tab is one of two Chart Tools contextual tabs.

Adding a Chart Element

Click the Add Chart Element button on the Chart Tools – Design tab to add and format chart elements including axes, axis titles, chart titles, data labels, and more. You can also modify chart elements by clicking the Chart Elements button to the right of a selected chart. See "Displaying, Hiding, and Modifying Chart Elements," earlier in this chapter, for more information.

Applying a Quick Layout

Click the Quick Layout button on the Chart Tools – Design tab to display a gallery of layout options you can apply to your chart. Pause over each option to preview its effect.

Applying a Chart Style

If you want to quickly dress up your chart, you can apply one of many chart styles designed to complement your presentation's theme. To do so, select one of the suggested styles in the Chart Styles group on the Chart Tools – Design tab. For more options, click the down arrow to the bottom-right of this group.

NOTE You can also apply chart styles by clicking the Chart Styles button that displays to the right of a selected chart.

Modifying Chart Data

PowerPoint enables you to edit the data in your charts at any time or refresh data from a linked Excel chart. You can do this by selecting an option in the Data group on the Chart Tools – Design tab. For example, this group enables you to switch rows and columns, edit data, or refresh data.

Changing the Chart Type

If you don't like the way your chart looks and would like to try a different chart type, click the Change Chart Type button on the Chart Tools – Design tab to open the Change Chart Type dialog box. This dialog box is nearly identical to the Insert Chart dialog box, covered in the "Inserting a Chart from Excel" section earlier in this chapter. Select a new chart type and then click the OK button to return to your slide.

Formatting Charts

The Chart Tools – Format tab, as shown in Figure 32.9, enables you to apply formatting to specific chart areas, such as the axes, legend, gridlines, and series.

FIGURE 32.9

Apply subtle or sophisticated formatting on the Chart Tools – Format tab.

To format specific chart areas, follow these steps:

1. Select the area of the chart you want to format from the drop-down list in the upper-left corner of the Chart Tools – Format tab. The options that appear in the menu vary based on the chart type. For example, a pie chart doesn't have axes.

2. Click the Format Selection button to open the Format pane. Again, the exact name of the pane and its content vary based on your chart type and what you selected to format. For example, Figure 32.10 shows the Format Axis pane, which opens if you choose to format a chart axis.

Select area to format

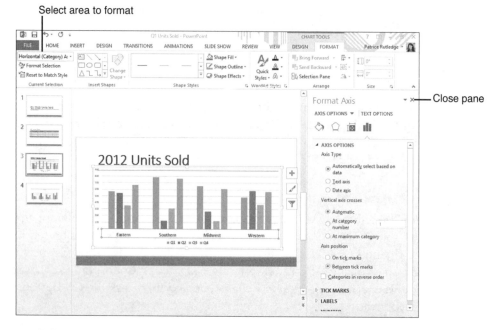

Close pane

FIGURE 32.10

The Format pane takes many forms, such as the Format Axis pane.

3. Specify your formatting changes on the Format pane.

4. Click the Close (x) button to apply your changes and return to your chart.

The Chart Tools – Format tab also offers features shared with the Format tabs that appear in context when you're performing other tasks in PowerPoint, such as inserting shapes, applying shape styles and WordArt styles, and arranging chart elements. See Chapter 5, "Working with Shapes and SmartArt," for more information about this tab.

Applying Chart Filters

Chart filters enable you to hide chart data without actually deleting it.

To apply a filter, follow these steps:

1. Select a chart and click the Chart Filters button to its right (see Figure 32.11).

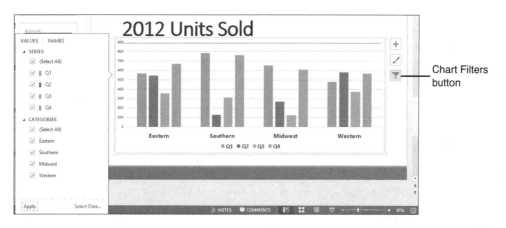

FIGURE 32.11

Filter the data that displays on your chart.

2. On the Values tab, deselect the series and categories you don't want to display.

3. Click the Apply button.

 NOTE Optionally, you can choose not to display series or category names on the Names tab. (PowerPoint displays numbers instead.) Or, you can click the Select Data link to open the Select Data Source dialog box, where you can add, edit, and remove data.

Saving Your Chart as a Template

If you make changes to your chart's design, layout, and format and would like to reuse it again, you can save it as a template.

To create a template based on your current chart, follow these steps:

1. Right-click the chart and select Save as Template from the menu that displays.

2. Verify that the default folder is the Charts folder. PowerPoint looks for chart templates in this folder when it populates the Templates section in the Insert Chart dialog box.

3. Enter a name for your template in the File Name field. This template now displays as a choice in the Insert Chart dialog box for future use.

4. Click the Save button to save your template and return to your chart.

THE ABSOLUTE MINIMUM

Here are the key points to remember from this chapter:

- Charts enable you to display, analyze, and compare numerical data in a graphical format.

- PowerPoint offers a variety of chart types, including column, pie, bar, and line charts.

- You can create a chart directly in PowerPoint or import a chart from Excel.

- PowerPoint's chart formatting tools are plentiful; you can apply a variety of chart styles, change chart colors and appearance, specify the exact chart content you want to display, and much more.

33

WORKING WITH AUDIO AND VIDEO

The selective use of audio and video is a great way to add impact to any presentation. With PowerPoint, you can insert audio and video from a variety of sources, including the Office.com clip collection and YouTube, edit your media files without having to use an external application, and create videos from your presentation.

Understanding Audio and Video Formats

PowerPoint offers a multitude of options when it comes to incorporating audio and video into your presentation, including several ways to insert clips and a vast array of formatting and playback options. PowerPoint also supports a variety of common audio and video file formats.

Table 33.1 lists the audio and video file formats PowerPoint supports.

TABLE 33.1 Audio and Video File Formats

Audio File Formats	Video File Formats
Audio Interchange File Format (.aiff), the standard audio format for Apple Macintosh computers	Advanced Systems Format (.asf), a Windows media file format for streaming media
Audio format used by Sun, Java, and Unix (.au)	Audio Video Interactive (.avi), a Windows video file format
Musical Instrument Digital Interface (.midi), an audio file format common with electronic musical instruments	Moving Picture Experts Group (.mpeg), a common movie file format
MPEG-1 Audio Layer 3 (.mp3), a common audio format for digital music	Windows Media Video (.wmv), a video file format developed by Microsoft for streaming video
Waveform Audio File Format (.wav), the standard audio format for Windows-based PCs	QuickTime video file (.mov), Apple's proprietary multimedia framework that handles both audio and video formats
Windows Media Audio (.wma), an audio format developed by Microsoft	Adobe Flash Media, multimedia format created with Adobe Flash (.swf)
QuickTime Video (audio component)	MP4 video (.mp4)

Inserting Audio Clips

PowerPoint offers three ways to insert audio clips into your presentation. You can insert an online audio clip from Office.com, insert an audio clip stored on your computer or network, or record an audio clip and insert it. When you select an audio clip on a slide, the player control bar displays below it. The Audio Tools – Format tab and Audio Tools – Playback tab also display. See "Formatting Audio and Video Clips" and "Specifying Audio and Video Playback Options," later in this chapter, for more information about these tabs.

Inserting Online Audio

To search for and insert an online audio clip from the Office.com royalty-free clip collection, follow these steps:

1. Navigate to the presentation slide where you want to insert your audio clip.

2. On the Insert tab, click the Audio button and select Online Audio.

3. Enter keywords related to the audio you want to insert in the text box and click the Search button (the small magnifying glass), as shown in Figure 33.1.

FIGURE 33.1

Add online audio to complement your presentation.

4. PowerPoint displays audio clips that match your search keywords. Select the audio clip you want and click the Insert button (see Figure 33.2).

 TIP Preview an audio clip by clicking it. Be aware that the preview takes a few seconds to load.

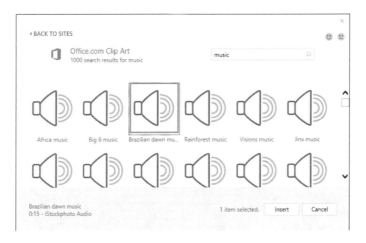

FIGURE 33.2

Select an audio clip from Office.com's extensive collection.

5. PowerPoint downloads and inserts the audio into your slide in the form of an audio clip icon (see Figure 33.3). Modify and format the audio clip as desired.

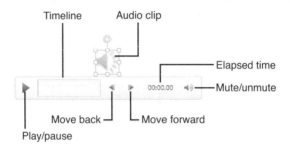

FIGURE 33.3

Play and control the playback of your audio clip.

Inserting Audio Clips from Your Computer

To insert an audio clip stored on your computer or on a network location, follow these steps:

1. Navigate to the presentation slide where you want to insert your audio clip.

2. On the Insert tab, click the Audio button and select Audio on My PC to open the Insert Audio dialog box, as shown in Figure 33.4.

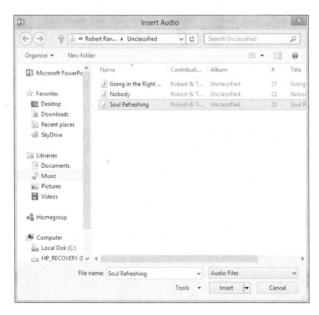

FIGURE 33.4

Insert an audio clip stored on your computer.

NOTE The Insert Audio dialog box shares many advanced options with the Open dialog box. See Chapter 26, "PowerPoint 2013 Basics," for more information about these options.

3. Navigate to the audio clip you want to insert and then click the Insert button. PowerPoint inserts the audio into your slide in the form of an audio clip icon (refer to Figure 33.3).

4. Modify and format the audio clip as desired.

You can reposition your audio clip elsewhere on your slide by clicking and dragging the clip to a new position.

 NOTE If you are upgrading to PowerPoint 2013 from PowerPoint 2007 or earlier, be aware that PowerPoint now embeds audio clips in the PowerPoint file itself.

Recording Audio Clips

You can record your own audio clips to insert in your PowerPoint presentation. You need to have a microphone (built-in or external) on your computer to do this.

To record an audio clip, follow these steps:

1. Navigate to the presentation slide where you want to insert your audio clip.

2. On the Insert tab, click the Audio button and select Record Audio to open the Record Sound dialog box, as shown in Figure 33.5.

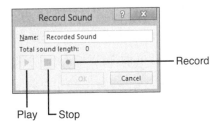

FIGURE 33.5

Record a sound to play with a particular slide.

3. Enter a description for this sound in the Name field.

4. Click the Record button to begin recording your sound.

5. Click the Stop button when you finish recording. To play back the sound, click the Play button.

6. Click the OK button to save the sound with the presentation; click Cancel to exit and start over.

An audio clip icon now displays in your presentation. You can reposition and resize it if desired. For example, you might want to place this icon in the lower-right corner of your slide to keep your audience focused on the slide content.

Deleting Audio Clips

To delete an audio clip from a slide, select it and press the Delete key.

 CAUTION Be aware that you can't undo an audio clip deletion. If you change your mind after deletion, you have to insert or record the clip again.

Inserting Video Clips

PowerPoint offers two ways to insert video clips into your presentation: insert an online video or insert a video clip from your computer.

Inserting Online Video

Inserting online video is an easy way to add a visual element to your presentation. PowerPoint enables you to insert video clips from an external website, such as YouTube. You can also search for videos on Bing, insert a video from one of your SkyDrive folders, or insert a video embed code.

To insert online video, follow these steps:

1. Navigate to the presentation slide where you want to insert your video clip.

2. On the Insert tab, click the Video button and select Online Video from the menu.

 TIP Another way to insert online video is to use a slide layout that includes the content palette and click the Insert Video button on the palette.

3. In the Insert Video dialog box, shown in Figure 33.6, you can do the following:

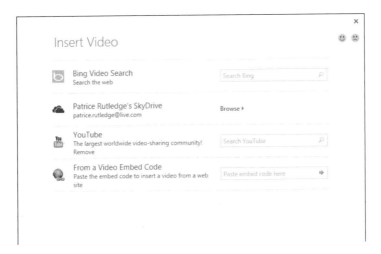

FIGURE 33.6

Insert videos from several online sources.

- Search for a video on Bing by entering keywords in the Search Bing field and clicking the Search button. PowerPoint displays matching videos from across the Web. Select the video you want and click the Insert button.

- Insert a video from your SkyDrive account by clicking Browse, selecting the video, and clicking the Insert button.

- Search for a video on YouTube by entering keywords in the Search YouTube field and clicking the Search button. PowerPoint displays matching videos. Select the video you want and click the Insert button.

- Enter a video embed code in the Paste Embed Code Here field and press the Enter key.

NOTE A video embed code enables you to share web videos in other locations, including PowerPoint presentations. Clicking a Share link or button usually leads to a video's embed code.

You can resize and reposition a video by dragging the handles that surround it when it's selected.

Inserting a Video Clip from Your Computer

To insert a video clip from your computer or a network location, follow these steps:

1. Navigate to the presentation slide where you want to insert your video clip.

2. On the Insert tab, click the Video button and select Video on My PC to open the Insert Video dialog box, as shown in Figure 33.7.

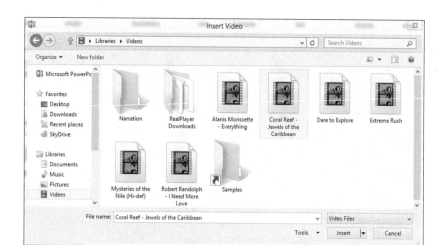

FIGURE 33.7

Select your own video to insert.

 NOTE The Insert Video dialog box shares many advanced options with the Open dialog box. See Chapter 26 for more information about these options.

3. Navigate to the video you want to insert and then click the Insert button. PowerPoint inserts the video into your slide, as shown in Figure 33.8.

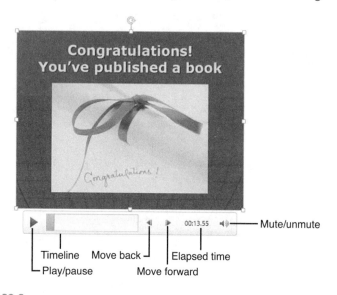

FIGURE 33.8

Insert your own video clip on a slide.

4. Modify and format the video clip as desired.

Select the video to display the player controls below it, including the Play/Pause button, a timeline, the Move Back and Move Forward buttons, an elapsed time counter, and a volume control. The Video Tools – Format tab and Video Tools – Playback tab also display.

Deleting a Video Clip

To delete a video clip from a slide, select it and press the Delete key.

Formatting Audio and Video Clips

The Audio Tools – Format tab and Video Tools – Format tab display when you select an audio or video clip on a PowerPoint slide. Figures 33.9 and 33.10 show these two tabs, which offer many options for formatting your media clips. With a few exceptions, these tabs are nearly identical and are also similar to the options on the Picture Tools – Format tab covered in detail in Chapter 4, "Working with Pictures." This chapter focuses on formatting issues unique to audio and video clips.

FIGURE 33.9

Format the appearance of an audio clip icon.

FIGURE 33.10

Dress up your video with a variety of video-formatting options.

Adjusting Audio and Video Clips

The Adjust group on the Audio Tools – Format tab and the Video Tools – Format tab enables you to remove background images from the audio clip icon, correct images, adjust color settings, and apply artistic effects. Be aware that not all these options are available, depending on the format of the image or video you want to modify.

See "Adjusting Pictures" in Chapter 4 for more information.

Specifying a Video Poster Frame

If you inserted a video clip, you can specify the appearance of the initial preview image, referred to as the *poster frame*. For example, you can display a static image from the video, a company logo, or even the photo of a speaker in the video.

To specify a poster frame for a selected video, go to the Video Tools – Format tab, click the Poster Frame button, and specify the poster frame source, such as the current frame or an image from your computer or the Web.

Working with Audio and Video Styles

The Picture Styles group on the Audio Tools – Format tab and the Video Styles group on the Video Tools – Format tab enables you to apply one of many preselected styles to your media clips, add a border around your clip, apply special clip effects, or modify your video shape. Note that for video, these effects apply to the video's preview image; for audio, the effects apply to the audio clip icon.

Figure 33.11 shows an example of the rotated, gradient style applied to a video clip.

FIGURE 33.11

Apply varied styles to your videos to give them a new look.

See "Working with Picture Styles" in Chapter 4 for more information.

Arranging Audio and Video Clips

The Arrange group on the Audio Tools – Format tab and the Video Tools – Format tab offers numerous options for arranging media clips. For example, you can align, group, and rotate images and send overlapping clips backward or forward to achieve a desired effect.

See Chapter 28, "Formatting and Organizing Objects, Slides, and Presentations," for more information about using the options in the Arrange group.

Resizing Audio and Video Clips

If you don't want to include an entire clip image in your presentation, you can crop it to your exact specifications. For example, you might want to zero in on an object in the center of a clip or remove extra content at the top of a clip. To do so, select the clip and click the Crop button on the Format tab. Handles surround the image, enabling you to specify the exact content you want to retain. Drag the mouse to determine your cropping area.

NOTE *Cropping a clip* refers to reducing the size of its physical image. If you want to play only a certain section of the clip's audio or video content, you need to trim it, which you can do on the Playback tab.

Alternatively, enter precise size specifications in the Height and Width boxes.

Specifying Audio and Video Playback Options

The Audio Tools – Playback tab or Video Tools – Playback tab appears when you select an audio or video clip on a PowerPoint slide. The Playback tab offers many options for specifying how you want to play your clips in an actual slide show. Figures 33.12 and 33.13 show these two tabs.

FIGURE 33.12

Specify how you want to play an audio clip.

FIGURE 33.13

On the Video Tools – Playback tab, you can trim video content and determine how to start your video.

 CAUTION Be aware that not all playback options are available for online clips. If a specific button isn't active for your selected clip, that feature isn't supported.

Playing a Clip

To play a clip directly on your slide, click the Play button on the Playback tab. Alternatively, click the Play button on the player control bar that appears below your clip. This is a good way to preview clips before actually running a show.

Adding a Bookmark

If you want to return to a specific place in one of your clips, you can bookmark it. To create a bookmark, play the selected clip and then pause at the location where you want to place the bookmark. Next, click the Add Bookmark button on the Playback tab. PowerPoint inserts a bookmark on the clip's timeline (a yellow circle). Figure 33.14 shows a sample bookmark.

Bookmark

FIGURE 33.14

Use a bookmark to easily return to a specific location in your clip.

Bookmarks are useful if you want to start playing your clip at a certain location or want to replay a specific segment for emphasis. You can also bookmark start and stop times if you want to trim your clip.

Editing Audio and Video Clips

In the Editing group on the Playback tab, you can trim your clip by specifying exact start and stop times. You can also add fade-in and fade-out effects to your clip in increments of seconds.

To trim a selected audio clip, click the Trim Audio button on the Audio Tools – Playback tab. The Trim Audio dialog box displays, as shown in Figure 33.15. To trim a selected video clip, click the Trim Video button on the Video Tools – Playback tab. The Trim Video dialog box displays, as shown in Figure 33.16.

FIGURE 33.15

Play only a certain section of an audio by trimming it.

FIGURE 33.16

PowerPoint makes it easy to trim your videos.

NOTE Be aware that trimming clips doesn't actually remove any content; PowerPoint just plays the trimmed portions. To physically remove trimmed content, you must compress your files. See "Compressing Media Files for Improved Performance" later in this chapter for more information.

Specifying Audio and Video Options

The Audio Options group and Video Options group on the Playback tab share many of the same buttons and features, including the following:

- **Volume**—Specify the volume level: low, medium, high, or mute.

- **Start**—Specify whether to start a clip automatically, start it with a mouse click, or play it across slides (audio only).

- **Play Across Slides**—Play audio across all slides (audio only).

- **Loop Until Stopped**—Repeat playing a clip until you manually stop it.

- **Hide During Show**—Hide the Audio Clip icon during a slide show (audio only). You should play your clip automatically if you select this option.

- **Play Full Screen**—Select this check box to play a video full screen during a slide show (video only).

- **Hide While Not Playing**—Hide the video preview image when it's not playing (video only).

- **Rewind After Playing**—Return to the beginning of a clip after you play it.

Compressing Media Files for Improved Performance

To improve the playback performance of your media files and save disk space, you can compress these files. To compress the media files in an open presentation, follow these steps:

1. Click the File tab to open Backstage view.

2. Click the Compress Media button, shown in Figure 33.17, and select from the following menu of options: Presentation Quality, Internet Quality, or Low Quality.

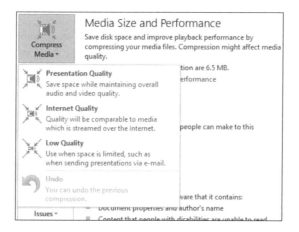

FIGURE 33.17

Compress your audio and video files to improve playback performance.

 CAUTION Be aware that the Compress Media button is available only if your presentation contains an audio or video file you can compress.

3. Review the Compress Media dialog box, which shows you the compression in progress. Depending on the number of media files in your presentation, this could take several minutes. When the compression process completes, the dialog box informs you how much space you saved, such as 1.4MB.

4. Click the Close button to close the dialog box.

Remember that compressing files affects presentation quality. Be sure to preview your presentation after compression to evaluate its effect.

 TIP To restore your presentation to its original status, select the Undo menu option.

Creating Videos from PowerPoint Presentations

PowerPoint lets you create full-fidelity video from your PowerPoint presentation in either a MPEG-4 Video (.mp4) or Windows Media Video (.wmv) format. You can distribute your video on the Web or mobile device, or through more traditional methods, such as on a DVD or through email.

TIP Before creating your video, decide what format you want to use and then verify that your slide content will work with this format. In addition, you need to create any timings or narration before creating your video. See Chapter 37, "Presenting a Slide Show," for more information.

To create a video, follow these steps:

1. Open the presentation you want to save as a video.

2. Click the File tab and select Export to open the Export window in Backstage view.

3. Select Create a Video. The right side of the page shows the Create a Video section, as shown in Figure 33.18.

4. From the first drop-down list, select one of the following video formats: Computer & HD Displays, Internet & DVD, or Portable Devices.

5. From the second drop-down list, select one of the following options:

   • **Don't Use Recorded Timings or Narrations**—Use timing specified in the Seconds to Spend on Each Slide box. The default is 5 seconds, but you can increase or decrease this as desired.

   • **Use Recorded Timings and Narrations**—Use the timings, narrations, and recorded laser-pointing directives you specified on the Slide Show tab. See Chapter 37 for more information. This option isn't available if you haven't recorded any timings or narrations.

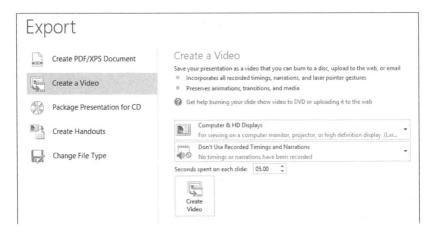

FIGURE 33.18

PowerPoint enables you to create videos from your presentations.

TIP If you would like to add timings and narrations, click the Record Timings and Narrations link to open the Record Slide Show dialog box. Click the Preview Timings and Narrations option to preview your presentation as it would display in your video with timings and narrations.

6. Click the Create Video button to open the Save As dialog box.

7. Enter a filename for your video, select a file type (MPEG-4 Video or Windows Media Video), and click the OK button. PowerPoint starts the video creation process. The time it takes to create your video depends on the number of slides in your presentation, your slide content, and the video format you choose.

From here, you can play this video on your computer, upload to your website or YouTube, burn it to a DVD, share to SkyDrive, or send it via email.

THE ABSOLUTE MINIMUM

Here are the key points to remember from this chapter:

- PowerPoint supports a variety of common audio and video file formats, including .mp3, .wav, .wma, .avi, .mov, and .mp4.

- You can insert an online audio clip from Office.com, audio stored on your computer or network, or audio files.

- Video options include inserting online video from Office.com or the Web and inserting a video clip from your computer.

- The Audio Tools – Format tab and Video Tools – Format tab display when you select an audio or video clip on a PowerPoint slide, offering a wide variety of media-formatting options.

- The Playback tab offers many options for specifying how you want to play your clips in an actual slide show.

- To improve the playback performance of your media files and save disk space, you can compress these files.

- PowerPoint enables you to create full-fidelity video from your PowerPoint presentation in either a Windows Media Video (.wmv) or MPEG-4 Video (.mp4) format.

IN THIS CHAPTER

- Understanding Animation and Transitions
- Setting Slide Transitions
- Applying Animations to Objects
- Customizing Animations on the Animation Pane
- Managing Animations

34

WORKING WITH ANIMATION AND TRANSITIONS

PowerPoint offers numerous options for animating your slide content and enlivening your presentation. You can animate the transition from one slide to another or animate how text, shapes, SmartArt, charts, and other objects display on a slide.

If the default settings don't meet your needs, you can also customize animations in a variety of ways using tools on the Animation pane, including special effects, timings, and more.

Understanding Animation and Transitions

Like most of PowerPoint's capabilities, animation can be either simple or complex. It all depends on how creative and sophisticated you want to make your presentation. Animation can definitely enhance any presentation, but as with any special effect, be careful not to overdo it. Too much animation can actually detract from your presentation. Animation also increases the presentation's file size.

PowerPoint offers two main ways to animate and add motion to your presentation:

- **Slide transitions**—Determine how to change from one slide to the next in your presentation. By default, when you move from one slide to another, the next slide immediately appears. With transitions, for example, you can make the old slide fade away to reveal the new slide or make the new slide move down from the top of the screen to cover the old slide.

- **Text and object animation**—Animate PowerPoint objects, such as text or shapes, using directional effects similar to slide transitions. For example, you can use an animation to wipe title text into your presentation. You can also specify more sophisticated animation options, such as the order and timing of multiple animation objects in one slide.

Setting Slide Transitions

Setting slide transitions is one of the most common animation effects. You can apply a slide transition to the entire presentation or just to the current slide. PowerPoint offers a variety of transition options, ranging from subtle to dynamic, including the capability to fade, wipe, reveal, or even introduce a slide with a honeycomb effect. If you aren't familiar with these effects, you can try them out on your slides before applying them. Most transitions enable you to choose a direction as well. For example, you can wipe up, down, left, or right.

 CAUTION As with so many PowerPoint features, use restraint with slide transitions. For the most professional results, choose one transition to use for every slide in a presentation.

To apply slide transitions, follow these steps:

1. On the Transitions tab, shown in Figure 34.1, choose one of the transitions that appears in the Transition to This Slide group.

FIGURE 34.1

Specify how you want to move from one slide to another slide during a presentation.

2. For more options, click the down arrow in the lower-right corner of the group and then choose one of the transitions from the gallery.

3. Click the Effect Options button to open a menu of effects that determine the direction your transition moves, such as from the top or from the bottom-right. Options vary based on the transition you select, and each includes an image that illustrates the direction.

4. To add a sound effect to your transition, select a sound from the Sound drop-down list. If you want to use a sound stored on your computer, choose Other Sound (at the bottom of the list) to open the Add Audio dialog box, select the sound to use, and click the Open button. If you want the sound to continue playing until the presentation encounters another sound file, select the Loop Until Next Sound option on the drop-down menu. See Chapter 33, "Working with Audio and Video," for more sound options.

 CAUTION Use sounds sparingly on slide transitions. They can unintentionally generate laughter or even annoyance in your audience.

5. In the Duration field, select the amount of time in seconds (or fractions of seconds) you want the transition to take introducing each slide.

6. If you want to advance to the next slide when you click the mouse or press a key (such as the spacebar, Enter, Page Up, or Page Down), verify that the On Mouse Click check box is selected and then skip to step 8. This is the default setting.

7. If you would rather have PowerPoint automatically change to the next slide after a specified amount of time, select the After check box and enter a specific time, in minutes and seconds, in the field beside it. Any timings you've already added to your slide show display in this box.

8. To preview your transitions, click the Preview button on the left side of the Transitions tab.

9. Click the Apply to All button to apply the transitions to all slides in your presentation.

TIP To remove slide transitions, click the None button in the Transition to This Slide group on the Transitions tab.

Applying Animation to Objects

You can apply basic animation to objects such as shapes, text placeholders, text boxes, SmartArt graphics, and charts using the options available in the Animation group on the Animations tab, as shown in Figure 34.2.

FIGURE 34.2

The Animations tab offers numerous options for adding motion to your slides.

To apply animations to objects, follow these steps:

1. Select the object or objects you want to animate. If you select more than one object, PowerPoint applies the animation to both objects at the same time. If you want the animations to occur in sequence, you must apply animation separately.

2. On the Animations tab, select the animation you want to apply from the Animation group. Several options appear on the Ribbon, but you can click the down arrow in the lower-right corner of the group and choose an option from the gallery (see Figure 34.3).

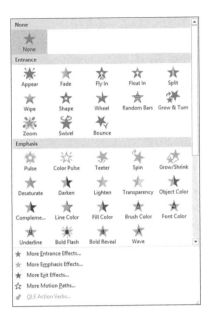

FIGURE 34.3

Choose from a variety of animation effects in the gallery.

3. Click the Effect Options button to choose the direction to apply the animation. The options that appear here vary based on the animation you chose. For example, if you choose the Fly In animation, this list includes eight options, including From Bottom and From Right. If the animation you selected doesn't offer effect options, you can't select this button.

 TIP If you're animating a chart, you can also specify a sequence. For example, you can animate a chart by series, by category, by element in a series, or as one object.

4. Click the Trigger button to specify what triggers this animation to start. Your choices include setting triggers based on the click of a specific object on the slide or on a bookmark.

5. Click the down arrow to the right of the Start button to specify when to start the animation: on a mouse click, with the previous animation, or after the previous animation.

6. Select a Delay setting, in seconds, between each animation. If you don't want a delay, select 00.00 in this field. Otherwise, you can specify delays in increments of 0.25 seconds or enter a custom increment.

7. Select a Duration setting, in seconds, to determine how long the animation should last. The smallest duration you can choose is 00.01, which introduces, and ends, your animation almost instantly. Otherwise, you can specify durations in increments of 0.25 seconds or enter a custom increment. If you choose a long duration, be aware that this creates a slow motion effect.

8. Click the Preview button to preview your animation choices.

Customizing Animations on the Animation Pane

The tools available on the Animations tab should suit most of your animation needs. However, if you want to customize your animations even more, you can do so on the Animation pane. For example, you use this pane to set animation effects for text, charts, SmartArt graphics, and media clips.

To open the pane (see Figure 34.4), click the Animation Pane button on the Animations tab.

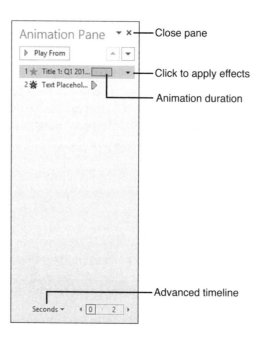

FIGURE 34.4

Further enhance your animation effects on the Animation pane.

 CAUTION Be aware that if you haven't applied any animations to the selected slide yet, the pane is empty and its features and buttons are inactive.

Each animation you applied from the Animations tab displays in the Animation pane in the order in which you applied it. The icon that precedes it tells you what kind of animation it is and corresponds to the icons that display in the Animation group on the Animations tab. The green bar that follows it indicates the duration of the animation. Pause the mouse over the animation in the list to display more information, such as the start option and effect type. If you have multiple animations in this list, the list is numbered, and the numbers also display on your slide to show where the animations are located. These numbers don't display in print or during a slide show, however.

Select an animated object in the list, and click the down arrow to its right to open a menu of additional options, described in more detail later in this section.

Click the Play All button to preview your animation effects. If you selected an animation on the pane, the Play From button displays instead.

Setting Additional Effects

To add additional effects to an animation listed in the pane—such as directional, sound, text, and color enhancements—click the down arrow to the right of an animation in the list and choose Effect Options from the menu that appears. A dialog box opens with the Effect tab selected (see Figure 34.5).

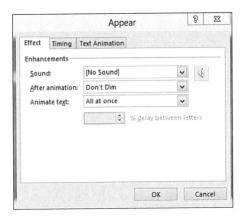

FIGURE 34.5

Continue to modify your custom animation with effect options.

The dialog box's name and content depend on the kind of animation event you're customizing. For example, if you choose the Appear entrance effect, the Appear dialog box opens.

Setting Timings

To set exact timing effects for your custom animations, click the down arrow next to an animation in the Animation pane and then choose Timing from the menu that appears. A dialog box opens with the Timing tab selected, as shown in Figure 34.6.

FIGURE 34.6

Make additional timing modifications on the Timing tab.

Remember that the name of this dialog box reflects the type of animation effect whose timing you want to customize. On the Timing tab, you can specify when to start the animation, enter the delay in seconds, choose a duration, specify what triggers the animation, and more.

Animating Charts

You can add more effects to a chart to which you've applied an animation. To do so, click the down arrow next to the chart in the Animation pane and then choose Effect Options from the menu. Figure 34.7 shows the dialog box that displays. Remember that the dialog box name reflects the type of effect you've applied, such as Fly In or Fade.

FIGURE 34.7

Animating a chart is another possibility.

Click the Chart Animation tab and, from the Group Chart drop-down list, indicate how you want to introduce the chart elements. Options include As One Object, By Series, By Category, By Element in Series, and By Element in Category.

 NOTE If you choose any option other than As One Object, the Start Animation by Drawing the Chart Background check box activates, letting you begin the animation with a chart background and then filling it in.

See Chapter 32, "Working with Charts," for more information about inserting charts in your presentation.

Animating Text

If the object you animate includes text, such as a text placeholder or text box, you can apply special text effects to your animation. To do so, click the down arrow next to the object in the Animation pane, choose Effect Options from the menu, and click the Text Animation tab. Figure 34.8 shows this tab.

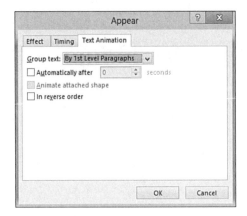

FIGURE 34.8

Emphasize specific words through text animation.

In the Group Text field, choose whether to animate as one object, all paragraphs at once, or by the level of paragraph (from 1st to 5th). You can also choose to animate text automatically after a certain number of seconds, animate an attached shape, or animate text in reverse order.

Depending on the type of text you animate, all these options might not be available. For example, let's say you want to animate a text box that includes several lines of text or perhaps a bulleted list. By choosing to animate by first-level paragraph, you can display each line individually rather than allow your audience to see your entire list at once.

Animating SmartArt Graphics

Animating SmartArt graphics is another animation customization you can apply. To do so, click the down arrow next to the graphic in the Animation pane, choose Effect Options from the menu, and click the SmartArt Animation tab.

From the Group Graphic drop-down list, choose the way you want to introduce the graphic onto the slide. The choices depend on the kind of SmartArt graphic you animate.

Animating Audio and Video Files

You can also add customized animations to a media clip such as an audio or video file. For example, to customize an audio clip animation, click the down arrow next to the clip in the Animation pane and choose Effect Options from the menu. The Play Audio dialog box opens, where you can customize audio effects, timing, and volume.

Viewing the Advanced Timeline

The Animation pane also displays the Advanced Timeline (refer to Figure 34.4), which lets you further customize timings by dragging the timeline's scrollbar.

To close the timeline, click the down arrow to the right of any object and then select Hide Advanced Timeline from the menu that displays. To display the timeline again, select Show Advanced Timeline from this same menu. (The wording of the menu option changes based on whether the timeline is visible.)

Managing Animations

After you create animations, it's easy to reorder, modify, or even remove them.

Reordering Animations

Your animations are numbered in the order in which you create them, but you can change this order if you prefer. To do so, select an animated object and click the Move Earlier button or Move Later button on the Animation tab.

You can also reorder animations on the Animation pane by using the Reorder arrow buttons at the top of the pane. Another option is to drag an animation to another location in the pane.

Modifying Animations

After you apply custom animations to a slide, you might decide that you want to modify them. For example, you might want to change the type of effect you applied from Fade to Float In or from Pulse to Grow/Shrink. To do so, select the object and choose a new animation effect from the Animation group.

Removing Animations

To remove an animation from a selected object or objects, click the None button in the Animation group. Alternatively, select the animated object in the Animation pane, click the down arrow, and select Remove from the menu. To remove all animations, select the first animation in the list, press the Shift key, select the last animation in the list, click the down arrow, and select Remove. If you make a mistake and want to restore your deletions, click the Undo button on the Quick Access Toolbar.

Reusing Animations with the Animation Painter

To copy an animation you added to one object and apply it to another object, you can use the Animation Painter button on the Animations tab. This button works in much the same way as the Format Painter button.

To apply the animation from a selected object to another object, click the Animation Painter button and then select the new object. To apply animations to more than one object, double-click the Animation Painter button and then select the new objects.

THE ABSOLUTE MINIMUM

Here are the key points to remember from this chapter:

- Slide transitions let you automate how PowerPoint moves from one slide to another.

- You can animate PowerPoint objects—such as text, shapes, SmartArt, and charts—using directional effects similar to slide transitions.

- The Animation pane helps you customize animations with special effects, timings, and more.

- Use the Animation Painter to save time and reuse animation effects you applied to other objects.

35

WORKING WITH SLIDE MASTERS

When you deliver a presentation, you want your audience to focus on the message and not be distracted by poor and inconsistent design from one slide to the next. Fortunately, PowerPoint makes it easy to achieve a consistent look in your presentation slides.

Slide masters help you achieve this uniformity by storing data about a presentation's theme and slide layouts—such as colors, fonts, effects, background, placeholders, and positioning—and applying it consistently throughout your presentation. Each presentation contains at least one slide master. In most cases, you won't need to do anything to the slide master but you can customize it if you choose. For example, you can change the default fonts, placeholders, background design, color scheme, or bullets, you can reposition placeholders, and you can add a logo. You can also create additional slide masters.

Modifying the Slide Master

To modify your slide master, go to the View tab and click the Slide Master button. PowerPoint displays the slide master layout and editing screen (see Figure 35.1).

Slide master thumbnail   Close and return to presentation

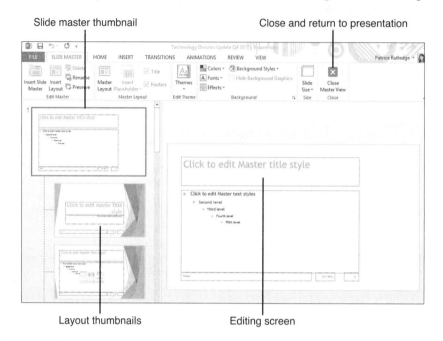

Layout thumbnails   Editing screen

FIGURE 35.1

The slide master editing screen helps you change the overall look and layout of your custom design templates.

 NOTE A template file (*.potx) can contain one or more slide masters. Each slide master can contain one or more sets of slide layouts, including custom layouts.

You can modify either the slide master, which affects the entire presentation's design, or the master for a specific slide layout, such as the title master or the title and content master.

 NOTE All changes you make to the title or other text while in the slide master editing screen apply to all slides in your slide presentation except those based on a specific layout master that overrides the slide master, thus helping you achieve consistency from slide to slide.

Place the mouse pointer over the thumbnails on the left side of the screen to display which thumbnail is for the overall slide master and which is for each layout master. Select the thumbnail to make formatting changes to the desired master. The master includes several areas you can modify: Title, Subtitle, Text, Date, Footer, and Number.

 NOTE In the Date, Footer, and Number areas, you normally don't add text but instead format the <date/time>, <footer>, and <#> placeholders. This information is added when you edit the header and footer. An exception might be the page numbering, where you can add and format "Page" before the <#> placeholder.

To modify an area, select it and apply the desired formatting changes from the Slide Master tab or the Format tab, which offers formatting options that should already be familiar to you. The Format tab appears when you click in the editing screen. Click the Close Master View button to exit and return to your presentation.

If you modify the slide master first, perhaps little needs to be changed for the title slide. However, you might make the title font larger, position it differently, or add a graphic object to the screen. Furthermore, you can delete the Date, Footer, and Number area boxes and create a different date or footer for the title slide.

 CAUTION Be sure that you have modified the slide master before changing the title layout. Initially, the title master uses the same fonts and other attributes as the slide master.

Adding a Slide Master

In PowerPoint, a template file (*.potx) can have one or more slide masters. To add a slide master, follow these steps:

1. On the View tab, click the Slide Master button to open the slide master editing screen.

2. Click the Insert Slide Master button in the Edit Master group on the Slide Master tab. A custom slide master displays. The thumbnails for the slide master and its related layouts appear below the thumbnails for your existing slide master. If you previously had only a single slide master, your new slide master will be numbered as Slide Master 2, as shown in Figure 35.2.

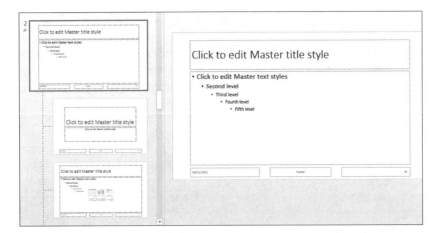

FIGURE 35.2

Easily identify multiple slide masters in PowerPoint.

3. Make any desired changes to the slide master and layouts just as you would with your original slide master. The Slide Master and Format tabs offer many formatting options.

4. Click the Save button on the Quick Access Toolbar to open the Save As dialog box.

5. Accept the default filename or enter a new name.

6. From the Save As Type drop-down list, choose PowerPoint Template and click the Save button. Your new slide master is now available in the template you saved.

Creating a Custom Layout

PowerPoint offers numerous predefined layouts—such as Title Slide, Title and Text, and Title and Content—that you can select by clicking the Layout button on the Home tab. These predefined layouts should be sufficient for most presentations, but sometimes you might need something a little different.

To create a custom layout, follow these steps:

1. Go to the View tab and click the Slide Master button. PowerPoint displays the slide master layout and editing screen.

2. Go to the Slide Master tab, select the thumbnail of the layout before which you want to add the custom layout, and click the Insert Layout button in the Edit Master group. A custom layout appears, as shown in Figure 35.3, whose thumbnail is just below the selected layout.

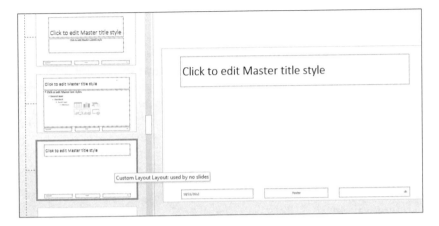

FIGURE 35.3

Create a custom layout if none of the standard layouts meets your needs.

3. By default, the custom layout contains a title placeholder and three footer placeholders for the date/time, generic footer, and slide number. To remove these placeholders, deselect the Title and Footers check boxes in the Master Layout group.

4. To add other placeholders, click the Insert Placeholder button in the Master Layout group. Options include the following placeholders: content, text, pictures, charts, tables, SmartArt, media, and online images.

5. Select a placeholder from the list, click a location on the slide layout, and drag the mouse to create an appropriately sized placeholder.

6. Continue adding placeholders and formatting your layout with the options on the Slide Master and Format tabs.

7. When you finish, select the thumbnail of the custom layout and click the Rename button in the Edit Master group on the Slide Master tab. The Rename Layout dialog box displays.

8. Enter a new name for your layout and click the Rename button.

9. Click the Save button on the Quick Access Toolbar to open the Save As dialog box.

10. Accept the default filename or enter a new name.

11. From the Save as Type drop-down list, choose PowerPoint Template and click the Save button. Your custom layout is now available when you click the New Slide button on the Home tab.

Managing Slide Masters

You can easily modify PowerPoint slide masters, including renaming, duplicating, deleting, or preserving them. You can also apply a theme to a slide master for a coordinated look.

Renaming a Slide Master or Layout

If you create a new slide master or layout, you'll probably want to rename it. To rename a slide master or layout, follow these steps:

1. On the View tab, click the Slide Master button to open the Slide Master editing screen.

2. Select the thumbnail of the slide master or layout you want to rename on the left side of the screen.

3. Click the Rename button in the Edit Master group on the Slide Master tab. The Rename dialog box opens.

 NOTE If you're renaming a slide master, the name of this dialog box is Rename Master. If you're renaming a layout, the name is Rename Layout.

4. Enter the new name for the slide master or layout and then click the Rename button.

Duplicating a Slide Master or Layout

Sometimes you want to create a slide master or layout that is similar to something that currently exists, yet requires a few small changes. Rather than starting from scratch, you can duplicate the existing master or layout and make your changes from there.

To duplicate a slide master or layout, follow these steps:

1. On the View tab, click the Slide Master button to open the slide master editing screen.

2. Select the thumbnail of the slide master or layout you want to duplicate on the left side of the screen.

3. Right-click the thumbnail and choose either Duplicate Slide Master or Duplicate Layout from the menu. Alternatively, press Ctrl+D on the keyboard to duplicate. A duplicate of your slide master or layout displays, which you can then customize.

Deleting a Slide Master or Layout

If you make a mistake or no longer need a slide master or layout, you can delete it. To delete a slide master or layout, follow these steps:

1. On the View tab, click the Slide Master button to open the slide master editing screen.

2. Select the thumbnail of the slide master or layout you want to delete on the left side of the screen.

3. Click the Delete button in the Edit Master group on the Slide Master tab. The slide master or layout is deleted.

Preserving a Slide Master

If you want to retain a slide master with your presentation even though you haven't applied it to any slides, you can choose to preserve it.

To preserve a slide master, follow these steps:

1. On the View tab, click the Slide Master button to open the slide master editing screen.

2. Select the thumbnail of the slide master you want to preserve on the left side of the screen.

3. Click the Preserve button in the Edit Master group on the Slide Master tab. The slide master is preserved.

Applying a Theme to a Slide Master

If you want to apply a new theme to a slide master, you can easily do so. When you apply a new theme to a master, the theme also applies to the layouts that comprise the master. Keep in mind that if you have only one slide master, applying a theme creates a second slide master with the chosen theme. If you apply a new theme to a slide master other than your original slide master, the master's theme changes to your new selection.

To apply a theme to a slide master, follow these steps:

1. On the View tab, click the Slide Master button to open the slide master editing screen.

2. Select the thumbnail of the slide master whose theme you want to change on the left side of the screen.

3. Click the Themes button in the Edit Theme group on the Slide Master tab.

4. Choose a new theme to apply from the gallery. If you selected a slide master other than the original master, the theme is applied to the master. Otherwise, PowerPoint creates a new slide master with the chosen theme.

See Chapter 27, "Customizing Themes and Backgrounds," for more information about PowerPoint themes.

Modifying the Handout and Notes Masters

In addition to the presentation itself, PowerPoint lets you modify the handout and notes masters. To modify the handout master, go to the View tab and click the Handout Master button. PowerPoint displays the Handout Master editing screen and Handout Master tab (see Figure 35.4).

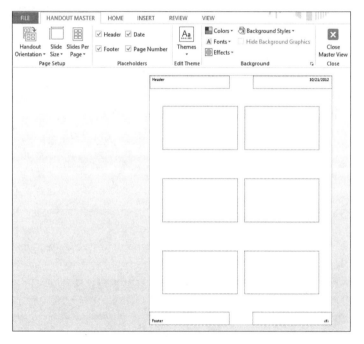

FIGURE 35.4

The handout master defines the default layout for your template's printed handouts.

On the handout master, you can perform the following tasks:

- Choose the number of slides you intend to include on each handout page by clicking the Slides Per Page button on the Handout Master tab. Choices include one, two, three, four, six, and nine handouts per page.

- Modify, reposition, or delete the Header, Footer, Date, and Page Area text boxes.
- Access the Format tab by selecting an object, where you can make edits to the text on the handout master.

 TIP You can easily change the number of slides to be included in the handouts in the Print dialog box when you actually print the handouts, without customizing the handout master.

To modify the notes master, go to the View tab and click the Notes Master button. PowerPoint displays the Notes Master editing screen (see Figure 35.5).

FIGURE 35.5

The notes master defines the default layout for your template's printed notes.

On the notes master, you can perform the following tasks:

- Reposition or resize the slide area, depending on how much area you want for the text (notes).
- Reposition or resize the notes area.

- Modify, reposition, or delete the Header, Footer, Date, and Page Area text boxes.

- Change the notes page orientation to either portrait or landscape.

- Access the Format tab by selecting an object, where you can make edits to the text on the handout master.

CAUTION Although you can change the background colors and color schemes for the handout and notes masters, you probably won't want to do so. Handouts and notes are usually printed, and background colors aren't necessary or wanted. You can, however, add a graphic element, such as a company logo, which then displays on each printed page.

THE ABSOLUTE MINIMUM

Here are the key points to remember from this chapter:

- The slide master editing screen helps you change the overall look and layout of your custom design templates.

- In PowerPoint, a template file (*.potx) can have one or more slide masters, giving you the capability to add slide masters to a presentation.

- If none of the predefined slide layouts works for your presentation, you can create a custom layout.

- PowerPoint makes it easy to modify, rename, duplicate, delete, or preserve slide masters. You can also apply a theme to a slide master for a coordinated look.

CREATING AND PRINTING PRESENTATION MATERIALS

PowerPoint enables you to print more than just slides. You can also print notes to remind yourself of what you want to say while presenting, handouts to give to your audience, and outlines to help you proof your content. PowerPoint also includes numerous customization options for printing auxiliary materials.

Understanding PowerPoint Printing Options

PowerPoint offers several options for printing your presentation, as follows:

- **Full page slides**—Print each slide on a single page.
- **Notes pages**—Print a single slide and its accompanying notes on one page. You create notes in the Notes pane, which is visible in Normal view. Figure 36.1 shows the Notes pane, where you can create detailed speaker's notes about your presentation. Notes are a useful way to remind yourself about what you're going to present. You can also use the Notes pane to provide additional details for your audience if you plan to distribute your presentation to them.

 NOTE If you choose to print three slides per handout, PowerPoint provides lined spaces to the right of each slide where you can write notes. If you choose another number of pages, you won't have this note space.

- **Handouts**—Print a specific number of slides per page (one, two, three, four, six, or nine), either horizontally or vertically. This can greatly reduce the number of pages and amount of printer toner required to print your presentation. When you print handouts, you see only the slides, not the accompanying notes.
- **Outlines**—Print your slide content without graphic formatting.

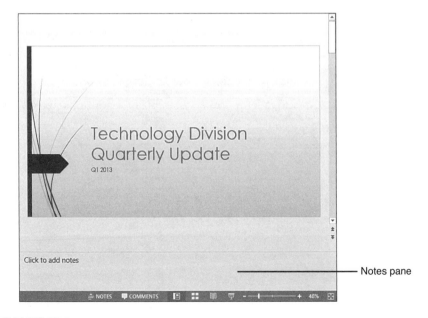

FIGURE 36.1

You can print the notes you add in the Notes pane.

To avoid wasting paper, first make sure that your PowerPoint presentation is ready to print. Set page and print options, customize headers and footers, and preview your presentation as you want it to appear when printed. Printing your presentation at least once is a good idea even if you don't plan on distributing handouts to your audience. When you proof a hard copy version, you often notice errors that you didn't catch on the screen.

 TIP Consider a greener alternative to printing a copy of your presentation for each member of your audience. You can save your presentation as a PDF (Portable Document Format electronic document) using the same formatting options as a print presentation (slides, handouts, notes pages, and outlines). See Chapter 26, "PowerPoint 2013 Basics," for more information about creating PDFs. Alternatively, consider posting a public presentation on the Web at SlideShare.net or a similar presentation-sharing site.

Printing PowerPoint Presentations

The Print window in Backstage view enables you to specify print settings, preview your slides, and print your presentation. Click the File tab and select Print from the menu, as shown in Figure 36.2.

Preparing to Print

Before you print, apply any special print settings. The Settings section includes five boxes with drop-down lists where you can specify these options (refer to Figure 36.2). The text that displays in each box varies depending on the last selection you made.

 NOTE You can customize printing defaults for the existing presentation in the PowerPoint Options dialog box. To access it, click the File tab, choose Options, and go to the Print section of the Advanced tab.

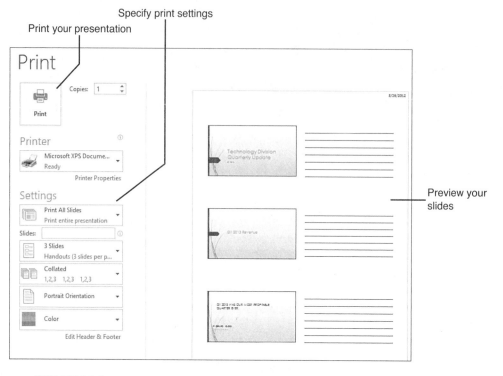

FIGURE 36.2

Prepare, preview, and print from the Print window in Backstage view.

Selecting Slides to Print

Click the first box in the Settings section to select the slides you want to print. Your options include the following:

- **Print All Slides**—Print the entire presentation.

- **Print Selection**—Print slides you select in Normal view or in Slide Sorter view.

- **Print Current Slide**—Print only the current slide that displays in the Print window.

- **Custom Range**—Print the slide numbers you enter in the Slides text box. For example, you could enter 1-4, 10 to print slides 1, 2, 3, 4, and 10.

- **Custom Shows**—Select a custom show to print. This option doesn't display if you haven't created at least one custom show. See Chapter 37, "Presenting a Slide Show," for more information about custom shows.

- **Print Hidden Slides**—Print slides you've hidden. See Chapter 28, "Formatting and Organizing Objects, Slides, and Presentations," for more information about hiding slides.

Specifying a Print Layout

Click the second box in the Settings section to select the print layout you want to use. Options include Full Page Slides, Notes Pages, Outline, as well as nine different handout layouts (see Figure 36.3).

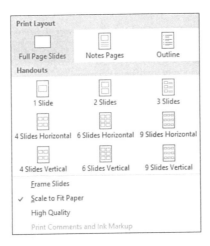

FIGURE 36.3

Your print layout options include nine different handout formats.

This menu also includes the following options:

- **Frame Slides**—Include a border around the slides.

- **Scale to Fit Paper**—Change the size of slides to fit the paper, making them either larger or smaller, as appropriate.

- **High Quality**—Print your presentation at the highest quality available with your printer.

- **Print Comments and Ink Markup**—Print comment pages and any ink markups you make onscreen with your presentation. This option is available only if your presentation contains comments or ink markups.

Collating Presentation Printouts

Click the third box in the Settings section to specify how you want to collate your printouts if you choose to print more than one copy of your presentation. Collating keeps multiple copies in sequence. If you print five copies of a presentation without collating, for example, you will print five copies of page one, five copies of page two, and so on.

Specifying Print Orientation

Click the fourth box in the Settings section to specify the orientation of your printouts: portrait or landscape. This option isn't available if you select Full Page Slides as your print layout. In this case, your slides print in landscape layout by default.

Specifying Colors Options

Click the fifth box in the Settings section to specify color options for your printed presentation. You can print in color, grayscale, or pure black and white.

 TIP Depending on the colors and shapes in your slide, the color option you select might produce different results. For example, on one slide, Color and Grayscale could produce similar results; on another slide, Grayscale and Pure Black and White could look alike. You need to experiment to see which option yields the optimal look in print.

In addition to previewing colors in the Print window in Backstage view, you can also preview from the View tab. To preview in grayscale, click the Grayscale button on the View tab. The Grayscale tab displays, offering additional grayscale and black-and-white options. Click the Back to Color View button to close.

Customizing Headers and Footers

You can add headers and footers to your slides, notes, and handouts when you print them. To do this, click the Edit Header & Footer link on the Print window in Backstage view. The Header and Footer dialog box opens, as shown in Figure 36.4.

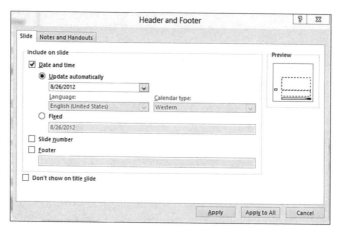

FIGURE 36.4

Indicate the headers and footers you want to print.

This dialog box includes two tabs with similar options: the Slide tab and the Notes and Handouts tab. You can add any or all of the following when you print slides, notes, handouts, or outlines: Date and Time, Slide Number, Header, Page Number, or Footer.

Previewing a PowerPoint Presentation

The right side of the Print window previews the way your presentation displays when printed, as shown in Figure 36.5.

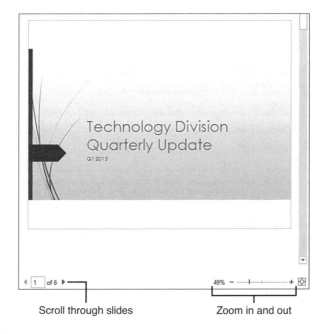

Scroll through slides   Zoom in and out

FIGURE 36.5

Preview before printing your presentation.

Any changes you make to your presentation settings are reflected in this view, so you can verify before printing whether the choices you make work for you.

Below the slide, you can click the left and right arrows to scroll through the presentation. You can also use the zoom control to reduce or enlarge the size of the slides.

 TIP Alternatively, click the Print Preview button on the Quick Access Toolbar (or press Ctrl+P) to open the Print window and preview your presentation.

Printing Your Presentation

After you specify your print settings and preview the results, it's time to print.

To print your presentation, follow these steps:

1. In the Print window in Backstage view (refer to Figure 36.2), select the number of copies to print. If you want to print more than one copy, remember to specify collation options. See "Collating Presentation Printouts," earlier in this chapter, for more information.

2. Select the printer to use from the Printer drop-down list. The list of options depends on what you connect to or install on your computer, such as printers, fax machines, PDF-creation software, and so forth.

3. Optionally, click the Printer Properties link to change the selected printer's properties and print parameters, such as page orientation (portrait or landscape).

4. Click the Print button to print your formatted presentation to the printer you selected.

 TIP Alternatively, click the Quick Print button on the Quick Access Toolbar to print your presentation based on the current default settings.

Creating Handouts in Microsoft Word

If you prefer, you can export the slides and notes from your PowerPoint presentation to Microsoft Word, where you can use Word's formatting to create more sophisticated handouts.

To create handouts in Microsoft Word, follow these steps:

1. Click the File tab and select Export from the menu.

2. In the Export window, select Create Handouts.

3. Click the Create Handouts button. Figure 36.6 shows the Send to Microsoft Word dialog box that opens.

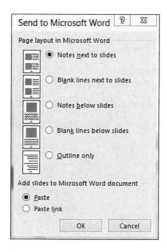

FIGURE 36.6

Create handouts in Microsoft Word from your PowerPoint presentation.

4. Choose one of the following page layout options: Notes Next to Slides, Blank Lines Next to Slides, Notes Below Slides, Blank Lines Below Slides, or Outline Only.

5. Specify whether you want to paste the slides into your Word document or paste as a link. If you link the slides, they update in Word whenever you make changes in PowerPoint.

6. Click the OK button to open a Microsoft Word document in the layout you specified.

THE ABSOLUTE MINIMUM

Here are the key points to remember from this chapter:

- PowerPoint offers several options for printing your presentation: full slides, notes pages, handouts, and outlines.

- Before printing, you should specify your printing parameters, such as print layout, collation, and colors.

- If you want to create more sophisticated handouts from your PowerPoint slides, you can export to Microsoft Word for additional formatting options.

PRESENTING A SLIDE SHOW

After you create all the slides in your presentation, you'll want to plan how to present them in a slide show. Fortunately, PowerPoint makes it easy to set up, rehearse, and present a show. In this chapter, you find out how to manage the slide show process, from setup to delivery, including how to present online and make the most of Presenter view.

Exploring the Slide Show Tab

In PowerPoint, all the tools you need to manage slide shows are on the Slide Show tab, shown in Figure 37.1.

FIGURE 37.1

Set up, manage, and run your slide shows from the Slide Show tab.

This tab is where you can set up and edit the slide show features you want to use, specify monitors, present online, and more.

TIP Before you deliver a PowerPoint presentation, think through its entire visual flow. This is the time to rehearse in your mind what you want to present and how you want to present it, as well as plan for the technical aspects of your presentation.

Setting Up a Show

Although you can deliver your presentation instantly by pressing F5, it usually makes sense to set it up ahead of time to specify the exact options you want to use. To set up a PowerPoint slide show, follow these steps:

1. On the Slide Show tab, click the Set Up Slide Show button. The Set Up Show dialog box opens, as shown in Figure 37.2.

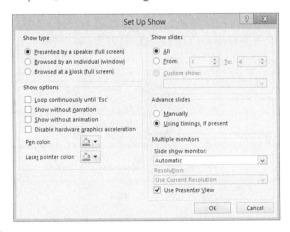

FIGURE 37.2

Use this dialog box to specify the type of presentation you want to make.

2. Select a show type. Options include the following:

    • **Presented by a Speaker (Full Screen)**—This is the default option and most common method of delivering a PowerPoint presentation—full screen in front of an audience.

    • **Browsed by an Individual (Window)**—This option lets someone view your presentation at any convenient time in a browser window with navigation elements such as a scrollbar.

    • **Browsed at a Kiosk (Full Screen)**—This method lets you create a self-running presentation. It displays full screen and loops continuously; after the final slide, the presentation starts over. Timings you set determine how long each slide is visible. You might set up a kiosk show as part of a tradeshow demonstration. You can add voice narration if you want, but be sure that your show plays where the narration will be audible.

 NOTE If you don't set slide timings when you choose the Browsed at a Kiosk option then slides won't move from one to the next unless you set up action buttons or hyperlinks to move from slide to slide.

3. Specify the show options you want to set. For example, you can loop your presentation continuously or temporarily deactivate narration or animation. You can also specify your preferred pen and laser pointer colors in this section.

4. Choose the slides you want to include in your presentation. Options include all slides, a certain range of slides indicated in the From and To boxes, and a custom show (which you can select from the drop-down list). The Custom Show option is active only if you've created a custom show. See "Creating Custom Shows," later in this chapter, for more information about custom shows.

5. To advance slides, choose either Manually or Using Timings, If Present. To advance the slide manually, you need to press a key or click the mouse. Choosing Manually in this field overrides any timings you previously set. See "Rehearsing Timings," later in this chapter, for more information about timings.

 TIP Be sure that you chose the Using Timings, If Present option if you want to browse at a kiosk. Otherwise, you can't browse manually at a kiosk unless you have a touchscreen device and have created hyperlinks.

6. Select the Use Presenter View check box if you want to use the enhanced Presenter view feature. With this option, you can use one monitor to display

just your slides and another to display speaker's notes, preview text, and the elapsed time of your presentation, among other useful tools. By default, when PowerPoint 2013 detects two displays, it automatically turns on Presenter view for the primary monitor. See "Exploring Presenter View," later in this chapter, for more information.

 TIP You can also set monitor options in the Monitors group on the Slide Show dialog box. By default, PowerPoint selects your monitor automatically, but you can specify a monitor if you prefer.

7. Click the OK button to close the Set Up Show dialog box.

Rehearsing Timings

PowerPoint can automate slide transitions, using transition timings that you set. PowerPoint shows a slide for the amount of time you choose and then transitions to the next slide. You can also set timings by rehearsing your presentation— PowerPoint keeps track of how long you spend on each slide. After you rehearse a presentation, you can save those timings.

To rehearse and set timings, go to the Slide Show tab and click the Rehearse Timings button. The presentation displays in Slide Show view, opening the Recording toolbar in the upper-left corner, as shown in Figure 37.3. This toolbar contains the buttons Next, Pause Recording, Slide Time, Repeat, and Elapsed Time, which enable you to control and navigate your recording as well as manage the time you spend on each slide.

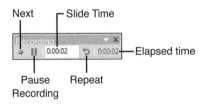

FIGURE 37.3

The Recording toolbar helps you rehearse and record slide timings.

Begin talking through your presentation, clicking the Next button in the toolbar (or clicking your mouse, or pressing any key) to advance to the next slide. If you need to stop temporarily, click the Pause Recording button. If you make a mistake and want to start over on your current slide, click the Repeat button.

The elapsed time of the current slide displays in the Slide Time box in the center of the toolbar. You can also enter a time manually in this box. The time field on the right side of the toolbar shows you the elapsed time of the entire presentation.

After you rehearse the last slide, PowerPoint asks whether you want to save the timings. If you click Yes, the presentation opens in Slide Sorter view with the timings displayed under each slide (see Figure 37.4). Alternatively, you can press the Esc key to stop rehearsal and optionally go to Slide Sorter view.

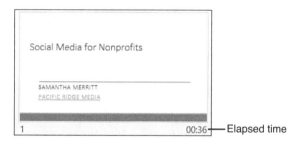

— Elapsed time

FIGURE 37.4

View the elapsed time for each slide narration in Slide Sorter view.

Using Timings

If you want to use slide timings during a slide show, verify that the Use Timings check box is selected on the Slide Show tab, which is the default setting. You can also choose whether or not to use timings on the Set Up Show dialog box.

Deleting Timings

To delete slide timings, click the down arrow below the Record Slide Show button on the Slide Show tab and select Clear from the menu that displays. From the submenu, choose to clear timings on the current slide or clear timings on all slides. If you haven't set automatic timings for your presentation, the Clear menu option isn't available.

Recording Voice Narrations

You can record your own voiceover to accompany a web-based presentation, an automated presentation (such as one you run continuously at a tradeshow booth), or a presentation delivered by a speaker that includes special recorded commentary by a particular individual.

Before recording your narration, create a script and rehearse it several times until it flows smoothly and matches your presentation.

To record a voice narration, follow these steps:

1. On the Slide Show tab, click the Record Slide Show button.

 TIP If you want to start recording from the current slide, click the down arrow below the Record Slide Show button and choose Start Recording from Current Slide.

2. In the Record Slide Show dialog box (see Figure 37.5), specify whether you want to record slide and animation timings, narrations and laser pointer, or both, and then click the Start Recording button.

FIGURE 37.5

Specify what you want to record in the Record Slide Show dialog box.

3. The presentation displays in Slide Show view, opening the Recording toolbar in the upper-left corner (refer to Figure 37.3).

4. Record your presentation as you move through the slide show, by clicking the Next button on the Recording toolbar or by pressing the Page Down button on your keyboard. The toolbar displays your elapsed time on the current slide (time indicator in the middle of the toolbar) as well as your overall elapsed time (on the right).

 TIP To pause your recording, click the Pause button on the Recording toolbar. When you're ready to resume recording, click the Pause button again.

5. When you reach the end of the presentation, it opens in Slide Sorter view with the slide timings listed below each slide (refer to Figure 37.4).

Rerecording Narrations

If you make a mistake in recording, you can rerecord your entire narration or rerecord a specific slide. To rerecord a specific slide, click the down arrow below the Record Slide Show button and choose Start Recording from Current Slide.

TIP To avoid overwriting the recording of the next slide, insert a blank slide after the one you want to rerecord.

Playing Narrations

To play voice narrations during a slide show, verify that the Play Narrations check box is selected on the Slide Show tab, which is the default setting. If you insert media clips, such as sounds, and then add a voice narration, the narration takes precedence over the media clips. As a result, you'll hear only the narration. To resolve this, delete the narration if the media clips are of more importance, or include the clips in the narration you record.

Deleting Narrations

To delete slide narrations, click the down arrow below the Record Slide Show button and select Clear from the menu that displays. From the submenu that displays, you can choose to clear narration on the current slide or clear narrations on all slides.

Creating Custom Shows

At times, you might need to deliver a presentation to several audiences, but modify it to suit each individual audience's needs. With custom shows, you can create a presentation once and then specify customized versions that include only the individual slides you need. This saves you from creating several nearly identical presentations or updating the same slide in multiple presentations.

To create a custom show, follow these steps:

1. On the Slide Show tab, click the Custom Slide Show button.

2. Select Custom Shows from the menu to open the Custom Shows dialog box.

3. Click the New button to open the Define Custom Show dialog box, shown in Figure 37.6.

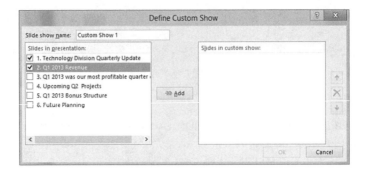

FIGURE 37.6

Add a new custom show in this dialog box.

4. Replace the default name in the Slide Show Name text box with a title for your show.

5. From the Slides in Presentation list, select slides to include in your custom show and click the Add button to copy these slides to the Slides in Custom Show list.

 TIP You can use the same slide more than once in a presentation. For example, you might want to show an Agenda slide at both the beginning and end of a presentation.

6. If you need to remove a slide from the Slides in Custom Show list, select it and click the Remove button.

 TIP Use the up and down buttons to the right of the Slides in Custom Show list to reorder a selected slide.

7. Click the OK button to save the custom show and return to the Custom Shows dialog box. From this dialog box, you can edit, remove, or copy any selected custom show.

 TIP Copying a custom slide show is useful if you want to create several similar versions of a custom show and don't want to repeat the same steps.

8. To preview what the show will look like, click the Show button. The show previews in Slide Show view.

9. Click the Close (x) button to close the Custom Shows dialog box.

To play a custom show, go to the Slide Show tab and click the Custom Slide Show button. Choose the show you want to play from the menu, and it begins automatically. You can also set up a custom show to play as the default show. See "Setting Up a Show" earlier in this chapter for more information.

Viewing Your Show

After you plan and set up your PowerPoint presentation, it's time to present it. To do this, press F5. Alternatively, click the From Beginning button or the From Current Slide button on the Slide Show tab (pressing Shift+F5 also accomplishes this).

 TIP   Before presenting your show live, you should preview it to test content, flow, and narration.

When you present a show, PowerPoint uses the settings you entered in the Set Up Show dialog box. For example, you can view in a browser or full screen, depending on what you entered in this dialog box. Whether you need to advance each slide manually depends on your choices in this dialog box.

 TIP   Displaying a scrollbar can make it easier for viewers to navigate your show. Specify whether to display a scrollbar in the Set Up Show dialog box.

Navigating a Show Full Screen

When a speaker presents a PowerPoint slide show, the presentation appears full screen. If you set up your show without automatic timing, you have to manually move among the slides during the show.

You have several ways to navigate your presentation full screen: using the invisible buttons in the lower-left corner of your screen, using the shortcut menu that displays when you right-click a slide, and using keyboard commands.

Navigating with Onscreen Buttons

To view PowerPoint's hidden navigation buttons, pause your mouse over the lower-left corner of your screen (see Figure 37.7). The following buttons display, from left to right:

- **Previous**—Return to the previous slide.

- **Next**—Move to the next slide.

- **Pen**—Display a brief menu with pen and arrow pointer options. See "Setting Pointer Options" and "Using the Onscreen Pen to Mark Your Presentation," later in this chapter, for more information.

- **See All Slides**—Display thumbnails of your presentation slides. Useful for moving to a slide out of sequence.

- **Zoom**—Zoom in to an area of a slide for closer viewing.

- **Menu**—Display a menu of options. See "Navigating with the Slide Show Menu" for more information.

FIGURE 37.7

Pause your mouse to view hidden navigation buttons.

Navigating with the Slide Show Menu

During a slide show, you can right-click anywhere on the screen to view a shortcut menu, as shown in Figure 37.8.

FIGURE 37.8

PowerPoint offers many shortcuts while you're presenting.

 CAUTION Although the options on this menu are useful, you'll probably want to avoid using most of these features during an actual presentation because a break in your flow can be distracting.

 TIP Navigating your slide show with keyboard commands is a third option. Right-click anywhere on the screen and choose Help from the shortcut menu to display a list of keyboard shortcuts within your slide show.

Setting Pointer Options

You can use or hide an arrow pointer during a PowerPoint presentation. The arrow pointer can help you draw the audience's attention to objects on your slides.

To activate the arrow, move the mouse. If the arrow doesn't display, right-click and choose Pointer Options, Arrow from the menu. The arrow displays as a standard mouse pointer arrow on your screen, which you can use to point to specific areas. To change the arrow to a laser pointer, press the Ctrl key and click the left mouse button.

By default, the arrow disappears after three seconds of inactivity, and it reappears whenever you move the mouse. This setting is fine for most presentations, but you can choose to have the arrow always or never appear. To do so, right-click and choose Pointer Options, Arrow Options from the menu that appears. Then choose one of these three commands:

- **Automatic**—Display the arrow when you move your mouse and hide it after three seconds of inactivity (default).

- **Visible**—Always display the arrow in your presentation.

- **Hidden**—Never display the arrow in your presentation.

Figure 37.9 shows the standard arrow pointer with which most people are familiar.

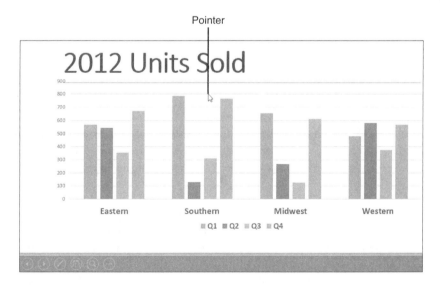

FIGURE 37.9

Use a pointer during your slide presentation.

Using the Onscreen Pen to Mark Your Presentation

Using the onscreen pen, you can actually mark right on your slides as you deliver a presentation. This feature works best if you have a pen tablet or a tablet PC, but you'll also get good value from it if all you have is a mouse.

To use the pen, right-click, choose Pointer Options, and choose the kind of ink to use (Pen or Highlighter). Your mouse cursor becomes a dot (when you choose a pen) or a colored bar (when you choose highlighter). Click and hold the mouse button and then drag the cursor to make your mark. Figure 37.10 shows some ink markings.

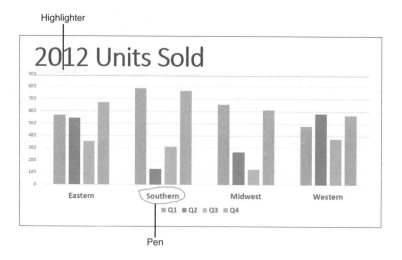

FIGURE 37.10

Use a pen or the highlighter to draw attention to elements in the presentation.

You can choose your pen's color by right-clicking your slide show screen and choosing Pointer Options, Ink Color. Select your preferred color on the color palette that displays. You can also preset the pen color in the Set Up Show dialog box.

When you don't need your ink markings anymore, you can erase them. To erase a specific ink marking, right-click and choose Pointer Options, Eraser from the menu that appears. The mouse cursor looks like an eraser. Click an ink marking to erase it. To erase all your ink markings, right-click and choose Pointer Options, Erase All Ink on Slide from the menu that appears or press the letter E.

After you finish delivering your presentation, PowerPoint asks whether you want to keep your ink annotations. If you click the Keep button, the annotations become drawing objects in the presentation.

Presenting Online

PowerPoint enables you to share your presentation in high fidelity with anyone on the Web, even if they don't have PowerPoint installed on their computer.

While presenting online, you can navigate with online buttons, the slide show menu, or keyboard commands, as described in the "Viewing Your Show" section earlier in this chapter.

 TIP Presenter view offers numerous features that enhance an online presentation. To start Presenter view manually, right-click and select Show Presenter View. Learn more in "Exploring Presenter View" later in this chapter.

To present online, follow these steps:

1. On the Slide Show tab, click the Present Online button.

2. Click the Connect button in the dialog box that displays (see Figure 37.11). If your presentation includes media files, this dialog box displays additional options.

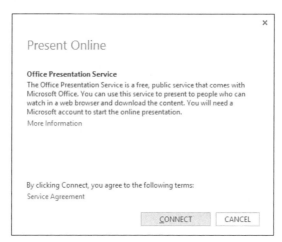

FIGURE 37.11

PowerPoint makes it easy to share your presentation on the Web.

 NOTE If you aren't already logged in to your Microsoft account, PowerPoint prompts you to do so.

3. Share the link in the Present Online dialog box with remote viewers (see Figure 37.12).

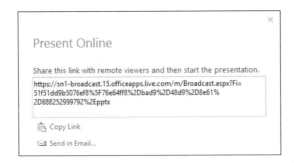

FIGURE 37.12

Share your presentation link to get started.

 TIP To send your link via your default email application (such as Microsoft Outlook), click the Send in Email link. To share using instant message or web mail, click Copy Link.

4. When you're ready to present, click the Start Presentation button.

5. PowerPoint starts your slide show on the Web, where your viewers can see it.

6. When you finish your presentation, right-click and select End Show.

7. Click End Online Presentation on the Present Online tab to disconnect all your remote viewers, as shown in Figure 37.13.

FIGURE 37.13

The Present Online tab provides several important tools, including a button to end your presentation.

8. Click End Online Presentation in the confirmation dialog box to confirm.

Exploring Presenter View

Presenter view enables you to display a full-screen presentation that your audience can see and another view that you, the presenter, can see with slide previews, speaker notes, a timer, and more. In PowerPoint 2013, you can use Presenter view even on computers with a single display. Figure 37.14 shows Presenter view.

FIGURE 37.14

Presenter view simplifies giving presentations.

To activate Presenter view, select the Use Presenter View check box on the Slide Show tab.

NOTE Another way to activate Presenter view is to right-click an in-progress presentation and select Show Presenter View from the menu.

In Presenter view, you can perform the following tasks:

- Display the taskbar (at the bottom of the window) by clicking Show Taskbar.

- Create meeting notes in Microsoft OneNote by clicking Share Meeting Notes. This option isn't available on computers that don't have OneNote installed.

- View display settings (such as swapping Presenter view and slide show view and duplicating the slide show) by clicking Display Settings.

- End the presentation by clicking End Slide Show.

- View your current slide in the main window.

- Use the buttons directly below the slide to display a menu of pen and pointer tools, view all slides, black or unblack the slide show, or view a menu of more slide show options.

- Navigate your presentation using the Advance to the Next Slide button and the Return to the Previous Slide button at the bottom of the window.

- Preview the next slide and any notes on the right side of the window.

- Change font size with the Make Text Larger and Make Text smaller buttons.

Packaging a Presentation onto a CD

Packaging your presentation onto a CD enables you to save your presentation, including its fonts and linked files, onto a CD, avoiding potential problems of presenting on a computer other than the one on which you created your presentation.

 NOTE The PowerPoint Viewer (PowerPointViewer.exe) lets people view a PowerPoint presentation when they don't have PowerPoint installed on their computers. You can freely distribute the viewer without any license fee. Although the viewer is automatically included on your presentation CD if you use Package for CD, you can also download it manually from the Microsoft Download Center (www.microsoft.com/downloads).

To package a presentation onto a CD, follow these steps:

1. Open a presentation to package.

2. Click the File tab and select Export to open the Export window in Backstage view.

3. Select Package Presentation for CD and then click the Package for CD button on the right side of the screen (see Figure 37.15).

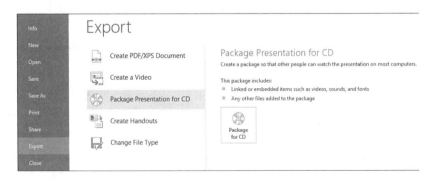

FIGURE 37.15

The Export window offers the option to package your presentation to a CD.

4. In the Package for CD dialog box, as shown in Figure 37.16, enter a name that describes the presentation you're packaging in the Name the CD field.

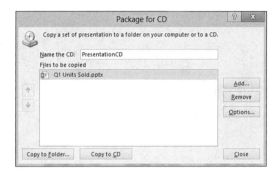

FIGURE 37.16

With Package for CD, you can deliver your presentation on another computer.

5. The current presentation's filename displays in the Files to Be Copied area. To package more presentations onto this CD, click the Add button. The Add Files dialog box opens. Select the presentations to package and click the Add button to return to the Package for CD dialog box.

6. If you are packaging more than one presentation, you can arrange the presentations in the order in which you want them to run. To move a presentation, select it and then click one of the arrow buttons on the left side of the dialog box to reposition it.

7. Click the Options button to open the Options dialog box, where you can specify any of the following options: link files, embed TrueType fonts, require a password, or inspect your presentation for private information before packaging.

8. Click the OK button when you're done to return to the Package for CD dialog box.

9. If you want to create a folder on your hard drive that contains everything that will be on the CD, click the Copy to Folder button. The Copy to Folder dialog box opens.

10. Type a name for the folder, choose where to add the folder, and click the OK button. PowerPoint creates the folder and copies all the files to it.

11. Place a blank writeable CD into your CD-R or CD-RW drive. If Windows asks you what to do with the CD, select Take No Action and then click the OK button. Go back to the Package for CD dialog box and click the Copy to CD button. PowerPoint writes the files to the CD.

When PowerPoint finishes creating the CD, it opens the CD drawer and asks whether you want to copy the same files to another CD. If so, place another writeable CD in the drive and click Yes. Otherwise, click No.

THE ABSOLUTE MINIMUM

Here are the key points to remember from this chapter:

- You'll find all the tools you need for managing slide shows on the Slide Show tab.

- Set up your show ahead of time in the Slide Show dialog box.

- PowerPoint can automate slide transitions, using the transition timing you set.

- You can record voiceovers to accompany any type of presentation.

- Custom shows enable you to deliver your presentation to several audiences without duplication of effort.

- You can navigate your slide show using onscreen buttons, the slide show menu, or keyword commands.

- PowerPoint enables you to share your presentation in high fidelity with anyone on the Web, even if they don't have PowerPoint installed on their computer.

- Presenter view displays a full-screen presentation that your audience can see and another view that you, the presenter, can see with slide previews, speaker notes, a timer, and more.

- The Package Presentation for CD feature makes it easy to deliver a presentation on a computer other than the one on which it was created.

38

OUTLOOK 2013 BASICS

Outlook is a *personal information manager* program or PIM for short. You can use it to record, track, and manage all types of personal information. Acting as both a project manager application and an email client, Outlook can help you organize appointments, plan and coordinate events, jot down notes, manage addresses and phone numbers, and track your many email messages. In short, Outlook is a powerful communications and organization tool, one that's sure to quickly become an indispensable part of your computing activities whether you use it on your computer, laptop, or tablet. In this chapter, you find out how to get started by putting the application to work for you.

Getting Started with Outlook

Millions of users make Outlook their go-to program all day long. People use it to collaborate with others or to help keep themselves on track, making it an essential part of their everyday routines at home or in the office, or both. Despite its widespread popularity, many users take advantage of only a small fraction of all the things Outlook can do to make life easier. Hopefully, this book pushes you out of the fraction group and into the well-informed and fully integrated group when it comes to using Outlook 2013.

You can use Outlook to

- Send, receive, and read email messages, reply to messages, forward and copy messages.

- Send file attachments, such as spreadsheets, documents, pictures, and presentations.

- Sort junk email from regular email and rid your Inbox of spam.

- Receive regular information from your favorite websites and social media networks using Really Simple Syndication (RSS) feeds.

- Create a corporate or personal signature to appear at the bottom of every message.

- Organize and archive messages, or remove emails you no longer want to keep.

- Schedule appointments or all-day events on your calendar, and turn on reminders to sound off and alert you to upcoming activities.

- Plan and coordinate meetings with other users and keep abreast of who is attending and who is not.

- Share your schedule with other users and view their schedules as well.

- Manage tasks you need to complete, and delegate them to others.

- Record contact information for all the people in your life, from colleagues and coworkers to friends and family.

- Quickly find a message, contact, attachment, or task using tags, categories, and search options.

Exploring Outlook

Outlook 2013 sports a modern, polished interface with a sleek ribbon full of tools and features, as shown in Figure 38.1.

Folder pane   Ribbon

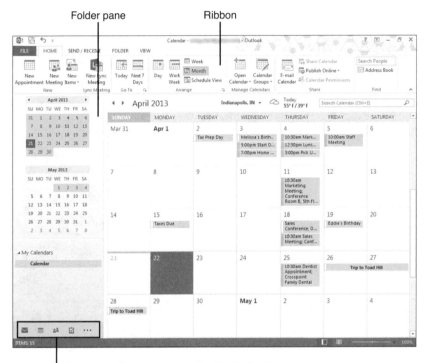

Component icons appear on the Navigation bar

FIGURE 38.1

Welcome to Outlook 2013.

Outlook acts quite literally like a personal assistant; you can open it every day and accomplish things you need to get done, from the urgent to the mundane. Outlook consists of several key components, which are called *modules*. Here's what you can expect with each module:

- **Mail**—Use this component to manage, send, and receive email messages. You can control junk email, organize messages into useful folders, and access multiple email accounts.

- **Calendar**—Use this component to keep track of your schedule, recording appointments, specifying all-day events, and assigning reminders when a date or scheduled time approaches.

- **People**—Use this component to manage all the people you contact, including friends, family, work colleagues, clients, and the like. Keep important information, such as phone numbers and emails, at easy reach, and add to the info as you go.

- **Tasks**—Help keep your important projects and To-Do lists organized with this component, which lets you monitor a task's status, due date, and share it with other users. Whether you're working on an important office assignment, or just trying to organize your daily activities, the Tasks component can help you stay on top of it all.

- **Notes**—Use this component to jot down notes for yourself and keep track of important information, such as ideas, questions, and quotes.

 NOTE   In previous versions of Outlook, the collection of names and addresses you recorded were called "Contacts." Now they're calling this component "People." What's the difference? Well, they've added a lot more to the module and the amount of information collected with people in your contacts list, making it easier than ever to get in touch with people and make sure you have all the information you need.

Exploring Outlook 2013 New Features

Microsoft has made quite a few improvements to Outlook 2013. For starters, you can utilize multiple email accounts, access social network feeds, and take advantage of cloud storage using your Microsoft SkyDrive account. In addition, the new Folder pane area is now dedicated to displaying folder structures, and the navigation pane of old has morphed into a Navigation bar.

Here's a rundown of some of the improvements and new features:

- You can quickly reply to a message using the new inline reply feature, which lets you respond with a click directly in the Reading pane.

- The message list now displays the message subject, sender, and first line of content so you can quickly check a message at a glance.

- You can also directly access commands to flag, delete, or mark your message from the message list.

- You can use the new quick peek feature to sneak a peek at current information for your calendar, contacts, or tasks.

- The new Weather bar in the Calendar module enables you to see the current weather conditions for a specified location, which is pretty handy if you want to know what the weather's doing for an appointment later in the day.

- The new People Card view shows a single contact's information gathered from multiple sources, such as social networks, Microsoft Lync, or Outlook, and you can easily initiate contact with a click.

- Outlook supports a variety of email accounts, including anything based on Exchange or Exchange ActiveSync-compatible, POP (Post Office Protocol), or IMAP (Internet Message Access Protocol). This means you don't have to have extra add-ins to connect to services such as Hotmail or Gmail.

- Quickly insert online pictures into your message body by searching for pictures among the Office Clip Art collection, your SkyDrive account, or using the Bing Image Search tool.

- You can assign a custom background design to the ribbon and title bar area of the program window to spruce things up on your screen.

- Use the new Navigation bar to easily switch between the Outlook components, and you can choose which items to appear by default.

Starting and Exiting Outlook

You can start Outlook the same as you start any other program on your computer. If you are using Windows 7, for example, you can apply any of these techniques:

- Click the Start button and type Outlook; then click Outlook 2013 at the top of the Start menu.

- Double-click the Outlook shortcut icon on the desktop (if there is one).

- Click the Start button, and then click All Programs, Microsoft Office 2013, and Outlook 2013.

If you are using Windows 8, try one of these methods:

- From the Windows 8 Start screen, type Outlook; then from the Apps search screen, click Outlook.

- If you added a tile for Outlook on the Start screen, you can click it to open Outlook on the desktop.

- In Desktop view, you can click Outlook's shortcut icon on the desktop, if available.

In Windows 8, Outlook launches over on the desktop, which means you can minimize and maximize the program window, and the taskbar shows the open Outlook program icon.

 NOTE If you're new to Windows 8, try the *Windows 8 Absolute Beginner's Guide,* available in fine bookstores online and off. It's sure to get you up and running fast with the latest Microsoft operating system.

After you open Outlook, the first thing you see is the Mail module, shown in Figure 38.2.

FIGURE 38.2

Viewing Outlook's Mail module.

When you're finished using Outlook, exiting is easy. Do any of the following:

- Click the Close icon in the upper-right corner of the program window.
- Click the Outlook icon in the upper-left corner and click Close.
- Right-click the Outlook icon on the taskbar and click Close Window.
- Click the File tab and click Exit.

As soon as you activate the Close command, Outlook closes entirely.

If you'd rather get the program window out of the way for a bit while you tackle other computer tasks, you can minimize the window; click the Minimize button. Minimizing the Outlook window reduces it to a button icon on the desktop taskbar. To open it again, click the icon.

It's a good idea to keep the Outlook program running in the background, even while you work with other programs. If you close it, you won't hear or see any reminders about pending appointments or emails received, thus making it difficult for your personal assistant to assist you.

Familiarizing Yourself with the Program Window

If you're new to using Outlook, take a few moments and familiarize yourself with the program window's many nuances, some of which are conveniently pointed out in Figure 38.3. For a refresher about the tools and features common to all Office applications, see Chapter 2, "Working with Office Applications."

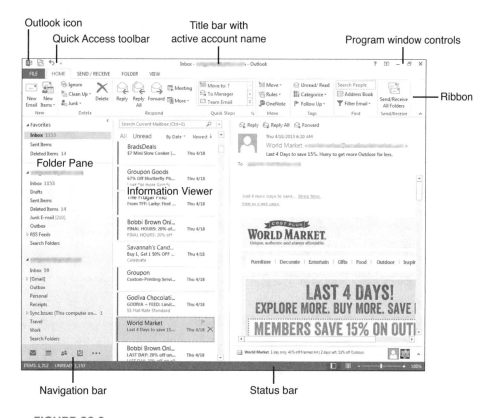

FIGURE 38.3

Familiarize yourself with the various window elements.

Let's go over the various elements you see onscreen and what they're used for in Outlook:

- **Outlook icon**—Click this icon to display a drop-down menu of program window controls, such as Minimize (reducing the window to an icon on the taskbar), Maximize (enlarging the window to optimize workspace), and Close (exiting the program).

- **Title bar**—Look for the name of your active account at the top of the program window, along with the name of the module you're currently viewing.

- **Folder pane**—This pane displays different folder structures depending on which module you're using. If it's Mail, the Inbox and subfolders appear for messages; if it's Calendar, navigation calendars appear. This pane can expand and collapse to free up onscreen workspace.

- **Information Viewer**—In the middle of the window, you do all your work, such as viewing messages or appointments.

- **Navigation bar**—Use this bar, which can expand or collapse, to switch between Outlook components. Each icon represents a module; click an icon to view the module.

- **Status bar**—The bottom area of the window displays status information, such as the amount of messages in the Inbox, and so on.

- **Program window controls**—Use these controls to minimize, maximize, and close the program window. These same controls are also available through the Outlook icon. In addition to window controls, you see icons for accessing Help and collapsing/expanding the ribbon.

You discover more about using the various Outlook elements as you tackle different tasks and features.

THE ABSOLUTE MINIMUM

Here are the key points to remember from this chapter:

- Outlook 2013 includes a lot of exciting improvements, including a new user interface, quick peeks, and a Weather bar. Outlook consists of several main modules: Mail, Calendar, People, Tasks, and Notes.

- Outlook is easy to launch, regardless of which operating system you're using.

- The program window layout is very intuitive; commands are located on the various tabs on the ribbon, the Folder pane displays your folder structure, and the Information Viewer area in the middle is where you view messages and appointments and such.

39

SETTING UP ACCOUNTS AND PERSONALIZING OUTLOOK

Before getting started with Outlook's Mail module, you need to set it up to work with your email account. In this chapter, you find out how to add email services, configure them to work with Outlook, and personalize the Outlook interface.

Understanding Email Services and Internet Access

If you're using Outlook at work, chances are Information Technology (IT) people or your network administrator set everything up for you. If you're using Outlook at home or you're your own network administrator in a small office situation, you're in charge of setting up Internet access and choosing email services. If you're the boss of your own connectivity destiny, then like most people, you probably use an outside source to access the Internet. These typically include a cable, satellite, or phone company (home or wireless). Companies that offer Internet access through their giant servers and networks are called Internet service providers, or ISPs. In most instances, these types of connections encompass access to the Internet for web surfing as well as for email. Many offer dedicated storage on their servers, too, so you can back up important files. Email comes in several types of accounts:

- **POP3**—Post Office Protocol 3; this is the most popular email account type. With it, your email messages are downloaded from the server hosting your account; you read and store them on your computer and not the mail server. This means you can read the messages on your computer only and the mail server keeps your email only until you download it (unless your provider has a web mail interface).

- **IMAP**—Internet Message Access Protocol; this type of account stores your emails on the mail server without your needing to download them onto your computer. The nice thing about this setup is that you can access your messages from any computer.

- **MAPI**—Messaging Application Programming Interface; this account type is a lot like IMAP, but with more features, especially if you're running Outlook with a mail server that uses Microsoft Exchange. MAPI accounts are generally associated with Microsoft Exchange.

- **HTTP**—This is a Web protocol, and you can use your browser to log on to the site and view mail. Yahoo! Mail, Hotmail, and Gmail are examples of web-based email services.

For a fee, ISPs offer the use of their equipment (giant servers and other computers and networks) and their connection to the Internet. Many include email as part of the package. Basically, this means you can set up an email address with them. On the downside, if you ever switch ISPs, you'll have to switch email addresses and notify everyone of the change. If this potentially poses a problem, you might consider getting an email account through a free service.

 TIP If you have your own website, you can set up Outlook to use an email address that comes with this domain. For example, if you purchase the domain www.annejones.com, you can set up the email address anne@annejones.com.

Microsoft offers free email through its Microsoft accounts. So, if you don't already have an email service, it's easy enough to set one up through Microsoft. Best of all, a Microsoft account works seamlessly with Outlook. Up until 2013, Microsoft's free perks included email through its Windows Live and Hotmail services. Users needed a Windows Live ID to sign into things like SkyDrive (cloud storage), Messenger (the instant messaging service), or Windows Phone (smartphone). You had to have another ID to use Xbox Live to play games online. Now the company has merged all these accounts into one service under the umbrella called a *Microsoft account*. The good news is if you already have an account through Windows Live or Xbox Live, you already have a Microsoft account. They're one and the same. You can use this account to access your data from any device, whether it's your Xbox, Windows Phone, or tablet, for example. You can also connect your Microsoft account to services like Facebook, Twitter, and LinkedIn.

If you don't have such an account yet, here is how to get one. Navigate to www.outlook.com and click the Sign Up Now link. You can then fill in a form and choose an email address, called a Microsoft account name. Figure 39.1 shows what the form looks like. You can even specify whether you want the new email account to use the outlook.com domain, hotmail.com, or live.com.

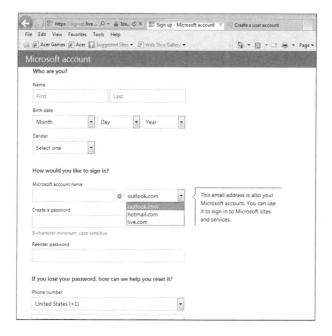

FIGURE 39.1

Signing up is simple; add your name information and choose an email address.

Your account name can be anything you want. Most people use their actual names or a combination of initials and such to create a unique email address. If you happen to choose something already in use by someone else, Microsoft prompts you to try another name. After you have a Microsoft account established, you can start using it to email with Outlook as long as you tell Outlook what the account is—learn more about adding and editing email accounts later in this chapter.

 NOTE You can have all the free email accounts you want, but they don't do you any good if you're not connected to the Internet. To find an ISP, check with your local cable or phone company. Cell phone companies also offer wireless connections you can use, such as setting up a hotspot in your house that all your household computing devices can access. If you're on the go all the time, you can also tap into free Wi-Fi services around town to surf the Internet and access your email accounts. (Wi-Fi stands for wireless fidelity, a technology that uses radio waves to provide high-speed Internet and network connections.) Just be sure to safeguard your computer when you do use Wi-Fi to prevent hacking (firewalls and virus protection, for example).

Adding Email Accounts to Outlook

You can use multiple email accounts with Outlook. This is extremely convenient. You might have a work account, for example, and a home account. Rather than having to check them separately, you can tell Outlook to work with both. Perhaps you have a special email account you use when signing up for online newsletters and advertising information. Or maybe each family member wants his or her own account. You can add additional accounts to Outlook and view your emails using the Mail module.

Outlook automatically configures your email accounts for you. All you need to specify is your email address and password; Outlook takes care of the rest. On the off chance it cannot establish a connection, you might need to gather up some additional information from your ISP and manually configure the account. This can include identifying your server type, the address of the incoming mail server and outgoing mail server, and any passwords required for each. The following sections cover both methods.

Automatically Configuring an Account

To have Outlook automatically set up an email account, you need to switch to Backstage view to get things started. Follow these steps:

1. Click the File tab.

2. On the Account Information screen, click the Add Account button.

3. The Add Account dialog box opens, as shown in Figure 39.2. Fill in your name in the first form field.

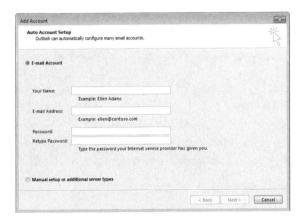

FIGURE 39.2

Use the Auto Account Setup tool to help you configure an account automatically.

4. Type the email address for the account you want to add.

5. Type the account's password.

6. Verify the password by typing it again.

7. Click Next to continue.

8. Outlooks checks the network connection, finds your settings, logs on to the mail server, and then displays a congratulations prompt. Click Finish (see Figure 39.3).

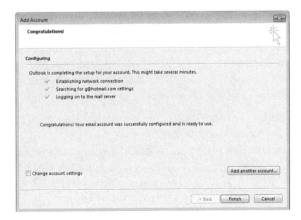

FIGURE 39.3

Outlook verifies your account and settings and logs on to the mail server.

TIP You can also set up a new account through the Add Account dialog box. On the Account Information screen in Backstage view, click the Account Settings button and then click the Account Settings command. This opens the dialog box listing all of your accounts. Click the New button to display the Add Account dialog box (refer to Figure 39.3).

You can now see your new email account listed in the Folder pane in Outlook's Mail module. When you click the Send/Receive All Folders button on the Home tab, Outlook checks the account for messages. Any messages received appear in the account's Inbox; click the Inbox to view the messages. Remember, each account's Inbox keeps a running list of messages received for that account.

NOTE If you mistype any part of your email address or password, Outlook won't be able to complete the automatic configuration. If you run into additional problems, you can try a manual setup, which is explained in the next section.

TIP One thing to consider when using multiple accounts is to make sure the correct account for new messages is selected before you send it off. If you're trying to keep things organized and precise, you don't want to send a business message from your personal account, for example.

Manually Configuring an Account

The manual route might be right for you if you know your email provider has some preferred settings or if you decide you want to control the details about the setup. For example, you might need to ascertain special incoming mail server or outgoing mail server info, or you might have to have special logon info. The first step in the manual process is to tell Outlook what type of email service you're adding. You can choose from a Microsoft Exchange Server (an Exchange account), Outlook.com or Exchange ActiveSync service (use this option if you have a free email through Microsoft), or a POP or IMAP service. If you're not sure, check with your email provider. They can provide you with all the pertinent info required.

After you've gathered all the correct information, you're ready to set up an account. Depending on which type of email service you're adding, different configuration steps appear. If you're adding an Exchange account, Outlook prompts you to close Outlook and use Windows Mail settings in the Control Panel. If you're adding an Outlook.com account, you must enter your server and logon information. If you're adding a POP or IMAP account, you need to specify the account type and the incoming and outgoing servers.

To start the process, click the File tab and click the Add Account button. So far, this is the same as having Outlook automatically configure the account. When the Add Account dialog box opens, however, you need to click the Manual Setup or Additional Server Types option, as shown in Figure 39.4. Click the Next button to continue.

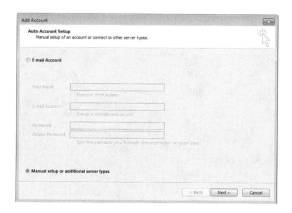

FIGURE 39.4

Choose the manual option to configure the email account yourself.

Next, select the type of email account you're adding (such as POP, IMAP, or Microsoft Exchange Server) and click Next.

Depending on what you're selecting, different options are shown. Figure 39.5 shows the POP and IMAP Account Settings you need to fill in, and Figure 39.6 shows the Server Settings fields for an Exchange ActiveSync service.

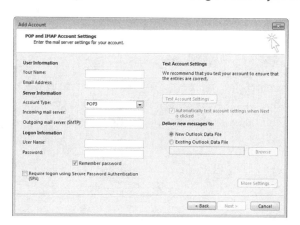

FIGURE 39.5

POP and IMAP settings.

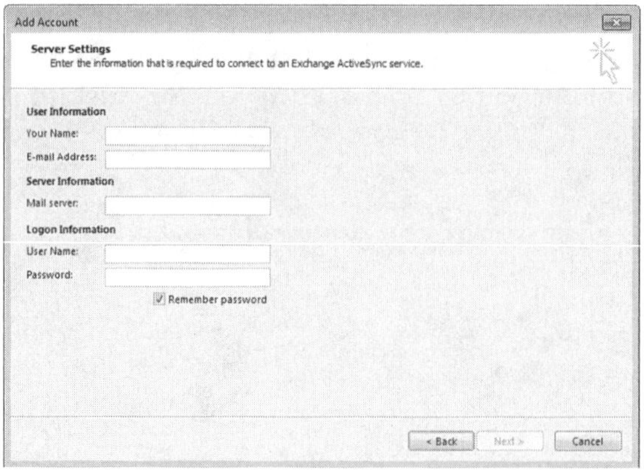

FIGURE 39.6

Exchange ActiveSync settings.

 TIP Click the More Settings button, if available, to add additional information.

After you've entered all the appropriate fields, you can click Next and Outlook establishes the network connection.

Editing Your Email Accounts

You can make changes to your email accounts through the Account Settings dialog box. This particular box keeps a list of all the accounts you're using. You can add new accounts from this dialog box, remove accounts you no longer use, or make changes to accounts. You can also reorder the way in which Outlook checks the accounts for new messages.

To access the dialog box, click the File tab to switch to Backstage view. Click the Add Accounts button, then click the Add Accounts command. A dialog box similar to Figure 39.7 opens, with the E-mail tab displayed.

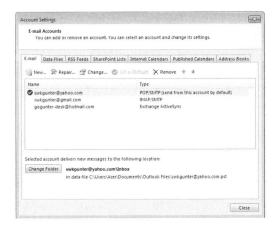

FIGURE 39.7

Use the Account Settings dialog box to make changes to your email accounts.

From the Account Settings dialog box, you can do any of the following:

- To add a new account to the list, click the New button and follow the steps for automatically or manually configuring a new email service to work with Outlook.

- To repair an account, select it in the list and click the Repair button. This reopens the setup box containing the information about the account, which includes the same form fields you used to enter information about the email service; you can recheck the information.

- To change an account, select it in the list and click the Change button. This displays detailed information about the account, and you can make changes, such as setting a new password.

- To remove an account, select it and click the Remove button. Outlook warns you that you're about to delete the account; click Yes to confirm deletion.

- To change the default account—the account listed to send from in the new message window—click the account and click Set as Default.

- To change the order of your accounts, click the up and down arrows to move the selected account up or down in the list.

Working with Outlook Panes

Now that you've set up your email account, it's time to take a look at the common components of Outlook so you know how to navigate them.

A common way to divide a program window into workable areas is to use *panes*. Most users are familiar with panes from web browsing. Typically, a navigational pane appears on the left or top side of a web page with links that, when clicked, display another page somewhere off to the right or below. Outlook uses panes to divvy up areas of the window. This section covers the various ways you can work with panes to navigate Outlook.

Working with the Folder Pane

The far left side of the program window features the Folder pane. This pane displays different aspects of your Outlook folder structure depending on which module you're viewing. For example, when viewing the Mail module, shown in Figure 39.8, the pane displays all your email account inboxes and their subfolders.

Click the Minimize button to collapse the pane.

FIGURE 39.8

You can expand and collapse the Folder pane as needed.

You can expand and collapse the pane to free up onscreen workspace. Click or tap the Minimize button located in the upper-right corner of the pane, pointed out in Figure 39.9. When collapsed, the pane folds to a skinny columnar display along the left side of the program window, like the example in Figure 39.9. To expand it again, click the Expand button.

Click the Expand button to expand the pane.

FIGURE 39.9

The Folder pane, collapsed.

 NOTE Notice when the Folder pane is collapsed, the Navigation bar runs vertically instead of horizontally—but only if the bar is displayed in Compact Navigation mode (icons instead of text labels).

You can also control the Folder pane using the Folder pane drop-down menu on the View tab, as shown in Figure 39.10. For example, you can turn the pane off entirely by selecting the Off option. To turn it on again, revisit the drop-down menu and choose Normal.

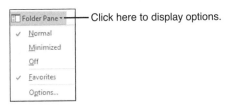

FIGURE 39.10

You can also control the Folder pane through the View tab.

You can also resize the Folder pane. Just move your mouse pointer over the pane's right border and drag it to a new size, wider or thinner. You can do the same thing with any pane in Outlook; drag the pane's border to resize the pane, whether it's the Reading pane, the message list, or the To-Do bar.

Working with the Reading Pane

In the main area of the Outlook window, called the Information Viewer, you can also control the view of the Reading pane. The Reading pane, which displays the contents of a selected message from the list, is an optional item. You can turn it on or off, or you can resize it. If you choose to have it on, you can have it display to the right of the message list or at the bottom of the main area. Figure 39.11 shows the Reading pane displayed at the bottom of the viewing area. The pane can be displayed in any module, but it appears by default when using Mail and Tasks.

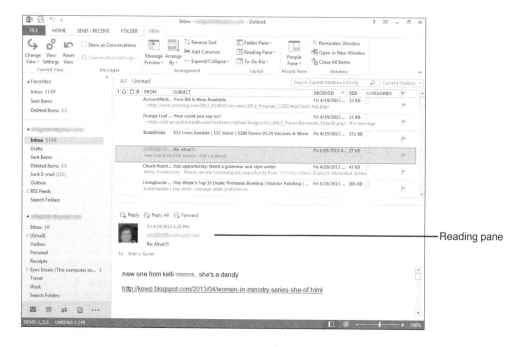

Reading pane

FIGURE 39.11

The Reading pane shows a selected message or file attachment.

To control the Reading pane, click the View tab and click the Reading pane drop-down arrow. Next, select a setting you want to apply. Outlook immediately changes the window to reflect your selection.

Working with the To-Do Bar and Peeks

You can use the To-Do bar to view sneak peeks of your calendar, people info, or tasks, or all three at the same time. A *peek* is a quick glance at current content, such as your calendar. Suppose you're busy typing a reply to an email and need to check your calendar to suggest a date. Rather than having to open the full Calendar module, you can use the peek feature to check the current month. For quick peeks, just hover the mouse over the module item on the Navigation bar, as shown in Figure 39.12.

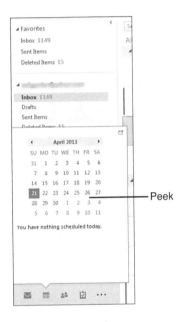

FIGURE 39.12

Outlook's peeks enable you to see your calendar, a contact, or a task list at a glance.

The To-Do bar opens a full pane for peeks, as shown in Figure 39.13. The To-Do bar is not turned on by default. To display it, click the To-Do Bar button on the View tab, and click which part you want to view. You can turn on just one peek or all three. A check mark next to the item's name indicates it's displayed; no check mark means the item is turned off. To turn them all off, click the Off command. To turn off individual peeks in the bar itself, you can click the peek's Close button.

To-Do bar

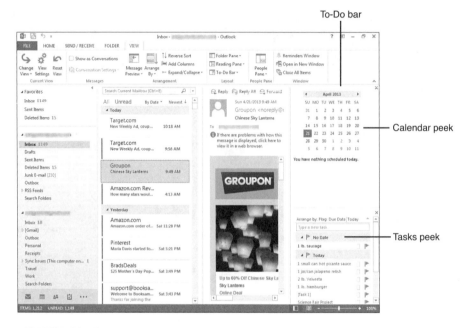

Calendar peek

Tasks peek

FIGURE 39.13

You can use the To-Do bar to keep different peeks in view.

 NOTE You can also turn on a People pane to view details about a particular contact. To learn more, check out Chapter 44, "Working with Contacts."

THE ABSOLUTE MINIMUM

Here are the key points to remember from this chapter:

- There are different types of email services, but Outlook can handily accommodate them.

- You can add multiple email services to Outlook and configure them automatically or manually.

- Outlook offers several panes and views that enhance navigation and usability.

IN THIS CHAPTER

- Composing and Sending Messages
- Reading and Replying to Messages
- Saving Messages
- Working with File Attachments
- Using Simple Message Tools

40

PERFORMING BASIC EMAIL TASKS

Outlook makes it easy to communicate with others via email. Using Outlook's Mail module, you can compose, send, receive, and read messages. Although basic email tasks can be simple and straightforward, Outlook offers numerous options and advanced features that enable you to customize your email experience. In this chapter, you explore these email nuances and ensure you can handle your incoming and outgoing communications with true finesse.

Composing and Sending Messages

You can compose a new email message using Outlook's Message window. The Message window has its own Ribbon with tabs that differ from those you find in Outlook's Mail module. These tabs include Message, Insert, Options, Format Text, and Review. Figure 40.1 shows a sample a Message window with a completed message.

Open a new Message window

Send the message

Type the recipient's email address here.

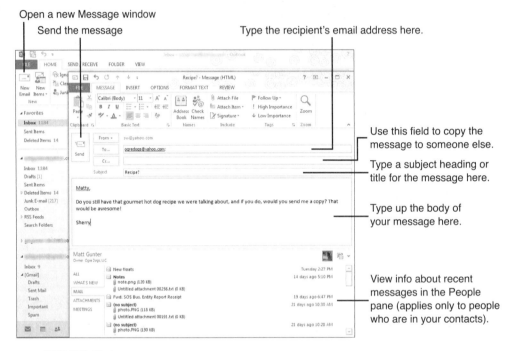

Use this field to copy the message to someone else.

Type a subject heading or title for the message here.

Type up the body of your message here.

View info about recent messages in the People pane (applies only to people who are in your contacts).

FIGURE 40.1

Here's a typical Message window.

You can use any of these methods to open a new Message window:

- Click the New Email button on the Home tab (refer to Figure 4.1).
- Press Ctrl+N on the keyboard.
- Click the New Items button in any Outlook module and choose E-mail Message from the drop-down menu.

Starting with an empty Message window (see Figure 40.2), type the email address of your recipient in the To field. If the recipient is already someone in your contacts list, you can click the To button and choose the person's name from the Select Names dialog box. Simply double-click the name of the person to insert it into the To field, and click OK to close the dialog box.

FIGURE 40.2

A blank Message form is ready for your input.

 TIP If you have more than one email service, you can change which one the message is sent from using the From drop-down menu at the top of the form. Click the button and choose a service.

Do you need to address the message to more than one person? That's easy; use a semicolon to separate email addresses in the To field. If you use the Select Names dialog box to add names, Outlook automatically inserts a semicolon for you, even if you insert only one name from your Address Book. (To learn more about building your contacts list in Outlook, see Chapter 44, "Working with Contacts.")

Do you want to carbon copy someone else on the message? The term *carbon copy* is a remnant of the days in which you had to use a sheet of carbon paper inserted between two sheets of paper in a typewriter to make a copy of a memo or letter. To Cc someone, click the Cc field and type the email address, or click the Cc button and choose people from your contacts list.

 TIP To blind carbon copy is to send a copy of the message to another user without the original recipient knowing or seeing the other person's inclusion. To send a blind carbon copy, click the Cc button to find the Bcc field in the Select Names dialog box.

After you enter the email address or addresses, you can move on to the Subject field and type in a title or subject heading for the message. This text identifies the message content for recipients; it's what they see when they view their incoming messages. It's a good practice to keep your subject titles brief and to the point.

Finally, click in the large, empty area of the Message window to type your message text. To move beyond sending a basic text email, see Chapter 42,

"Working with Advanced Email Features." Not everybody's email services can read all message formatting, so keep that in mind before you start trying to format a message like a Microsoft Word document. You can choose between three overall message formats in Outlook:

- **HTML**—This format, which is a web page format, supports text and paragraph formatting (such as bold, italic, text alignment, fonts and sizes, background colors, and the like). Most email readers support HTML, and if one doesn't, the message appears as plain text.

- **Rich Text**—This format supports more attributes than HTML, such as borders and shading. On the downside, this format is usually compatible only with Outlook and Microsoft Exchange Server. The text is converted to HTML for other email readers.

- **Plain Text**—This is the most basic of the formats; no attributes appear in plain text messages, just straight up text. This format is supported by all email readers.

You can control the message's format by clicking the Format Text tab and then making your selection from the Format group of buttons.

After you've completed your message, click the Send button or press F9. If you're connected to the Internet, Outlook immediately sends the message. If not, the message remains in the Outbox folder until you're ready to send and receive messages.

 TIP If you're piling up messages in your Outbox, you can press F9 or click the Send/Receive All Folders button on the Quick Access toolbar when you finally connect to the Internet and are ready to send.

Reading and Replying to Messages

All the emailing activities you perform happen in the Mail module, Outlook's email component. You learned a little about how the Folder pane works in Chapter 39, "Setting Up Accounts and Personalizing Outlook." That's where all the Inboxes for each email account you use are listed. That's also where your list of incoming messages piles up. To view a list of messages for a particular account, click the account's Inbox. The message list that appears shows you who sent the message and gives you a peek at the first line. You can scroll up and down to view the list of messages.

If you turn off the Reading pane, you can see more details about the messages displayed across the width of the viewing area (the Information Viewer), such as date and time sent, message size, priority levels, or flagging. You can also see paper clip icons representing file attachments. Figure 40.3 shows an example of the message list expanded.

Column labels

FIGURE 40.3

You can view your list of messages expanded if you close the Reading pane.

Notice that the message details are organized into columns with labels. If you want, you can resize the columns if you need to view more or less of a certain detail. Click and drag the column label's border to resize the column. You can also use the column headings to perform sorts on a particular column. For example, you can sort your list by date or sender, and so on. You might choose to sort your list alphabetically by sender name, for example, to help you see who sent you what. Outlook displays two buttons at the top of the list to view all messages or just the unread messages.

You can tell which messages are read or unread based on their appearance in the list. If they appear bold and in blue, they're unread. If they are not bold and have no color, you've read the message already (refer to Figure 40.4). If the Reading pane is displayed and the message list is less wide to accommodate it, a blue vertical bar on the left side of the message indicates an unread message.

To select a message, click it. This makes it active, and you can perform actions on it. To open it entirely, double-click it. This opens the message in a Message window, similar to Figure 40.4. The window is the same as the one you use to compose new messages. To close it and return to viewing your message list, click the window's Close button.

FIGURE 40.4

You can also open a message in its own window to read.

If the Reading pane is open, you can also view a selected message's content there. Figure 40.5 shows an example of the Mail module with the Reading pane displayed. (The pane can be displayed to the right or at the bottom of the window—your choice.) If the People pane is displayed, you can see contact information pertaining to the sender and reply directly in the Reading pane. To toggle the pane on or off, click the View tab, click the People pane button, and choose a setting.

From the Reading pane, you can navigate messages using these techniques:

- Scroll through longer messages using the scrollbars or click the scroll arrows.

- Move up or down a long message one page at a time by pressing the spacebar on the keyboard. At the end of the message, press the spacebar again to open the first page of the next message.

- Use the Zoom tool on the status bar to zoom your view of the Reading pane display; drag the slider left to reduce the size of the text, or drag the slider right to magnify the text.

- Choose between displaying the Reading pane on the right side of the pane or at the bottom of the pane by clicking the Reading Pane button on the View tab and making your selection.

Unread   Read   Column labels

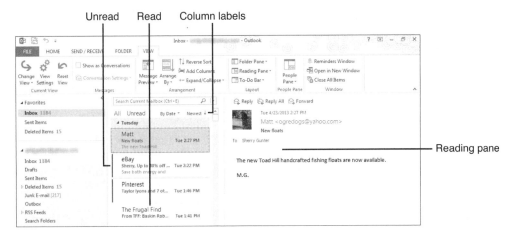

FIGURE 40.5

You can use the Reading pane to view a selected message's content.

NOTE If you turn the People pane on, it appears directly below the Reading pane. The People pane displays information about the message sender, including references to previous correspondence. If you keep info about the person stored in your contacts, you can view it in the People pane. For example, if the person's contact record includes a picture, the image appears in the People pane. You can expand and collapse the People pane using the tiny arrow icon in the upper-right corner of the pane. You can also control the pane through the View tab; click the People pane button and choose Normal (expanded), Minimized (collapsed), or Off.

Checking for New Messages

You can tell Outlook to check for messages, or you can set the program up to check them automatically at a designated interval. By default, Outlook is set up to check for new email every 30 minutes.

To check for new messages manually, use one of these methods:

- Click the Send/Receive All Folders button on the Quick Access toolbar; you can do this no matter which Outlook module you're viewing.

- Click the Send/Receive All Folders button on the Home tab when viewing the Mail module (see Figure 40.6).

- Click the Send/Receive All Folders button on the Send/Receive tab.

- Press F9 on the keyboard.

FIGURE 40.6

Look for the Send/Receive All Folders button to download new email messages.

Of course, you must be connected to the Internet to receive messages from your email services.

To set up an automatic email check or to change the default setting, click the File tab to visit Backstage view, and then select Options. This opens the Outlook Options dialog box. Click the Advanced tab, and then scroll down to the Send and Receive group of options. Click the Send/Receive button to open the Send/ Receive Groups dialog box. Here you can turn off automatic mail retrieval or specify a different interval for downloading messages. You can even set options for retrieving email from individual email accounts.

To turn off the default retrieval, deselect the Schedule an Automatic Send/Receive check box. You can also reset the interval to another setting, such as every 60 minutes. You can tell Outlook to retrieve mail whenever you exit the program window, too. Click Close to exit the dialog box, and click OK to exit the Outlook Options dialog box.

Replying to a Message

One of the best aspects of email is the capability to send messages back and forth. You can keep replying to an original message as long as you need to, with both parties sending their responses back and forth, thus creating a conversation of sorts. By default, Outlook includes the original message content in the message body of each response. New responses are added to the top of the message, and the conversation scrolls along newest to oldest.

New to Outlook 2013, you can reply directly to a message from the Reading pane without opening a Message window. With the Reading pane turned on, select the message from the list to view it in the pane, as demonstrated in Figure 40.7, and then click the Reply or Reply All button at the top of the pane. Reply sends a response to the sender, whereas Reply All sends the response to everyone referenced on the sender's list (the To field).

Reply tools

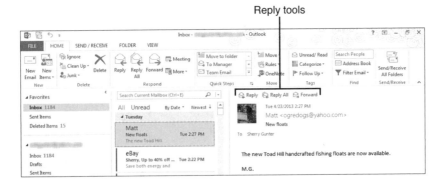

FIGURE 40.7

Look for message reply buttons at the top of the Reading pane.

Outlook displays mini form window fields and you can type your reply, similar to Figure 40.8. Outlook also automatically adds an RE: prefix to the subject title, which stands for Reply, Regarding, or Referencing (depending on who you ask). After typing in your reply text, click Send.

Pop out the reply in its own message window
Send your message
Forego the reply entirely

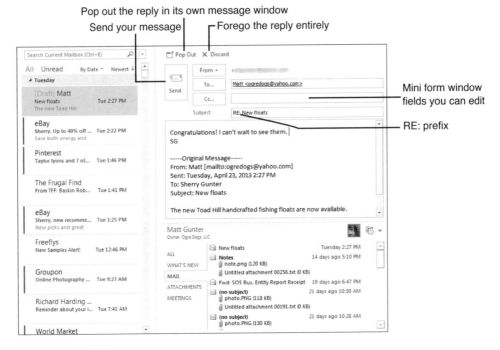

Mini form window fields you can edit

RE: prefix

FIGURE 40.8

Type your reply directly into the Reading pane.

You can click the Pop Out button to pop out the reply into its own window, which enables you to access all the additional message tools. If you decide you don't want to carry through with creating a reply message, click the Discard button to remove it.

You can also reply to a message by double-clicking it in the message list to open it in its own window, and then click the Reply or Reply All button.

Forwarding a Message

You can also forward a message to a new recipient. For example, you may want to forward a funny email you received from your coworker to your friend, or forward a message about a new product to your boss. When you forward a message, Outlook adds a FW: prefix to the subject title, which stands for Forward, naturally. Figure 40.9 shows an example.

To forward a message from the Reading pane, click the Forward button at the top of the pane. This command displays the same mini form window fields that appear when you click Reply or Reply All. Type any message text you want to include with the forwarded text, and click Send.

FIGURE 40.9

You can also forward a message from the Reading pane.

To forward a message from a message window, double-click the message from the list and click the Forward button on the Message tab.

Deleting a Message

You can remove messages from the list and place them in the Deleted Items folder to permanently delete later. Deleting messages as you read them can help you manage your Inbox. To delete a message, select it and use one of these methods:

- On the right side of the highlighted message (see Figure 40.10), click the Delete button.

- Right-click the message and choose Delete.

- On the Home tab, click the Delete button.

You can empty the Delete Items folder periodically to clean out messages. See Chapter 41, "Managing Email," to learn how to permanently delete messages.

 TIP If you accidentally delete a message you still wanted to see in your message list, click the Deleted Items folder in the Folder pane, select the message, and drag it back to the Inbox.

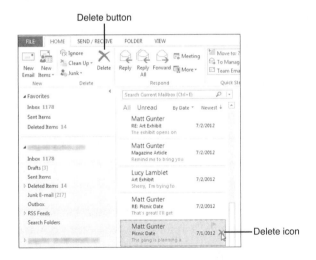

FIGURE 40.10

Look for a Delete icon when you hover your mouse pointer over a message.

Saving Messages

Unlike some of the other Microsoft Office programs, such as Word or Excel, you don't have to worry about saving files much in Outlook. Items you create, such as messages, tasks, and contacts, are saved when you add them to the modules. You don't have to save your work before exiting Outlook, for example. If you want to save a message manually, however, you can do so.

Saving a Draft Message

If you're in the middle of composing a message and need to step away before completing it and sending it, you can save it. The Message window form has a Save button on its Quick Access toolbar which, when clicked, places the message in the Drafts folder, shown in Figure 40.11. (Each email account you work with in Outlook has its own Drafts folder.) The Message window stays open, however, so you can keep working on it. If you happen to close the window, the message still sits in the Drafts folder waiting for you.

Drafts folder

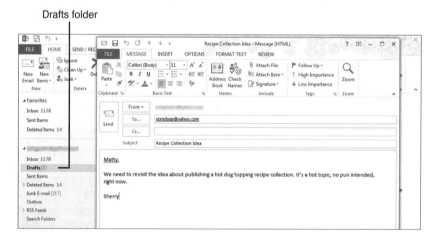

FIGURE 40.11

The Drafts folder stores your in-progress messages.

This feature is handy when you want to work on a message and keep it around temporarily until it's ready for sending. You can reopen it anytime and work on it more. Click the account's Drafts folder and double-click the message you want to edit. When it's finally ready to go out, click the Send button.

 TIP If you decide not to use the draft message after all, you can delete it from the Drafts folder. Click the message in the Drafts folder list of messages and then click the Delete button. Outlook moves the message to the Deleted Items folder.

Saving a Message File

You can also choose to save an Outlook message as a message file. You might, for example, save a message to use in another program, or maybe you've written a masterful message that needs to be saved for posterity. Aside from the obvious ways to retain a message (print it on paper), you can save it as a file on your computer or other storage device, or export it to another program.

When saving a message as a file, you have the option of controlling what sort of file format is used. You can save it in a variety of formats, including text only, Outlook template, Outlook message format, HTML, or MHT (MIME HTML, which is similar to HTML but without an additional folder for support files).

To save a message, follow these steps:

1. With the Message window open, click the File tab.

2. Click Save As.

3. Navigate to the folder and drive to which you want to store the file (see Figure 40.12).

4. Enter a name for the file in the File Name box.

5. Optionally, click the Save as Type drop-down arrow and specify a file type.

6. Click Save.

Outlook saves the message as directed.

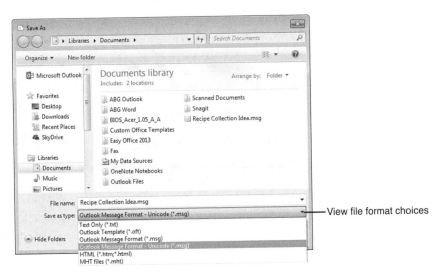

FIGURE 40.12

You can specify a file format for the messages you save as files.

Working with File Attachments

You can attach files to your emails to send to others and receive file attachments, too. *File attachments* are files created in other programs that you want to send along with a message. File attachments can be pictures, word processing documents, spreadsheets, slideshow presentations, desktop publishing documents, and so on. For example, suppose you want to send an email to a new client and include an electronic copy of your latest product list or a picture of your top-selling widget. You tell Outlook what file you want to include and it attaches to the message as a file the recipient can open and view.

 CAUTION File attachments increase the overall size of your email message. This is something to consider if your email service sets limits to how much data you can send. Some files are obviously bigger than others, with picture files often being the largest.

At the other end of the spectrum, you can open attachments you receive from others and save them on your computer for viewing and using. You can easily see if a message in your list has an accompanying attachment; Outlook displays a paper clip icon when a message has a file attachment.

 TIP You can email attachments directly from the other Microsoft Office programs. Suppose you want to send a Word document; just click the File tab, select Share, click Send Using E-Mail, and then choose Send as Attachment.

Attaching a File

To attach a file, follow these steps:

1. From the Message window, select the Message tab (if it's not already displayed).

2. Click the Attach File button (see Figure 40.13).

3. In the Insert File dialog box, navigate to the folder or drive containing the file you want to attach and select the filename.

4. Click Insert.

Outlook attaches the file. Now you can send the message when you're ready.

Attach File button

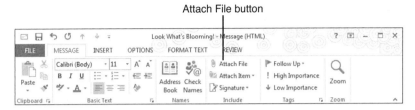

FIGURE 40.13

Look for the Attach File button.

If you've chosen HTML or Plain Text as the email's format, the attached file's name appears in the Attached box in the message header area, just below the subject title, as demonstrated in Figure 40.14. If the message format is in Rich Text, the attachment appears as an icon in the message body.

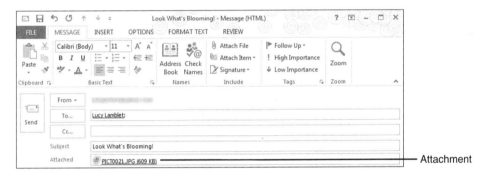

Attachment

FIGURE 40.14

A file attachment shows up here.

Opening an Attachment

When you receive a message with a file attachment (which is marked as a paper clip icon in your message list), you can choose to view the attachment in several ways. You can preview some types of files, such as PDF files, Word documents, and Excel workbooks, in Outlook's Reading pane. Figure 40.15 shows an example of what this looks like. Click the attachment and instead of showing the message text in the Reading pane, a preview of the attachment fills the area, and an Attachments tab appears on the Ribbon. To switch back to the message content again, click the Show Message button on the Attachments tab (see Figure 4.15) or click Message in the Reading pane's header area.

To open a file attachment in its own program-appropriate window, double-click the file attachment. Depending on the file type, a program window opens to view the file.

To save the attachment to your computer and work with it later, right-click the attachment and choose Save As. You can then navigate to the folder or drive you want to save to and activate the Save command.

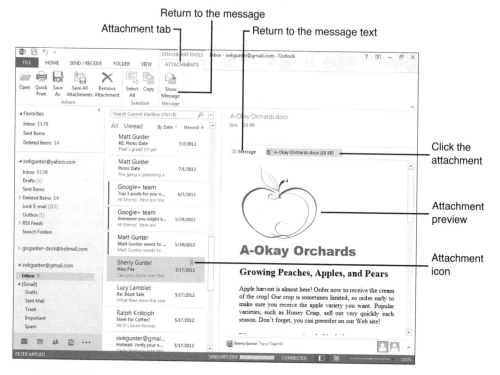

FIGURE 40.15

You can preview an attachment directly in the Reading pane.

 NOTE Outlook might prompt you about viewing attachments from unsafe sources. This is a precaution against computer viruses and hacking. If you trust the source, you can continue with the preview. If not, stop to run a virus check using your computer's virus protection software.

Using Simple Message Tools

In this section, you explore some useful tools you can use to process messages in the message list.

Marking Messages as Read or Unread

As you're working with messages in the list, Outlook notifies you which messages are read and which ones are unread. Learning to ascertain which ones you've read already can help you eliminate wasted time reviewing unimportant messages. Every new message that arrives in your Inbox (or Inboxes, if you're using multiple email accounts) is marked with a blue vertical line and bold blue header text. This indicates that the message is unread. As soon as you open it, or preview it for a margin of time, Outlook marks the status as read, indicated by the lack of the blue vertical line.

On some occasions you might want to mark a read message as unread to remind yourself to view the message again. Or you might want to mark an unread message as read.

To change the message status, use one of these methods:

- Click the blue vertical bar to mark the message as read (see Figure 40.16).
- Right-click the message and choose Mark as Unread or Mark as Read.
- Select the message and, on the Home tab, click the Unread/Read button.
- Press Ctrl+Q to mark a selected message as read.
- Press Ctrl+U to mark a selected message as unread.
- To mark everything in a folder as read, right-click the folder name and choose Mark All as Read.

You can also mark groups of messages by selecting the group first before applying a new status.

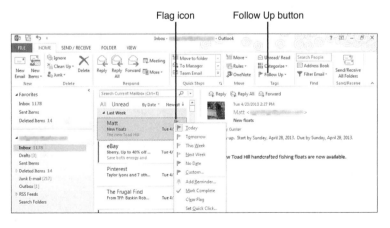

FIGURE 40.16

Marking messages as read and unread can help you review which messages require your attention.

Flagging Messages

You can flag a message with a reminder so you can revisit it later to address it or take care of a task. Flagging is a great tool to help you stay on top of things you need to do or people you need to reply to with haste. Any messages you flag are added to your Task list. (See Chapter 45, "Working with Tasks and To-Do Lists," to learn more about working with tasks in Outlook's Task module.)

To flag a message, use one of these techniques:

- Hover the mouse pointer over a message until you see a Flag icon (see Figure 40.17); click it and choose how you want to mark the message.

- Right-click the message and choose Follow Up; then click a flag.

- On the Home tab, click the Follow Up button, and then click a flag.

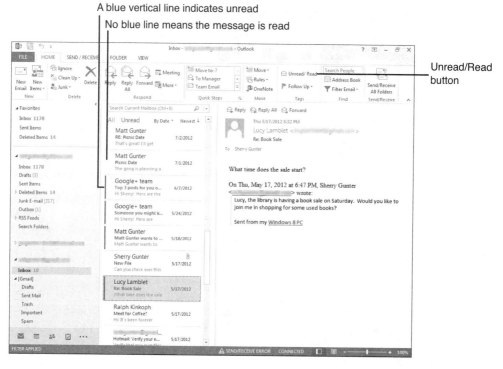

FIGURE 40.17

Flagging messages marks them so you can return later.

To remove a flag, hover over the flag icon in the message list and click it to turn it off.

Categorizing Messages

You can color code your messages to help you determine actions you need to take on them. Outlook offers six preconfigured category colors, and you can rename them to suit your own workflow or create new ones. You can learn more about using categories in Chapter 48, "Using Color Categories," but for now, you learn how to apply them to your messages.

Select the message you want to categorize and then click the Categorize button on the Home tab. Click a color category and Outlook immediately assigns it to the message, adding a color box to the listed item and adding a color bar to the message content. The first time you use the feature, Outlook might prompt you to give the color category a unique name. You can do so then, or you can change it later (see Chapter 48).

You can also right-click a message in your list and choose Categorize, and then specify a color.

THE ABSOLUTE MINIMUM

Here are the key points to remember from this chapter:

- You can compose new email messages in the Message window, which includes its own unique ribbon of message-related tools.

- To check for new email messages and send any existing ones waiting in the Outbox, click the Send/Receive All Folders button.

- If you want to save a message that's not ready for sending, save it as a draft.

- You can attach files you create in other programs to send along with your email message.

- Flag and categorize messages to help you manage tasks and keep on top of things you need to do.

MANAGING EMAIL

As your email messages start piling up, you eventually need to plan ways to manage them or your Inbox is going to seem like it's bursting at the seams. Thankfully, Outlook makes it easy to choose how you want to organize and store messages. In fact, this is where Outlook puts the word "manage" in personal information manager and kicks it into high gear.

Although it may be tempting to let messages turn into a mountain in your Inbox, don't. You can opt for a variety of handy methods for dealing with them efficiently. In this chapter, you discover essential techniques for keeping ahead of your email stack.

Organizing Messages with Folders

Every message you receive for a particular email service appears in the account's Inbox folder listed in the Folder pane. In the same way you use folders to organize files on your computer, you can use folders in Outlook to store and sort email messages.

Each email account includes a set of default folders, one of which is the main Inbox for the account. Other folders might include Drafts, Sent Items, Deleted Items, Junk E-mail, and Outbox. (These vary depending on your email service.) Most preexisting folders are self-explanatory based on their names alone, but you can also add more folders to help you better organize your messages. For example, you might want to keep all your departmental emails in a folder labeled Sales Department, or all your business correspondence in a folder labeled Clients. You can create as many folders as you need, even for temporary projects and tasks.

Making a New Email Folder

To create a new folder, follow these steps:

1. With the Mail module displayed onscreen, click the Inbox folder under the email service you want to add a folder to (see Figure 41.1).

2. On the Folder tab, click the New Folder button.

New Folder button

FIGURE 41.1

Start by choosing which email account you want to add a folder to.

3. Outlook opens the Create New Folder dialog box, as shown in Figure 41.2. Type a name for the new folder in the Name box.

4. Leave the other settings intact. (Mail and Post Items is selected in the Folder Contains box, and the Inbox you selected in step 1 is highlighted in the Select Where to Place the Folder list box.)

5. Click OK.

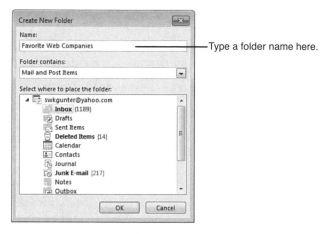

FIGURE 41.2

Use the Create New Folder dialog box to make new folders.

Outlook adds the new folder to the Folder pane, similar to Figure 41.3. Now you can start moving messages to the folder as needed.

 TIP You can also right-click the Inbox name and choose New Folder from the context menu that pops up; then type in a new folder name directly without using the Create New Folder dialog box.

 TIP Adding folders is a key part of using Outlook's other message management features, such as rerouting incoming emails to designated folders. Sometimes it helps to plan what types of folders you might need later, such as a work project or important client you're corresponding with. You can always remove folders you no longer need and archive any old messages.

New folder

FIGURE 41.3

Outlook adds the new folder to the list.

Moving a Message to Your New Folder

To move a message to a folder, you can drag and drop it in place. You can also use this method:

1. Click the title of the message you want to move.

2. On the Home tab, click the Move button.

3. Select the name of the folder where you want to place the message (see Figure 41.4).

If the folder you want to use isn't listed in the Move menu, click the Other Folder option and use the Move Items dialog box to choose your folder.

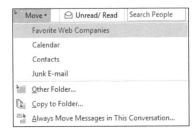

FIGURE 41.4

Use the Move menu to move selected messages around in your folder structure.

Working with Folder Contents

You can right-click a folder to open a menu of options that enables you to rename, copy, move, or delete it. From this menu you can also create a new folder, clean out junk mail, or mark all messages as read.

 TIP Your Sent Items folder keeps a copy of all the emails you send. This feature is turned on by default, which makes it a nice safeguard in case you need to find a message later.

Routing Messages with Quick Steps

You can use Outlook's Quick Steps feature to perform multiple actions on your email messages with just one click. For example, you might want to flag a message for follow up later *and* move it to a special folder. Rather than do the two actions separately, why not do them at the same time?

Outlook stores Quick Steps in the Quick Steps gallery on the Home tab when you're using the Mail module. You can scroll through the gallery to view them or expand the gallery to view all of them at once. Outlook even includes a few preset Quick Steps you can take advantage of:

- **Move To**—If you find yourself moving messages to the same folder over and over, designate it as the Move To folder and use this Quick Step to immediately relocate messages.

- **To Manager**—This opens a message form that's automatically preset with a designated recipient, such as your manager (hence the name), along with the forwarded message.

- **Team Email**—Use this Quick Step to send a new message to everyone on a team. All the member's email addresses are saved and preloaded, ready to go.

- **Done**—This marks the selected message as read, completed (with a Mark Complete flag), and moves it to a designated folder—three things at once.

- **Reply and Delete**—This one opens a reply form to send back a reply and also moves the original message to the Deleted Items folder.

To practice using one of the default Quick Steps, you can try out the one that moves messages. While viewing your Inbox messages in the Mail module, select the message you want to dispatch. (Click it or tap it to select it.) Next, make sure the Home tab is displayed and click the Move to: ? Quick Step from the Quick Step gallery, as shown in Figure 41.5. If the Move to: ? option isn't in view, scroll through the gallery to locate it.

Quick Steps gallery

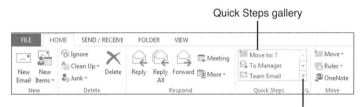

Click here to expand the gallery and view all the Quick Steps

FIGURE 41.5

Use the Quick Steps gallery to apply automated tasks to your messages.

When you activate the option, the First Time Setup dialog box appears, similar to Figure 41.6. The same box opens for some of the other Quick Steps the first time you use them—that's because you first need to specify people or folders so Outlook can carry out the actions. To designate a folder to move the selected message to, click the drop-down arrow and specify a folder name.

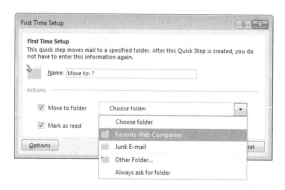

FIGURE 41.6

Use the First Time Setup dialog box to tell Outlook which folder to move messages to.

The Mark as Read check box is also conveniently selected. You can leave it checked if you want to consider the message read; uncheck it if you want to move it and treat it as not read yet.

Finally, click the Save button. Outlook saves the folder name as your designated folder and adjusts the Quick Step name accordingly. The next time you want to move a message, click the option listed in the Quick Steps gallery, and Outlook takes care of the relocation for you. You can use the Quick Steps gallery on the Home tab to make your selection, or you can right-click the message, choose Quick Steps, and then choose the name of your step.

To build a custom Quick Step, choose the Create New option from the Quick Steps gallery. This opens the Edit Quick Step dialog box, shown in Figure 41.7, and you can choose actions, folders, even type ToolTip text to remind you what the step does when you hover the mouse pointer over the Quick Step name.

You can open the Manage Quick Steps dialog box (see Figure 41.8) to make changes to actions associated with Quick Steps or remove Quick Steps you no longer want. From the Quick Steps gallery, select the Manage Quick Steps option to display the dialog box. Choose which Quick Step you want to edit and then click the Edit button to make changes to the associated actions; you can also click the Delete button to remove the Quick Step entirely from the list. You can also duplicate a Quick Step and tweak it slightly to create a new step.

FIGURE 41.7

Build your own Quick Steps with the tools in this dialog box.

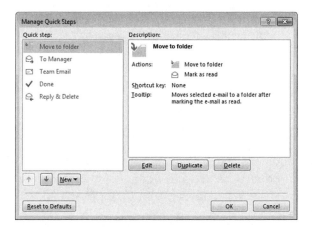

FIGURE 41.8

Manage your Quick Steps from this dialog box.

 TIP   If you don't like the order of your Quick Steps in the gallery, you can reorder them in the Manage Quick Steps dialog box. Use the arrow buttons to reposition how a step is listed in the bunch.

Managing Incoming Messages with Rules

Outlook enables you to set up rules for your email messages, such as telling all the emails from a certain friend to go to the Boring folder, or put all the messages from your boss into a Do This Now folder. You can set rules in Outlook that help you sort through your email and put them in special locations, among other actions. Rules can help you move, copy, delete, reply to, forward, and redirect your email. You can choose from Outlook's preset rules or create brand new ones.

You can build rules with help from Outlook's Rules Wizard, a step-by-step process for creating a rule. (Click the Advanced Options button in the Create Rule dialog box to summon the wizard for help.) However, one of the easiest ways to build a rule is to use an example of an existing message you want to create a rule for, such as an email from a certain person that you always want routed to a certain folder, and build on it. With the Mail module displayed, follow these steps:

1. Select the message you want to turn into a rule.

2. On the Home tab, click the Rules button (see Figure 41.9).

FIGURE 41.9

Activate the Rules menu to find the Create Rule command.

3. Select Create Rule to open the Create Rule dialog box, shown in Figure 41.10.

4. Use the conditions check boxes to set the criteria for the email. You can specify messages from that particular sender, identify subject matter to recognize, or who the message was originally sent to, for example.

5. Under the Do the Following group, choose what you want Outlook to do when it encounters these same message types in the future, such as moving them to a specified folder.

FIGURE 41.10

The Create Rule dialog box is the place to set criteria for a message rule.

6. Click OK and the rule is set for any incoming messages resembling the criteria you specified.

7. Outlook asks if you want to run the rule immediately. Click the check box and click OK to do so, or click OK to exit without running the rule yet.

You can manage any rules you create using the Rules and Alerts dialog box, which you can open by clicking the Rules button on the Home tab and selecting Manage Rules and Alerts.

Controlling Junk Email

Junk email is a broad term covering advertising emails, unsolicited bulk emails, spam, or just about anything sent to your email address without your consent. Billions of spam emails are sent daily, and they're not always just about advertising something. Spam email can also be criminal in nature, generated by hackers and "phishers" trying to steal your identity or personal information for nefarious reasons. Thwarting junk email from reaching your Inbox requires some filtering on Outlook's part. Although it can't catch everything all the time, Outlook's filtering tools do a pretty good job of sorting out the bad stuff and placing it in a special folder marked for such unworthy messages.

You can even fine-tune the sensitivity settings to low or high to suit your needs. Choose from the following options:

*   **No Automatic Filtering**—This setting means there's no filtering happening at all. Junk mail can flow freely into your Inbox.

*   **Low**—Some junk mail still gets through, but the worst of it is tossed away.

- **High**—The most ruthless setting; no junk gets through, and sometimes even legitimate emails are dumped here. (Be sure to check the Junk E-mail folder periodically to see if anything important gets tossed in by mistake.)

- **Safe Lists Only**—This setting allows only emails from specified companies and individuals (from your safe recipients list) to make it into your Inbox. You first have to identify senders in a special Safe Senders list (sort of like a guest list for your email, and only the invitees make it into the party).

In addition to setting a filtering level, you can also choose to permanently delete junk email when it's found, disable links in suspected phishing messages, or display a warning prompt for suspicious domain names for a heads up.

To adjust your junk mail settings, follow these steps:

1. From the Mail module, click the Junk button on the Home tab (see Figure 41.11). If you have more than one email service, select the account's Inbox first.

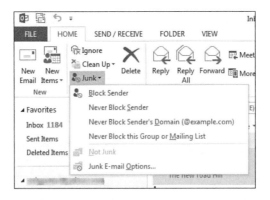

FIGURE 41.11

Look for the Junk drop-down menu on the Home tab.

2. Select Junk E-mail Options. The Junk E-mail Options dialog box opens to the Options tab, as shown in Figure 41.12.

3. Click a protection level.

4. Click OK.

You can also help Outlook identify junk email by pointing it out when you find it in your Inbox. Right-click the message from the list, click Junk, and then choose the Block Sender option.

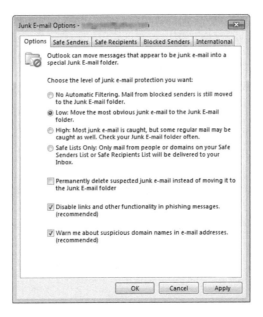

FIGURE 41.12

Set any junk email protection levels in this dialog box.

If you find the filter dumping legitimate messages into the Junk E-mail folder, display the folder's contents (click the folder name in the Folder pane), right-click the message from the list, and choose Never Block Sender or Not Junk.

 TIP If you're concerned Outlook might identify email messages from someone as junk, such as the weekly family updates from Uncle Marvin, you can add the individual to your Safe Recipient's list. From the Junk E-Mail Options dialog box (see Figure 41.14), click the Safe Recipients tab and click Add, and then type in the user's address.

Archiving Messages

Deleting old messages is a great way to clean out your Inbox, but sometimes you need to keep selected old messages, especially if you need to refer to them to recall an exchange. Archiving is a great solution for these messages.

You can archive manually or automate the task. Outlook's AutoArchive tool is perfect for taking care of archiving tasks in the background without any help from you. You can set different archiving tasks for different folders. For example, you can instruct the tool to automatically archive messages in your Inbox that are older than 3 months and move them to a special archive folder.

By default, Outlook is set up to archive messages to a file named archive.pst. You can specify another location for your archive files as well as specify more descriptive filenames.

Manually Archive Messages

If you're doing a little folder cleaning, you can manually archive messages. For example, you might be wrapping up a work project and need to put all the email messages associated with it into an archive file.

To manually archive messages, follow these steps:

1. Click the File tab.

2. Select Info to open the Account Information screen.

3. Click Cleanup Tools.

4. Click Archive to open the Archive dialog box shown in Figure 41.13.

FIGURE 41.13

Use the Archive dialog box to manually archive old messages.

5. Click the folder you want to archive.

6. Choose a cutoff date, such as items older than 6 months.

7. Choose an archive file location (click the Browse button, navigate to the location, and specify a more descriptive filename), or use the default filename and locations.

8. Click OK and Outlook archives the messages.

Setting Up Automatic Archiving

You can instruct Outlook to perform automatic archiving for you. You can set automatic archiving for individual folders or the Inbox in general. To set up automatic archiving, follow these steps:

1. Select the folder or subfolder you want to archive, such as your Inbox or an old project folder.

2. On the Folder tab, click the AutoArchive Settings button.

3. Outlook opens the Junk E-mail Properties dialog box to the AutoArchive tab of tools, as shown in Figure 41.14. Click the Archive This Folder Using These Settings option.

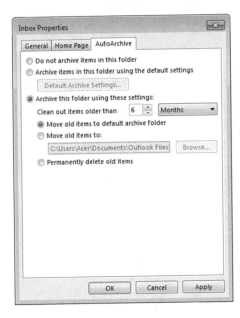

FIGURE 41.14

Use the AutoArchive feature to automatically archive old messages.

4. Specify the age of the messages, such as older than 3 months.

5. Specify a location for the archived file, or use the default location.

6. Click OK.

> **TIP** To check out how much room is being consumed in your Inbox, click the File tab, click the Cleanup Tools button, and then click Mailbox Cleanup. This opens the Mailbox Cleanup dialog box. Click the View Mailbox Size button to check out how much room is taken up by your messages in the various folders. Based on what you see, you might decide you need to clean up some folders and archive old messages.

THE ABSOLUTE MINIMUM

Here are the key points to remember from this chapter:

- You can use Outlook's folder hierarchy to organize messages in an orderly fashion; just add new folders when you need them and move messages around.

- Use Outlook's Quick Steps to perform multiple actions on your messages, such as sending particular ones to a certain folder and flagging them with priority status.

- You can use message rules to direct the flow of incoming email, such as sending messages from your colleague to a project folder.

- Turn on Outlook's filtering tools to stop the flow of junk email to your Inbox.

- You can archive older messages to get them out of the way, yet keep them available if you need to refer to them again.

42

WORKING WITH ADVANCED EMAIL FEATURES

Outlook offers many extra features you can use to enhance your email messages, automate replies, and take your email tasks to the next level. For example, you can assign email priority and sensitivity levels, use Quick Parts to automate repetitive tasks, insert a digital signature automatically at the bottom of all your messages, request delivery receipts, and even subscribe to and read your favorite RSS feeds right in Outlook.

Setting Priority and Sensitivity Options

One way to add urgency or attention to an email you send is to assign a priority level. Priority levels come in three settings: High, Normal, and Low. Normal is the default setting, so you don't have to specify it when creating a regular message. When you assign High status, for example, the recipient can immediately determine how important the message is and the urgency of a timely response. With High priority, Outlook adds a red exclamation point to the message that's visible in the recipient's email Inbox.

To assign a priority level to your message, click the Message tab and choose a priority level in the Tags group of tools (see Figure 42.1). Click the High Importance button to assign High priority level, or click Low Importance to mark the message as low-level priority. You might set low priority in your office environment to help your coworkers or boss recognize the message as lower in the chain of importance.

Assign a priority level using these buttons.

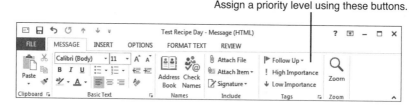

FIGURE 42.1

You can find two of the three priority levels available as buttons on the Message tab.

In the lower corner of the Tags group, click the Message Options button to open the Properties dialog box shown in Figure 42.2. From here, you can click the Importance drop-down arrow and choose a priority level.

While you're looking at the Properties box, you can also use the controls found within to set a sensitivity level for a message. Click the Sensitivity drop-down arrow (refer to Figure 42.2) and choose a setting. Like the priority level setting, Normal is the default sensitivity setting. You can also set Personal, Private, or Confidential. Be warned, however, that these settings don't necessarily protect your email message from prying eyes; rather, they just alert the recipient regarding the nature of the message. If you use Outlook in an office or corporate setting, check with your administrator concerning any policies for confidential emails.

Click here to set a priority level.

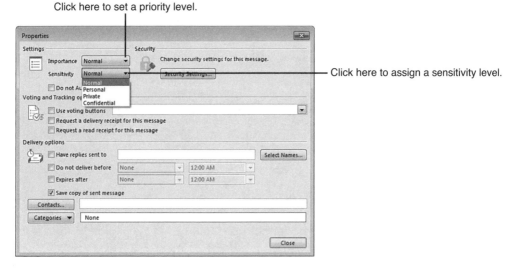

Click here to assign a sensitivity level.

FIGURE 42.2

The Properties dialog box offers all three priority levels in a drop-down list of options.

Using Quick Parts

To help you build better, faster emails, you can save text you type in repeatedly with your messages into reusable blocks, called *Quick Parts*. Microsoft's Quick Parts feature is available throughout the Office suite and is used to insert all kinds of elements, such as headers and footers, salutations for letters, page numbers, and so on.

To turn text into a building block, follow these steps:

1. Select the message text you want to turn into a Quick Part.

2. On the Insert tab, click the Quick Parts button.

3. Select Save Selection to Quick Part Gallery. This opens the Create New Building Block dialog box, as shown in Figure 42.3.

4. Type a name for your building block.

5. Optionally, fill out any additional details you want to save along with the text element.

6. Click OK to save the building block.

Any time you want to add your building block to a message, click the Quick Parts button on the Insert tab and choose your item from the gallery.

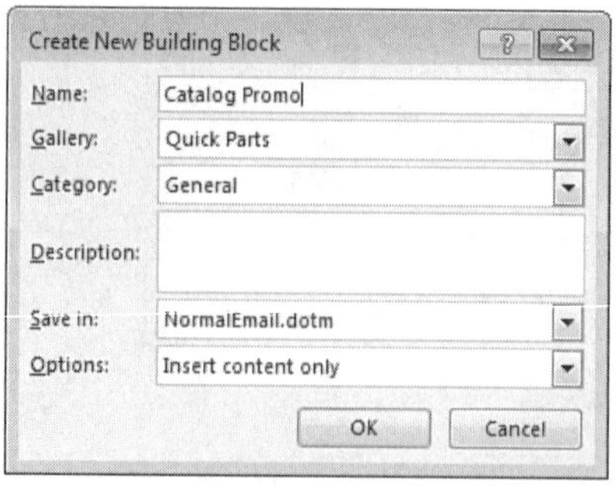

FIGURE 42.3

Create your own Quick Parts using this dialog box.

To remove a Quick Part you no longer need, click the Quick Parts button, right-click the Quick Part and choose Organize and Delete. This opens the Building Blocks Organizer. Select your Quick Part and click the Delete button to remove it. You can also use this dialog box to view a list of all your Quick Parts and manage them.

Adding Signatures

A digital signature is a portion of text you add to the end of every email message, a salutation of sorts that uniquely identifies you as the sender. Some people use signatures to include company information, such as the name and web address, whereas others use signatures to include contact information, such as addresses and phone numbers. It's not uncommon to see signatures with famous quotes, logos and graphics, and sales information. You can instruct Outlook to add a default signature to every new message you create, or you can choose to add one manually when you need it.

To create a signature, follow these steps:

1. Click the File tab.

2. Select Options to open the Outlook Options dialog box (see Figure 42.4).

3. In the Compose Messages group on the Mail tab, click the Signatures button to open the Signatures and Stationary dialog box.

4. Click New to open the New Signature dialog box.

Click to display the Mail options.

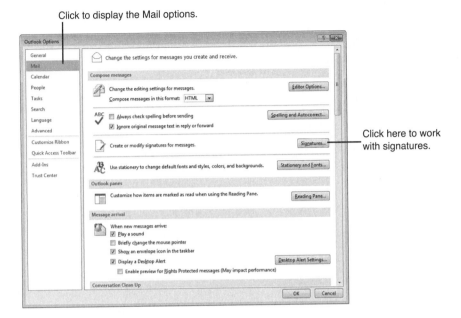

FIGURE 42.4

Use the Outlook Options dialog box to start access signatures.

5. Type a name for the new signature.

6. Click OK.

7. Type your signature text and format it any way you want using the formatting tools (see Figure 42.5). You can change text color, make text bold or italic, or set a different font or size.

8. Click OK.

9. Click OK again to close the Outlook Options dialog box.

The next time you compose a new email message for that particular account, Outlook automatically inserts the signature into the email's message body.

To edit signatures or assign new ones to your accounts, reopen the Signatures and Stationary dialog box and make your changes. You can delete signatures, edit existing signatures, or change which accounts they're associated with.

Use the formatting tools to spruce up your signature.

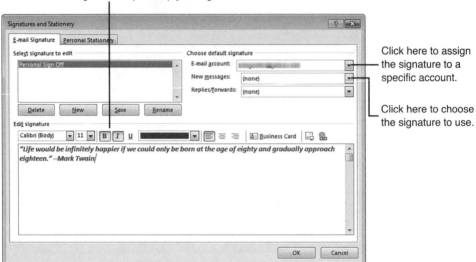

Click here to assign the signature to a specific account.

Click here to choose the signature to use.

FIGURE 42.5

You can add and edit signatures with this dialog box.

Controlling Replies, Forwarding, and Receipts

You can control how Outlook handles replies and forwarding with the options in the Outlook Options dialog box. By default, Outlook is set up to include the original message text in any replies. You can change this. For example, you might prefer to send the original text as an attachment instead.

To open the Outlook Options dialog box, click the File tab and select Options. On the Mail tab, scroll down to the Replies and Forwards group of tools, as shown in Figure 42.6. Click the When Replying to a Message drop-down list and make your selection. You can make similar changes to how the message text is handled when forwarded. Click OK to exit the dialog box and apply the changes.

You can also request delivery receipts or read receipts with your messages. When you activate these features, the recipient's email server generates a response when the person receives or views the email message. This can help you keep track of whether someone has read your message. You can also assign a delivery reply to another email address, or a day or time for delivery, or even a delivery expiration. These particular tracking controls appear in the Properties dialog box for the Message window. Check out Figure 42.7 to view them.

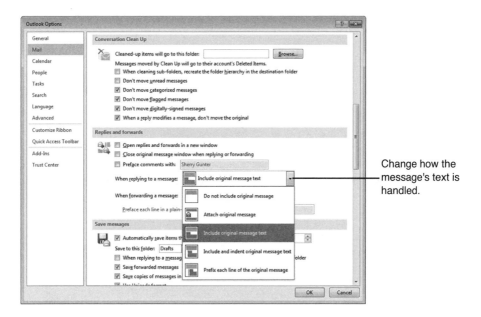

Change how the message's text is handled.

FIGURE 42.6

Control how replies and forwards appear using these options.

Click here to request a delivery receipt

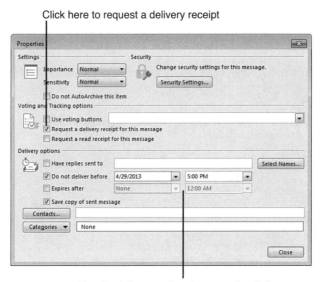

Use the delivery options to customize delivery

FIGURE 42.7

The Properties dialog box has delivery options.

TIP To view additional tracking options, open the Outlook Options dialog box (click File, Options). On the Mail tab, scroll down to the Tracking group to view additional settings for receipts.

Working with RSS Feeds

RSS (Really Simple Syndication) is a technology that enables web content to be converted into a feed that is viewed as message posts. You can receive RSS feeds for blogs, podcasts, news, and so on. You can use Outlook to check the latest updates of your favorite RSS feeds. Feeds you subscribe to appear in the RSS Feeds folder in the Mail module.

You can conduct a web search to find popular RSS feeds to try if you don't already have a few favorites. You need the RSS feed location, or URL, to connect to the feed.

To subscribe, follow these steps:

1. Click the File tab.
2. On the Account Information screen, click the Account Settings button.
3. Select Account Settings.
4. The Account Settings dialog box opens; click the RSS Feeds tab (see Figure 42.8).

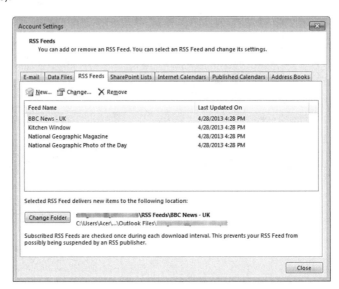

FIGURE 42.8

The Account Settings dialog box is your gateway to signing up for RSS feeds.

5. Click New.

6. Type the RSS Feed address (see Figure 42.9).

FIGURE 42.9

You need to know the RSS feed web address to subscribe.

7. Click Add.

8. The RSS Feed Options dialog box displays with a general name for the feed already assigned (see Figure 42.10). Click OK to continue.

9. The RSS Feed is added to the list box; click Close.

10. Click the Send/Receive tab.

11. Click Send/Receive All Folders to update the latest posts.

12. Click the RSS Feeds folder in the Folder pane to view the RSS feed subfolders to which you are subscribed (see Figure 42.10).

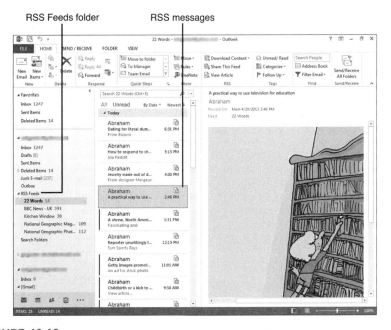

FIGURE 42.10

View your RSS feeds in the RSS Feeds folder.

13. Click the folder you want to open.

14. Click the message you want to view.

15. The Preview pane displays the message.

 TIP If you no longer want to subscribe to an RSS Feed, reopen the Account Settings dialog box to the RSS Feeds tab, select the Feed Name, and then click the Remove button.

THE ABSOLUTE MINIMUM

Here are the key points to remember from this chapter:

- The Format Text tab and Insert tab in the Message window offer a variety of tools to enhance your message appearance and content.

- You can assign priority levels and sensitivity settings to messages to help alert the recipient to a message's importance.

- Use Quick Parts to speed repetitive text entry in your messaging tasks.

- Add unique digital signatures at the end of your messages to personalize your emails.

- Request receipts to verify the recipient has received or read your email.

- Subscribe to your favorite RSS feeds directly in Outlook and read the latest updates from the RSS Feeds folder and your Reading pane.

43

USING THE CALENDAR

The Outlook Calendar helps you keep track of your appointments, dates, and other scheduled events with ease. With a digital calendar, you don't have to worry about making room on your wall or desk for a regular calendar. You can view everything at a glance or with a quick click. As an added benefit, you can view your calendar on the go using your favorite mobile device.

Displaying Your Calendar

With Outlook's Calendar tool, you can conveniently maintain your calendar on your computer. To get started, click the Calendar icon at the bottom of the Folder pane, as shown in Figure 43.1.

Views are listed in this group of tools.

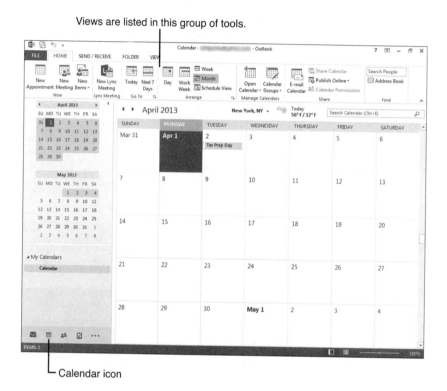

Calendar icon

FIGURE 43.1

Outlook's Calendar displays your calendar by weekly, monthly, or daily view.

When you switch to Calendar, Outlook presents you with a default view that lays out your digital calendar in an easy-to-read design. Depending on how you want to view your information, Calendar offers several views you can toggle among:

- **Day**—Displays a single day on the calendar with times listed in hourly increments and subdivided into half-hour increments. (You can change the increments to suit your needs.)

- **Work Week**—Also displays a week of your calendar, but from Monday through Friday.

- **Week**—Displays a week view of your calendar, starting with Sunday and ending with Saturday.

- **Month**—Displays a full month of days.
- **Schedule View**—Displays your schedule in a horizontal layout, handy for viewing multiple calendars for scheduling meetings with other users.

View modes are available in two places. The Home tab displays the five view modes in the Arrange group (refer to Figure 43.1), whereas the View tab lists them in the Arrangement group. To switch between view modes, click the view you want to display. For example, to see your calendar in Month view, click the Month button.

TIP If you have a different set of days for your workweek instead of the traditional five, you can customize your calendar's work week display. Click the File tab and select Options to display the Outlook Options dialog box. Next, click the Calendar tab. Under the Work Time heading, choose which days constitute your work week. You can also change the work hours for your Day and Week views, or even change the default first day of the week. After you make your adjustments, click OK to apply the changes.

In addition to the view modes, you can also activate a sneak peek mode and check your calendar from any Outlook module using a pop-up display. To do so, hover your mouse pointer over the Calendar icon located at the bottom of the Folder pane, as shown in Figure 43.2. The sneak peek lets you know if you have any appointments or meetings scheduled for the day, and it clues you into the current date.

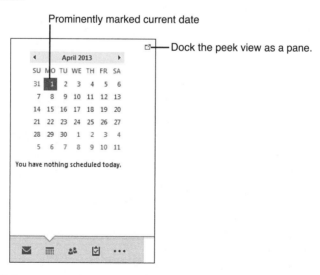

Prominently marked current date

Dock the peek view as a pane.

FIGURE 43.2

You can also sneak a peek at your calendar using the Calendar icon.

Recording Events and Appointments

The true heart of Outlook's Calendar module is its capability to manage your busy schedule. You can add both events and appointments, and there's a distinction between the two. *Events* are all-day activities, whereas *appointments* earmark both a date and a time on your schedule. You can use a form, which appears as a separate window of tools, options, and fill-in-the-blanks, to include details and specify whether it's an event or an appointment you're recording. The form is the same whether you're creating an event or an appointment, but the outcome differs depending on whether you check one particular box.

Recording Events

It's incredibly easy to add an event. As mentioned, *events* are all-day activities, such as a conference, trip, birthday, or anniversary. As such, Outlook displays events a little differently from a scheduled appointment (which occurs at a designated time in the day). In Month view, events appear highlighted in a color bar on the date, whereas in Day, Work, and Work Week view, the event appears at the top of the schedule, also in a color bar. Figure 43.3 shows an example of an event.

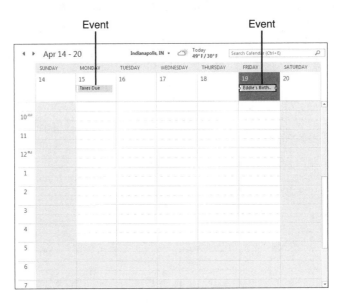

FIGURE 43.3

Events appear as headlines on your calendar.

The simplest way to record an event is to type it directly on the calendar. To add an event in Month view, click the date on the giant calendar display and type your event title, such as **Bob's Birthday**, **Sales Conference**, or **Author Appreciation Day**. Press Enter and the event is added.

You can use the same method to add an event in Work Week or Week view, but click the day's date at the top of the schedule and type the event name, similar to Figure 43.4.

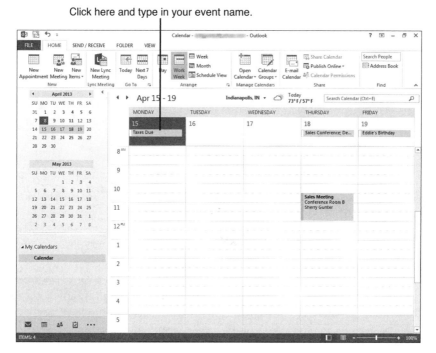

FIGURE 43.4

In Week or Work Week view, the event appears as a header at the top of your schedule.

To add an event in Day view, navigate to the date and click the area at the top, just below the day's date (see Figure 43.5). Type an event name and press Enter.

Click here and type in an event name.

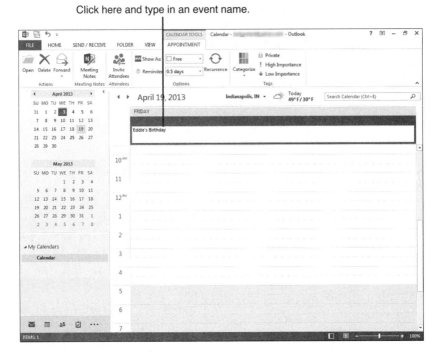

FIGURE 43.5

In Day view, the event appears as a header at the top of your schedule.

You can add multiple events to a single day, or make an event span as many days as you need. For example, your sales conference might cover three days of the week, or a vacation might require seven days. If an event requires more details, such as a location or multiple days, you can open the event and add more information.

To utilize the form method of recording an event, double-click the date. If you're viewing your calendar in Day, Week, or Work Week view, double-click the date at the top of the view, not a time slot in the schedule. By default, the All Day Event check box is already selected for you in the form, as shown in Figure 43.6. This indicates that the item is an event and not an appointment. If you deselect this check box, the item becomes an appointment.

Click here to save the item.

Click here to remove the event.

Access tools and features on the Event tab.

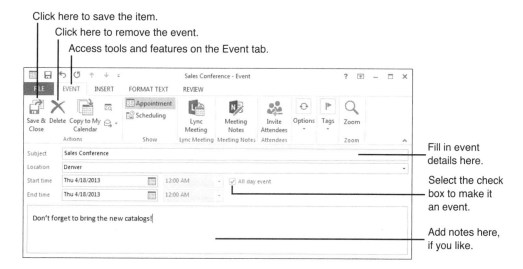

Fill in event details here.

Select the check box to make it an event.

Add notes here, if you like.

FIGURE 43.6

Use the window to add more details to an event.

You can tap into additional features and tools in the window's tabs to customize an event. To fill out the details, click in a form field and type. For example, type a name for the event in the Subject box or a location for the event in the Location box. When you type in a subject, the window's title bar changes to reflect the event's name.

If the event spans several days, choose a start and end date. The large notes area lets you jot down any additional notes about the event (such as "Don't forget to pick up my tux before leaving town for the wedding"). When you finish, click the Save & Close button.

Anytime you want to view information about a particular event, hover your mouse pointer over it to see a quick peek of details, such as whether a reminder is set. (Read more about reminders later in the chapter.) If you click an event, the Appointment tab appears on the Ribbon with tools for setting reminders, recurring status, or tagging the event with priority settings.

 TIP To quickly expand an event from one day to two or more, hover over the left or right edges of the event name in Month, Week, or Work Week view, and then click and drag across the other days you want to include.

TIP You can also use the Event window to remove the event; open the event and click the Delete button on the Event tab to remove it from the calendar. Or, for a quicker delete, right-click the event name and choose Delete.

If you want to create a recurring event—one that happens with regularity, such as a birthday, anniversary, or tax day—you can assign it recurring status using the Event window (see Figure 43.7). With the Event window open, click the Options button on the Event tab and select Recurrence. This opens the Appointment Recurrence dialog box, shown in Figure 43.8.

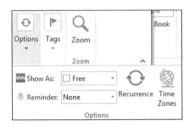

FIGURE 43.7

Look for reminders and recurrence settings in the Options list.

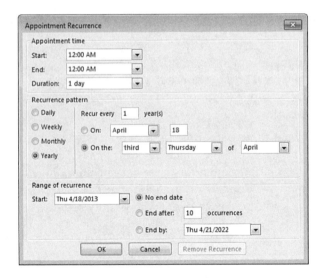

FIGURE 43.8

Use the Appointment Recurrence dialog box to set up a recurring event.

To change the recurrence pattern, choose how often the event appears on the calendar and then fine-tune the settings based on the type of pattern you choose.

For example, if you're setting a weekly event, such as "Half Price Tuesday" or "Carpool Day," you can specify on which day of the week the event always occurs. Click OK to save your changes.

 TIP You can also set recurring status using the Appointment tab. Click the event from any calendar view to display the tab. Then click the Recurrence button to open the Appointment Recurrence dialog box.

If you ever need to remove a recurring event, open the Event window again and display the Recurrence dialog box, this time clicking the Remove Recurrence button.

 NOTE The Calendar module does not show any holidays. You can add them though, with a few easy steps. Click the File tab and select Options to open the Outlook Options dialog box. Click the Calendar category and scroll down to the Calendar Options group. Click the Add Holidays button. Specify a country and click OK. Outlook then populates your calendar with the appropriate holidays.

Recording Appointments

Appointments in Outlook are any item you add to your calendar that require a designated date and time, such as doctor appointments, lunch dates, meetings, a project deadline, and so forth.

You can use a special form to fill out appointment details and save it to your calendar. To open the Appointment window, click the New Appointment button on the Home tab or press Ctrl+N.

The Appointment window, as illustrated in Figure 43.9, offers the same tools and options as the Event window. If you click the All Day Event check box, the form becomes an Event form, but if the box is unchecked, the window is the Appointment form.

You can fill out as many details about the appointment as you need. For example, click in the Subject box and type a title or description of the appointment. Assigning a title can help you quickly see what type of appointment it is from any of the calendar views. Brief titles work best, such as Staff Meeting or Dentist Appointment. When you type a subject, the window's title bar changes to reflect the new title.

Click to save the item.

Click to remove an appointment.

Access tools and features on the Appointment tab.

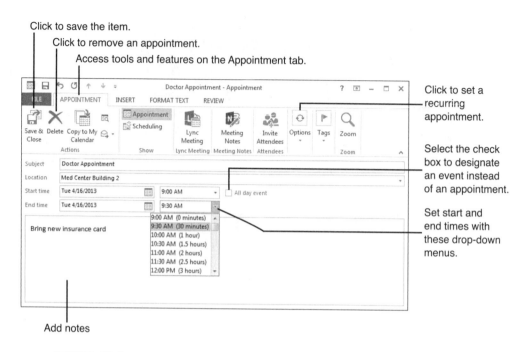

Click to set a recurring appointment.

Select the check box to designate an event instead of an appointment.

Set start and end times with these drop-down menus.

Add notes

FIGURE 43.9

Use the Appointment window to create a scheduled appointment.

If your appointment needs to specify a location to help you keep track of where you need to be, click in the Location box and include information such as a conference room number, address, building, restaurant, street, or city.

Next, specify a start and end date and time for the appointment. To change the date, type directly in the fields or click the tiny calendar icon at the end of the box and choose a date from the pop-up calendar. If you already double-clicked the correct date for the appointment, Outlook displays the date in the Start Time and End Time boxes.

You can set both a start time and an end time for the appointment to specify a duration. To change the time, click the time drop-down arrows and choose a time from the list, or just type the time directly into the boxes. By default, time is listed in increments of 30 minutes, so you can set an appointment for 11:30, for example. If you want to use 15-minute increments, type the specific time, such as 11:15. If you're sharing your calendar information with others, the appointment time appears as "busy" in your schedule.

You can type any notes about the appointment in the wide-open notes area. For example, you might want to jot down items you need to bring to the appointment, such as an insurance card your dental office may require, or information about what you're going to do at the appointed time.

When you're finished filling out appointment details, click the Save & Close button. Outlook closes the form and adds the appointment to your calendar, as shown in Figure 43.10. The time span you indicated when setting a start and end time show up as a block of light-blue color.

Appointment

FIGURE 43.10

Behold, the appointed time and place.

To revisit the appointment details, double-click the appointment to reopen the form. For even quicker details, you can also hover your mouse pointer over the appointment in your calendar to see a quick peek. Also, when you select an appointment, which just takes a click, Outlook displays an Appointment tab on the Ribbon. This tab is the same as the Appointment tab in the Appointment window. You can use the tools to help you work with the appointment, such as setting a recurrence, tagging it, or setting up a reminder.

TIP You can quickly print your appointment's details to take with you or hang on a bulletin board for a reminder. Right-click the appointment and choose Quick Print from the pop-up menu.

If you need to move an appointment, you can click and drag its left edge and drop it where you want it in the schedule, whether it's a new time slot or a new date.

Setting Reminders

If you need some help remembering appointments and events, you can assign a reminder. When you set a reminder, Outlook displays a pop-up alert box, similar to Figure 43.11, telling you that it's time for the appointment or event and even plays a special sound. You can set reminders as far out as a week before the appointed date, or you can set a reminder to appear 5 minutes before the appointment. You decide how much lead time you need. The only caveat to reminders is that you need to have Outlook open and running in the background on your computer system; otherwise, you won't hear or see the reminder alert until the next time you open the Outlook program window.

FIGURE 43.11

A reminder alert.

By default, Outlook automatically adds a 15-minute reminder to your appointments, but no reminder is added to events, so if you want one, you have to add it. Here are several ways to handle reminders:

- To add a reminder from the window, click the Options button and choose when you want to be reminded by clicking the Reminder drop-down arrow and making a selection.

- To add a reminder to an existing appointment or event already on your calendar, click the item to display the Appointment tab on the Ribbon. Next, click the Reminder drop-down arrow and make a selection.

- When the reminder alert appears, you can turn it off by clicking the Dismiss button, or you can put it off for a little longer using the Snooze button (just like the button on your alarm clock). You can even specify when you want to be reminded again.

Setting Up Meetings

Using Outlook's emailing capabilities and contacts list, you can set up meetings with other people and keep track of who is attending and who is not. You can view other users' calendars and schedule meetings at the most convenient time for everyone. For example, if you have a sales meeting with Joe on Friday, and you know Joe's email address or he's already one of your Outlook contacts, you can create an email invitation to let Joe know about the meeting. A great thing about this is that you can do all of it from within the Calendar module's screen.

Sending an Invite

To create a meeting and send an invite, you can use the Meeting form, a special window for both emailing a message and scheduling the meeting on your calendar. Figure 43.12 shows an example of the window, which looks like the other windows used to create events and appointments. A meeting is just like an appointment, but it involves more people and emailing features.

To create an invite, follow these steps:

1. On the Home tab, click the New Meeting button.

2. Add the email addresses for the people you want to invite. If they happen to be Outlook contacts, you can click the To button and specify attendees from your address book.

3. Type a title for the meeting in the Subject field.

4. Type a location for the meeting.

5. Indicate a start and end date and time for the meeting.

6. Type your email message text.

7. Click Send.

Outlook sends the email and adds the meeting to your own calendar.

Add your attendees
email addresses.

Set a date, start, and end times.

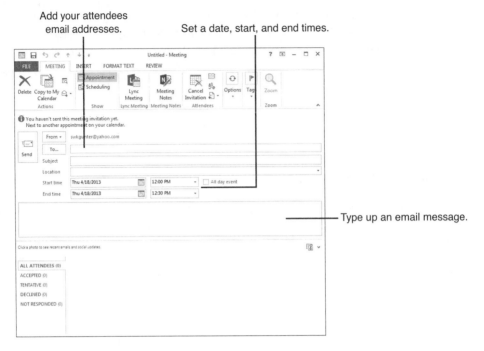

Type up an email message.

FIGURE 43.12

Use the Meeting form to set up a meeting date and email the attendees.

Tracking Invites

You can keep track of people who respond to your meeting request or manage their attendance using the Tracking feature in Calendar. You can find the tool on the Meeting tab, a special tab that appears when you click a meeting on your calendar. The tab offers tools to help you manage the meeting, including adding or removing attendees, canceling the meeting, or following up with additional emails.

To open the Tracking feature, click the Tracking button, as shown in Figure 43.13. You can use the list box area to make changes to the status of your attendees. Click the Response box to display a drop-down menu and choose whether the person has accepted, declined, is tentatively coming, or you've received no response (None). The tabs at the bottom of the window also let you see the status for a particular response at a glance.

Turn on tracking.

Manually change an attendee's status
by clicking here and making a selection.

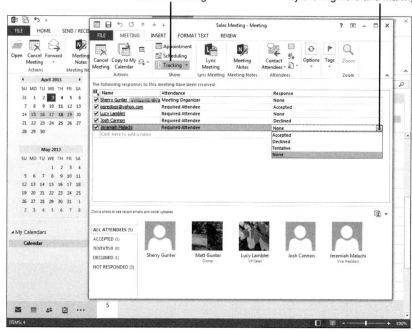

FIGURE 43.13

Use the Tracking feature to manage attendance for your meeting.

You can use the tools in the Meeting window's Tracking display to send out more emails, such as a reminder or date change; you can also cancel the meeting entirely. Here are a few actions you can take:

- To email a particular person in the list, hover the mouse pointer over the person's name and click the Email icon that appears.

- To email everyone, click the Contact Attendees button on the window's Meeting tab.

- To cancel the meeting and email everyone, click the Cancel Meeting button on the Meeting tab.

- To invite more attendees, click the Forward button and email others.

- Another way to invite someone else is to type the person's name at the bottom of the list. Outlook prompts you to save the changes and send the user an invite.

- To view your original invitation, click the Appointment button on the Meeting tab.

To reopen the Meeting window anytime, double-click the scheduled meeting on your calendar.

 TIP If you use Microsoft's OneNote program, you can create meeting notes and share them with others. Click the Meeting Notes button on the Meeting window's Meeting tab.

Sharing Your Calendar

The Calendar module offers several ways to share your calendar with others. An obvious way is to email it. You can choose which part of your calendar to include, such as a range of dates, the current date, and so on. Outlook then places the specified calendar portion in an email window, similar to Figure 43.14, which you can then address and add any additional message text. Your calendar appears not only in the message area, but also as a file attachment.

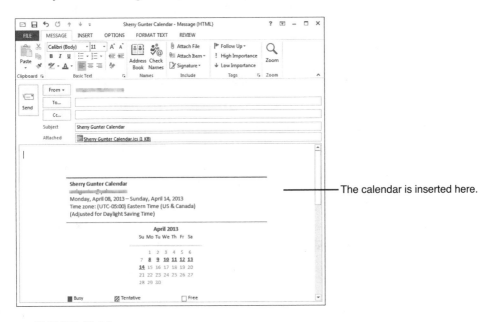

The calendar is inserted here.

FIGURE 43.14

Share your calendar via email.

To email your calendar, click the E-mail Calendar button on the Home tab. The Send a Calendar via E-mail dialog box appears, as shown in Figure 43.15. A message window opens with the calendar included. Now you can fill in the rest of the information to create your email message.

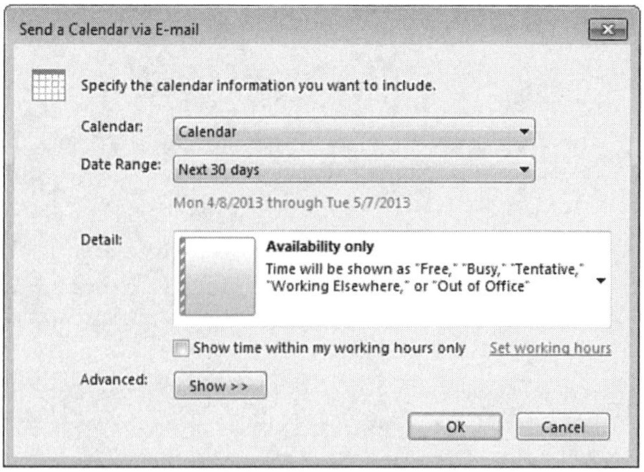

FIGURE 43.15

Use this box to specify which dates to include.

To publish your calendar online, you first need to know the WebDAV server address—that's a server that supports Web Distributed Authoring and Versioning protocols. Check with your server administrator to find out the details, but if you're good to go, click the Publish Online drop-down arrow on the Home tab and click Publish to WebDAV Server. The Publish Calendar to Custom Server dialog box opens, as shown in Figure 43.16. Type in the web address for the location of the server and choose the date range you want to publish. Click OK to post the calendar online.

FIGURE 43.16

Use this box to specify which dates to include.

NOTE You can save your calendar to another folder or drive, or export it as a file. For example, you might save it on a USB flash drive to share it with a colleague. To save your calendar to another location, click the File tab and select Save Calendar to open the Save As dialog box. Navigate to the folder or drive you want to save to and click Save. Calendars are saved in the iCalendar Format (.ics). To export a calendar, click the File tab and select Open & Export. Choose an export action and follow the onscreen prompts to complete the process.

THE ABSOLUTE MINIMUM

Here are the key points to remember from this chapter:

- You can use Calendar's view to see your schedule by month, week, work week, or day.

- An event is an all-day activity on your schedule, such as a birthday or conference, whereas an appointment is a designated time slot on your schedule.

- You can use special forms for recording details for events and appointments you add.

- Set up meetings with other users by coordinating a date and sending out an email invitation, and then track the responses to manage attendance.

- Share your calendar with others directly through email, or publish it to a server that supports calendar formats to share your schedule online.

44

WORKING WITH CONTACTS

Contact management is one reason many people choose Outlook over other email clients. Not only can you store email addresses, phone numbers, and mailing addresses in contacts, but you can also store personal information such as your contacts' birthdays, anniversary dates, and spouses' or children's names.

You can use contacts as an email addresses book, or to address letters in Word. Smartphones and tablets can synchronize their address books with Outlook contacts. This chapter shows you how to create and manage your contacts.

Creating Contacts

Before you can use contacts to address email or letters, you need to create some contacts.

Creating a New Contact in a Contact Form

To create a new contact using the contact form, follow these steps:

1. On the Home tab, click the New Items button and then select Contact from the menu. Alternatively, press Ctrl+Shift+C to open this form.

 TIP When you are viewing the Contacts folder, you can also click the New Contact button or use the Ctrl+N keyboard shortcut to open the contact form.

2. In the contact form (see Figure 44.1), enter your contact's name.

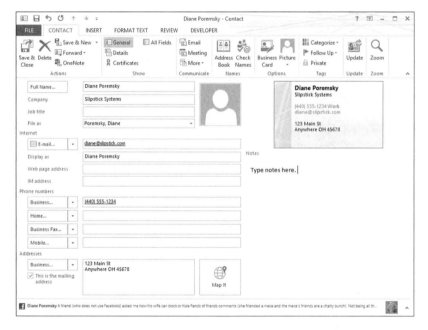

FIGURE 44.1

An Outlook contact form contains fields for email addresses, phone numbers, and mailing addresses.

3. On the General page, complete the other fields as needed. The General page of the contact form includes fields for your contact's name, the employer,

3 physical addresses, 19 phone numbers, 3 email addresses, notes, websites, and instant message (IM) addresses. You can also add photos or images to a contact, which display on email messages from the contact.

4. Double-click the picture icon to add a photo or image. This image displays in the message header in the Reading pane or opened message.

5. Double-click the business card to open the Edit Business Card dialog box (see Figure 44.2).

FIGURE 44.2

Use the Business Card editor to customize the business cards.

6. Enter the fields you want to display on your business card. Optionally, click the Image button to add a logo. Click OK when you're finished to return to your contact form.

7. Click the Details button to open the Details page (see Figure 44.3).

FIGURE 44.3

The Details page has fields for office and personal information.

8. Enter the birthday and anniversary dates. On the Details page, enter additional information, such as birthday and anniversary date, spouse's name, manager's name, assistant's name, and so forth. Outlook creates automatic recurring events in the calendar when you enter the birth date and anniversary of a contact.

9. Click Save & Close when you are finished.

 NOTE In addition to the contact form, Outlook 2013 also uses a contact card to display your contacts. Contact cards display contact information when you move the cursor over an email address in Outlook. The contact cards display the contacts in a simpler card format; however, not all contact fields are available on contact cards.

Creating a New Contact from an Email Message

Although you can create a new contact by opening a new contact form and typing in the contact information, you can also create contacts for people who send you email messages. When you use this method, the name and email address fields are filled in automatically.

To create a new contact from an email message, follow these steps:

1. Select a message.

2. Right-click a name and email address in the From, To, or CC field.

3. Choose Add to Outlook Contacts.

4. Fill in the desired fields by clicking the plus sign (+) before each section you want to add, such as Phone, IM, Work, Address, or Birthday.

TIP   Drag the lower-right corner to resize the form.

5. If you want to add a contact photo or an attachment, click the link under View Source to open the full contact form (see Figure 44.4). See "Creating a New Contact in a Contact Form" earlier in this chapter for more information.

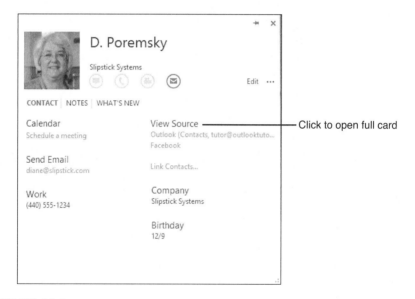

FIGURE 44.4

A completed contact card; open the full card by clicking the Outlook link under View Source.

6. Optionally, click the ellipsis (…]) to add the contact to the People Peek Favorites or to link the contact to other contacts. You might have additional options listed, including adding the contact to LinkedIn, Facebook, or other social networks. If you have Skype or Lync installed, you can link the contact to those services and tag a contact so you are alerted when they come online. If Business Contact Manager (BCM) is installed, you can add the contact to BCM from here.

7. Click Save to save the contact to your Contacts folder.

8. The contact card remains open onscreen. Click Close (x) to close it.

TIP If you want to create a contact for someone who sent you an email, and the email message contains a mailing address or other information you want to keep with the contact, drag the email message to the Contact button in the Navigation pane. A new contact is created using the sender's name and email address; the message body is added to the notes field on the contact.

Creating a New Contact from the Same Company

When you need to create several contacts from the same company, click Save & New in an existing contact form, and then select Contact from the Same Company. This opens a new contact form with the company name, business address, and phone number fields from the first contact. See "Creating a New Contact in a Contact Form" earlier in this chapter for more information about completing this form.

Working with Contact Groups

If you send messages to the same group of people frequently, you can create a Contact Group. When you send a new message to the group, you select the Contact Group instead of each address individually.

Creating a Contact Group

To create a new Contact Group, follow these steps:

1. In the Contacts folder, click the New Contact Group button. Alternatively, press Ctrl+Shift+L.

2. Type a name for your Contact Group in the Name field.

3. Click the Add Members button and choose From Outlook Contacts (see Figure 44.5).

FIGURE 44.5

Create a new Contact Group.

4. Double-click each address that you want to include in the group, or select the contacts and click the Members button to add the names to the Members field.

5. Click OK when you are finished selecting names to return to the contact group.

6. To add addresses of people who are not in your Contacts folder, click the Add Members button, select New Email Contact, enter the name and email address, and click OK.

7. Click Save & Close.

Creating a Contact Group from a List

If you have a list of addresses in Excel or Notepad, you can add your Contact Group in one step. The list needs to be comma or semicolon separated or have one address per row.

To create a Contact Group from a list, follow these steps:

1. In the Contacts folder, click the New Contact Group button.

2. Copy the list of email addresses.

3. Click the Add Members button and choose From Outlook Contacts.

4. At the bottom of the dialog box, paste the list in the Members field and press OK.

5. If you want to add notes about this contact group, click the Notes button.

6. Click the Save & Close button when you're finished.

Using a Contact Group

You can send email to the group or create a meeting invitation by clicking the Email or Meeting buttons on the contact group form, but it's usually easier to select or type the group address in the To, CC, or BCC field of an email or meeting request.

After addressing a message with the Contact Group, you can click the plus sign beside the group name to expand the list and see the individual names.

If you need to remove a member from the Contact Group, select the name or address and click the Remove Member button on the Contact Group tab.

Don't click the large X icon labeled Delete Group, unless you want to delete the entire group. Surprisingly, this happens a lot. If you make this mistake, find the group in the Deleted Items folder and drag it back to the Contacts folder.

 TIP Select more than one name at a time by holding down the Shift or Ctrl key as you select names. You can double-click names to add them to the Members field.

When you update a contact with a new email address, any groups the contact belongs to are not automatically updated. You need to click the Update Now button to update the contact group. Repeat this for every Contact Group the contact belongs to (see Figure 44.6).

Click Update Now to update the Contact Group

FIGURE 44.6

Choose the Update Now button to update the Contact Group with new addresses.

Managing Your Contacts

Outlook offers several options for viewing and managing your contacts. You can

- View your contacts in the People Hub, new to Outlook 2013, by clicking the People button on the left side of the screen. Each contact in the People Hub displays data from all sources Outlook links together. For example, if you have an Outlook contact for a person, and are friends on Facebook and LinkedIn, contact information from all three sources displays on one contact card in the People Hub (see Figure 44.7). The contact card includes links to each data source as well as an Edit link to update the contact.

FIGURE 44.7

Outlook 2013's new People Hub. Click the blue links to create a new meeting, send email to the contact, or view the full contact.

- View mail, meetings, and attachments sent by the contact on the People pane at the bottom of messages or contacts, shown in Figure 44.8. The People pane displays only mail, meetings, or attachments from the person, not messages you sent to them or other Outlook items. You can open, reply, or forward messages from the People pane, but you can't delete items. If you have a social networking account, such as LinkedIn or Facebook, you can sign in to your account and see updates and the profile picture of contacts or people who send you email.

FIGURE 44.8

Email, meetings, and attachments from the selected person are listed in the People pane.

- View a list of contacts in the Outlook Address Book by clicking the Address Book button on the Home tab. You can also open this dialog box by using the keyboard shortcut Ctrl+Shift+B.

- View contacts using People Peek (see Figure 44.9), a new Outlook feature that works like this: When you hover over the word People, a window pops up that lists your Favorite contacts. If you use Lync, your favorite Lync contacts are listed here as well. To add a contact to the People Peek, right-click a name or email address in a message or right-click a photo in the People Pane and choose Add to Favorites.

FIGURE 44.9

Add your favorite people to the People Peek.

- Configure how you work with your contacts by clicking the File tab, selecting Options, and selecting the People tab on the Outlook Options dialog box. These settings affect how addresses are sorted in the Address Book and Contacts folder. The most important options for most users are the default Full Name and File As Order.

- Search for contacts using the Search People field at the end of the Home tab or using the Search Contacts field in the Contacts folder. When you use Search People, the search results contain matches for the first, middle, or last names or company name. Search Contacts searches by more fields and you can use criteria to limit the search results.

THE ABSOLUTE MINIMUM

Here are the key points to remember from this chapter:

- You can create new contacts using the contact form or from an email message.

- Contact Groups enable you to easily send messages to a group of people.

- Outlook offers several ways to view and manage your contacts including the People Hub, the People pane, an address book, or People Peek.

45

WORKING WITH TASKS AND TO-DO LISTS

Tasks and to-do items help you organize and prioritize your work. With reminders set, you won't forget what is on your list. Both tasks and to-do's display in the Tasks peek, so you always know what needs your attention.

What is the difference between a task and a to-do? You create tasks using a task form and save them in a Tasks folder, tracking them until they are complete. To-do's are messages that are flagged for follow up.

Although tasks have a lot in common with appointments, they serve a different purpose. Typically, you use tasks to track activities you need to complete but don't need to do at a specific time. Tasks can be open-ended with no start or due date, or you can set start and due dates.

Creating Tasks

You should create tasks for items that don't have a set time to be completed. You only need to complete the Subject field for your task and save it. Optionally, you can also include a due date, start date, reminder, and category. As you work on the task, you can update the Status and % Complete fields.

To create a task, follow these steps:

1. On the Home tab, click the New Items button and select Task from the menu. Alternatively, press Ctrl+Shift+K.

2. Enter a subject for your task (see Figure 45.1).

3. Using the Tab key, navigate to the Start Date field and type or select a start date.

4. In the Due Date field, type or select a due date.

5. Select a Priority, if desired.

6. Select the Reminder check box and choose a date and time.

FIGURE 45.1

Outlook offers several task options.

 NOTE Tasks use the default reminder time specified on the Tasks tab of the Outlook Options dialog box, but you can assign a different default time manually to any task.

Outlook can set the due date based on the start date. For example, to create a task that starts next Friday and is due two days later, enter **next friday** in the Start field, and then press Tab to go to the Due Date field and enter **2d**.

Entering Task Details

Optionally, you can click the Details button on the Task tab to open the Details page (see Figure 45.2), which contains fields useful for billing purposes: hours worked, mileage, and billing information. The Total Work and Actual Work fields use the Work Hours setting from the Tasks tab on the Outlook Options dialog box to calculate the days worked. For example, if you have the work hours set to the default of 8 hours per day and 40 hours per week, when you enter 12 hours in the work field, Outlook converts it to 1.5 days.

The Create Unassigned Copy button is available only when you send a task request; use it to create an unassigned copy of the task on your Task List.

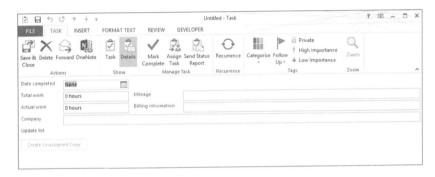

FIGURE 45.2

Use the Details page to record or review hours worked and other billing information.

Creating Recurring Tasks

When you need to repeat a task over several days or weeks, you can create a recurring task. Outlook generates the next task in the series when you mark the task complete.

 NOTE When you have recurring tasks with reminders, don't dismiss the reminder in the Reminder window because this will turn the reminder off for future tasks in the series. Snooze it instead or mark the task complete to remove it from the Reminder window.

To create a recurring task, follow these steps:

1. From an open task form, click the Recurrence button on the Task tab or press Ctrl+G to open the Task Recurrence dialog box (see Figure 45.3).

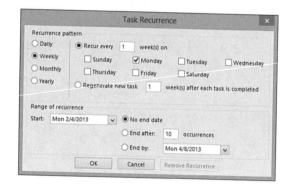

FIGURE 45.3

Use the Task Recurrence dialog box to create recurring tasks.

2. Select the desired recurrence pattern. Choices are Daily, Weekly, Monthly, or Yearly.

3. Select the frequency. When you select the Recur Every option, the next task is generated as soon as you mark the previous task complete. With Regenerate New Task After Each Task Is Completed, the next task is not generated until the period of time passed.

4. Select a start date for the recurrence range and an end date. It's highly recommended that you always set an end date. For long-running tasks, end recurrences at the end of each year and re-create the task at the beginning of each new year.

5. Click OK to close the Task Recurrence dialog box.

6. Click the Save & Close button when you finish the task.

7. When you complete the task, mark it complete to generate the next occurrence.

Completing Tasks

As you work on a task, you can change the % Complete field to reflect how much work you've done toward completing it. Although it's not necessary when working on your tasks, if you're working on a shared task or you are assigned a task by someone else, updating the % Complete field helps others gauge how much you have left to do. The list contains 25, 50, 95, and 100, or you can type any whole number into the field.

You can also set a status for the task, choosing from the following: Not Started, In Progress, Completed, Waiting on Someone Else, or Deferred.

When the % Complete field is changed and the Status field is on the default of Not Started, the status updates to In Progress or Completed. Status selections are unchanged when another status is selected and the % Complete field is updated to anything except 100% Complete, at which time the status changes to Completed.

When the task is complete, you can mark it complete using one of several methods:

- To mark the task complete in the reminder window, don't click the Dismiss button; this removes only the reminder. Instead, right-click the task and choose Mark Complete (see Figure 45.4).

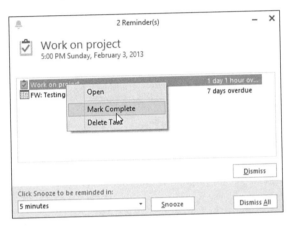

FIGURE 45.4

Right-click a task reminder and select Mark Complete.

- On opened tasks, click the Mark Complete button on the Task tab or set % Complete to 100.
- In the Tasks folder or To-Do Bar, you can click the flag, click in the Complete column (if shown in the view), click the Mark Complete button, or right-click the task and choose Mark Complete.

Using Task Requests

You can assign new or existing tasks to other Outlook users. They receive the task by email and can accept or decline the assignment.

When status updates are enabled, each time the recipient updates the status of the task, updates are sent back to you, and the copy of the task in your Tasks folder is updated.

Creating a Task Request

To assign a task to someone else, follow these steps:

1. On the Home tab, click the New Items button, and select Task Request from the menu. Alternatively, you can press Ctrl+Alt+Shift+U or click the Assign Task button on an open task to convert it to a task request. If you change your mind, click the Cancel Assignment button to convert the task request to a regular task. Figure 45.5 shows a sample task request.

FIGURE 45.5

Create a task request to assign tasks to other people.

2. Enter the recipient's name in the To field. Although you could send the task to several people, you won't receive updates when the task request is sent to more than one person.

3. Enter the subject, start and end dates, and priority.

4. Select the Keep an Updated Copy of This Task on My Task List check box if you want to add the task to your Task List. If this option is selected, then updates the recipient makes are reflected on your copy.

5. Select the Send Me a Status Report When This Task Is Complete check box if you want to receive an email notification when the task is completed.

6. To create an unassigned copy of the task in your Task List, click the Details button and then click Create Unassigned Copy.

7. Click the Send button when you're finished creating the task.

After receiving the task, the recipient can either accept or decline it by clicking the appropriate button in the Reading pane or opened task. If the task is declined, you can take ownership of the task again by clicking the Return to Task List button.

Accepting or Declining a Task Request

When a task request arrives in your Inbox, you can click either the Accept button or Decline button in the Reading pane or on an opened message (see Figure 45.6).

FIGURE 45.6

You can accept or decline a task assignment in the Reading pane.

If you accept the task, Outlook adds it to your Task List. If you decline the task, Outlook moves it to your Deleted folder. Optionally, you can edit your response before sending it to the person who created the task request.

Viewing Tasks

There are several ways you can view your tasks:

- In the Tasks folder
- In the Tasks peek (see Figure 45.7)
- Using the Daily Task List in the calendar (see Figure 45.8)
- On the Outlook Today page

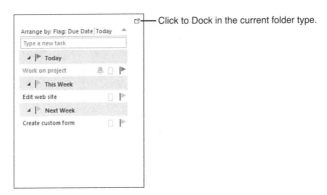

FIGURE 45.7

Hover over the word Tasks to display the Tasks peek. Click the Dock icon to pin it open.

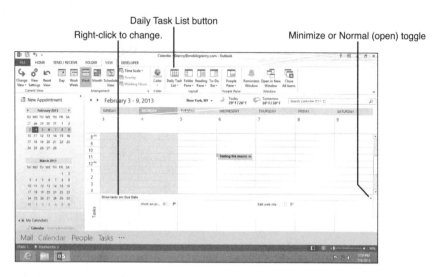

FIGURE 45.8

Current tasks are shown under the date when you view your calendar in the day or week view.

The Task List in the Tasks peek displays tasks from all Tasks folders in your profile and all flagged messages, contacts, and other Outlook items.

When the peek is docked, you can resize the task section by pulling the separator up or down.

You can display your tasks in the Daily Task List at the bottom of the day or week calendars. The Daily Task List is not available in the monthly view.

If the Task List is not visible on the day or week calendars, switch to the View tab and expand the Daily Task List button; then select Normal. Click the icon on the right side of the Daily Task List to minimize the list and click it again to restore it.

The Task List supports two views: Show Tasks by Start Date or Show Tasks by Due Date. You can hide completed tasks in either view. Right-click the bar separating the Task List from the calendar to change the order or show/hide completed tasks. You can also change the view from the View tab by clicking Daily Task List and then clicking Arrange By.

The Outlook Today screen lists the tasks that are due today or overdue. You can mark tasks complete from the Outlook Today screen or open a task by double-clicking it in the list. This screen shows only the tasks in your default mailbox or .pst file. The To-Do List shows the tasks in all folders.

TIP If you don't like the predefined views in the Tasks folder or To-Do List, you can customize the views or create a new view by clicking the Change View button on the View tab.

NOTE To configure task options, click the File tab, select Options, and go to the Tasks tab on the Outlook Options dialog box. Here you can set reminders on tasks with due dates, specify default reminder times, select task colors, and more.

Creating To-Do Items

A to-do item is a flagged message or contact. It acts like a task, supports reminders, and displays with your tasks in the To-Do List, but the item you flagged remains in its own folder.

Setting a flag on a message is easy: Move your mouse over the message in the message list, and then click the Quick Flag icon when it comes into view to use the default flag or right-click the Quick Flag icon to choose a different flag (see Figure 45.9).

FIGURE 45.9

Move your mouse over a message to display the Quick Flag icon. Click or right-click it to set a flag.

Optionally, click the Follow Up button on the Home tab to flag an open message or contact (see Figure 45.10).

From this menu, you can select one of the following dates: today, tomorrow, the end of this week, the end of next week, or a custom date. You can also set a flag without a due date. In addition, most Follow Up menus also include the option to mark an item complete, clear a flag, or set a quick click.

CAUTION Outlook.com and Internet Message Access Protocol (IMAP) accounts do not support all of the Follow Up options. You are limited to setting a flag and clearing it. You can't customize the flags or choose a due date.

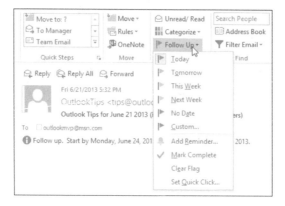

FIGURE 45.10

Select a follow-up date.

When you no longer need a flag, click the Follow Up button and choose either Mark Complete or Clear. Choosing Mark Complete keeps the item in the To-Do List for future reference, whereas Clear removes the flag and removes the item from the To-Do List.

 CAUTION Don't delete the item from the To-Do List; this deletes it from Outlook.

THE ABSOLUTE MINIMUM

Here are the key points to remember from this chapter:

- Outlook makes it easy to create tasks, including recurring tasks and tasks with reminders.

- Track task progress using the % Complete field.

- You can assign new or existing tasks to other Outlook users, who are notified by email and can accept or decline the assignment.

- There are several ways you can view your tasks: in the Tasks folder, in the Tasks peek, on the Daily Task List in the calendar, or on the Outlook Today page.

- A to-do item is a flagged message or contact. It acts like a task, supports reminders, and displays with your tasks in the To-Do List.

IN THIS CHAPTER

- Configuring the Social Connector
- Managing Social Connector Security

46

USING SOCIAL CONNECTOR

Outlook's Social Connector does a little of everything. It displays a person's recent activities, including email, appointments, and attachments, in a pane at the bottom of an email message or contact. If you have a Facebook or LinkedIn account and have Outlook signed into the accounts, you also see updates the person posts to these social networks.

When you first open Outlook, the Social Connector is empty, displaying only email to or from the sender or recipients of the selected email messages. If you look at a contact, the Social Connector shows messages sent or received by the contact or meetings with the contact. Activity feeds and profile photos from networking sites, such as Facebook, LinkedIn, or SharePoint Server, are displayed in the Social Connector's pane after you configure Outlook to connect to the social networking service.

Configuring the Social Connector

Out of the box, the Social Connector's People pane acts like a search folder—messages and meetings between you and the sender are displayed in the People pane. Selecting a message in the list opens the message.

When a message is sent to more than one person, each person is listed in the People pane, and selecting any of the pictures or the icon representing the person displays your activities with that person: sent or received messages, social networking feeds (based on social network security settings), appointments, or sent or received attachments.

If you don't want to see the People pane, you can turn it off or minimize it. See the "Showing or Hiding the Social Connector Pane" section later in this chapter.

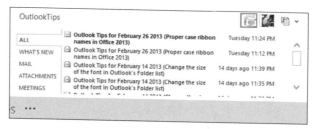

FIGURE 46.1

The People pane displays at the bottom of the Reading pane and contacts.

 TIP You can use the People pane without connecting to social networks. The People pane displays Outlook items—email, meetings, and email attachments—and the sender or recipient's photo when a photo is added to that contact.

To view updates from social networks in the pane, you need to configure the social providers in Outlook. Outlook 2013 includes Facebook, LinkedIn, and SharePoint providers with the default installation, and you can go online to download additional connectors (when available).

 NOTE To see your contacts' Facebook profile pictures or activity feeds, they need to have public profile pictures and have email addresses configured in their Facebook accounts.

Setting Up Social Networking Accounts

Before you can view profile photos and status updates for people who send you email, you need to connect Outlook to the social network. To do so, follow these steps:

1. On the View tab, expand the People pane button by clicking the caret icon to its right.

2. Select Account Settings from the menu.

3. Click to select a social network you want to use.

4. Enter your name and password (see Figure 46.2).

5. Click Connect to link the social network to Outlook.

6. If you want the social network to be the default source for contact photos, select By Default, Show Photos and Information from This Network When Available.

7. Select the next social network and repeat the process.

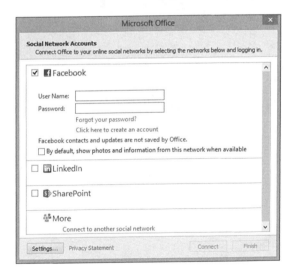

FIGURE 46.2

Sign in to the social networks. Outlook 2013 includes Social Connector providers for Facebook, LinkedIn, and SharePoint server.

TIP If you are unable to connect Outlook to Facebook and you receive an "invalid username or password" message, check your security settings at Facebook. You need to give Outlook permission to access Facebook.

If you want to remove a social network, select the network and click the X on the right to delete your username and password for the social network.

If you change your username or password on the social network, change it in the Social Connector by clicking the Paper icon. In the Settings dialog box, click the Options button to view or change the settings Office applies to data shared between Office and the social network (contacts, profile photos, and status updates).

Turning Off Contact Photos

Although the Social Connector displays contact photos, the option to display photos throughout Outlook and other Office applications is a People option. If you don't want to see the photos, you can disable this feature.

To turn contact photos off, click File, and select Options to open the Outlook Options dialog box. On the People tab, deselect the Show User Photographs When Available check box (see Figure 46.4). You must restart Outlook for this to take effect.

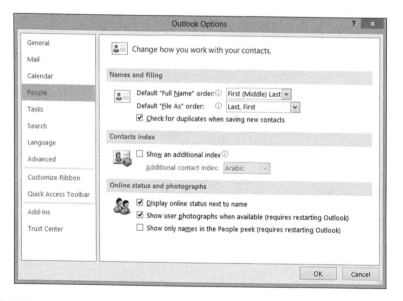

FIGURE 46.4

Outlook gives you the option not to display contact photos.

Showing or Hiding the Social Connector Pane

As useful as the People pane might be, you probably won't want it open all the time. You can minimize and open the pane by clicking the caret icon on the right edge of the pane (see Figure 46.5).

If you want to turn the People pane off, you need to click the People Pane button on the View tab.

Minimize button

FIGURE 46.5

Open and minimize the People pane using the caret on the right.

When the pane is open, you can drag the upper edge to make the panel larger or smaller. This can be helpful when you are reviewing a list of messages in the People pane.

Managing Social Connector Security

Most questions about Social Connector security are about Facebook. This is because Facebook contains more personal information, whereas LinkedIn targets businesspeople. In either case, if you don't want people you correspond with to see your profile photo or status updates, you need to make your profile private.

Managing Facebook Security

When you install the Facebook provider, Outlook displays the profile photos and status updates of people who send you email or are in your contacts in the People pane. This occurs only for people whose profiles are publicly searchable and who have associated the email address with their Facebook account.

Just being Facebook friends with people is not enough to ensure that their status updates or profile pictures are visible when they send you email. The email addresses you have for the people must be linked to their Facebook accounts, and the correct Facebook profile privacy settings must be set (see Figure 46.6).

The address associated with Facebook must be the same email address used for email (or on the contact record in Outlook), or registered as a secondary address in the Facebook Profile.

General Security	**Privacy Settings and Tools**			
Privacy Timeline and Tagging Blocking	**Who can see my stuff?**	Who can use your future posts?	Friends of Friends	Edit
		Review all your posts and things you're tagged in		Use Activity Log
Notifications Mobile Followers		Limit the audience for posts you've shared with friends of friends or Public?		Limit Past Posts
	Who can look me up?	Who can look you up using the email address or phone number you provided?	Friends	Edit
Apps Ads		Do you want other search engines to link to your timeline?	Off	Edit

FIGURE 46.6

Adjust security settings in Facebook to prevent people you send email to from seeing your Facebook status in the People pane.

NOTE If the email address used to send messages or listed on the contact is not registered with the social network, the user's activities don't appear in the People pane.

If you want your activities to appear for your colleagues at work, add your work email address as an additional email address under account settings for the social network. Or, to ensure business colleagues can't see your Facebook posts, don't link your business address to your Facebook account.

NOTE Even people who do not use Outlook or the Social Connector need to check their Facebook and LinkedIn settings; otherwise, people they send email to might be able to see their profile picture or feeds.

Who Sees Your Photo and Your People Pane Content?

A surprising number of people see the search results in the People pane and are concerned that their replies include all these messages. However, no one except you sees this list of messages. Other Outlook users you send email to see a similar list, but it contains only the email in their mailboxes. You see only what is in your mailbox or what they have allowed on social networking sites. Others see only what is in their mailboxes or what you allow on social networking sites. You can't "see" messages in their mailboxes, even if you use Exchange server.

THE ABSOLUTE MINIMUM

Here are the key points to remember from this chapter:

- You can use the Social Connector People pane to view recent messages sent to or from a message's sender or recipients. You don't need to sign into a social network to view messages, appointments, or attachments associated with a contact.

- Even if you decide not to use the People pane or log into a social network, anyone with Outlook might be able to see your profile photo and status updates if your profile is set to public and your email address is in your social network profile.

47

SYNCHRONIZING AND SHARING OUTLOOK DATA

When you use more than one computer, or if you have a smartphone or a tablet, you might want to sync your Outlook data with the other computer or smartphone. You also might want to share your calendar and contacts with another user or use the data in another program. If you have an Exchange Server mailbox, syncing your mailbox to other computers is as easy as configuring your account in Outlook. Sharing your calendar and contacts with other users is also easy, as long as the other users also have mailboxes on your Exchange Server.

Sharing Calendar and Contacts

Most people who use Outlook on more than one computer want to use their calendar and contacts on their other computers or share them with other people. Sharing works best if you use an Exchange Server mailbox or an Outlook.com email account, because Outlook stores your email, calendar, and contacts on the mail server and synchronizes to any computer or device.

If you use a POP3 (Post Office Protocol 3) email account, your choices are to leave the mail on the server and download it on each computer or use a utility to sync your email, calendar, and contacts. IMAP (Internet Message Access Protocol) accounts sync email only; you need to use a utility or another method to move your calendar and contacts between computers and devices.

Syncing with Smartphones and Tablets

The easiest way to sync your mailbox with smartphones or tablets, or even other computers, is with an Outlook.com or Exchange Server mailbox, such as Office365. Apple, Android, Windows Phone, and Blackberry 10 smartphones and tablets sync directly with Outlook.com and Exchange Server mailboxes.

If you're using an IMAP account, email syncs to all your devices, and changes you make on one device, such as reading a message or replying, are seen on your other devices. If your email account supports only POP3 accounts, you need to configure Outlook to leave mail on the server so it's available to download on all devices.

 NOTE If you want the best experience using email, calendaring, and contacts on multiple computers and portable devices, you need to use an Exchange Server mailbox, such as offered by Office365 for business users. The accounts are targeted to businesses, but can be used by individuals as well.

Apple iPhone and iPad users who do not use Outlook.com or Exchange mailboxes can share Outlook Calendar, Contacts, and Tasks using the iCloud add-in. The iCloud moves appointments, contacts, and tasks to an iCloud data file in Outlook, which then syncs to the iCloud and all Apple devices linked to your Apple ID account.

The iCloud works well, but many users don't like that all appointments, contacts, and tasks are removed from Outlook's folders, even though they are still visible in Outlook.

Android and Windows Phone users need to use a third-party utility to sync with Outlook if they don't have Outlook.com or Exchange server mailboxes. You can find a list of third-party utilities at www.slipstick.com/smartphones.

Sharing with a Second Computer

If you're sharing with a second Outlook account on another computer, one of the easiest ways to share is to copy the PST file to the other computer and open it in the profile. Click the File tab, select Open & Export, click Open Outlook Data File, and select your PST file.

Moving the Data File

Before you can move the data file, you need to find it on your hard drive. The easiest way to do this is by using the Account Settings dialog box.

1. Click the File tab.

2. On the Account Information screen, click the Account Settings button and select Account Settings from the menu.

3. In the Account Settings dialog box, select the Data Files tab.

4. Select the .pst file.

5. Click the Open File Location button to open Windows Explorer to the location of the .pst file (see Figure 47.1).

6. Close the Account Settings dialog box.

7. Close Outlook, and then copy the .pst file.

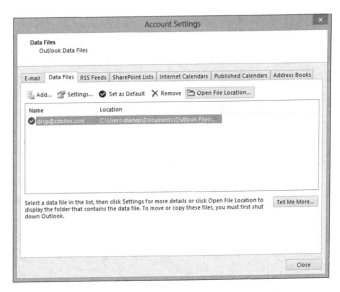

FIGURE 47.1

Use the Account Settings dialog box to move the data file.

Copy the data file to the second computer. You can put it anywhere on the hard drive, but it's best to use the default location for .pst files and place it in the My Documents\Outlook Files folder. This makes it easier to make a backup copy of your Outlook data (which you should do on a regular basis).

Open the data file in your profile by clicking Outlook's File tab, selecting Open & Export, and then clicking Open Outlook Data File to select your .pst file.

 NOTE You can use only .pst files in other profiles. IMAP, Outlook.com, and Exchange offline files can't be opened in other profiles.

Using Export and Import

Although it's best to move the entire .pst to a new computer to preserve views and other hidden data, as well as the modified dates, it is easier to export if you need to move your calendar and/or contacts to another computer also using Outlook. When you use the data in another copy of Outlook, export in Outlook Data File (.pst) format. Use CSV format when the data is used in other programs.

To export Outlook data, open the Import/Export wizard by clicking the File tab, selecting Open & Export, and selecting Import/Export. In the wizard, choose Export to a file and click Next. If you are using the data in Outlook, choose Outlook Data File (.pst).

Sharing a Calendar

You can use several options when you need to share a calendar in Outlook 2013. In addition to exporting the calendar or copying the .pst file, you can share the calendar by email or publish it to a WebDAV server.

To access these options, right-click the Calendar folder and choose Share.

Sharing by email creates an iCalendar (.ics) file of your calendar and inserts it in an email message; it also creates a planner-style calendar in the message body. For more information on these options, see Chapter 43, "Using the Calendar."

Using Outlook.com to Share Calendar and Contacts

Outlook 2013 syncs with the Outlook.com calendar and contacts using the Outlook.com Exchange ActiveSync (EAS) account type. When you use a POP3 or IMAP email account, you can use an Outlook.com account to sync your appointments and contacts with other computers and smartphones.

All you need is a Microsoft account. Although you could use an Outlook.com or Hotmail address, you can create a Microsoft account using any valid email address because you use this account only for appointments and contacts, not email.

If you don't have a Microsoft account for your email address, go to https://signup.live.com/signup.aspx and complete the form to create one, entering your email address in the Microsoft account name field.

After the Microsoft account is created and verified, log in to http://outlook.com to begin using the account. Next, you need to add your Microsoft account to Outlook. If you need to add a POP3 or IMAP account, you can use Auto Account Setup. If you aren't using Auto Account Setup, you must set it up manually. For a reminder of how to set up accounts, see Chapter 39, "Setting Up Accounts and Personalizing Outlook."

Before closing the Account Settings dialog box, switch to the Data Files tab. Select the new account's data file and click Set as Default so appointments display on the Calendar Peek and new appointments and contacts are added to the Outlook.com folders and sync to the server. Now you can close the dialog box.

When you return to Outlook, you have two accounts in the folder list: your Internet Service Provider (ISP) or "real" email address for email and the Outlook.com account for calendar and contact sync. Both accounts have the same email address.

It's confusing to have two accounts with the same address in your profile, but you can rename the Microsoft account. To do this, open the Send/Receive Groups dialog box using Ctrl+Alt+S and then click Edit. Select your Microsoft Account and click the Account Properties button in the upper-right corner. Enter a user-friendly name for the account on the General tab in the dialog (see Figure 47.2). Click OK to change the name.

You need to close and restart Outlook to finalize the changes.

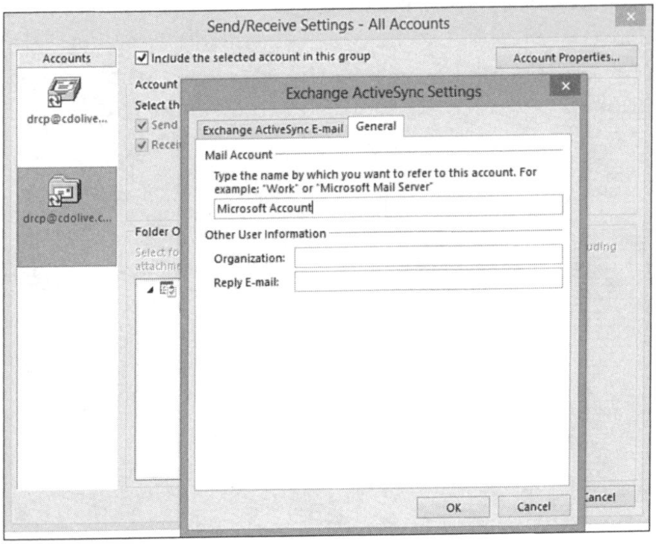

FIGURE 47.2

Change the account's display name to a friendlier name.

Moving Data to the Microsoft Account Data File

Next, move or copy existing appointments and contacts to the Microsoft Account data file. This is easier if you use a List view and then select all and drag to the folders. To do so, follow these steps:

1. Switch to the Calendar folder.

2. Select the View tab.

3. Click the Change View button and select List.

4. Select an appointment and press Ctrl+A to select all.

5. Use the Move button the Home tab or drag the appointments with your mouse to move them to the new calendar folder.

6. Switch to the Contacts folder, select all contacts, and move to the new contacts folder.

Using Contacts in Other Programs

You can use contacts in other programs by exporting to a CSV file. You can even use a List view and then select all the contacts to copy and paste them into any application that accepts paste. Most applications can import (and export) CSV files.

To copy and paste a List view, create a custom view containing only the fields you need (see Chapter 52, "Working with Views"). Select the contacts you need using Select All (Ctrl+A) or hold Ctrl as you click specific contacts. Use Ctrl+C to copy the selected contacts and paste into any application that accepts paste. If you paste Outlook data into Word, you need to paste as text.

THE ABSOLUTE MINIMUM

Here are the key points to remember from this chapter:

- You can use Outlook's calendar and contacts on other computers.

- It's possible to sync calendar and contacts to any smartphone. If you use Outlook.com or Exchange Server, you can sync over-the-air and do not need to use an add-in.

IN THIS CHAPTER

• Assigning Color Categories to Outlook Items

• Managing Color Categories

48

USING COLOR CATEGORIES

Color categories take categories to a new level by highlighting the item with color when you assign a category. This enables you to color code Outlook items so it's easier to visually identify them, or use Instant search to find the items within a specific category.

You can "group" categories that have similar purposes by assigning them the same color or color family. For example, suppose you are working on several projects for a client and created categories for each project, calling them Project1, Project2, and Project3. You are using the blue category colors for this client. Project1 is active and uses the dark blue category color. Project2 and Project3 are still in the planning stage and the category color is light blue. All email, appointments, and tasks that are associated with these projects are assigned the appropriate category. When you glance over your calendar, you know which client and project the appointment is for, just by seeing the category color.

Assigning Color Categories to Outlook Items

Assigning a color category to an email message, appointment, task, or contact is simple. First, select what you want to categorize. Like all things in Windows, there are several ways you can assign a category:

- Right-click a message in the message list and choose Categorize, and then select a category from your list of categories (see Figure 48.1).

- Click the Categorize button on the Home tab and choose a category from the menu.

- Click in the category column to apply the Quick Click category or right-click to choose from your list of categories.

- When an Outlook item is open and has a category assigned, double-click or right-click the category in the message header to access the Category menu.

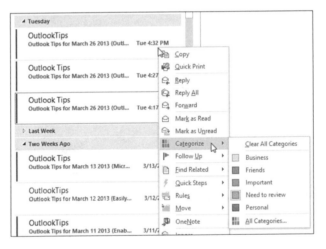

FIGURE 48.1

Right-click a message and choose Categorize; then select a category from the menu to add it to the email message.

After you assign a category to a selected item, the category is highlighted with a pale blue border on the Categorize menu or has a check mark beside the category name in the Color Category dialog box.

The 15 most recently used categories are shown on the Categorize menu in alphabetical order. Select All Categories from the bottom of the Categorize menu to open the Color Category dialog box. In this dialog box, you can select a category from your entire list of categories, including those not listed in the menu. The Clear all Categories command removes all categories assigned to the currently selected item.

 NOTE The first time you select each one of the default color categories, Outlook displays the Add New Category dialog box so you can give the category a more descriptive name.

 TIP Another option for color categories is to use them to create contact groups, which is preferable to using multiple folders to group similar contacts. Each contact can belong to multiple categories.

Using the Quick Click Category

Outlook has a handy little feature to help you out, called the Quick Click Category. You set your most frequently used category to use the default color category. Then when the Category field is shown in a view, you can click in the color category column to add the color category to the item, saving time and a lot of mouse clicks.

To set one of your most frequently used categories to the Quick Click, follow these steps:

1. On the Home tab, click the Categorize button to expand the category menu.

2. From the menu, select Set Quick Click.

3. In the Set Quick Click dialog box, shown in Figure 48.2, choose the color category you want to use as your default category and click OK.

4. Click the color category column. Outlook adds this color category, enabling you to categorize an item as the default color. If you click again, the category is removed from the color category column.

FIGURE 48.2

Select a Quick Click color category.

The Quick Click Category field is supported only in single line List views; it is not available in the Compact view, which is the default view in all Mail folders. Turning the Reading pane off switches the Inbox to a single-line view.

Clicking in the Category field toggles on and off the category assigned to the Quick Click. Right-click the Category field to select from the list of most recently used categories. Selecting a category from the Category menu toggles the category on and off, enabling you to add more than one category to the selected item (see Figure 48.3).

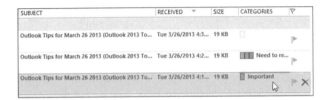

FIGURE 48.3

When the view shows the Category field, you can click in it to apply the Quick Click category.

NOTE The Color Category Picker is not available in Internet Message Access Protocol (IMAP) accounts. You can assign keyboard shortcuts to color categories, and then use the shortcuts to add categories.

Creating Additional Color Categories

Outlook comes with six predefined color categories. You can add as many additional categories as you need and assign keyboard shortcuts on up to 11 categories. You are limited to 25 colors, but each color can be assigned to multiple categories.

To create a new color category, follow these steps:

1. On the Home tab, click the Categorize button to expand the Category Picker.

2. Select All Categories to open the Color Categories dialog box.

3. Click New.

4. In the Add New Category dialog box, type a name for your new category (see Figure 48.4).

5. Select a color.

6. Select a shortcut from the list of available Shortcut Keys, if desired.

7. Click OK to create the category.

FIGURE 48.4

Use the Add New Category dialog box to create new color categories or edit existing categories.

If you decide you want to delete the category, change the category name, use a different color, or assign (or change) the shortcut key, select the category name and use the buttons on the right. When you choose Rename, you edit the name in place (see Figure 48.5).

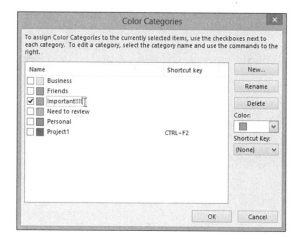

FIGURE 48.5

Rename color categories using the Color Categories dialog box.

TIP If you assign keyboard shortcuts to your frequently used color categories, you can assign categories without using the mouse.

Managing Color Categories

In this section, you explore how to upgrade to color categories, share categories, and remove categories.

Upgrading to Color Categories

When you import an Outlook Personal Folders file (.pst) that has categories assigned to items, you need to use Outlook's Upgrade to Color Categories command to add these categories to your Master Category list. Outlook assigns random colors to the categories.

When some of your categories are not listed on the Master Category list, or are not assigned a color, you need to follow these steps to add the Categories to the Master Category list. If you aren't sure, go ahead and run Upgrade to Color Categories; it's completely safe to use.

1. Right-click the top-level folder in your mailbox. This is the folder that displays your email address; if it's your default data file, clicking this folder opens the Outlook Today screen.

2. From the menu, click Data Files Properties.

3. Click the Upgrade to Color Categories button (see Figure 48.6).

FIGURE 48.6

If you previously used Outlook, upgrade your categories to color categories before creating new color categories.

If you don't use the Upgrade to Color Category option, categories not in the master list are colored white and marked "not in Master Category list." These one-off categories cannot be used on other Outlook items until they are added to the Master List.

Sharing Color Categories

Color categories are stored in the mailbox and are available only to the current mailbox. If you have multiple accounts in your Outlook profile, each account has its own set of color categories. If you want the same categories available in each account, you need to create the categories in each account.

This same limitation applies to shared mailboxes and folders; when you share folders in an Exchange mailbox with coworkers, they won't be able to see the colors assigned to categories or create and edit existing categories unless they have Owner permission to your mailbox.

 TIP   Outlook doesn't provide a built-in method to share categories with other people. It's possible to create a list of your categories and add the list to the Master Category list using a macro or a third-party utility. You can find a macro that does this at http://slipstick.com/categoriesmacro and a list of utilities at http://slipstick.com/categories.

Removing Categories

To clear one or all categories assigned to an item, follow these steps:

1. Select the categorized item.

2. On the Home tab, click the Categorize button to expand the menu.

3. To remove one category, select it from the menu.

4. To remove all categories, select Clear All Categories (see Figure 48.7).

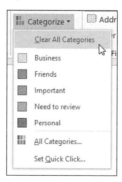

FIGURE 48.7

Use Clear All Categories to remove all categories from an item.

THE ABSOLUTE MINIMUM

Here are the key points to remember from this chapter:

- You can organize your Outlook items by creating new categories and editing existing categories.
- Assigning color to categories, creating color contact groups, and sharing contact colors can help you organize your appointments, email, and contacts.

WORKING WITH NOTES

Outlook notes, which resemble online sticky notes, offer a handy way to securely store bits of text and information. If you used notes in a previous version of Outlook, be aware that Outlook 2013 has streamlined notes' functionality to focus on simplicity.

TIP If you need a full-featured online notebook, check out OneNote 2013, covered in Part VI, "Microsoft OneNote 2013," of this book.

Exploring Outlook Notes

Outlook notes are useful for storing small pieces of text. You can add contacts or categories to your notes and locate the note quickly using the Find functionality. Because URLs in notes are clickable, you can paste a URL in a note and include comments about the site. You never have to remember to save notes; Outlook automatically saves them as soon as you move focus away from the note.

To simplify things and make Outlook's options less overwhelming, Microsoft removed all the note options in 2013. A medium yellow note is your only choice, although you can drag the edges of a note to make the note larger (or smaller) and Outlook remembers the note size.

Notes use a simple text editor that doesn't support rich text formatting. As a result, you can't highlight words or phrases with different colors or fonts or include images in a note. This doesn't mean notes aren't useful—as an electronic version of sticky notes, simple is better. Notes are great for small snippets of text—usernames and passwords, email settings, and other short blocks of text are well suited for notes.

The Notes feature is not listed on the Folder bar by default. Click the three dots on the bar and select Notes to open the Notes folder (see Figure 49.1). To create the maximum number of visible items or change the order of the folders on the Folder bar, click the three dots on the bar and select Navigation Options. This enables you to see Notes on the Folder bar.

FIGURE 49.1

Select Notes from the Folder bar to view your notes.

Creating a Note

To create a note in the Notes module, click the New Note button on the Home tab. Alternatively, use the keyboard shortcut Ctrl+Shift+N to create a new note. A blank note opens, as shown in Figure 49.2, where you can type or paste note content.

Click icon for options.

2/5/2013 9:15 PM

FIGURE 49.2

An Outlook note has a simple interface and no toolbar.

The status bar displays the time and date the note was last modified. The Modified Time field is updated to the current time when you edit a note.

 NOTE   If it's important for you to know the date a note was created, type the date into the note body—don't rely on the Created and Modified Date fields in Outlook.

When you're done creating your note, you can use the Esc key or Alt+F4 to close it.

Outlook uses the first line of the note for the name of the note. The maximum length for the name is 256 characters, unless you begin a new paragraph. If you want a shorter name, press Enter to begin a new line.

Emailing Notes

It's easy to send your notes to other people; just drag and drop the note on the Inbox or any mail folder. A new message form opens with the text of the note in the body of the message. The first line of the note is used for the subject, and the note's last modified date is added to the message.

When you select multiple notes and drop them on the Inbox, one message is created with the contents of the notes in the message body. The subject field is left blank.

You can send notes as attachments, too. If you've already started an email message, click the Attach Item button in the message window and select Outlook Item from the menu.

Organizing Your Notes

Whenv you have a lot of notes, you can organize them, either using folders or views. In some cases, creating additional note folders makes sense, but you can create custom views to show certain notes. In the Current View group (see Figure 49.3), you see the predefined views that are included with Outlook 2013:

- **Icon**—Display notes as icons.

- **Notes List**—Similar to the view used in the Inbox. Arrange by category or created date.

- **Last Seven Days**—A filtered view that shows only new notes.

You can customize these views or create new custom views. Right-click the Current View group and select View Settings from the menu to customize a view.

FIGURE 49.3

Select your preferred notes view.

THE ABSOLUTE MINIMUM

The key points to remember from this chapter include the following:

- Outlook notes are simple, online sticky notes that enable you to store small pieces of text.

- Create a new note using the keyboard shortcut Ctrl+Shift+N.

- Drag and drop a note on the Inbox or any mail folder to email it to someone.

- If you have a lot of notes, you can organize them using folders or views.

50

USING FOLDERS

Many users like to file their mail into folders, if only to keep the Inbox empty. While using too many folders isn't a good idea because it makes managing Outlook items more difficult (especially contacts), filing mail into a few folders can be useful.

Creating New Folders

You can create as many folders as you need at either the Inbox level or as a subfolder to any other folder. The default folder type is the same type as the parent folder or parent module. You can create subfolders of any type under any folder. For example, you can create contacts and calendar folders under the Inbox.

 NOTE Is there a limit to the number of folders you can create in Outlook 2013? No! The data file format Outlook 2013 uses supports unlimited subfolders and Outlook messages or other items per folder. The default file size is 50 GB, but you can increase that.

 TIP Some people like to create a folder for each person they receive email from, but this makes it harder to work with long email exchanges when several people are replying because each message is stored in a different folder. If you want to move messages out of the Inbox to keep it clean, move the messages to a folder named "Completed." Or use separate folders for personal and business messages, plus one for receipts for online purchases. In general, it's usually better to use fewer folders and instead group contacts or appointments using color categories (see Chapter 48, "Using Color Categories").

To create a new mail folder, click the New Folder button on the Folder tab or right-click an existing folder and choose New Folder from the menu. Type the name for your folder in the folder list (see Figure 50.1).

FIGURE 50.1

Outlook adds new Mail folders directly to the folder list in the Mail module.

When you're working in other modules and choose New Folder by right-clicking or from the Folder tab, the Create New Folder dialog box opens (see Figure 50.2). Type a name for your folder, verify the desired folder type is selected in the Folder Contains drop-down list, and specify where to place the folder. If you want it at the same level as the Inbox, select the top level of the mailbox. Click OK to create the folder and exit the dialog box.

FIGURE 50.2

Choose any folder type in the Create New Folder dialog box.

After creating folders, you can move them to another position in the folder list by dragging the folder with your mouse.

 TIP If you have a habit of accidentally picking up folders and dropping them inside other folders, try enabling the mouse's ClickLock feature in Control Panel, Mouse. With ClickLock enabled, you need to click once to pick up a folder and click again to drop the folder.

Managing Folders

In addition to creating new folders, you can move, copy, rename, and delete your folders. These commands are available on the Folder tab and on the context menu when you right-click a folder.

When you delete a folder, it's moved to the Deleted Items folder. Calendar, Contact, or Tasks folders won't be visible in the Deleted Items folder when you are using the Mail pane. You need to switch to the folder list to see the non-mail folders.

 TIP If you need to delete a lot of folders, drag the folders into one folder and then delete that folder or drag the folders into the Deleted Items folder. This avoids the annoying "Are you sure?" dialog box that opens when you use the Delete command.

If you need to move a folder a short distance on the folder list, you can drag it with your mouse. Use Outlook's Move Folder and Copy Folder commands when you need to move the folders a longer distance because it uses the Folder picker, which is usually easier than dragging a folder up or down the folder list.

In addition, the Folder tab, shown in Figure 50.3, offers numerous tools for creating, renaming, moving, deleting, and searching folders.

FIGURE 50.3

The Folder tab contains the commands you need to manage your Outlook folders. This figure shows the commands for an Internet Message Access Protocol (IMAP) account.

THE ABSOLUTE MINIMUM

Here are the key points to remember from this chapter:

- You can create as many folders as you want or need; however, sorting mail and contacts using folders can make it harder to manage your data. Having fewer folders is better.

- Outlook offers numerous ways to manage your folders, including the commands found on the Folder tab.

51

USING SEARCH

Finding your messages in a large mailbox isn't difficult when you use Instant Search. If you use the same search over and over, you can create a search folder, which contains always-up-to-date search results.

Outlook also offers several other ways to find things in your mailbox, including the Find Related command and the People pane. Although these methods use essentially the same search criteria, each has unique benefits.

Using Instant Search

Instant Search is a quick and easy way to find your messages, contacts, or appointments. Simply type a keyword in the Search field or refine the search query using field names and wait a few seconds for Outlook to find items matching the keyword. If you don't refine the search to specific fields, Outlook searches all common fields.

The Search tab, shown in Figure 51.1, displays when you click in the Search field or press Ctrl+E on your keyboard so you can select the fields to refine the search. After you learn the common field names, it's usually faster to type the query into the Search field.

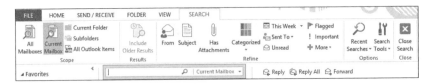

FIGURE 51.1

Click in the Search field to show the Search tab.

Choose the folders you want to search in the Scope group on the left side of the Search tab. Options include All Mailboxes, Current Mailbox, Current Folder, Subfolders, or All Outlook Items.

To set a specific scope as your default search scope, click the Search Tools button on the Search tab and select Search Options from the menu to open the Outlook Options dialog box. On this tab, you can configure the search options, including the default scope, the search term highlight color, and whether to include the Deleted Items folder in the results.

Using Instant Search Queries

Instant Search includes a number of commands you can use to refine a search. You can insert these commands by clicking buttons on the Search tab or you can type the query into the search field directly. Typing the query is a faster and more efficient way to do a search, when you know the commands to use.

To search by a field name, type the Outlook field name in the search field. Don't use a space in multiple-word field names.

```
from:john

firstname:mary
```

To search between (but not including) two dates use the following format with any date field. This example will find messages received 1/2/2013 through 4/14/2013.

```
received:(>1/1/2013 AND <4/15/2013)
```

To include the two dates in the results, add an equal sign or use two periods between the dates. These two queries will find messages received 1/1/2013 through 4/15/2013.

```
received:(>=1/1/2013 AND <=4/15/2013)
```

```
received: (1/1/13..6/15/13)
```

To find messages of a certain size or within a size range use the greater than (>), less than (<), and equal (+) symbols or two periods.

```
size:10kb
```

```
size:=50KB<60kb
```

```
size:3mb..12mb
```

In addition to greater than, less than, and equal symbols, you can use commas, AND, or OR operators between search terms.

```
from:(mary NOT smith)
```

```
cc:(mary AND sue)
```

```
to:(mary OR billy)
```

You can use some natural language words with Instant search. Search recognizes days of the week (Sunday, Monday, Tuesday), the months (March, April, May), as well as today, tomorrow, yesterday, week, next month, last week, past month, and coming year. The space between multiple word phrases is optional: thisweek, nextmonth, lastweek, pastmonth, and comingyear are valid in Instant Search.

```
received:(last week)
```

```
start:(nextmonth)
```

Using Partial Word Searches

Instant Search can't do the type of partial word search most people want, with the search term found anywhere in the word. Instant search looks for the search term at the beginning of each word. This means searching for **ann** would include Anniversary in the results but not MaryAnne. The search engine sees most punctuation as the end of a word, so it would find **ann** in Mary-Anne.

Finding Related Messages

Find Related is a predefined Instant Search query. You can access it by right-clicking a message in your mailbox or by clicking the Related button on the Message tab in an open message. The Find Related command enables you to find related messages in a conversation or from a specific sender.

Searching on the People Pane

If you need to find recent messages, attachments, or appointments from a specific person, view the People pane (see Figure 51.2) at the bottom of the Reading pane in an open message from that person.

Drag the top edge to make
the pane larger or smaller.

Click anywhere in this top section
to minimize and maximize the pane.

Click a picture or icon to view messages
and other items from the selected person.

Click the arrow to minimize
and maximize the pane.

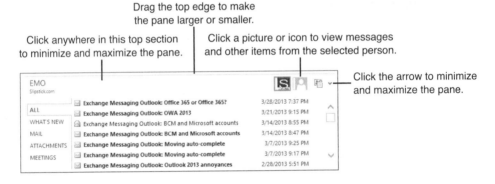

FIGURE 51.2

The People Pane displays recent messages from the sender or any recipient of the current message.

The People pane lists the sender and each person the message was sent to, represented by a contact photo (if available) or a generic people icon. Click the photo or icon to view messages from that person and click any message to open it.

Minimize and maximize the People pane by clicking the top of the bar (or use the arrow on the right side). You can adjust the height of the maximized window by dragging the top edge. To turn the People pane off completely, click the People Pane button on the View tab and select Off from the menu.

The People Pane works best when you need to find recent messages as it is limited to the 100 most recent items, including Facebook or LinkedIn status updates.

Creating Search Folders

If there is an Instant Search you use a lot, you can create a search folder for it. Search folders are virtual folders that can display messages from any folder in the data file (unlike Instant Search, which can search all data files in the profile). If a search folder is used at least once every 8 days, the folder watches for messages meeting the condition of the search and adds them to the search results.

To create a search folder, follow these steps:

1. Right-click Search Folders in the folder list.

2. Choose New Search Folder.

3. In the New Search Folder dialog box, shown in Figure 51.3, select from one of the predefined searches or create a custom search folder.

4. Choose your search criteria.

5. Click OK to close the dialog box.

6. Right-click the new search folder and choose Show in Favorites.

FIGURE 51.3

Create search folders for frequently used searches.

 NOTE   Search folders are limited only to email. You can't use them with other Outlook item types. Search folders display the results of a search; messages are not moved to search folders.

THE ABSOLUTE MINIMUM

Here are the key points to remember from this chapter:

- Instant Search is fast and powerful enough for most search needs.

- Find Related is a predefined Instant Search query that enables you to find related messages in a conversation or from a specific sender.

- View recent messages, attachments, or appointments from a specific person on the People pane at the bottom of an open message.

- If there is an Instant Search you use a lot, you can create a search folder for it.

WORKING WITH VIEWS

Outlook contains a lot of data, including all your email, contacts, appointments, and tasks—often several years' worth of data. If you send and receive a lot of email, you could have thousands of messages in your Inbox to sort through. Views can help you manage your email, calendar, and contacts, making it easier to find the information you need. You can use Outlook's default views or create your own custom views, with conditional formatting to color code items or filters to show only the item you want to see.

Managing Views

The View tab in Outlook 2013, shown in Figure 52.1, makes it easy to select a view and to create your own customized views.

FIGURE 52.1

The View tab has the commands you need to change the view and arrangement of your email messages.

Changing Views

Changing the view in Outlook is simple: On the View tab, click the Change View button and select a new view from the menu (see Figure 52.2).

FIGURE 52.2

Click Change View to select a new view.

Outlook includes several predefined views for each folder type, such as the monthly calendar view for the calendar folders and the business card view for the contacts folders. One or more list views are available for each folder type.

Items in a list view can be grouped together by the category, date, subject, or several other fields. Outlook 2013 refers to this as *arrangement*. The fields you can arrange by vary with the folder type, but you have category and date arrangements available in each folder type (see Figure 52.3).

FIGURE 52.3

Use the Arrangement group to change how you group Outlook items.

Applying Views to Folders

After you change a view on one folder, you can apply the view to many other folders at once. You need to view the folder whose view you want to apply to other folders.

To apply views to any or all folders of the same folder type, follow these steps:

1. Open the folder whose view you want to apply to other folders.

2. On the View tab, click the Change View button.

3. Select Apply View to Other Folders.

4. In the Apply View dialog box, select the folders you want to apply the view to.

5. Select the top-level folders and select the Apply View to Subfolders check box to apply the view to all folders of that type within your mailbox or data file.

6. Click OK when you are finished selecting folders. This applies the current view to all the selected folders (see Figure 52.4).

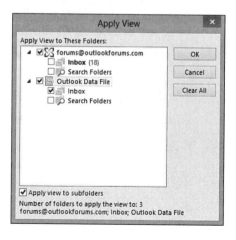

FIGURE 52.4

Select the folders to apply the view to, and then press OK.

TIP When you use a list view, if you press and hold Shift as you click field names, you can sort by multiple fields.

Resetting Views

Although a rare occurrence, occasionally one or more views become corrupt and prevent Outlook from displaying the folder contents. To fix it, press the Reset View button on the View tab, as shown in Figure 52.5.

FIGURE 52.5

Click Reset View to restore the view to its default settings.

Copying Views

Imagine this scenario: You spent an hour creating a number of conditional formatting rules in one of Outlook's default views. Because Outlook does not offer an easy way to lock a view, you accidently reset the view and lost all your hard work.

Although you can't lock views to prevent changes, you can make copies of custom views to use as backups if the original is lost or changed.

Create a copy of the current view from the View tab by clicking the Change View button and selecting Save Current View as a New View.

If you want to copy other views, select Manage Views and use the Copy button in the Manage All Views dialog box to create a copy of the view you select.

Creating Custom Views

You can use customized views to show or hide Outlook items meeting certain conditions. You can use custom views to filter contacts before doing a mail merge. If you use the same search queries over and over, you can use a custom view as a more permanent instant search.

Views offer seven areas you can customize:

- **Columns**—Add the fields you want to see in your view.
- **Group By**—The default setting is to Automatically Group According to Arrangement.
- **Sort**—Change the sort order of your Outlook items.
- **Filter**—Create filters to show or hide Outlook items. Choose from preselected options or use the Advanced tab (and Structured Query Language (SQL) tab, when available) to create your own filters using any available field.
- **Other Settings**—The options available in Other Settings depend on which folder you view. Use this dialog box to change fonts and customize your layout.
- **Conditional Formatting**—Conditional formatting changes the color or font of an item in List view when the item meets the conditions in the conditional formatting rule. Not all views support conditional formatting.
- **Format Columns**—Use this to change the format used in columns containing dates or numbers or to change Yes/No fields to check boxes or words.

To create a custom view, you need to switch to the View tab. Click View Settings to customize the current view or click Change View, Manage Views to create a new custom view.

To create a new custom view, follow these steps:

1. On the View tab, click the Change View button.
2. Select Manage Views.
3. Click New.
4. Enter a name for your view.
5. Select the type of view.
6. Select who can see the view.
7. Click OK.
8. In the Advanced View Settings dialog box, select the Columns (fields) to use in the view (see Figure 52.6).
9. Configure the other options, including filters and conditional formatting.
10. Click OK to close the Advanced View Settings dialog box.
11. Click OK to close the Manage All Views dialog box.

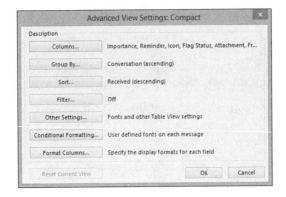

FIGURE 52.6

Create a custom view in Outlook 2013.

Using Conditional Formatting

Use conditional formatting to format messages or other Outlook items that meet specific conditions. For example, messages from your boss can be shown in the message list with a larger red font, and messages from friends can use a smaller purple font (see Figure 52.7).

Conditional formatting rules are part of a view; if you change the view, you lose the conditional formatting rules.

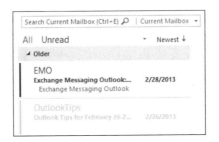

FIGURE 52.7

Use colors to highlight messages for better visibility.

 NOTE Outlook includes default conditional formatting rules for read, unread, expired, and overdue messages. The formatting can be changed, but the conditions cannot be changed.

To create a conditional formatting view, follow these steps:

1. On the View tab, click the View Settings button.

2. In the Advanced View Settings dialog box, click the Conditional Formatting button.

3. Click Add to create a new Conditional Formatting rule.

4. Enter a name for the rule (see Figure 52.8).

5. Click the Font button to open the Font dialog box. Select a color, font, and font size and click OK to close.

6. Click the Condition button to open the Filter dialog box. Create your filter and click OK to close.

7. Click OK to close the Conditional Formatting dialog box.

8. Click OK to close the Advanced View Settings dialog box.

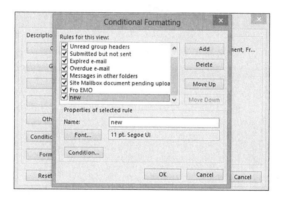

FIGURE 52.8

Create a conditional formatting rule.

NOTE To create a filter for an email address or part of an address, use the From field on the Messages tab. To use the display name, use the Advanced tab and select the From field from the list of fields.

THE ABSOLUTE MINIMUM

Here are the key points to remember from this chapter:

- Use views to sort and filter Outlook items instead of using multiple folders.

- Don't be afraid to customize the views. If you mess up a view, reset the view and start over.

- Use conditional formatting to highlight messages in color so they are easier to find.

ONENOTE 2013 BASICS

Microsoft OneNote enables you to create digital notebooks that contain text, links, pictures, audio, video, screen clippings, digital handwriting, external files, and more. OneNote makes it easy to keep all your information and research about a specific topic in one searchable, shareable place. In this chapter, you find out how to create basic OneNote notebooks, apply an optional template, and create sections, pages, subpages, and tags.

Creating a New Notebook

When you first open OneNote, a sample notebook displays (see Figure 53.1). After exploring this sample, you'll probably want to create your own notebook.

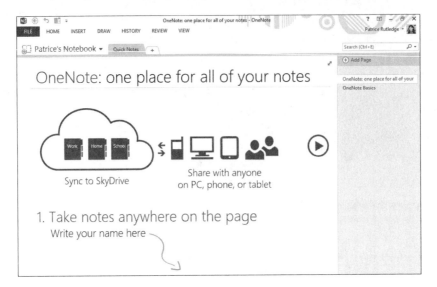

FIGURE 53.1

Explore OneNote's sample notebook.

To create a new notebook, follow these steps:

1. On the File tab, click New.

    TIP You can also click the down arrow next to your sample notebook and select Add Notebook to open the New window.

2. In the New Notebook window (see Figure 53.2), select a location to store your new notebook: your SkyDrive account, your computer, or another place you designate.

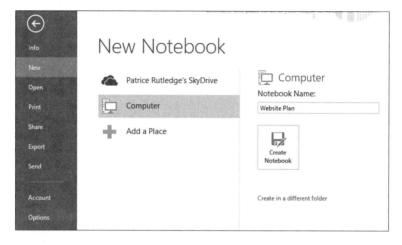

FIGURE 53.2

Get started with OneNote by creating a new notebook.

3. Enter a name for your notebook.

 NOTE OneNote saves your notebook in the default location for the option selected. If you want to specify another folder, click the Create in a Different Folder link.

4. Click the Create Notebook button.

Figure 53.3 shows what a new blank notebook with an untitled section and untitled page looks like.

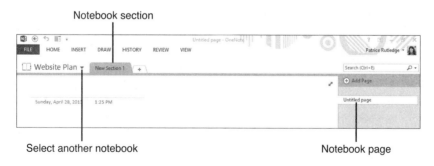

FIGURE 53.3

OneNote creates a notebook that's a blank canvas.

From here, you can

- Add content to your notebook.
- Add new sections, pages, and subpages.
- Rename your section and page titles.

 TIP   To select a different notebook, click the down arrow to the right of the current notebook tab and select a notebook from the list.

Adding Notes to Your Notebook

To add a text note in your notebook, click the location where you want to insert it and start typing. OneNote displays a note container that expands as you type (see Figure 53.4).

Sunday, April 28, 2013   1:25 PM

New Website Schedule

FIGURE 53.4

OneNote places text in a container that you can move around the page.

To move the note, drag the top of the container to a new location on the page.

To resize the note, drag either side with your mouse.

Formatting Notes

Similar to other Office applications, you can format text in OneNote using the text-formatting tools on the Home tab. For example, you can apply bold, italic, fonts, and colors using the options in the Basic Text group.

 NOTE   See Chapter 3, "Working with Text," to learn more about formatting text in Microsoft Office applications.

Applying Text Styles

With OneNote, you can quickly apply a style to text by selecting the text you want to style and then selecting your preferred style in the Styles group on the Home tab (see Figure 53.5). For example, you can apply styles for headings, citations, quotes, or code. The default style is Normal.

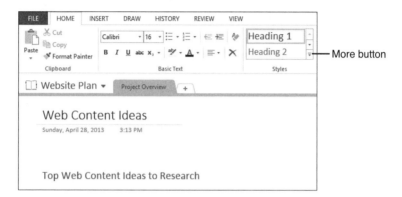

FIGURE 53.5

Format text quickly by applying a style.

TIP   To remove a style from selected text, click the More button in the Styles group (it's in the lower-right corner) and select Clear Formatting.

Saving Notebooks

OneNote saves your notebooks automatically to the location you specified during setup. You don't need to take any action to save notebook content.

Working with Sections

A OneNote section contains multiple pages or subpages and serves as an organization tool for your notebooks. Section tabs display at the top of each notebook and are color coded.

Creating a New Section

To create a new section, click the Create a New Section icon to the right of the section tabs (see Figure 53.6). Replace the default section title, such as New Section 1, with your preferred title.

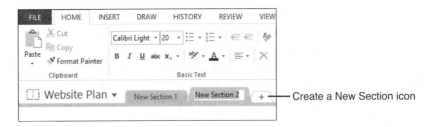

FIGURE 53.6

Organize your notebooks in sections.

Modifying Sections

OneNote offers many options for modifying a notebook section when you right-click it (see Figure 53.7).

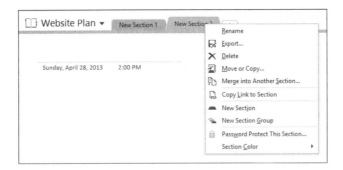

FIGURE 53.7

This shortcut menu offers many section formatting options.

You can

- Rename a section by right-clicking it and selecting Rename from the menu. The section title is highlighted and you can replace it with new text.

- Delete a section by right-clicking it and selecting Delete from the menu. OneNote asks for confirmation before deleting.

- Move a section by dragging it to a new location with your mouse. If you want to move a section to another notebook, right-click it and select Move or Copy from the menu. In the Move or Copy dialog box, select the location where you want to move the section and click the Move button.

- Copy a section by right-clicking it and selecting Move or Copy from the menu. In the Move or Copy dialog box, select the location where you want to place the copy and click the Copy button.

- Merge one section into another by right-clicking it and selecting Merge into Another Section from the menu. In the Merge Section dialog box, select the section you want to merge into and click the Merge button. OneNote prompts you to confirm this action and asks if you want to delete the first section.

- Create a section group by right-clicking a section tab and selecting New Section Group from the menu. Creating a section group is particularly useful if your notebook contains more sections than you can view on a single screen.

- Protect a section with a password by right-clicking it and selecting Password Protect This Section from the menu. The Password Protect pane opens where you can specify your password.

- Change a section's color by right-clicking it and selecting Section Color from the menu. Select one of the available colors to apply it to your section tab.

Working with Pages

Each notebook section can include multiple pages or subpages, which help label and organize your content.

Inserting a New Page

To better organize your notebook content, you can add one or more pages.

To insert a page into a notebook, go to the page tab list, select the location where you want to place your new page, and click the Add Page button (see Figure 53.8).

FIGURE 53.8

Add one or more pages to your notebook sections.

Inserting a Page Based on a Template

OneNote offers numerous page templates that give you a head start in creating a page for a specific task. Sample OneNote templates include the following: project overview, simple to do list, formal meeting notes, or detailed lecture notes. You can also use a design-based template, such as a page with blue stripes or flat squares. Downloading a template from Office.com is another option.

To insert a page based on a template, follow these steps:

1. On the Insert tab, click the Page Templates button.

2. In the Templates pane, click the down arrow next to each category to view related templates, as shown in Figure 53.9.

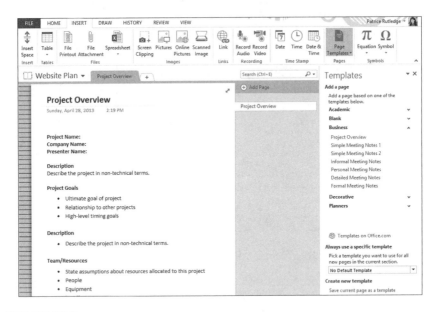

FIGURE 53.9

Get a jumpstart on a new page by using a template.

3. Select the template you want to apply to your page.

4. Click the Close button (x) in the upper-right corner of the pane to close it.

 TIP Click the Templates on Office.com link in the Templates pane to search online for more template options.

Modifying Pages

OneNote offers many options for modifying a notebook page when you right-click it in the page tab list, as shown in Figure 53.10.

FIGURE 53.10

Choose from several options when you right-click a page in the page tab list.

You can

- Rename a page by right-clicking it and selecting Rename from the menu. The page title is highlighted and you can replace it with new text.

- Delete a page by right-clicking it and selecting Delete from the menu. OneNote deletes pages automatically, but if you make a mistake you can click the Undo button in the upper-left corner of the screen to restore it.

- Move a page by dragging it to a new location on the page tab list with your mouse. If you want to move a page to another notebook, right-click it and select Move or Copy from the menu. In the Move or Copy dialog box, select the location where you want to move the page and click the Move button.

- Copy a page by right-clicking it and selecting Move or Copy from the menu. In the Move or Copy dialog box, select the location where you want to place the copy and click the Copy button.

- Make a page a subpage by right-clicking it and selecting Make Subpage from the menu. OneNote indents the selected page below the page that precedes it. Creating subpages is a good idea when you have too much content for a single page and want to divide this content into specific topics related to the main page.

- Promote a subpage back to a page by right-clicking it and selecting Promote Subpage from the menu.

Working with Tags

Tags make it easier to search for specific information, particularly in a notebook that contains a lot of data.

Applying a Tag

To apply a tag, select the content you want to tag and, on the Home tab, select an appropriate tag from the Tags group (see Figure 53.11). To view more options, click the More button. Sample tags include To Do, Important, Question, Remember for Blog, Idea, and Website to Visit.

FIGURE 53.11

Tags make it easier to find your content in a large notebook.

TIP To quickly apply the To Do tag to selected content, click the To Do Tag button on the Home tab. OneNote inserts a check box on all To Do items, so that you can check it off when completed.

Removing a Tag

To remove a tag, select the tagged content, click the More button in the Tags group on the Home tab, and select Remove Tag.

Creating Custom Tags

If none of OneNote's existing tags suits your needs, you can create your own tags. To create a custom tag, follow these steps:

1. On the Home tab, click the More button in the Tags group.

2. Select Customize Tag.

3. In the Customize Tags dialog box, click the New Tag button (see Figure 53.12).

FIGURE 53.12

Create a custom tag if the default tags don't suit your needs.

 TIP If you want to create a tag that's similar to an existing tag, select it in the Customize Tags dialog box and click the Modify Tag button.

4. In the New Tag dialog box (see Figure 53.13), enter a name for your tag; select its symbol, font color, and highlight color; and click OK.

FIGURE 53.13

Define your new tag's name, symbol, and colors.

5. Click OK to close the Customize Tags dialog box. Your tag is now available in the Tags group on the Home tab.

Finding Tags

OneNote offers built-in tag search functionality to help you find the content you tagged. This is particularly useful for large notebooks with lots of tags.

To search for tags, click the Find Tags button on the Home tab. The Tags Summary pane opens; in it you can search a specific section, page, or notebook. Optionally, you can also create a summary page of tagged content by clicking the Create Summary Page button.

THE ABSOLUTE MINIMUM

Here are the key points to remember from this chapter:

- A OneNote notebook contains all the information you want to store for a specific topic or project, and it is divided into sections and pages.

- A section contains multiple pages or subpages and serves as an organization tool for your notebooks. Section tabs display at the top of each notebook and are color coded.

- Each notebook section can include multiple pages or subpages, which help label and organize your content.

- Tags make it easier for you to search for specific information, particularly in a notebook that contains a lot of data. OneNote offers numerous ready-made tags as well as the capability to create your own custom tags.

54

INSERTING NOTEBOOK CONTENT

In addition to inserting notes, OneNote enables you to insert a variety of other content including external files, images, and links. You can also record and insert your own audio and video files, add timestamps to date your content, insert symbols, and draw freehand on your notebook pages.

Inserting Files

From the Files group on the Insert tab (see Figure 54.1), OneNote enables you to insert three kinds of files: file printouts, file attachments, and Excel spreadsheets.

FIGURE 54.1

Insert files—and other content—from OneNote's Insert tab.

Attaching a File

If you want to keep all your documents related to a single topic in one place, you can attach them to a notebook page. To do so, follow these steps:

1. On the Insert tab, click the File Attachment button.

2. In the Choose a File or Set of Files to Insert dialog box, select your files (see Figure 54.2).

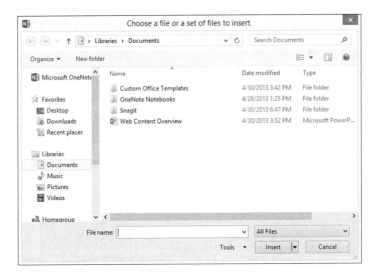

FIGURE 54.2

Select one or more files to attach.

3. Click the Insert button.

4. Specify your attachment preference, as shown in Figure 54.3:

    • **Attach File**—OneNote inserts an icon that you can click to open the file.

    • **Insert Printout**—OneNote inserts the content (including its formatting) of the file as a note.

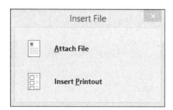

FIGURE 54.3

Choose to insert a file attachment icon or printout.

 TIP Another way to insert a file printout is to click the File Printout button on the Insert tab.

Inserting an Excel Spreadsheet

If you want to take advantage of Excel's formatting and calculation features in your table, you can insert an Excel spreadsheet in your OneNote notebook.

To insert a new spreadsheet, follow these steps:

1. On the Insert tab, click the Spreadsheet button and select New Excel Spreadsheet from the menu. A blank spreadsheet displays, as shown in Figure 54.4.

 TIP To insert an existing spreadsheet, click the Spreadsheet button on the Insert tab and select Existing Excel Spreadsheet from the menu.

FIGURE 54.4

Create a new Excel spreadsheet in your notebook.

2. Using the resizing handles (the small white squares), resize your spreadsheet to fit your page.

3. Click the Edit button in the upper-left corner of the spreadsheet to open it in Excel.

4. Enter and format your cell data as you would in any other Excel spreadsheet.

5. When you're finished, save your spreadsheet and click the Close button (the large X in the upper-right corner) to close Excel and return to OneNote.

Inserting Images

The Images group on the Insert tab (refer to Figure 54.1) offers four buttons that enable you to insert images in your notebook:

- **Screen Clipping**—Drag your mouse to select the content to include in your screen clipping.

- **Pictures**—Select and insert pictures from your computer or network location.

- **Online Pictures**—Select and insert pictures from the Web, including pictures from the Office.com clip art collection, your SkyDrive account, and other locations such as Bing Image Search and Flickr.

- **Scanned Image**—Connect to a scanner or camera to insert an image.

> **NOTE** The first three options are common Office tasks and are covered in other chapters in this book. See Chapter 4, "Working with Pictures," for more information about inserting pictures. See Chapter 5, "Working with Shapes and SmartArt," to learn how to insert a screen clipping.

Inserting Links

A common item you might want to include in a notebook is a website link related to your notebook's topic. You can also insert links to other OneNote pages, sections, or notebooks.

To insert a link, follow these steps:

1. On the Insert tab, click the Link button.

2. To insert a Web link, insert the link address and optional display text (see Figure 54.5).

FIGURE 54.5

List important website links in your notebooks.

TIP Click the Browse the Web button to open your default browser and search the Web for the desired link. If you want to include a long URL, copying and pasting it helps ensure accuracy.

3. To insert a link to a OneNote location, select the location in the Or Pick a Location in OneNote section.

4. Click the OK button.

Recording Audio and Video

In addition to static content, you can also insert audio and video clips in OneNote. For example, rather than writing a note, you might want to record your comments about a particular topic. Another option is to record a presentation or lecture.

Recording an Audio Clip

If you have a microphone (built-in or external) on your computer, you can easily record audio.

To record an audio clip, follow these steps:

1. On the Insert tab, click the Record Audio button. OneNote displays the audio icon on your page, opens the Audio & Video – Recording tab, and starts recording (see Figure 54.6).

FIGURE 54.6

Add audio notes to your notebook.

2. Record your audio.

 NOTE During recording you can adjust your audio settings by clicking the Audio & Video Settings button on the Audio & Video – Recording tab.

3. On the Audio & Video – Recording tab, click the Stop button when you're done recording.

To play an audio clip, select it and click the Play button on the Audio & Video – Playback tab. On this tab, you can also pause, rewind, and fast forward your audio clip (see Figure 54.7).

FIGURE 54.7

Play back your audio files using the options on the Audio & Video – Playback tab.

Recording a Video Clip

You can record video clips using your computer's webcam and insert them in your OneNote notebooks.

To record a video clip, follow these steps:

1. On the Insert tab, click the Record Video button. OneNote opens a video window, displays the Audio & Video – Recording tab, and starts recording (see Figure 54.8).

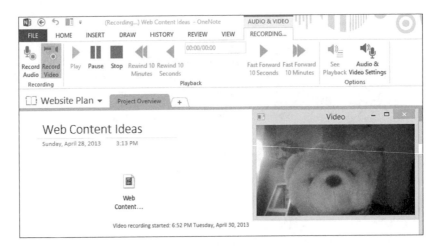

FIGURE 54.8

Record video clips using your computer's webcam.

2. Record your video.

 NOTE During recording, you can adjust your video settings by clicking the Audio & Video Settings button on the Audio & Video – Recording tab.

3. On the Audio & Video – Recording tab, click the Stop button when you're done recording.

To play a video back, select it and click the Play button on the Audio & Video – Playback tab. On this tab, you can also pause, rewind, and fast forward your video (refer to Figure 54.7).

Inserting Other Notebook Content

In addition to inserting files, images, links, audio, and video, OneNote offers a few other content options. For example, you can also insert spaces, tables, timestamps, symbols, and equations.

Inserting Extra Space

If you want to insert a note or other content between existing content on a page, you can insert extra space. To do so, follow these steps:

1. Click where you want to insert space.

2. On the Insert tab, click the Insert Space button.

3. Drag the arrow to insert the desired amount of space and release, as shown in Figure 54.9.

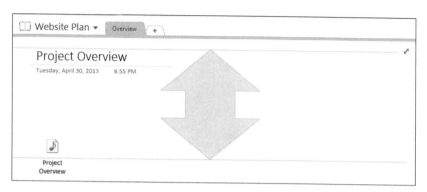

FIGURE 54.9

Drag the arrow to insert a space.

Inserting a Table

By inserting a table, you can display related data in columns and rows. After creating a basic table, enhance it using the tools on the Table Tools – Layout tab.

To insert a table, follow these steps:

1. On the Insert tab, click the Table button.

2. In the gallery that displays (see Figure 54.10), select how many columns and rows to include. OneNote highlights the selected cells.

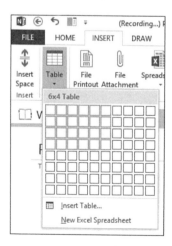

FIGURE 54.10

Specify the number of rows and columns in your table.

3. Click the gallery. OneNote inserts the table on your notebook page, as shown in Figure 54.11.

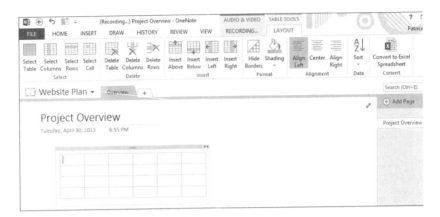

FIGURE 54.11

Get started with a blank table.

From here, you can

*   Enter content directly in your table cells.

*   Format table content using the tools on the Home tab. (See Chapter 3, "Working with Text," for more information.)

*   Select your table to display the Table Tools – Layout tab (refer to Figure 54.11), where you can insert and delete rows and columns, format borders, apply shading, align and sort cell content, and convert your table to an Excel spreadsheet.

Inserting a Timestamp

If you want to attach a date or time (or both) to any of your notebook content, you can use a timestamp. To do so, on the Insert tab, click one of the following buttons: Date, Time, or Date & Time (refer to Figure 54.1). OneNote displays the timestamp on your page with the current date and/or time (see Figure 54.12).

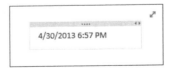

FIGURE 54.12

Add a timestamp to associate a date with your notebook content.

You can drag a timestamp to another location on a page, just as you can with any other content in a container.

TIP If you need to change a timestamp, select it and enter a new date or time. This is most useful when you need to enter a date in the past or future.

Inserting Symbols and Equations

The Symbols group on the Insert tab (refer to Figure 54.1) enables you to insert equations or symbols into your notebook. For example, you can click the Equation button to insert a common equation such as the Pythagorean theorem or click the Symbol button to insert symbols such as the Euro, trademark, or copyright sign.

Using OneNote Drawing Tools

Using the drawing tools on OneNote's Draw tab, you can add freehand drawings and shapes to your notebook pages.

NOTE Working with shapes is a task common to multiple Office applications. See Chapter 5 for more information.

Inserting a Drawing

OneNote offers two standard drawing tools with several color choices: a thin pen 0.5 mm wide and a thick highlighter 4.0 mm wide.

To insert a drawing, on the Draw tab, click a drawing tool in the Tools group (click the More button for more options). Start drawing on your page with your selected tool. Figure 54.13 shows a sample drawing.

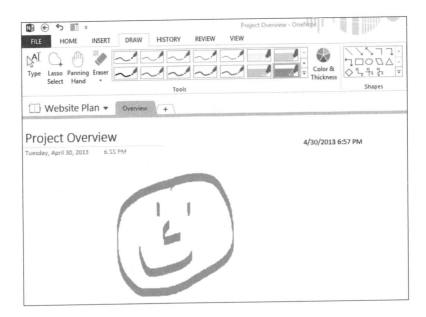

FIGURE 54.13

Use the Draw tab to add freehand drawings to your pages.

 TIP If the default options don't meet your needs, click the Color & Thickness button on the Draw tab to open the Color & Thickness dialog box (see Figure 54.14) where you can customize pen and highlighter thickness as well as line color.

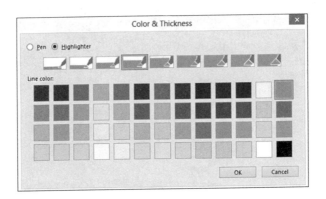

FIGURE 54.14

Customize the color and thickness of the pen you're using.

CAUTION It takes time to master these drawing tools, particularly if you aren't experienced with using similar tools in other applications.

Erasing a Drawing

If you decide you no longer want a drawing on your page, you can erase it.

To erase a drawing, follow these steps:

1. On the Draw tab, click the down arrow below the Eraser button (see Figure 54.15).

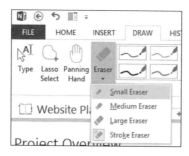

FIGURE 54.15

Select the eraser option that best fits what you want to erase.

 TIP Click the upper part of the Eraser button to bypass selecting your eraser type and use the last selected option.

2. Select the type of eraser you want to use: a small, medium, or large standard eraser or a stroke eraser (erases an entire drawing when you click it).

 NOTE The eraser doesn't erase text or other page content, only drawings and shapes.

3. Drag the eraser with your mouse to remove your desired content.

THE ABSOLUTE MINIMUM

Here are the key points to remember from this chapter:

- OneNote enables you to insert three kinds of files: file printouts, file attachments, and Excel spreadsheets.

- You can add images to OneNote, including screen clippings, pictures on your computer, pictures from the Web, and scanned images.

- Inserting a link to a website or other OneNote content is another possibility.

- In addition to static content, you can also record and insert audio and video clips in OneNote. The Audio & Video – Recording tab and Audio & Video – Playback tab offer additional tools to help you customize and manage your media files.

- Other content you can insert in a OneNote notebook includes spaces, tables, timestamps, symbols, and equations.

- Using the Draw tab, you can add freehand drawings and shapes to your notebook pages.

55

VIEWING AND MANAGING NOTEBOOKS

After you figure out how to create a basic notebook and insert notebook content, it's time to move on to OneNote's more advanced features. In this chapter, you see how to display Full Page view, dock OneNote to your desktop, integrate with Outlook, use the Send to OneNote tool, protect your notebook content, and view notebook history.

Displaying Full Page View

OneNote's default view is Normal view, which displays the Ribbon and navigational tabs. Optionally, you can avoid distractions by switching to Full Page view, which displays only your current page.

To switch to Full Page view, click the Full Page View button on the View tab (see Figure 55.1).

FIGURE 55.1

The View tab offers options for viewing and managing your notebooks.

Figure 55.2 shows a sample of this view. When you're ready to switch back to Normal view, click the Normal View button in the upper-right corner of the screen.

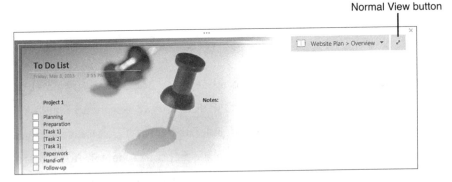

FIGURE 55.2

Avoid distractions with Full Page view.

Docking OneNote to Your Desktop

If you want to work in other applications yet keep OneNote open and handy for taking notes and inserting content, you can dock it to your desktop.

To do so, click the Dock to Desktop button on the View tab.

Figure 55.3 displays OneNote docked to the right side of your desktop while you work in Excel.

FIGURE 55.3

Dock OneNote to the right side of the screen while you work in other applications.

To return to Normal view, click the Normal View button in the upper-right corner of the screen.

Using Linked Note Taking

Docking OneNote to your desktop activates Linked Note Taking, which creates an automatic link to the content that displays in your main window when you enter a note in the docked OneNote window. For example, if you have a document open in Microsoft Word and enter a note about it in your docked OneNote window, OneNote adds a link to the Word document automatically (see Figure 55.4).

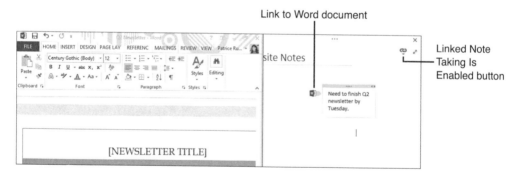

FIGURE 55.4

One Note adds an automatic link to any content you're viewing when you add a note.

 NOTE When OneNote is docked, click the Linked Note Taking Is Enabled button to view a menu of options. From here, you can view linked files, delete links, turn off Linked Note Taking, or go to the Advanced tab of the OneNote Options dialog box where you can specify your Linked Note preferences.

Setting Up OneNote Pages

You can customize the appearance of your OneNote pages using the buttons in the Page Setup group on the View tab (see Figure 55.5). These buttons include the following:

FIGURE 55.5

Customize your notebook pages with the options in the Page Setup group.

- **Page Color**—Change the color of your page to one of the pastel shades on the palette that displays. To remove a color, select the No Color check box on the palette (the default option).

- **Rule Lines**—Add rule lines (similar to a real notebook page) or grid lines (useful for placing images). If you apply rule lines, the Rule Line Color menu option becomes active, where you can choose from an extensive list of line color options, as shown in Figure 55.6.

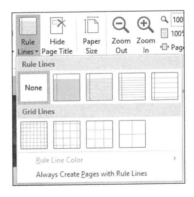

FIGURE 55.6

Adding rule lines or grid lines is another page option.

- **Hide Page Title**—If your page title includes content, hiding it deletes this content. To restore the page title field, click the Hide Page Title button again.

- **Paper Size**—Display the Paper Size pane, as shown in Figure 55.7, where you can specify the page size, orientation, and print margins.

FIGURE 55.7

Modify the default size of your pages on the Paper Size pane.

Working with Microsoft Outlook

OneNote offers full integration with another Microsoft Office application: Outlook. You can email pages directly from OneNote and send OneNote to-do lists to your Outlook calendar.

Emailing a Page

You can email a notebook page to someone directly from OneNote by following these steps:

1. On the Home tab, click the Email Page button. An Outlook message window opens (see Figure 55.8) that displays your page content in the message area and your page title as the message subject.

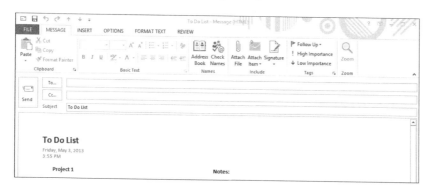

FIGURE 55.8

Send an Outlook message directly from OneNote.

NOTE If you have any attachments on your page, they're attached to the message.

2. Enter the email address of your recipient in the To field.

 NOTE As with any Outlook message, you can email more than one recipient and copy recipients using the Cc field.

3. Optionally, add any additional text.

4. Click the Send button to send your message.

 TIP Another option is to save a notebook, section, or page as a PDF and email it to someone. See Chapter 2, "Working with Office Applications," for more information.

Sending a Task to Outlook

If you use Outlook to manage tasks, you can send a OneNote to-do list (such as a note assigned the To Do tag) to Outlook as tasks by following these steps:

1. Select the content you want to send to Outlook.

2. On the Home tab, click the Outlook Tasks button.

3. From the drop-down list, select a timeframe, such as Today, Tomorrow, or Next Week (see Figure 55.9).

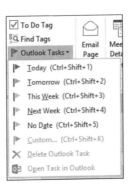

FIGURE 55.9

Select a timeframe for this to-do list.

OneNote inserts flags next to the selected content (see Figure 55.10) and adds the tasks to your Outlook To-Do List.

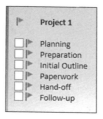

FIGURE 55.10

Flagged content in OneNote.

Using the Send to OneNote Tool

The Send to OneNote tool enables you to send content to a OneNote notebook while working in other applications. Minimized on your desktop, this tool is available whenever you use OneNote. If it doesn't open automatically when you start OneNote, you can open it by pressing ⊞+N on the keyboard or clicking the Send to OneNote Tool button on the View tab.

Sending a Screen Clipping to OneNote

If you're working in another application or find something interesting on the Web, you can send a clipping to a OneNote notebook. To do so, follow these steps:

1. Open the application from which you want to take a screen clipping. For example, you might want to capture something from another Office application or from an external website.

2. Open the Send to OneNote window and click the Screen Clipping button (see Figure 55.11).

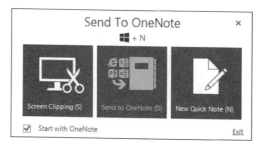

FIGURE 55.11

The Send to OneNote tool offers three options for sending content to a OneNote notebook.

3. Select the area you want to include in your notebook using your mouse pointer (which now appears as a crosshair), as shown in Figure 55.12.

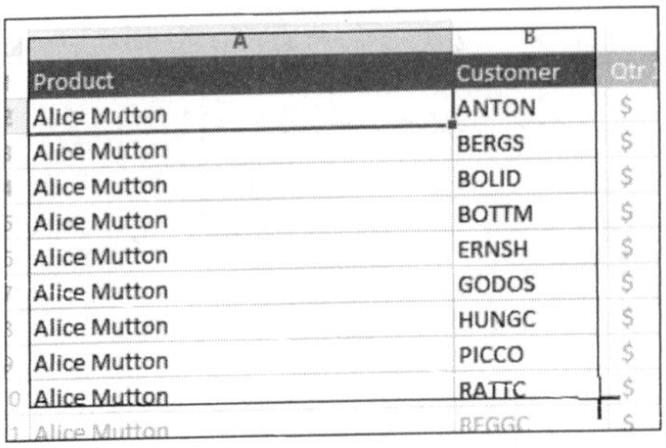

FIGURE 55.12

Select the content you want to clip.

4. In the Select Location in OneNote dialog box (see Figure 55.13), specify where you want to insert your clipping.

FIGURE 55.13

Specify a location for your new content.

5. Click the Send to Selected Location button. OneNote inserts the screen clipping in the specified location.

NOTE   See Chapter 5, "Working with Shapes and SmartArt," for more information about inserting screen clippings in Office applications.

Sending Content to OneNote

You can also use the Send to OneNote tool to insert actual content from another application (not just a screen clipping).

To send content to OneNote, follow these steps:

1. Open the content you want to send to OneNote. In this example, you send a PowerPoint presentation to OneNote and insert it as a printout.

2. Open the Send to OneNote window and click the Send to OneNote button (refer to Figure 55.11).

3. In the Select Location in OneNote dialog box, specify where you want to insert this content.

4. Click the OK button. OneNote inserts the content in the specified location.

 NOTE   See "Inserting Files" in Chapter 54, "Inserting Notebook Content," for more information about inserting printouts.

Creating a Quick Note

A third option the Send to OneNote tool provides is sending quick notes to OneNote. Use a quick note when you want to send a note to OneNote without sending a clipping or printout.

To send a quick note, follow these steps:

1. Open the Send to OneNote window and click the Send to OneNote button (refer to Figure 55.11).

2. In the window that opens (see Figure 55.14), enter your note.

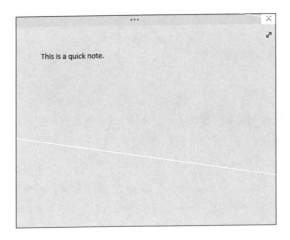

FIGURE 55.14

Take quick notes and store them in OneNote.

 TIP Click the top of the window to display the OneNote Ribbon.

3. Click the Close button (X) in the upper-right corner of the window. OneNote places your note in the Quick Notes section, which is below your notebook list (see Figure 55.15).

FIGURE 55.15

View your quick notes.

You can keep your notes in the Quick Notes section or move them to another notebook.

Protecting Notebook Sections with a Password

Applying a password to a specific section is a good idea if you want to prevent unauthorized people from viewing your content. This feature is particularly useful for notebooks you share with others.

To apply a password to a section, follow these steps:

1. On the Review tab, click the Password button. The Password Protection pane opens, as shown in Figure 55.16.

FIGURE 55.16

Protect notebook sections with a password.

2. Click the Set Password button.

3. In the Password Protection dialog box (see Figure 55.17), enter and confirm your password and click OK. Passwords are case sensitive.

FIGURE 55.17

Enter and verify your password.

CAUTION Be sure to keep your password in a safe place. OneNote doesn't have a "lost password" feature and can't restore content if you forget your password.

4. If section backups exist, OneNote opens the Existing Section Backups dialog box and prompts you to delete unprotected backups.

NOTE After applying a password to a section, the Change Password button and Remove Password button become available on the Password Protection pane in case you want to modify your password settings.

TIP To lock all sections, click the Lock All button (or press Ctrl+Alt+L on your keyboard).

Viewing Notebook History

The History tab in OneNote enables you to review changes to your notebook content, including recent edits, edits by author, and page versions. These tools are most useful if you're collaborating and sharing a notebook with others. If you're the sole author of your notebook, you're less likely to need these features.

NOTE For more information about sharing and collaborating in OneNote, see Chapter 2 and Chapter 6, "Using Microsoft Office on the Web and Mobile Devices."

The History tab offers the following buttons, as shown in Figure 55.18:

NOTE The History tab is new to OneNote 2013. In previous versions, this functionality was available on the Share tab.

- **Next Unread**—View the next page with notes you haven't read.
- **Mark as Read**—Mark this page as read. This button acts as a toggle. Clicking a read page marks it as unread.
- **Recent Edits**—View recent edits by a specified date, such as today, yesterday, in the last 30 days, and so forth.
- **Find by Author**—Open the Search Results pane where you can search for changes by a specific author.

- **Hide Authors**—Hide authors' initials next to their changes in a multi-author notebook. Also acts as a toggle; clicking again shows authors.

- **Page Versions**—Displays a list of page versions on the page tab list by author and date. Click the lower portion of the Page Versions button to display a menu, which enables you to delete versions in a section, section group, or notebook. You can also disable history for the open notebook.

- **Notebook Recycle Bin**—View the notebook recycle bin. OneNote deletes content permanently after 60 days. To empty your bin immediately, click the lower portion of the Notebook Recycle Bin button and select Empty Recycle Bin from the menu. You can also right-click content in the recycle bin to restore it to OneNote.

FIGURE 55.18

View notebook history including page versions and recent edits.

THE ABSOLUTE MINIMUM

Here are the key points to remember from this chapter:

- If you want to avoid distractions and display only your current page, switch to Full Page view.

- Dock OneNote to your desktop if you want to work in other applications yet keep OneNote open and ready for taking notes and inserting content.

- Docking OneNote to your desktop activates Linked Note Taking, which creates an automatic link to the content that displays in your main window when you enter a note in the docked OneNote window.

- Using the buttons on the View tab's Page Setup group, you can change page background color, add rule lines and grid lines, hide page titles, and more.

- When you integrate OneNote with Outlook, you can email notebook pages and convert OneNote to-do lists to Outlook tasks.

- Send screen clippings, printouts, and quick notes to OneNote while working in other applications using the handy Send to OneNote tool.

- Apply a password to a specific section if you want to prevent unauthorized people from viewing your content, particularly if you share notebooks with others.

- The History tab in OneNote enables you to review changes to your notebook content, including recent edits, edits by author, and page versions.

Index

N

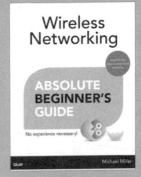

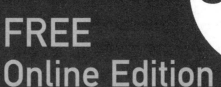